This textbook has been written to help teachers and students to pilot their way through the enormous and ever expanding literature on the French Revolution.

The author makes a conscious effort to combine social and political interpretations of the origin of the Revolution and offers a synthesis which takes full account of current debates. He also seeks to restore the Revolution to its domestic environment. Notwithstanding the powerful contemporary myth of rupture, the author argues that the dramatic events of 1789 need to be considered alongside the reform achievements of Bourbon absolute monarchy. The result is a new account of the gestation of the Revolution which is both up-to-date and satisfying in its range of vision.

Reform and Revolution in France, 1774–1791

Reform and Revolution in France

The Politics of Transition, 1774–1791

P. M. Jones

University of Birmingham

CAMBRIDGE
UNIVERSITY PRESS

Published by the Press Syndicate of the University of Cambridge
The Pitt Building, Trumpington Street, Cambridge CB2 1RP
40 West 20th Street, New York, NY 10011-4211, USA
10 Stamford Road, Oakleigh, Melbourne 3166, Australia

First published 1995

Printed in Great Britain at the University Press, Cambridge

A catalogue record for this book is available from the British Library

Library of Congress cataloguing in publication data
Jones, P. M.
Reform and Revolution in France: the politics of transition, 1774–1791
/ P. M. Jones
    p.   cm.
Includes bibliographical references and index.
ISBN 0 521 45322 4. – ISBN 0 521 45942 7 (pbk.)
1. France – History – Revolution, 1789–1799 – Causes.
2. France – Politics and government – 18th century – Social aspects.
3. Political participation – France – History – 18th century.
4. Monarchy – France – History – 18th century.
5. Nationalism – France – History – 18th century.   I. Title
DC138.J68 1995
944.04–dc20   94-44077 CIP

ISBN 0 521 45322 4 hardback
ISBN 0 521 45942 7 paperback

CE

For Isobel

Contents

List of illustrations

Preface

Every year thousands of items of literature about the French Revolution appear in print. Even scholars of the period find the task of choosing what to read and what to discard a daunting exercise. For teachers and students the challenge can be insurmountable. The present book has been written with the needs of the latter firmly in mind. It knits together a considerable amount of research, often of a fairly unyielding or inaccessible character. The aim is to provide an account of the gestation of the French Revolution which is both up-to-date and satisfying in its range of vision.

Studies of the turbulent history of late eighteenth-century France are prone to suffer from two shortcomings in particular. They tend either to begin, or to end, in 1789, thereby placing 'old' and 'new' regimes in two water-tight compartments. Moreover, a tendency to emphasise political explanations and narratives at the expense of socio-economic factors has become apparent of late. Of course there are good, even telling, arguments to support these perspectives. This book makes no claim to redirect the thrust of modern scholarship. On the other hand, it does seek to balance arguments envisioning a total rupture in 1789 with evidence of continuity. Similarly, a conscious effort is made to link together the socio-economic and the political legacies of Bourbon absolutism. Only by this route does it seem possible to explain why the outcome of the crisis was not reform 'from above', but full-blown revolution.

The opening chapters of the book provide a structural anatomy of France in the latter half of the eighteenth century. The country's institutions of government, social make-up and economic characteristics are each examined in turn. Chapter 4 shifts the presentation into a dynamic mode and explores the pressure for reform that the monarchy itself did so much to promote. The inevitable contradictions that resulted from piecemeal, or faint-hearted, reform within a state still nominally absolutist form the subject-matter of chapter 5. The nerve-racking leap from antiquated notions of the polity to a conception of the nation containing unlimited potential for revolutionary change is described in chapter 6. That leap accomplished, chapter 7 investigates the ideological construction of the new regime, the process of bargaining with new political forces and the attempt to anchor the freedoms proclaimed in 1789 by means of a fresh set of institutions.

Acknowledgements

The writing of a book is usually a solitary business. But the effort is sustained by the imagined dialogue which the historian conducts with his sources. This work of synthesis is the product of many such conversations, nearly all of them anonymous. May these 'voices' find appropriate acknowledgement of their contribution in the endnotes and in the bibliography. However, the character of my book has also been shaped by more immediate and identifiable sources. Innocent, yet probing, questioning by generations of French Revolution 'Special Subject' students has left a perceptible mark. The same can be said of scholarly exchanges with Malcolm Crook, William Doyle, Melvin Edelstein, Alan Forrest, John Harris, Peter McPhee, John Markoff and other academic historians too numerous to mention. In particular, I feel indebted to the regulars of the George Rudé Seminar whose biennial gatherings have been a fount of refreshment to many French historians. The meeting held in Adelaide in 1992 provided the first opportunity to test some of the ideas that have germinated in this book. Subsequent scholarly encounters in Washington DC (Annual Meeting of the American Historical Association, 1992) and Atlanta (Annual Meeting of the Consortium on Revolutionary Europe, 1993) pushed the process of intellectual gestation a stage further.

On a more concrete level, specific debts have been incurred which demand acknowledgement. In 1992 the fellows of the British Academy made available funds to meet some of the research costs of this book, just as they responded to claims upon their resources made in earlier years. I am profoundly grateful for their continued support. Similarly, the Faculty of Arts Research Grants Committee of Birmingham University has made it possible for me to attend a satisfying number of French history conferences over the years. I also owe a debt of gratitude to John Markoff of the University of Pittsburgh (and to his publisher Pennsylvania State University Press) for allowing me to reproduce several of the figures in his forthcoming book.

Introduction

Historians may be forgiven for supposing that great events must have great causes; their status as professional investigators of the past demands as much. Fortunately, few serious students of the French Revolution have ever doubted the proposition. The events of the 1790s seem to mark a watershed between the old world and the new and they cry out for a major effort of explanation. This book joins many others in seeking to clarify the circumstances that produced the upheaval of 1789. Stated simply, it is about the transition from 'administrative' to constitutional monarchy in France between 1774 and 1791. Few things are as simple as they appear, however, and the present volume also puts forward an argument spurred by the scholarly discussions which marked the bicentenary of the French Revolution.

After three decades of research along pathways strewn with discarded theories, the enquiry into the origins of the French Revolution stands at the crossroads, unsure in which direction to proceed. Signposts beckon enticingly towards the 'political', the 'social' and even the 'cultural', but it is far from clear where they will lead. The old certainties sustaining the social or, more often, the socialist interpretation have crumbled amid a welter of new research which has yet to be welded into a constructive alternative. Teachers and even textbook writers find themselves in the uncomfortable position of relying on elderly models of causality which they know to have been undermined in detail. May the present writer not fall into the same trap! For this book is written with the needs of students and teachers very much in mind. It aims to bridge the principal fault line of modern research into the French Revolution, or what a recent scholar termed the 'two distinct centres of gravity at the heart of the debate, the one "political" and the other "social"'.[1] Specifically cultural explanations, it is true, receive shorter shrift: in this author's view they offer nothing which cannot be subsumed within the 'social', broadly defined. Whether the pages that follow amount to a satisfying synthesis is for the reader to judge. Probably they do not, for positions rigidly adhered to become irreconcilable which is another way of saying

1

that some of the basic assumptions in the debate over the French Revolution are beyond the reach of historical proof. And in any case, the book has a thesis of its own to advance which challenges the current thrust of research at the most fundamental level.

If proponents of the 'social' as opposed to the 'political' agree on nothing else, they agree that 1789 marked a moment of discontinuity. The late Albert Soboul, like nearly all the Revolutionary scholars of his generation, believed the crisis to have been engendered by a class conflict which was resolved when the bourgeoisie overthrew the aristocracy and consolidated its political and economic supremacy. As a Marxist, indeed, Soboul tended to see this event in apocalyptic terms, as a classic 'bourgeois revolution' which signalled the destruction of feudalism and the emergence of capitalist modes of production and exchange. Embedded firmly in what is often termed the 'orthodox' or social interpretation of the French Revolution, then, is the notion that 1789 marked a sharp break with what contemporaries were pleased to call the 'ancien régime'. Yet, curiously, this is precisely the position that vehement critics of the social interpretation have opted to defend. Impatient with notions of socio-economic causality and of seismic shifts from feudalism to capitalism, they prefer to depict the Revolution as a political watershed, as a dramatic moment of renewal in which old ideas were discarded and new practices elaborated. François Furet, whose secular dogmatism comes close to rivalling that of Albert Soboul, even invites us to comprehend 1789 as the 'birth of political modernity'.[2] Amid the turmoil of a lightning scene change, the stage of history was cleared for the institutions and ideologies of the modern age. The methodology of Marxism is jettisoned, only to be replaced by a neo-Whig theory of development in which the basic frame of reference remains the same.

This book challenges the 'rupture' thesis as starkly presented above. It puts the case for viewing the years associated with the reign of Louis XVI as a whole, not two uneven and disjointed epochs. As such it is a study straddling conventional periodisation, an enquiry into outcomes which pursues answers deep into the fabric of the *ancien régime*. Enmeshed in a web of socio-economic and institutional contradictions, the French monarchy, it is argued, entered a phase of rapid evolution in the 1770s and 1780s. Each attempt to extricate itself in one direction tended to inhibit movement in another, and the energies released gave depth and purpose to the upheaval of 1789. Studied from this angle the Revolution loses the sharp focus in time that we associate with the taking of the Bastille or the 4 August decrees: it ceases to be an event purely and simply and becomes part of a process. That process is here dubbed the transition from administrative to constitutional monarchy, a process completed only in 1791 when the antique Estates General (renamed the National Assembly) fulfilled its pledge to endow France with a written constitution.

Contemporaries appear to have experienced less difficulty in recognising the hybrid and makeshift character of the new regime than have historians subsequently. The term 'revolution', in the singular, entered political vocabulary quite quickly, it is true, but the phrase 'ancien régime' was slow to acquire the resonance of a global repudiation of the past. For as long as the new regime incorporated the institution of monarchy, the old regime had to be defined with care. The deputies of that first legislature were uncomfortably aware of the ambiguous position which they occupied. Most were cautious pragmatists, far removed in outlook from the zealots and iconoclasts of later years. Their job was to manage the transition so that regeneration could commence under the aegis of beneficent institutions. But this task would fall to a subsequent and post-Revolutionary legislature according to the neat (and optimistic) formulation of the deputy Le Chapelier.[3] In the meantime extempore politics would determine the order of the day.

The perception of the historian Alexis de Tocqueville is relevant here, for he was the first non-contemporary to grasp the organic quality of the political transition. The Revolution simply 'came out of'[4] the preceding regime: in the earlier stages, at least, it was the metamorphosed product of powerful forces unleashed during the reign of Louis XVI. Albert Sorel, another nineteenth-century observer, made a similar point albeit on a broader canvas. Comparing governmental practices across the watershed, he drew attention to 'the permanence of the same pressures, the propensity of accumulated habits, the strength of tradition'.[5] Both of these historians were schematisers, of course, and some of their generalisations have proved vulnerable to more recent research. Indeed, a reassessment of Tocqueville's thesis on centralisation will be offered in the chapters that follow. Nevertheless, both writers have contributed powerfully to the thinking that lies behind this study. Their emphasis on continuities provided the initial encouragement to try and penetrate beyond the rhetoric of rupture.

A more important influence than either of these authorities, however, has been the renewed interest in institutional history. Over the past few years a younger generation of scholars has revitalised research into the late *ancien-régime* monarchy. The reform initiatives of the 1770s and 1780s, the dilemmas of institutionalised 'privilege' and the tensions generated by the growth of a definably 'public' opinion have all been found worthy of study in their own right, instead of being bracketed to an expiring *ancien régime* or a beckoning Pre-Revolution. Not every historian would find the phrase 'administrative monarchy' an apt description of the direction in which government was proceeding in these decades; courtly politics based on patronage and private interest continued to exert a powerful hold. Yet scholars now seem willing to allow 'superstructures' an active if not a determining role in the historical process. In particular, the agency of 'state' seems generally recognised and it is a contention of this study that the Bourbon administrative machine – at several levels – played an important part in the unfolding drama.

The reinterpretation of the final decades of the old monarchy as a period that witnessed significant reforms necessarily reopens the question of 'enlightened absolutism'. This concept fell from favour among historians in the 1960s, but it now shows signs of making a comeback. French historians, it should be said at once, never showed much interest in the question. They had their Revolution and their *ancien régime* and nothing could be permitted to blur the distinction. The classical texts of republican historiography were austerely teleological: Lavisse labelled the period 1781–9 'The Agony of the Old Regime', while Sagnac put the monarchy on borrowed time from Maupeou's coup in 1771 with the heading 'Towards the Revolution'.[6] The temptation to view the reforms of the 1770s and 1780s as minor, manipulative and cynical proved irresistible, as did the corollary notion of renewal solely through the cathartic act of revolution. Not surprisingly, therefore, synthetic studies of 'enlightened absolutism' scarcely mention the case of France. According to one influential textbook writer, 'it is almost a truism that the French government for most of the eighteenth century before 1789 was distinguished less by reform than by a remarkable lack of it'.[7]

Louis XVI was no philosopher-king, to be sure. Nor did his ministers act under the immediate influence of enlightened authors, save for the possible exception of Turgot. Nonetheless, the middling reaches of the royal administration fairly hummed with reformist activity as this study will seek to demonstrate. By the mid-1780s, moreover, public opinion had become an inescapable factor in the process of ministerial decision-making. Daniel Hailes, England's perspicacious diplomat at the Court of Versailles, alluded repeatedly to a spirit 'of discussion of public matters which did not exist before'.[8] None of this energy was coordinated, of course; at least not until Calonne's 'great project' placed root-and-branch reform on the agenda of state in 1787. Nevertheless, we should not belittle the substance of the issues raised and the progress registered even before the onset of the Revolutionary climacteric. The impetus for change came from several directions and, sometimes, from within corporate bodies which were themselves vulnerable to social criticism. 'Privilege', it is worth remembering, posed no insuperable barrier to reformist modes of thought. Even the magistrates of the sovereign courts, so often condemned as selfish protagonists of an 'aristocratic revolution' in government, expressed a breadth of interests which resists neat classification. The latest historian of the *parlements* calls those bodies to account less for their defence of 'privilege', than for their adherence to a static, non-evolving form of monarchism incapable of surmounting the pressures of the age.[9]

This study will examine closely the institutional tensions which the Bourbon monarchy sought both to exploit for fiscal advantage and to overcome for the sake of administrative efficiency. The failure to reconcile these divergent tendencies helps to explain the isolation of successive ministers of the crown when hard decisions had to be taken. However, we need also to look at the subaltern agencies of reform. As a body of men with considerable powers of initiative, the royal provincial intendants have not been well served by historians. *Parlementaire* rhetoric against the supposed organs of 'ministerial despotism', allied to Tocqueville's scathing and overstated descriptions of administrative centralisation, has reduced their role to that of robots. Yet the actions of these men contributed powerfully to the formation of a reform constituency in the second half of the eighteenth century. They launched discussions, tried out ideas and reported their experiences to central government. Some of those ideas germinated, many more remained dormant until the socio-political impediment to structural reform was thrust aside in 1788–9. Of course, not all the intendants were reformers and their formidable authority in the countryside could be used to contain as well as to promote pressures for change. On balance, however, they represented the single most effective force for a recasting of the functions and responsibilities of government in the mould of 'enlightened absolutism'. It will be argued that the speed and relative unanimity with which France was reconstructed between 1789 and 1791 owed much to men like Turgot in the Limousin, the Chaumont de la Galaizière in Lorraine, Bertrand de Boucheporn in Corsica and Bertier de Sauvigny *fils* in the *généralité* of Paris.

If the record of the intendants remains largely unexplored and hence unsung, that of central government has been minutely analysed. The verdict has not been flattering to Louis XVI and his ministers: inadequate budgetary controls over expenditure, factional instability at Court, stop–go reform policies and a general failure of political leadership have all been adduced as factors critical to the collapse of Europe's most powerful monarchy. No doubt; but a focus on the final, rather desperate years of absolute monarchy in France produces an unduly pathological reading of events. Widen the chronological focus and we find a state venturing upon the path of renewal, only to be dragged under by forces unleashed by that very process of modernisation. Tocqueville's dictum[10] concerning the dangers faced by governments seeking to reform themselves is apposite here, and it serves as a further reminder that the Revolution emerged organically from the bosom of the *ancien régime*.

Recognition of the substance of *ancien-régime* reform legislation is slowly gaining ground, aided by the revival of scholarly interest in the career of Jacques Necker.[11] Calonne's ministerial career must surely be next in line for reassessment. But sustained commitment to root-and-branch reform can be traced back to Henri Bertin's tenure of the post of controller-general between 1759 and 1763. Bertin's efforts were concentrated in the field of economic policy and more especially in a desire to accomplish the restructuring of France's agricultural economy. Together with fellow royal bureaucrats Daniel Trudaine and the marquis d'Ormesson and a group of agronomists, he spent two decades pressing the case for the 'new agriculture' in the corridors of power. Agricultural societies were founded in the major towns, incentives introduced to encourage the clearance of waste, and between 1769 and 1781 a steady flow of royal legislation promoted enclosures, the partition of commons and the curtailment of collective rights such as free grazing which sapped the profits of freehold tenure. Bertin retired in 1781 and the agricultural reform lobby momentarily lost its privileged access to the councils of state, but in 1785 a savage drought prostrated the countryside and seriously perturbed the whole economy. Agricultural reform returned to the agenda of state, and the debate continued in the committee rooms of the National Assembly within a frame of reference little different from that established in the 1760s and 1770s.

It is true that reforming absolutism generated high hopes but small achievements in the agrarian sphere, yet so did the Revolutionary Assemblies. The continuities of policy formulation are the point that needs to be emphasised. The history of fiscal reform during these years might easily invite the opposite conclusion, for it is generally taken for granted that the Revolutionaries completely remodelled the taxation system which they inherited. Unglamorous and technical in nature, fiscal history has attracted few takers in recent decades and much remains to be discovered. Nevertheless, it is still worth trying to probe beyond the spectacular clashes that fiscal reform provoked in the 1770s and 1780s in order to capture the underlying trend. The first point to note is that the transition to a new tax regime was neither quick nor painless. Direct taxes to replace the old *taille, capitation* and *vingtièmes* only came into force in 1791, and the new levies owed much to ideas put into circulation by the physiocrats some thirty and forty years earlier. Turgot was the first royal minister to distil a coherent plan of action from this body of thought: while still intendant of Limoges he demonstrated empirically the nefarious consequences of determining tax liability on the basis of presumed wealth and prejudice. His *Mémoire sur la surcharge*, penned in 1766, can be construed as a powerful plea for scientific taxation resting on a nationwide assessment of land holdings and values. Therein lay the germ of Napoleon's cadastral survey. Turgot also campaigned for a unitary land tax calculated on net rather than gross income and applicable to each and every landowner irrespective of birth or station. All these ideas, as we shall see, would enter the realm of practical politics between 1787 and 1791.

Whether Turgot's reformist vision extended to the political reconstruction of Bourbon government, or merely some kind of streamlined administrative super-monarchy, is an open question. He was dismissed from office after only twenty-two months and his comments while in retirement on Necker's scheme for Provincial Assemblies leave the matter unresolved. Yet no minister with an appetite for tax reform and the commutation of the *corvée* could have been unaware of the sociopolitical implications of such changes. Fiscal privileges and exemptions from labour service on the highways formed part of the 'constitution', as Keeper of the Seals Miromesnil remarked to the king in 1776, and to abolish these ancient rights was tantamount to unravelling the social fabric of the kingdom. Moreover, Turgot had other changes in mind on the eve of his downfall: measures to extinguish royal tolls and customs barriers, and perhaps legislation to curtail the burden of seigneurial dues on agriculture.

The intellectual debate on the utility of feudalism can be said to have started in earnest when Pierre-François Boncerf, a senior official in the Finance Ministry, published a brochure entitled *Les Inconvénients des droits féodaux* (1776). The Parlement of Paris, which was locked in a struggle with Turgot over the Six Edicts, condemned the tract to be burned in the belief that it was dealing with one of the minister's new-fangled schemes. In fact, reform of the seigneurial regime was another idea whose time was approaching. The physiocrats had long stigmatised forms of surplus extraction assessed on total yields with no allowance made for variable production costs; and feudal dues, like the ecclesiastical tithe, were notoriously vulnerable to this criticism. In 1779 a disciple of Quesnay, Guillaume-François Le Trosne, published a massive tome bearing the title *De l'administration provinciale et de la réforme de l'impôt* to which was appended an audacious essay denouncing both the theory and the practice of feudal tenure. The whole system, that is to say both the dues themselves and all ancillary running costs, he argued, placed an intolerable burden upon the wealth-producing sector of the economy. There followed a series of detailed recommendations for the redemption of harvest and casual dues which foreshadowed the liquidation legislation of the National Assembly.

The actual politics of the liquidation operation were infinitely complex, of course, and Turgot made virtually no headway on this front during his brief spell in ministerial office. His successor, Necker, contrived the only major alteration of the seigneurial regime when he persuaded the king to emancipate vassals of the Royal Domain from the servitude of *mainmorte* in 1779. As the preamble to the edict made clear this was to be a policy of reform by emulation, but it misfired. Only a trickle of seigneurs followed the royal example, and in the province of Franche-Comté where most of the population subject to *mainmorte* resided, the Parlement of Besançon managed to block the reform for nearly a decade. Even as feudalism was crumbling from below, the National Assembly displayed a marked reluctance to convert the fiery abolitionist rhetoric of 4 August 1789 into concrete legislation. *Mainmorte* was outlawed, more or less, but harvest and casual dues had to be bought out by vassals, failing which they would remain in force.

More important than any of the reforming initiatives mentioned so far, were efforts to remodel the institutions of local government which sought to alter the face of absolute monarchy in the decade before the Revolution. As usual the physiocrat writers led the way, but it fell to Jacques Necker to convert the blueprints of Dupont de Nemours and Le Trosne into a viable scheme of 'representative' bodies to mediate between the organs of central government, the intendants and the *parlements*. These Provincial Assemblies, two of which came into being in 1778–9, offered a bright hope for the social and political regeneration of the kingdom and they cemented Necker's contemporary reputation as the preeminent reform statesman of his generation. Subsequent historians have been less generous with their praise, notably Pierre Renouvin,[12] the only scholar to have studied the experiment in a systematic fashion. However, it is clear that Necker's stock is rising: both of his most recent biographers believe that the Provincial Assemblies offered a means of resolving the tensions engendered by the transition from administrative to constitutional monarchy. The present study examines this proposition closely, while trying to recapture the ripple of excitement and anticipation that Necker's and Calonne's local government reforms provoked.

Necker resigned in 1781 amid mounting opposition to his plans to multiply Provincial Assemblies across the kingdom. But in a sense his work was done: the two prototype assemblies provided a political model which others would copy and improve upon. As the years passed they served to focus the arguments of reformers and to whet the public appetite for participation in the affairs of government. When, in 1787, Calonne decided to bid for this constituency of public-minded individuals with an elaboration and extension of Necker's Provincial Assemblies, Thomas Jefferson's shrewd-minded correspondent, John Adams, was moved to remark: 'All Europe resounds with Projects for reviving States and Assemblies, I think; and France is taking the lead. How such Assemblies will mix, with simple Monarchies, is the question.'[13]

That was indeed the question. *Parlementaire* critics had dubbed Necker's initial creations 'a monstrous coupling of republican and monarchical principles',[14] yet by the end of 1787 around twenty of these bodies had come into existence. Moreover, they were flanked by Department and Municipal Assemblies established within the subdivisions of the *généralités*. Membership of the top two tiers was determined by a combination of royal appointment and cooption, but Calonne planned to substitute an electoral procedure after a trial period of three years. As for the Municipal Assemblies, they were thrown open to election from the outset. Such changes were not cosmetic: Calonne's speech to the assembled Notables made clear that the time for half measures had long since passed. Nor were they purely 'administrative' as is sometimes suggested. Integral to the local government reforms launched by Calonne was a theory of representation that implied a renegotiation of the foundations of monarchical power.

This issue of representation brings the discussion full circle, for it throws a bridge from the 'social' to the 'political' and invites a further and final comment upon the rupture thesis. Under reform proposals tabled by Calonne and implemented by his successor, Loménie de Brienne, tens of thousands of ordinary Frenchmen went to the polls in the summer and autumn of 1787 and thereby gave expression to an embryonic theory of representation based on individuals rather than interests or orders. They were only electing Municipal Assemblies, to be sure, but a broad swathe of contemporary opinion concluded that France was finally embarked upon the transition to constitutional monarchy. 'I think it possible', confided Thomas Jefferson, 'this country will within two or three years be in the enjoiment of a tolerably free constitution.'[15] Obviously contemporaries could have no knowledge of what the immediate future held in store, and Jefferson went on to express his admiration for the lack of violence and bloodshed attending the transition. Yet this note of optimism serves as a salutary reminder to the historian girded with the analytical tool of retrospective vision. France in the 1780s presented all the signs of a country caught in the throes of institutional renewal, a renewal that did not wait upon the 'birth of political modernity' at a signal given by the National Assembly.

Agrarian and fiscal reforms, the burgeoning debate over feudalism, the emergence of representative institutions; all of these developments, and many others besides, tend to blur the conceptual clarity of the rupture thesis. Even François Furet, a firm believer in the vision of discontinuity, has acknowledged the instrumentality of the Bourbon monarchy in procuring change and progress. He likens it to an 'ongoing workshop of "enlightened" reform' and draws specific attention to Calonne's achievement in generalising a hierarchy of deliberative assemblies. The setting up of these bodies consummated a kind of 'revolution before the Revolution' we are told.[16]

This is all very well, but it produces a logical tension in some of the most recent writing on the French Revolution which is not easily resolved. If the old monarchy contrived, through its reformist labours, to assemble the rudiments of liberal democracy, what price the invention of modern political culture in 1789? A partial solution to the problem might dwell upon the underlying purpose of 'enlightened absolutism', for it is far from certain that any of Louis XVI's ministers actually willed the establishment of a constitutional monarchy. Their notions of 'representation' coincided imperfectly with those that would surface under the pressure of events in the Estates General. Indeed, it has been suggested that the history of both the theory and the practice of representation in France should be dated more properly from the famous declaration of the deputies of the Third Estate on 17 June 1789 explicitly vesting sovereignty in the social body of the nation.[17] According to François Furet, this date marked the inception of a new form of absolutism based on sovereignty of the people. Its institutional counterpart followed on 4 August when the deputies mounted their celebrated attack on 'privilege'.

These debates are important for they help us to determine where to place the boundary posts between the old regime and the new. Furet's arguments bracket the National Assembly firmly to the new regime, and contain a gloomy prognostication about the subsequent course of events. They imply that Revolutionary France was proto-republican almost from the outset: the repudiation of the Monarchiens in the late summer of 1789 would merely underscore the constitutional rupture.

The present study adopts a rather different tack. While sifting through the arguments of both 'orthodox' and 'revisionist' historians in an effort to discover some congruity of interpretation, it formulates instead an altogether less apocalyptic vision of the process of change.

1   Government

The notion that the ills of *ancien-régime* France could be attributed to
defects in her institutions of government is as old as the Revolution
itself. Unversed in the sophisticated theories of socio-economic causa-
tion that have gripped the imaginations of historians in more recent
times, contemporaries tended to blame the 'constitutions' of states when
seeking an explanation for civil commotions. Enlightened writers taught
that ideas alone were capable of setting the world to rights, and what
better arena for a demonstration of the corrective power of ideas than
the business of government. In any case, the world of real politics
seemed to offer unprecedented scope for renewal in the 1770s and
1780s. The intervention of France in the American colonists' revolt
against Great Britain relayed garbled messages concerning 'representation' and the right of consent to taxation to every corner of Europe. And
such messages fused with domestic pressures which were also nudging
Old World monarchies in the direction of institutional reform. Political
economy – the science of measurement and mobilisation of the wealth of
nations – issued from these preoccupations and served to redouble
interest in the functions and responsibilities of government. When
Arthur Young ventured upon his travels in France, he did so in the hope
of determining 'the connection between the practice in the fields and the
resources of the empire'. Having chronicled the habits of a state
fundamentally at odds with the productive energies of its population, his
conclusion was unequivocal: 'the more one sees, the more I believe we
shall be led to think, that there is but one all-powerful cause that
instigates mankind, and that is GOVERNMENT!'[1]

Defining France

Political arithmeticians absorbed by concerns very similar to those of
Arthur Young made strenuous efforts to count, to map and to measure
in the second half of the eighteenth century. According to *abbé* Expilly,
the population of mainland France amounted to a little over 24 million

in 1778. Lavoisier, the chemist and polymath savant, deduced a figure of 25 million some ten years later. Neither calculation can be relied on today, for modern demographers are agreed that the population living within the borders of France cannot have numbered fewer than 28 million on the eve of the Revolution. Nevertheless, the preoccupations of men such as Expilly and Lavoisier reveal a determination to measure and to quantify that was fast becoming a hallmark of the age. Under this utilitarian onslaught, both the role and the machinery of government were found to be in need of adjustment. The conceptual vocabulary of the *ancien régime* with its fluid notions of 'territory', 'jurisdiction' and 'sovereignty' had also to be brought into sharper focus. The defining of territory was already far advanced by the time the Revolution broke. Cassini de Thury began work on a revised national grid of maps in 1750 and upon his death in 1784 only Brittany remained uncharted. Turgot, meanwhile, had set up a Topographical Bureau with a specific remit to mark out the frontiers of French territory. Even though France was one of the oldest and most cohesive states of Europe, the task was not an easy one. The surface area of the country was known (to a surprising degree of accuracy), but land borders were ragged in the extreme. In the North-East, the frontier with the Austrian Netherlands was not sharply defined, nor was it entirely clear where the possessions of the king of France ended and those of the elector of Trier began. Foreign enclaves complicated matters further: the county of Montbéliard owed allegiance to the duke of Württemberg, the princes of Nassau owned the county of Saarwerden and the principality of Salm, while Mulhouse was linked to the Helvetic Confederation. All of these entities were surrounded by territory that was indisputably French. The Pyrenean frontier exhibited a similar porosity, but the most sizeable lacunae in French jurisdiction were to be found around Avignon in the Rhône valley where a pontifical state, known as the Comtat Venaissin, had existed since the fourteenth century. In common with all these enclaves, it would be overrun by French troops during the Revolution.

As the Bourbon monarchs pressed ahead with their state-building ambitions, these discrepancies came to be frowned upon. In the 1760s and 1770s steps were taken to straighten out the border in the North-East. But the meaning attached to such concepts as 'sovereignty' and 'jurisdiction' remained far from agreed. Royal administrators were groping towards a rationally ordered state, whereas vested interests in the realm knew that their best hope for survival lay in diversity. They clung to ancient jurisdictional rights and exploited the ambiguities of sovereignty to the full. Several provinces resisted the suggestion that they formed part of the kingdom of France until the very end of the *ancien régime*; instead they invoked a purely dynastic link to the French crown: 'Navarre is by no means a province of France; it is a separate kingdom subject to the king of France, but distinct from and independent of the kingdom of France.'[2] The indignation of the Estates of Navarre at being lumped together with the rest of France for the purposes of electoral consultation would have been well understood. Even in 1788, most French men and women were not yet accustomed to thinking in the neat categories of administrative monarchy. Sovereignty and the 'patrie' (homeland) were local constructs which not even the Estates General was empowered to override. When a Robespierre or a Mirabeau spoke of their 'nations' on the eve of the Revolution, they had in mind not France, but Artois and Provence.

A glance at the internal architecture of the country will bring out these points more forcefully. If France was 'invented' as certain sociologists have argued, it was, above all, the product of conquest.[3] By a process of internal colonisation, performed over many centuries, the core kingdom of the Capetian monarchs expanded to fill out the roughly hexagonal chunk of territory that we know today. In terms of geographical configuration, late eighteenth-century France differed little from its twentieth-century counterpart. The duchy of Lorraine was the last sizeable province to fall under the control of the kings of France, in 1766, following the death of Stanislas Leszczynski. Two years later the Republic of Genoa ceded sovereignty over the island of Corsica to the French crown. This left the duchy of Savoy and the county of Nice which were seized during the wars of the Revolution, but not durably united to France until the following century.

Attrition, conquest and dynastic alliance produced a realm of impressive dimensions, then. But the process did not imply a commensurate degree of internal unification. Paradoxically, France remained a fundamentally disunited state in which centrifugal pressures threatened, at intervals, to get out of control. Instead of harmonizing institutions as military and diplomatic power expanded, the monarchy deemed it expedient to leave the privileges and immunities of each newly acquired territory more or less intact. As a result, the Bourbons found themselves ruling over a considerable empire which, in reality, resembled nothing so much as a patchwork quilt of interlocking and sometimes overlapping jurisdictions, all stitched together with the tenuous thread of regalian justice and administration. A realm of some 500,000 square kilometres, France undoubtedly experienced difficulties in coming to terms with obstacles of terrain and topography. But these impediments were no greater than those facing other continental states and, in any case, Bourbon administrators made substantial headway in constructing roads to link outlying provinces and cities during the second half of the eighteenth century. Between 1765 and 1780 the journey time of coaches plying between Paris and Toulouse was cut by half to only seven days. Climate left a deeper imprint, however, for no other country of Europe experienced the range of weather patterns to which France was susceptible. The North, West and South-West received moist and temperate Atlantic airstreams for most of the year, whereas the South and the South-East were subject to Mediterranean influences which could be felt as far inland as Lyon. One of the consequences was an agriculture of extraordinary diversity, and one which confounded attempts by government ministers to devise all-purpose reforms. Cereal husbandry was practised almost everywhere, of necessity. But the regions best adapted to wheat cultivation lay to the North and East of the country. Then as now, the West and the western flanks of the central highlands were better suited to pastoral farming, although rye was grown for daily subsistence. In the South-East, the valley of the Rhône and on the plains bordering the Mediterranean, olive orchards and vines tended to compete with the arable.

The flux of political power across the centuries had deeply etched the human landscape of France as well. In the southernmost third of the country codified or Written Law prevailed (see map 1). A legacy of ancient Gaul, Roman or Written Law brought a standardised formality to collective relationships which included rigid rules governing matters such as property transmission. By contrast, the rest of France was a land of customary practice. Even though all the Customs had been written down by the eighteenth century, they varied significantly from region to region. On the eve of the Revolution some 60 General Customs and perhaps 300 local variants still carried the force of law. Statute law made by the king-in-council topped off this edifice, of course, but the royal writ could not be assumed to pass without challenge. Linguistic frontiers divided the population of this supposedly united kingdom, too. Expressed in spatial terms, the principal frontier spanned the country in a broad arc running from East to West (see map 2). To the north lay the historic lands of France and the *langue d'oïl*; to the South the patois-speaking civilisation of the *langue d'oc*. But pockets of non-French and non-patois speakers existed at the extremities of the kingdom as well. Breton was spoken in Lower Brittany, Basque along the Atlantic frontier with Spain, Catalan in Roussillon and German in Alsace and parts of Lorraine. The *ancien-régime* monarchy was inclined to ignore these linguistic discrepancies provided official documents were drafted in French and religious instruction was given in that language, more or less. Only after 1789, with the inception of politics for the masses, did language become a test of national allegiance.

Map 1   Division between Written and Customary Law

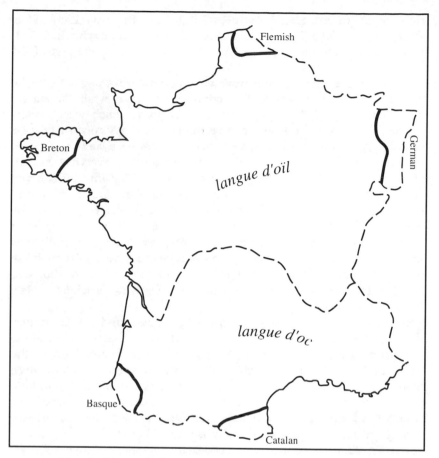

Map 2   Linguistic frontiers

Fundamental to the definition of France was the notion of the
'province'. It gave shape and meaning to the *ancien-régime* vision of
nationhood and provided a secure anchorage for much else besides.
Pierre Doisy's dictionary listed fifty-eight provinces, but that was in
1753 – before the annexation of Lorraine and Corsica.[4] Most of the
provinces had been ruled by the house of France for centuries,
although Flanders, Artois, Alsace, Franche-Comté and Roussillon
were all additions of the seventeenth century. By their very nature,
however, provinces were not territories of even weight and consequence. Some, like Gascony, Champagne or Languedoc, were vast
while others were quite tiny. Their boundaries could be blurred, too,
for the Bourbons tended to shun the province as a unit of administra-

tion. Some of the largest entities (Burgundy, Brittany, Languedoc, Provence) retained Provincial Estates, but the monarchy had succeeded in abating provincial independence in much of the rest of the country.

In what sense, then, did the provinces still signify? Among the elite the embers of provincial particularism continued to glow, while the masses derived a sense of belonging from the Customs which were usually provincial in scope. Large provinces remained shadowy constructs as far as ordinary country dwellers were concerned, however, and the *pays*, or district, was more likely to define the horizons of everyday life. In vernacular usage, the province of Gascony subdivided into thirty-seven *pays*, that of Champagne into around thirty and Normandy into a dozen or so. As for Languedoc, it encompassed subprovinces such as the Rouergue and the Velay whose territory had scarcely altered since the Romans. Time conferred legitimacy upon these ancient jurisdictions and we should not underestimate their capacity to focus and to mobilise public opinion. As the strength of absolute monarchy began to ebb, long dormant traditions of provincial dissidence emerged to provide a vehicle for political reform.

Belatedly, the monarchy acknowledged the fund of legitimacy invested in the concept of the province. First Necker and then Calonne contrived to set up Provincial Assemblies which would harness the underused energies of provincial elites to the government interest (see below pp. 38–43). But this was to renege upon both the theory and the practice of absolutism. For much of the *ancien régime* successive Bourbon monarchs laboured long and hard to remodel the map of France in such a way as to neutralise or obliterate rival sources of authority. Military control was exercised through a system of royal governors, each appointed to supervise a specific region. By the seventeenth century the whole of the kingdom was divided into military *gouvernements*, although their boundaries fluctuated a good deal. Eventually, in 1776, a thorough reorganisation created thirty-nine military zones ranked according to importance. As the danger of internal rebellion diminished, the relevance of the *gouvernements* declined in proportion. Policing now became a matter of ensuring the efficient collection of taxes. With this end in mind the monarchy had established fiscal jurisdictions known as *généralités*. In the later seventeenth century – by which time the *généralité* had acquired a precise territorial format – thirty such units existed. Additions (notably Nancy and Bastia) and modifications raised this figure to thirty-three on the eve of the Revolution (see map 3).

Contemporaries sometimes confused the *généralités* with the

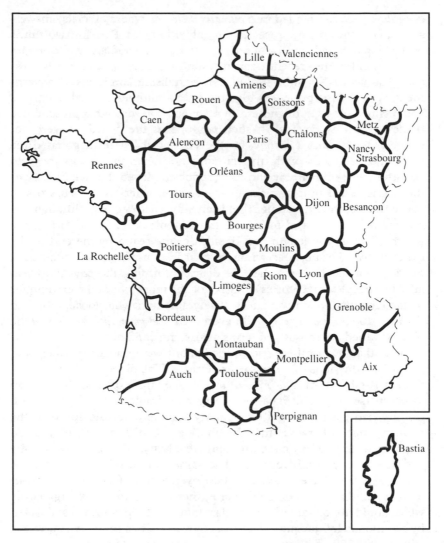

Map 3 *Généralités*

provinces, not surprisingly since ministers such as Necker and Calonne
would deliberately engineer confusion in the labelling of the Provincial
Assemblies. In reality, of course, they were superimpositions like so
much of the military and civilian apparatus of the Bourbon state. The
bulk of the country was made up of provinces which had long since
forfeited their privileges in matters of taxation. In such regions, the

généralités were subdivided into *bureaux d'élection* where officials, answerable only to the crown, proceeded to gather in taxes. Perhaps two-thirds of the kingdom had thus been reduced to the status of *pays d'élections*; in the remainder the revenue-raising status of the *généralité* was less straightforward. Notwithstanding the centralising ambitions of government, several large provinces together with a number of smaller entities had retained the right of consent to royal taxation through representative bodies known as Estates. In such *pays d'états* the *généralités* were not divided into *bureaux d'élection*, for the Provincial Estates negotiated the tax burden directly with the crown and determined how best to apportion it. Both Brittany and Languedoc employed the civil diocese as the district fiscal unit in place of the *élection*, while the procurators of Provence distributed taxation between fifty *vigueries*. So, although the monarchy had managed to impose the administrative framework of the *généralité* across the length and breadth of the realm by the end of the *ancien régime*, the subsidiary units were far from uniform. A fundamental divide remained between the 179 districts forming the *pays d'élections* and the straggle of territories situated for the most part at the extremities of the kingdom which were collectively and somewhat loosely dubbed the *pays d'états* (see map 4). And even then, the *généralités* as well as the *élections* varied enormously in terms of size and configuration.

Older than any of these fiscal jurisdictions were the ecclesiastical and judicial subdivisions of *ancien-régime* France. The dioceses were perhaps the most stable territorial units of all, for they were often Gallo-Roman in origin (see map 5). Papal boundary modifications in the fourteenth century had generated a litter of petty bishoprics in the south of the country, but otherwise the distribution of dioceses displayed an impressive degree of cohesion and regularity. On the eve of the Revolution they numbered 135. The same can be said of the parishes which may well have totalled 40,000 by the end of the *ancien régime*. Though differing considerably in size, they tended to evolve organically which could not be said of the secular units of administration established by the monarchy. Jacques Necker acknowledged as much when, in the winter of 1789, he stipulated that the process for the election of commoners to the Estates General should begin with an assembly of the parish. Equally, Revolutionary legislators were forced to concede the primacy of the parish when planning a new system of local government based on the commune.

This blurring of jurisdictions was typical of an age in which the separation of powers had little meaning, and it applied equally to what might be described loosely as the judicial machinery of the Bourbon state. At the helm stood the king in whose name a battery of

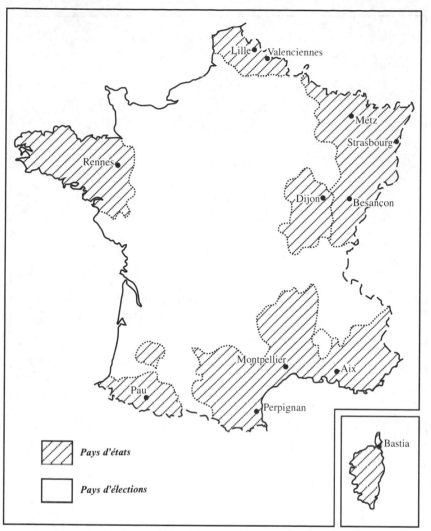

Map 4   *Pays d'états* and *pays d'élections*

appeal courts dispensed justice and much else besides. The most
significant were the thirteen *parlements* or general courts which received
appeals from well-defined catchments (see map 6). That of the
Parlement of Paris was the largest and it transcended provincial
boundaries to embrace a quarter of the entire kingdom. By comparison
the others were junior partners, although the Parlement of Toulouse
exercised jurisdiction over the whole of Languedoc and a considerable

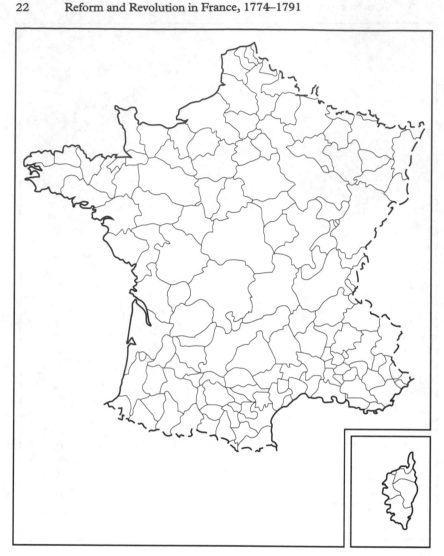

Map 5   Dioceses (before 1789)

swathe of the adjoining province of Guyenne. The smallest jurisdictions
were those on the periphery (Arras, Alsace, Roussillon and Corsica),
representing recent acquisitions of the crown. Here the appeal courts
were not called *parlements*, but they differed little from their counterparts
in terms of function. Subordinate to these august tribunals there existed
an array of about 430 *bailliage* or *sénéchaussée* courts whose sentences

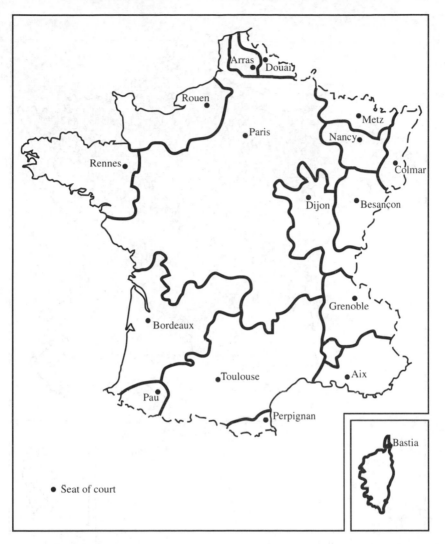

Map 6 *Parlements* and other sovereign courts

remained subject to appeal. Each possessed a territory which was often irregular and even disjointed, particularly in the North and East of the kingdom (see map 7). Nevertheless, these ancient subdivisions became the constituencies in which electors of the Third Estate conducted their deliberations in the spring of 1789. With a few exceptions, the scope of royal justice ceased at the level of the *bailliage or sénéchaussée* seat.

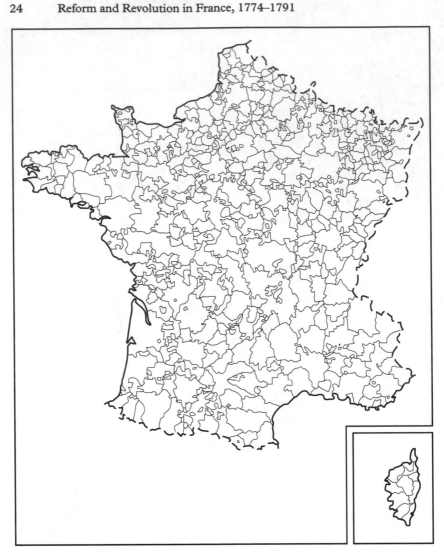

Map 7   *Bailliages* and *sénéchaussées*

Beyond lay the villages in which seigneurial courts provided the primary means of judicial redress.

Institutions

The territorial and jurisdictional complexity of *ancien-régime* France was reflected in the institutions of government. Indeed, the very notion of 'government' lacked clarity. The physiocrat author J. C. V. de Gournay drew attention to the growing fashion for government by office-bound officials in the 1750s and he invented the word 'bureaucracy' to describe this new and unwelcome form of interventionism. But government – in the sense of administration – was not by any means a royal prerogative. All sorts of bodies exercised powers of administration, sometimes on behalf of the crown and sometimes independently. The church, the *parlements*, the Provincial Estates and secular seigneurs generally, all performed considerable administrative tasks, for instance. And in any case, the crown's own organs were not clearly assorted. Because the function of 'government' grew out of that of justice, most administrative agencies possessed powers of justice and could operate as tribunals when the need arose, whereas courts such as the *parlements* also exercised responsibilities which had nothing whatever to do with litigation. Such overlaps, together with the profound lack of uniformity across the realm, make it difficult to analyse the institutional structures of the Bourbon state in coherent terms. The approach adopted here is to start at the grass-roots and to work up the social and political scale.

At village level, corporate life was conducted within three institutions: the parish, the *communauté d'habitants* and the seigneurie. The parish can be defined as a community of the faithful grouped around a church, an incumbent priest and a burial ground. The *communauté d'habitants* originated in the modicum of collective organisation required for the regular payment of direct taxes to the crown, while the seigneurie consisted of a community of vassals owing dues as well as obedience to a specific lord. The functions, personnel and territory of these institutions might easily overlap, but they were not necessarily conterminous. In Brittany the parish assemblies (known as *généraux*) dealt with secular as well as spiritual matters, but elsewhere it was more usual to encounter an interdependence of civil and seigneurial apparatus at village level. For example, the seigneurial *mandements* of the Velay subprovince of Languedoc were also employed by the monarchy as a unit for tax gathering. This symbiosis deserves particular attention, for it was in the area of tax extraction that the stresses and strains of administrative modernisation became most apparent.

To judge from Edme-Gilles Guyot's postal directory published in 1754, country dwellers paid tax in no fewer than 50,000 localities on the eve of the Revolution.[5] Nobody knew how many *communautés d'habitants* there were, least of all the controller-general and his officials in the provinces. The historian Alexis de Tocqueville's vision of the tax-raising arm of government sucking communities dry with the remorseless efficiency of a machine falls short of the reality as far as the *pays d'états* were concerned. And in any case, the fisc was not without rivals in the shape of the seigneur and rooted traditions of municipal autonomy. Municipal independence was not a significant phenomenon in the North and East, it is true. Here the organs of community life remained underdeveloped owing to the pervasive institutional presence of the seigneurie. Villages had syndics and tax collectors, of course, but they were reputed legal minors and were required to submit their transactions to seigneurial officers for authentication. In the Artois, for example, village assemblies met infrequently and only at the behest of seigneurial personnel.

Seigneurs interfered in the corporate life of their vassals in the South, too, but with less success. In Provence, Languedoc and parts of Guyenne even quite small villages maintained institutions that might amount to a miniature municipal body. Consuls were elected rather than nominated by outsiders, and were often flanked by subordinate officers such as a clerk, a forest guard and perhaps a market inspector. The consuls remained responsible for the collection of taxes, but enjoyed many other powers, too. Most important in this region of Written Law, they were regarded as magistrates with the authority to take legally binding decisions. It was this power to take decisions which began to disrupt relations between village elites, their seigneurs and officials of the crown from the middle decades of the eighteenth century. Local bigwigs chafed at the restrictions imposed by the seigneurial regime. In the East, particularly, bitter disputes over the management of commons and forests pitted villagers against seigneurs and the entrepreneurs to whom they so often leased their rights. In such circumstances vulnerable communities appealed to the royal intendants, but the intendants also had an axe to grind. As the interventionist ambitions of central government expanded in the second half of the century, the intendants made a determined effort to extend their supervisory powers (*tutelle*) over the *communauté d'habitants*. In the *pays d'élections* and in recently annexed regions such as Franche-Comté, this was not too difficult to achieve. The *pays d'états* remained problematic, however. In Brittany and also in Languedoc powerful Provincial Estates kept the intendants at bay, whereas conditions in Burgundy made possible the steady encroachment of officialdom upon the affairs of everyday life. Here villagers pledged their independence to the intendant in return for protection from their seigneurs. Administrative *tutelle* increased, but seigneurial interference in the activities of the *communautés d'habitants* was greatly curbed.

Urban institutions of government differed almost to infinity as Tocqueville correctly observed. Renewable municipal bodies were certainly more common in the South than elsewhere, if only because many villages could boast a municipal superstructure; otherwise almost any generalisation is hazardous. Perhaps one further general statement could be ventured: the century seems to have occasioned a shift towards oligarchy. Wealth began to outclass rank as a criterion for municipal office, while the institutions securing popular participation in the decision-making process (notably the general assembly of inhabitants) tended to wither. One example must suffice and it concerns the little town of Le Malzieu in the Massif Central. According to an anonymous note penned shortly before the Revolution the town's affairs were managed by a body consisting of three consuls, three ex officio councillors (the judge, procurator-fiscal and syndic of the Chapter) and twelve elected councillors. A three-tier franchise grouping the bourgeoisie and senior professionals, the merchants (together with lesser professionals), and the crafts and trades supplied candidates, in equal proportions, to vacant posts. And it had been the practice for half the councillors to stand down each year. However, 'since it doubtless appeared inconvenient to convene general assemblies with such frequency, each councillor gradually assumed the right to appoint his successor',[6] who, out of gratitude, then proceeded to nominate his benefactor. As a result, the town council had become a self-perpetuating oligarchy.

Oligarchy and also venality were the defining characteristics of urban municipal government, then. Venality because the monarchy persisted in converting municipal posts into a capital resource and selling them off. Between 1692 and 1771 a bewildering procession of new offices were created, deleted and then re-created in a fiscal pantomime which tried the patience of long-suffering urban elites to the limit. The Controller-General Laverdy tried to put an end to this confusion and to endow royal policy with a consistency of purpose stretching beyond the day-to-day needs of the exchequer. Laverdy, it should be said, was a former magistrate of the Parlement of Paris whose commitment to an organic vision of government left little room for fiscal expedients, or indeed for the concentration of power in the hands of the intendants. In 1764 and 1765 he promulgated edicts which amounted to a significant reform of municipal administration. The trade in municipal offices was abolished and a complex process of election introduced for the designation of mayors, councillors and aldermen (*notables*). Moreover, towns were divided according to size with a standard municipal format prescribed for each category. Such arrangements would have dealt a mortal blow to self-serving oligarchies of the type ensconced in Le Malzieu which is exactly what they were intended to do. But Laverdy had fixed his sights on the creeping interventionism of the intendants as well. To borrow from the language of eighteenth-century politics, his reform set out to bolster the 'jurisdictional' power at the expense of the 'ministerial' (see below pp. 46–7). The intendants lost some of their powers to examine and approve municipal accounts which were transferred to local courts, and thence to the judicial hierarchy presided over by the *parlements*.

Not surprisingly, the Parlement of Paris registered the edicts forthwith and the measures won support in Franche-Comté, too. Elsewhere they encountered objections which were sometimes overcome with more specialised legislation, as in Languedoc in 1766. In the event, however, the experiment was overturned by Terray in 1771. Acute fiscal pressures appeared to justify the return to a regime of venality, but Terray was a known supporter of 'ministerial' power in any case. Nevertheless, the retreat left the institutions of urban life in complete disarray with some towns boasting councils elected in accordance with Laverdy's edicts, others functioning according to ancient custom, and still more staffed with venal office-holders. These were the conditions that provoked a flurry of writings on the subject of municipal reform in the 1770s, notably the *Mémoire sur les municipalités* drafted by Dupont de Nemours in 1775 at the behest of Turgot. But no new legislative proposal emerged from the bureaux of central government until Calonne revealed to the Assembly of Notables his scheme for Provincial Assemblies in early 1787. Only then was Laverdy's pioneer application of the electoral principle rehabilitated.

Compared with the organs of local government, the intendants and the subdelegates were upstarts. The intendants were royal administrators and law enforcement officers in the provinces whose plenipotentiary powers became permanent from the middle decades of the seventeenth century. The subdelegates originated in an order-in-council of 1642 permitting intendants to 'delegate' their authority to subordinate officials. Both institutions were simply superimposed upon the existing administrative and judicial apparatus whose powers they tended to usurp. Thus the intendants were allocated to the *généralités* and took over the tax-raising responsibilities hitherto exercised by the *bureaux des finances*, while the subdelegates sprouted in the *élection* subdivisions of the *généralité* and thereby diminished the role of the *bureau d'élection* courts. At least, this was the theory: the reality on the ground was never quite as clear cut. Brittany avoided the creation of an intendancy until 1689, whereas the province of Languedoc – long since divided into two *généralités* – only had one intendant who resided in Montpellier. As for the subdelegations, that is to say the portions of territory administered by the subdelegates, they soon ceased to correspond with the *élections* which were too unwieldy for the purposes of general administration. In any case the *pays d'états*, together with several frontier provinces, had never been divided into *élections* and here the subdelegations owed something to local units of jurisdiction (civil dioceses, *vigueries*, *bailliages*, etc.). If Corsica is included in the calculations, the agents of administrative monarchy numbered some 33 intendants and 704 subdelegates on the eve of the Revolution (see map 8).

Although there were many practical limitations upon their power, these men came close to providing the Bourbons with a unified system of government. On their shoulders rested the hopes of reforming absolutism in the third quarter of the eighteenth century (see below pp. 122–7). Equally they attracted the scorn and enmity of all those bodies whose ancient jurisdictional rights they challenged and deflected. For, after tentative beginnings during which their role was confined to one of 'inspection', the intendants evolved into a corps possessed of wide-ranging powers and an almost unlimited scope for treading on the toes of others. Matters of taxation, *tutelle* and general 'police' absorbed the bulk of their energies, but they turned their attentions increasingly towards ameliorative projects of social welfare. They could even be called upon to outflank the *parlements* and publish royal edicts as happened when Lamoignon issued his judicial reforms in May 1788. A growth in security of tenure undoubtedly served to enhance their authority, too. Of the sixty-eight intendants who held office during the reign of Louis XVI more than half remained in the same post for over ten years and nearly a fifth more than twenty-five years. All were nobles by this date, as well as men of considerable substance. Their employees, the subdelegates, were also well embarked upon the road to professionalisation with posts passing from father to son or son-in-law more often than not. However, they were recruited from less exalted social milieux.

Alongside the overlapping structures of the administrative edifice there existed a parallel judicial hierarchy ranging from petty seigneurial assizes to the *parlements*, the most senior courts of the realm. These bodies dispensed what might be termed 'ordinary' or general purpose justice, but they were flanked by quasi-judicial institutions with the more specific remit of interpreting and fashioning administrative law. Although the *ancien régime* never admitted a clear distinction between law and administration, it helps to treat separately these courts specialising in the area of 'extraordinary' justice.

The common people sought redress first and foremost on an informal, person to person basis. But if that failed they pursued their grievances before seigneurial assizes that met at intervals in the small towns and villages. Where seigneurial lordship had not been fragmented, in the

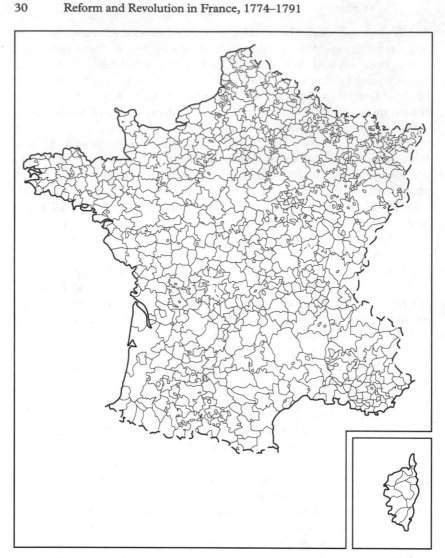

Map 8   Subdelegations

Velay or the Gévaudan, for example, such courts functioned fairly
smoothly and there may have been as many as 80,000 in operation by
the end of the *ancien régime*. In some localities, however, the institution
had fallen into disrepute. Seigneurs were accused of abandoning all
attempts at law enforcement, or of leasing their rights to ruffianly bands
of lawyers who preyed upon the peasantry. It is true that the judicial

competence of seigneurial courts was extremely limited, which could encourage either neglect or abuse. Most seigneurs' judicial rights did not extend beyond the levying of paltry fines for the non-payment of feudal dues. The gibbet was strictly a matter for display.

The crown viewed these petty tribunals with undisguised hostility and contrived to undercut their activities by widening the scope of the royal courts in the 1770s and the 1780s. On the other hand, the *parlements* showed signs of wishing to reform seigneurial justice in order to make it more resistant to the encroachments of Bourbon absolutism. In 1768 the Parlement of Dijon took steps to expand the assizes of Bresse and Bugey from occasional courts of pleas into regularly assembled administrative bodies with wide powers of law enforcement. The reality of the situation militated against a significant expansion of royal justice in the countryside, however, for the crown's courts were confined to the *bailliage* and *sénéchaussée* seats and a number of other towns. In the small subprovince of the Velay, for instance, there existed 155 seigneurial jurisdictions, but only one royal court in addition to the seneschalcy seat of Le Puy. Brittany, a vast province in comparison with the Velay, possessed a score of royal seats of justice by the end of the *ancien régime*, but 90 per cent of litigation was dealt with by seigneurial assize courts whose numbers ran to thousands.

Nevertheless, the *bailliage* and *sénéchaussée* courts were vigorous institutions whose competence was growing in the eighteenth century. They possessed the right to preempt more serious cases from seigneurial jurisdiction and they steadily centralised the dispensation of royal justice in their own hands, leaving the lesser royal courts (known variously as *prévôtés royaux*, *vigueries*, *vicomtés* and *châtelainies*) without much of a role to perform. In recognition of their enhanced status, some of the *bailliage* and *sénéchaussée* tribunals had been granted the power to judge certain categories of offence without appeal (to the *parlements*). These were dubbed *présidial* courts and they numbered around a hundred at the end of the *ancien régime*. The prestige conferred by membership of such bodies were considerable and they provided a ready avenue of social promotion to the small-town bourgeoisie who could not yet aspire to the office-holding magistrature of the *parlements*. The senior judge in a *sénéchaussée* court was called the lieutenant-general and he would be flanked by a variable number of auxiliary judges, counsellors, barristers and prosecutors. Altogether the *bailliage* and *sénéchaussée* courts were serviced by some 2,700 judges of varying descriptions who represented perhaps half of the practising magistrates in the kingdom.

The offices of judge, barrister and prosecutor were all venal and changed hands for significant sums of money by the end of the *ancien régime*. On the other hand, they brought exemption from many fiscal obligations and rich pickings in terms of influence and inducements. They did not confer noble status, however, and established nobles were only attracted to the most senior positions within the court hierarchy. In the provinces of Burgundy and Poitou, according to one calculation, no more than 6 or 7 per cent of *sénéchaussée* magistrates were of noble birth.[7] By and large, then, the *bailliage* and *sénéchaussée* courts remained the preserve and pastime of well-to-do members of the Third Estate and it comes as no surprise to find that the legislators of the Revolutionary Assemblies were drawn predominantly from this social and professional milieu.

Nearly all sentences pronounced by the *bailliage* and *sénéchaussée* courts were subject to appeal before the *parlements*, and sentences prescribing corporal or dishonourable punishment were appealed automatically. The *parlements* can be defined as courts of final appeal for all matters falling within the jurisdiction of 'ordinary' justice. Only an order-in-council emanating from the highest level of government could revoke their *arrêts* or judgements. In addition, however, the *parlements* exercised wide-ranging powers of 'police' which, in eighteenth-century parlance, could cover market practices, guilds, local government finance, servitudes and customary rights, and public decency, as well as an habitual concern with law and order. The scope and antiquity of these powers made it inevitable that the *parlements* should come into conflict with the intendants, just as their right to inspect new laws could jeopardise relations with the monarch. By the end of the *ancien régime* thirteen such institutions existed, the last having been established at Nancy in 1775. Equivalent in all but name, however, were the four *conseils souverains* set up in Colmar, Perpignan, Arras and Bastia in order to endow newly annexed regions with courts of final appeal. All of these bodies were staffed by men who had bought their positions, and offices in the sovereign courts conferred personal nobility without exception. Collectively, therefore, the 1,200 *parlementaire* magistrates made up the core element of what was termed the 'nobility of the robe', although many would have qualified for noble status on other grounds. From their midst were drawn the intendants and thence a goodly number of the ministers of the crown. Chancellor Maupeou, the man who would throw this comfortable world into turmoil in 1771 by exiling the *parlements* and abolishing venality of office, was himself a first president of the Parlement of Paris.

The courts dispensing 'extraordinary', that is to say more specialised, royal justice present a much less coherent picture. The *prévôté* tribunals which functioned as the judicial arm of the *maréchaussée* or mounted police force were among those most likely to touch the lives of ordinary people. They judged summarily and without appeal in a manner similar to courts martial. Distributed by *généralité*, the *prévôtés* attracted a growing volume of criticism in the eighteenth century. The officials administering the salt monopoly were also empowered to try offenders, in this instance individuals suspected of infringing the rules governing the distribution and sale of salt. These *grenier à sel* courts were to be found primarily in the northern sector of the country, the so-called *pays de grande gabelle* (see below p. 93), where salt was forced on consumers at very high prices. Their ruthlessness in policing the monopoly and in pursuing delinquents was a source of widespread concern by the end of the *ancien régime*. Country dwellers with a fondness for the hunt, or for fishing, scavenging and stock grazing out of season might easily fall foul of the royal Waterways and Forests administration (not to mention their seigneurs). The Eaux et Forêts exercised control over the wooded properties of the Royal Domain and a more general jurisdiction over all the forests of the kingdom. Inevitably, these powers implied a judicial competence and the right to try offenders which was vested in *maîtrise* courts. Following Colbert's restructuring of the administration in the late seventeenth century, their numbers rose to around sixteen on the eve of the Revolution. While inland waterways remained the preserve of the Eaux et Forêts, nearly all types of coastal and maritime activity fell within the jurisdiction of admiralty courts of which there were about fifty in 1789. These bodies handled all cases to do with ship-building, maritime contracts, coastal fishing, port repairs and improvements, and much else besides. Their sentences were subject to appeal before the *parlements*.

The ubiquity of fiscal institutions combining administrative and judicial functions has already been mentioned. At the base the *bureaux d'élection* employed a variable number of personnel in a judicial capacity. Over a score of magistrates handled cases in the *élection* of Paris, but a dozen was more usual in the provinces. Since nearly all the personnel were office-holders, the size of these courts tended to reflect the revenue hunger of the monarchy as much as anything else. Certainly their business load was diminishing as the intendants and subdelegates ate into their traditional areas of jurisdiction. Nonetheless, they performed a useful social role in providing small-town elites with an accessible rung on the ladder of advancement. The next tier of fiscal bureaucracy offered more substantial rewards to the ambitious and well-heeled bourgeois, for the most senior offices in the *bureaux des finances* conferred nobility, albeit at one remove. Twenty-six *bureaux des finances* existed at the end of the *ancien régime*, roughly one per *généralité*, and each contained between twenty and thirty magistrates. Although they possessed wide powers in matters of taxation, including oversight of customs duties and the salt monopoly, the omnicompetent interventionism of the intendants had turned the principal office of *trésorier de France* into a sinecure to all intents and purposes.

The noble status attaching to the post of *trésorier de France* derived from the fact that holders were reputed also to be members of the *chambres des comptes* and the *cours des aides*. These bodies were deemed to be sovereign courts on a level with the *parlements*: as such they stood at the apex of the fiscal judiciary. The *chambre des comptes*, as its name implies, originated in Paris as an audit commission entrusted with the task of scrutinising the returns of royal accountants. But as the power of the house of France expanded 'branches' were established in the provinces, numbering ten or eleven by the end of the *ancien régime*. As time passed their powers of examination gradually became redundant, although they retained the right to remonstrate with the monarch on matters within their legal competence. In terms of antiquity and precedence, the *cour des aides* of Paris played second fiddle to the *chambre des comptes*. Nevertheless, there was some overlap between the two institutions, and, indeed, between them and the *parlements*. By the close of the *ancien régime* the original *cour* had multiplied in the provinces and they functioned as final appeal courts for litigation arising out of the major state taxes. During the eighteenth century, the *cours des aides* were buffeted by both the *parlements* and the intendants in protracted quarrels over competence and jurisdiction.

There existed several other institutions with specialised judicial powers, but sufficient has been said to demonstrate that justice, whether 'ordinary' or 'extraordinary', was big business in *ancien-régime* France. Literally so in some instances: when the Parlement of Dijon was sent into exile in 1788, central government found it necessary to allocate to the intendant the sum of 18,000 *livres* for support of the poor. If the *bailliage* and *sénéchaussée* courts contained around 2,700 judicial personnel, the *parlements* about 1,200 magistrates and the more specialised bodies no fewer than 1,500 individuals of similar description, it will be evident that the country was fairly bulging at the seams with judges. Judges were more numerous than policemen, many times more numerous if seigneurial judges are included. Moreover, whole towns lived off the courts housed within their walls and, by the same token, whole towns found themselves contemplating economic ruin as the deputies of the National Assembly strove in 1789 and 1790 to rationalise the administrative and judicial structures of the kingdom. To take two examples, Angers – the capital of Anjou province – boasted no fewer than fifty-three different bodies with judicial powers, while Besançon practically lived off its courts. A century after the annexation of Franche-Comté, the city boasted a *parlement,* a *présidial,* a *maîtrise* and several *bailliage* and *prévôté* courts, not to mention ecclesiastical, municipal and University tribunals. During the same period its population doubled: as true a measure as any of the role of institutions in the life of the *ancien régime.*

It has already been suggested that the province constituted the basic building block of the Bourbon state. But most provinces had forfeited all right to administrative independence by the eighteenth century. Only four entities could boast Provincial Estates of any consequence: Languedoc, Brittany, Burgundy and Provence. Among these, the Estates of Languedoc enjoyed a unique reputation for effective and enlightened regional government. They met in Montpellier every year on a summons of the monarch for the specific purpose of giving consent to royal taxes. However, their role was not limited to a power of consent: the Estates also controlled the machinery for the distribution and collection of taxes across the province, exercised jurisdiction in matters of fiscal litigation and initiated an assortment of public works. It was the energy brought to this latter task that so impressed contemporaries. Arthur Young was lost in admiration for the 'magnificent causeways'[8] of Languedoc. The vigour and sophistication of administration in the province owed much to the constitution of the Estates, for they met in common session and reached decisions by majority verdict. The Third Estate, moreover, controlled half the votes which ensured a degree of consensus even though the senior clergy tended to dominate the proceedings. As the campaign to redesign the institutions of local and regional government gathered momentum in the 1770s, it is scarcely surprising to find the Estates of Languedoc invoked as a political model. After all, they embodied in a fruitful partnership the two reforms that would become the rallying cry of Third Estate pamphleteers in the winter of 1788–9.

By contrast, the Provincial Estates of Brittany had a reputation for unbridled independence. They met every two years to endorse a grant or 'donation' of monies to the royal exchequeur in lieu of direct taxation. These sums were covered by means of a hearth tax (*fouage*) that fell most heavily upon the rural poor, and by means of an excise duty on alcoholic drinks. However, since 1733, the province had also possessed a permanent committee or *commission intermédiaire* which maintained administrative continuity between the sessions of the Estates. It was this body that patiently chipped away at the authority of the intendant in the province over the course of the eighteenth century. In 1785 the Estates finally won total control of the highways, much to the chagrin of the intendant Bertrand de Molleville. The embarrassments of the crown in dealing with this unruly province stemmed mainly from the composition of the Estates, however. Virtually all nobles were entitled to attend the sessions, whereas representation of the Third was confined to forty-one towns. Voting by order was prescribed, it is true, but the nobility were generally able to determine the outcome. In a province stuffed full of country gentlemen, it was not unusual for 600 or 700 nobles to attend the sessions, whereas the clergy's muster was limited to fifty-six and that of the Third Estate to forty-six. Two developments of fateful consequence ensued. The crown became increasingly impatient at its inability to subject the province to a pro rata share of direct taxation, while Breton town and country dwellers moved closer to confrontation with the nobility over *fouage* assessments. On the eve of the Revolutionary crisis, Bertrand de Molleville wrote feelingly from Rennes: 'in no other province is there less of an inclination to make sacrifices for the public good; this appears to me to stem from the fact that the nobility, which is all powerful, regards industry and commerce as alien objects'.[9]

The Burgundian Estates met every three years amid much pomp and ceremony. All gentlemen in possession of four generations of noble status were entitled to attend, providing that they were also fief-owners in the province. By contrast clerical representation was limited to the bishops, the canonry and a fixed quota of lesser beneficed clergy, while representation of commoners was confined, as usual, to the mayors of a number of privileged towns. Little real power remained to this body, however, for the day-to-day administrative burden was shouldered by an institution known as the Elus généraux which acted on behalf of the Estates during the long intervals between sessions. The Elus numbered nine in all, but included the intendant and several royal appointees which reduced considerably the scope for truly independent action. In any case the king levied the *taille* throughout the province, although the Estates had won exemption from drinks taxes (*aides*) and paid the *capitation* and the *vingtième* in a beneficial lump sum form. Unlike his counterpart in Rennes, the intendant of Dijon could usually rely upon the Estates to do his bidding; the constitutional challenge came rather from the urban and rural bourgeoisie, and the parish clergy who felt excluded from the system of representation.

Strictly speaking, the Estates of Provence no longer existed in the eighteenth century. Nevertheless, the province retained substitute institutions of self-government until the very end of the *ancien régime*. The original Estates fell victim to Richelieu's centralising policies in 1639 and they were replaced by an organ comprising a deliberative body called the Assemblée générale des communautés and an executive termed Les Procureurs du pays. The former was quasi-representative in as much as it grouped together ex officio members such as the archbishop of Aix, a handful of elected clerics and nobles, and the first consuls of some of the principal towns. The latter body amounted to a steering committee of eleven permanent officials under the supervision of the archbishop. Although these institutions served to curb the strength of the nobility, the powers of the intendant were slow to expand in proportion. An attempt to convert the province into a *pays d'élections* proved unsuccessful, with the result that the intendant remained excluded from the business of direct tax assessment. The Assemblée also asserted its independence in matters of roads and bridges, on which it spent considerable amounts in the closing years of the *ancien régime*. This truce in the long conflict between ministerial and jurisdictional authority was dramatically broken in 1787 – a year which witnessed the retreat of absolute monarchy on several fronts. In the face of a mounting clamour from the disenfranchised Provençal nobility, ministers allowed the Estates to reassemble in accordance with ancient precedents granting all fief-owning noblemen the right to participate (see below p. 148).

Lesser Provincial Estates existed in at least sixteen other regions on the eve of the Revolution. They were to be found, for the most part, in frontier provinces whose annexation had been consummated with a reciprocal pledge to preserve local privileges. The majority continued to exercise the right to negotiate with the monarch over the apportionment of taxes, and all were dominated by a narrow elite drawn principally from among the clergy and the nobility. Ministers tended to regard these archaic institutions with mixed feelings. On the one hand they could pose an obstacle to fiscal reform, although the crown usually managed to tax adequately the *pays d'états* by one means or another. Brittany was the only major province to escape the clutches of a revenue-hungry government. On the other, the Provincial Estates did provide a model of political representation, albeit one grossly biased in favour of the privileged orders. As the physiocratic plea for elected assemblies of undifferentiated landowners began to make headway in governing circles (see below p. 111), ministers came to view the Estates in a more sympathetic light. The introduction of Estates to Corsica in 1775 is telling in this respect, for the island became something of a show-case for new ideas on government and taxation. Bertrand de Boucheporn, the energetic intendant sent out to supervise the transition to French-style institutions, made use of the opportunity to press for a strict equality of representation within the Estates.

By 1787, then, the long history of the Provincial Estates seemed about to start on another chapter. Pressure for a wholesale restoration (of those bodies abolished, or prorogued, in the sixteenth and seventeenth centuries) was mounting, and ministers were toying with plans for a fundamental restructuring of regional and local government in which the Provincial Estates would have played a major role. 'My objective', Calonne informed the king in late 1786, 'is to garner the support of landowning taxpayers who, through their regularly elected representatives, would be confined to advising the government in a consultative capacity, without, at the same time, giving them either the right or the ambition to govern themselves'.[10] The question was whether the Estates could be relied upon to perform this role. An edict restoring these ancient bodies might be interpreted as a sign of weakness and would do nothing to build a political consensus unless they could be made truly representative. On the other hand an alternative institutional model beckoned in the shape of Necker's Provincial Assemblies. As Calonne pondered his options on the eve of the Assembly of Notables, the future of administrative monarchy hung in the balance.

The Provincial Assemblies were the last and most significant administrative innovation of the *ancien régime*. They can be traced back to a policy document drafted by Necker for the king's eyes only in 1778. In it the director-general argued a case substantially the same as that to be put before the monarch by Calonne some eight years later: His Majesty's subjects were alienated and divided and it was time to harness their latent energies to the common cause of enlightened absolutism. Provincial Assemblies grouping equal numbers of clerics and nobles and a double representation of the Third Estate would permit the wealthiest and most civic-minded members of society to play a real part in the business of government. Voting by head and in common session would maximise public-spiritedness, while royal nomination and a ban on venality would preclude any danger of insubordination. No doubt the intendants and the *parlements* would find the presence of the new bodies irksome, but in Necker's judgement these were precisely the institutions that impeded the rejuvenation of the monarchy. Turgot, watching the experiment unfold from his retirement, was dubious: by their mere existence the Assemblies would serve to undermine monarchical authority. Indeed, if thirty such Assemblies were to unite and form a Congress on the American model, they might contrive the utter destruction of monarchy.

In the event, Necker confined his ambitions to the creation of four Provincial Assemblies in the first instance. Only two of these bodies ever saw the light of day, while the struggle to establish a third – in the Bourbonnais – triggered his resignation amid a chorus of opposition from the *parlements* and the intendants. The Provincial Assembly of the Berry came into being in the autumn of 1778 when the king instructed sixteen landowners to assemble in the town of Bourges and to proceed to the nomination of a further thirty-two individuals in order to bring the Assembly to full strength. Although cooption rather than election determined membership, the royal edict stipulated that the new body should contain twelve non-noble rural landowners, twelve urban bourgeois, twelve nobles and twelve provincial clerics. This determination to ensure an adequate representation of articulate public opinion is what marks out the experiment with Provincial Assemblies, for at that time only the Estates of Languedoc could boast a doubled representation of the Third Estate allied to voting by head in a common session. It is true that Necker refrained from abolishing the distinction between the orders, but he nonetheless appears to have regarded those appointed to his Assemblies as an undifferentiated elite. This has prompted a recent historian to dub them 'modern, deliberative bodies'[11] having little in common with the traditional Provincial Estates. Such a judgement seems excessive, but they certainly contained the potential to evolve into institutions of a modern, representative character.

In fact, the Provincial Assembly (or Administration) of the Berry was something of a misnomer for it corresponded not to the province of the Berry, but to the *généralité* of Bourges. Similarly, the Provincial Assembly of Haute-Guienne, which came into being the following year, redefined the *généralité* of Montauban for all practical purposes. Necker's intentions in seeking to appropriate the untarnished image of the province are not difficult to fathom, but the new bodies remained tied closely to the machinery of absolutism for all the camouflage. They could promote public works, encourage agricultural reform and assist in the task of provisioning during times of harvest scarcity like any Provincial Estates. They could discuss and even reapportion the major state taxes, but they were not permitted to challenge the overall load. Necker specifically warned the officers of the Provincial Assembly of Haute-Guienne that the granting of a lump sum payment facility for the *vingtième* did not entitle them to haggle over the amount. On the other hand, the intendants were convinced that their powers had been eroded. When the Provincial Assembly of Haute-Guienne commissioned a village-by-village study of tax assessments, both the intendant and the *cour des aides* in Montauban grew restless. The intendant tried to prevent the Assembly from publishing its deliberations, and it was the outright refusal of the intendant of Moulins to countenance the creation of a similar body on his territory that curtailed the experiment in 1781.

Necker's fall eased tensions and his successor, Joly de Fleury, took steps to reassure the intendants as to the plenitude of their authority. Nevertheless, the two prototype Provincial Assemblies survived and even flourished; a beckoning invitation to further local government reform. That invitation was taken up by Calonne in his speech before the Notables in February 1787. Calonne envisaged not one but three tiers of assemblies located at the level of province, *élection* and parish. These bodies would be created, moreover, in all the *pays d'élections* without exception. Influenced by Dupont de Nemours and the physiocratic writers, he planned to staff the assemblies with landowners regardless of social rank. In answer to the criticism levelled at Necker's creations, these representatives would be elected – initially at parish level only but eventually at the higher levels too. Calonne's immediate objective was to obtain consent for a wider definition of public taxation which was unlikely to be forthcoming if the assemblies were thought to be a tool of the government. On the other hand, his proposal implied the creation of perhaps 22,000 parish assemblies, 700 *élection* assemblies and a score of Provincial Assemblies which might easily slip out of the consultative role assigned to them.

The Notables applauded this hefty administrative reform while expressing concern at the radical departure from traditional notions of representation by order. In this respect they proved more perspicacious than their overeager minister. After Calonne's fall his replacement, Brienne, returned to the constitutionally less risky ground of representation by order within the Provincial Assemblies, moderated by a doubling of the Third and voting by head in common session. As such the reform went ahead. An edict of June 1787 announced that the king wished to continue the work begun by Necker and to extend a network of assemblies to all provinces not already endowed with Provincial Estates. In practice this presupposed the creation of rather more assemblies than a tally of provinces would indicate, for the thinking of ministers remained rooted in the institutional categories of absolute monarchy. *Généralités* rather than provinces were the true denominator of Calonne's reform. Hence the province of Normandy, which was divided into three *généralités*, gave birth to three Provincial Assemblies meeting in the intendancy seats of Caen, Alençon and Rouen. The latter body proved the most sensitive creation owing to the proximity of the Parlement of Rouen which would really have preferred a revival of the Provincial Estates. In the event, the edict proclaiming the establishment of the Provincial Assembly of Upper Normandy arrived for registration in August 1787 when most of the magistrates were on vacation. It was passed – under some pressure – and the new body held its inaugural session later that same month.

One of the first tasks of the provincial councillors was to bring to life the intermediate bodies described variously in the documents as 'District' or *élection* Assemblies. Their members were either appointed or coopted in the first instance, but Calonne had made it clear that the government planned to make both Provincial and *élection* Assemblies elective by means of a process of retirement and renewal commencing in 1791. In the *généralité* of Châlons-sur-Marne a regulation prescribed the formation of assemblies in all fourteen *élection* subdivisions, but the bizarre configuration of the *élections* prompted a flexible misinterpretation of the reform in several areas. Upper Normandy was divided into ten 'departments', each embracing two or three *élections*, while 'District' Assemblies emerged as a solution to ragged fiscal frontiers in Alsace and Lorraine. However constituted, most of these bodies held inaugural sessions in the autumn of 1787, and would meet again the following year before the Revolution supervened. Like the Provincial Assemblies, they were empowered to establish permanent committees (*commissions inter-médiaires*) which would handle business during the interval between sessions.

In the event, much of that business concerned the Municipal Assemblies: the bottom and most innovative tier of Calonne's local government reform. Unlike the Provincial and *élection* Assemblies, the new municipalities were thrown open to election from the start. Depending upon the size of the community, up to nine councillors were to be chosen henceforth by means of a ballot in which all adult males paying taxes to the value of 10 *livres* or more were entitled to participate irrespective of 'estate and rank'.[12] The transition from a status-based mode of representation to one based on wealth was not complete, for both the seigneur and the parish priest obtained an ex officio right of representation. Also the reform did not apply to towns and smaller localities where there were already established municipalities. Nevertheless, the edict commenced the civic existence of the village, notwithstanding the claims of the Revolution to the contrary. In common with hundreds of villages in northern, eastern and central France, the first entry in the municipal register of Rennemoulin on the outskirts of Versailles was made not in 1790 but during the summer of 1787.[13]

The censitary, or tax-paying mode of representation brought into being a new set of problems, however, which the *élection* assemblies spent much of their short lives trying to sort out. Who was qualified to vote? How should votes be expressed? How many councillors were to be permitted? What should be done about resignations? Many of these difficulties had been anticipated in the framing of the various edicts and regulations, but others appear to have taken ministers by surprise. A fundamental source of confusion pertained to the territorial definition of a Municipal Assembly. The legal instruments equated the municipality with the parish, but it transpired that ministers had really intended to institutionalise the fiscal entity known as the *communauté d'habitants* or *collecte*. In several regions of the country the parish and the *collecte* did not reliably coincide as the *élection* assembly of Saint-Flour in the Auvergne was at pains to point out. The perennial *ancien-régime* ailment of overlapping jurisdictions also resurfaced in the form of tension within the municipalities between the old village syndics and their newly elected replacements (see below pp. 145–6). A year after the implementation of the reform the permanent officials of the *élection* assembly of Laon complained that the old syndics were refusing to stand down and, indeed, were still receiving orders from the intendant.

Calonne's local government reform project made faltering progress at the lower reaches, then. Large swathes of rural France were municipalised, but in an approximate fashion and only after considerable delay in some regions. The weekly meetings prescribed in the regulations were rarely held and such municipal registers as were kept provide the historian with sparse and unenlightening fare. The higher authorities accused the new *élus* of foot-dragging; in reality they possessed neither the capacity nor the resources adequately to perform the tasks required of them. On receiving a fourteen-point questionnaire from the Provincial Assembly of the Soissonnais with instructions to forward it to the municipalities, the officers of the Laon *élection* assembly expressed misgivings lest 'the number of questions to start off with should cause the members of the municipalities to take fright'.[14] Far better to accustom them to official correspondence bit by bit. On the other hand, the novelty of elective village institutions made a deep impression. The subdelegate of Saint-Flour in the Auvergne reported that the hustings had provoked 'a terrible combustion in the parishes and appeared to threaten both the tranquility of the countryside and the cohesion of the towns'.[15] Town dwellers, it is true, had good grounds for complaint against a reform which offered them nothing. But even once the initial excitement of the elections had ebbed, villagers seem to have remained alert to the potential of the new municipalities as vehicles for the expression of civic identity. In several provinces the parish *cahiers* of 1789 urged the king to expand their powers, which suggests that the assemblies were playing a part in stoking up the atmosphere of expectation that gripped the countryside on the eve of the Revolution.

The introduction of assemblies to the *généralités* and *élections* paid more immediate dividends. Ministers had hoped to mobilise educated public opinion in the cause of reform from above and they were not disappointed. Following the inaugural session of the Provincial Assembly of the Auvergne, Lafayette reported to Thomas Jefferson that the members 'were disposed to act with zeal, and good harmony, whereby many abuses may be destroyed, liberal principles be adopted, and a great deal of good be done'. He went on to applaud the 'good understanding' reached between the ancient nobility and the Third Estate, while pointing out that it did not extend to nobles of more recent origin.[16] By the end of that year some twenty Provincial Assemblies had mushroomed, and Jefferson was not alone in supposing that a combination of devolution and representation would shortly accomplish a political reformation of the kingdom. Necker's return to power in the late summer of 1788 seemed to promise as much and the minister soon began to cast around for a means of boosting the elective component of Calonne's assemblies. He seems even to have contemplated using the Provincial Assemblies as electoral constituencies for the forthcoming Estates General. On the other hand, opinion had begun to shift in favour of a wholesale restoration of Provincial Estates, a prospect which Brienne had been forced to concede several months earlier. This presented the government with something of a dilemma: Provincial Estates were undoubtedly more 'constitutional' than Provincial Assemblies, but they were unlikely to sanction the kind of reformation upon which ministers were now embarked. Piloting a way through this institutional maze would absorb much of Necker's time and energy during the autumn and winter of 1788–9 (see below pp. 157–8).

Calonne, Brienne and Necker held, in sequence, the most powerful office under the crown and it is important to conclude this institutional anatomy of the *ancien régime* with a description of the apparatus of central government. The king was the primary institution of state and in his official capacity he functioned in three spheres; that is to say he appeared at Court, he presided over royal Councils and he conducted private cabinet business with his ministers. Unlike his great-grandfather, Louis XVI performed the public duties of kingship dutifully rather than enthusiastically. He was serious-minded and highly educated, but reluctant to apply himself, to make up his mind and to adhere to decisions when placed under pressure to do otherwise. Much of the business of government went on around him, although this is more a comment upon the ramifying bureaucracy of administrative monarchy than a judgement upon the incumbent of the throne. Originally the kings of France ruled through a single 'great council', but by the late eighteenth century five more specialised royal councils had come into being, although their functions overlapped a good deal.

Major issues of state and of foreign affairs, in particular, were decided in the Conseil d'Etat which was a direct descendant of the old medieval Council. The king presided over this body which met in an upstairs room of the château of Versailles, hence its alternative title of Conseil d'en-haut. Originally the senior royal Council had exercised control over domestic affairs as well, but by the eighteenth century two more specialised institutions claimed authority in this sphere: the Conseil des Dépêches and the Conseil royal des Finances. The former, as its name implies, received despatches sent in from the provinces by the intendants and the governors. It handled business to do with the *parlements*, the Provincial Estates, the church, the municipalities and much else besides. The Conseil royal des Finances, whose title was often abbreviated to Conseil royal, tended to operate in the same area but with a different emphasis. State finances and those of the royal household fell within its purview, as did economic policy until 1730 when a separate Conseil royal de Commerce was established. This latter Council was reabsorbed into the Conseil royal des Finances in 1787. All of these bodies were only supposed to meet in the personal presence of the monarch, but there also existed several Councils whose sessions were chaired by the chancellor acting in the name of the king. By far the most important was the Conseil d'Etat privé (also known as the Conseil des Parties) whose function was to dispense the king's privy justice, that is to say appellate justice above and beyond the competence of the *parlements*. This Council conducted judicial reviews, heard appeals against judgements of the intendants and was empowered to issue resolutions quashing the rulings of the courts.

Here we have the broad categories of conciliar government, then. But power tended in practice to be wielded by a restricted number of high officials who acted independently of the Councils, and it is to these individuals that we must turn next. Highest in prestige, if not always in terms of effective power, were the ministers who sat alongside the king in the Conseil d'Etat. These included the secretaries of state for Foreign Affairs, for War, for the Navy and for the Royal Household. The controller-general was not, automatically, a minister, nor could he sit by right in either the Conseil d'Etat or the Conseil royal des Finances. In practice, though, he performed the tasks of Minister of Finance whatever his precise status. Until the very end of the *ancien régime* the fiction that decisions were taken by the king-in-council was retained despite overwhelming evidence to the contrary. In reality the day-to-day business of government was conducted at three levels: by the king in weekly cabinet discussions with individual ministers, by the controller-general on his own initiative, and by the six powerful under-secretaries (*intendants des finances*) or divisional heads of the controller-general's department. These latter were not employees of the crown, but venal officials with near total control over the activities of their respective divisions. From their offices scattered around Paris, they fed business to the controller-general who, in turn, might lay it before the king. Thus the Councils were not so much altered in function as bypassed. They survived as a convenient camouflage for an increasingly bureaucratic style of government. Laws and edicts were often promulgated as 'arrêts du conseil' without ever having been submitted for conciliar approval. The imprimatur of the Conseil royal des Finances, in particular, became little more than a rubber stamp: barely one finance measure in twenty was ever brought before the Council.

The culprit, in the view of the sovereign courts at least, was the controller-general. In 1775 the *cour des aides* of Paris penned a blunt remonstrance to Louis XVI blaming the decline of conciliar government upon the busybodying officials of the Contrôle Général. It is true that the expanding competence of successive controllers-general, as fiscal considerations became all-embracing, did much to determine the restructuring of the machinery of state. Necker, the last Finance Minister of the *ancien régime*, presided over a 'ministry' employing 360 clerks divided between roughly thirty-eight bureaux. These bureaux were mostly located in Paris and between them they handled business spanning the entire spectrum of government activity, even foreign affairs. More an administrative empire than a ministry in the modern sense, the Contrôle Général des Finances has been described as 'a rambling agglomeration of commissions, services, semi-independent functionaries' which was held together by a general staff of senior officials known as *premiers commis*. Outsiders, and above all the magistrates of the *parlements* and the *cours des aides*, viewed this concentration of ministerial power with unconcealed alarm, but despite all the efforts at reform in the 1770s and 1780s the Contrôle Général never became a streamlined institution of state. Ministers of the calibre of Turgot and Necker only succeeded in dominating this ramifying bureaucracy with the utmost difficulty; their successors scarcely even tried.

A well-ordered state?

Rambling and inefficient though the machinery of government may appear, it is important to keep matters in perspective. By European standards France was an impressively well-ordered state. The Bourbons very nearly succeeded in welding together a realm which, in its late eighteenth-century form, displayed unmistakable characteristics of modernity. Sovereign control over territory was no longer a matter for serious dispute, despite a residue of geographical and administrative untidiness, and the native population no longer challenged the taxing prerogative of the crown. How many *ancien-régime* rulers could claim as much? On the other hand, the doctrine of state service was less developed in France than in the Germanic lands, even though French institutions were widely copied. The physiocrats sketched out a philosophy of rational government comparable, in some respects, to the theories of the German cameralists, but they could never secure the unflinching support of ministers. The French administration remained in a state of imperfect modernisation; bureaucratic in tendency and yet prevented from further evolution by the sapping effects of Court intrigue, vested interest and venality of office.

This crisis afflicting the institutional fabric of the Bourbon state had deep roots. In fact it developed in tandem with the growth of absolute monarchy. However, the frictions within the machinery of government reached a new pitch of intensity in the 1770s and 1780s, decades that witnessed mounting public concern over the issue of 'despotism' and vigorous attempts to break through the institutional gridlock. But public concern did not translate into a neat recipe for administrative reform, for at its heart the blockage was social and not institutional. The provincial elites on whom the monarchy relied for the smooth running of government adopted a contradictory posture. As men of the Enlightenment they favoured administrative reform on intellectual grounds, but at the same time opposed it on political grounds. Fear of the likely despotic tendencies of a government unrestrained by vested interests provided some justification for this attitude, but many members of the intelligentsia were office-holders whose views were tempered by more immediate considerations. However desirable in the abstract, reform from above threatened the 'constitution' of the kingdom; it also threatened livelihoods and lucrative networks of patronage.

No one identified the dilemmas confronting those who would reform the machinery of government with more acuity that Auget de Montyon. On the strength of many years experience as an intendant and councillor of state, he penned a remarkable study devoted to what he described as the 'science of administration'. Therein we find a valuable generalisation which helps to make sense of the frictions and tensions that accompanied the growth of administrative monarchy. Montyon depicts the apparatus of state (under Louis XVI) as caught in the turmoils of a transition. An organic, particularist and fundamentally juridical style of rule was being challenged by an impersonal, homogenising and fundamentally administrative approach to the task of government. Neither tendency could be said to predominate, resulting in a 'fairly continuous and often too intense war between two powers, the *jurisdictional* and the *ministerial*'.[17] The office-holding magistrature of the sovereign courts behaved as watchdogs of the jurisdictional interest, whereas the intendants together with the impersonal bureaucracy of the Contrôle Général symbolised the competing claims of administrative monarchy.

The expanding supervisory role of the intendants has already been mentioned, but it should not be exaggerated. As servants of the crown, they were tied closely to the life-cycle of absolute monarchy. The power of the monarchs of France determined the power of the intendants and not vice versa. Alexis de Tocqueville rightly detected a centralising urge emanating from the very heart of government, but he was wrong to suppose that the work of administrative centralisation was all but complete by the end of the *ancien régime*. On the contrary, the royal power wielded by the intendants fluctuated dramatically in the second half of the eighteenth century. And even when constant, the intendants were still required to negotiate the king's business with established elites in large parts of the kingdom. In the face of opposition from the Breton Estates, the intendants could do little. Even holding on to royal power in this region proved problematic, for the Estates were ever on the look out for signs of weakness. Having won the right to conduct business between sessions by means of a permanent committee (*commission intermédiaire*), they went on to wrest control of the highways, as we have seen. Bertrand de Molleville glumly concluded that there remained little left for him to do in the province.

The reaction of the man who was effectively Brittany's last royal intendant is interesting, for he clearly felt betrayed. He conceived his task as being to defend and, if possible, to extend the authority of central government, and it was not made easier by the gratuitous sacrifice of power by the king and his ministers. His dismay captures the more general sense of disillusionment which overtook the corps of intendants as the shadows lengthened around the *ancien régime*. Could inept decision-making be the prelude to a wholesale retreat from the hallowed principles of absolute monarchy? The signals emerging from the palace of Versailles in 1786 and 1787 were disturbing to say the least. Individual intendants resolved the tensions inherent in their position in different ways, of course. Some were liege-men to the core. Others tended to identify with the interests of the region in which they found themselves, thereby jeopardising their primary function as enforcement officers of the crown. It is said that Tourny, intendant of the *généralité* of

Tours, drew a distinction between the king's interest and the public interest. Whenever the two were in conflict, he pursued the latter. By the reign of Louis XVI, according to the Russian historian Paul Ardascheff, a significant evolution had taken place: the intendants had ceased to function as the eyes and ears of central government. Instead, they had become representative of the provinces.[18] This inversion of Tocqueville's thesis is thinly supported by facts and liable to the charge that it mistakes local aberrations for a general trend. On the other hand, it does serve to remind us that the 'king's interest' had become decidedly difficult to identify by the end of the *ancien régime*. During the last feverish years of the old monarchy, many intendants found themselves defending a conception of the royal prerogative which Louis XVI and his ministers seemed no longer to share.

More important for our purpose is the band of intendants who, in the absence of clear guidance from the centre, set about elaborating policies which they perceived to be in the best interests of the monarchy (see below pp. 124–7). Thus Turgot began work on a scheme to distribute more equitably the burdens of road-building (*corvée*); the new intendants of Corsica supervised the introduction of Provincial Estates based on equal representation, and Bertier de Sauvigny *fils* pushed ahead with major revision of the *taille* in the *généralité* of Paris. In Lorraine intendant Chaumont de la Galaizière *fils* both encouraged ministers in the direction of agrarian reform and set an example on his own lands. As for the feudal regime, many intendants perceived the interests of good government to be best served by the curtailment of seigneurial control over the rural community, if only for fiscal reasons. In extreme cases this resulted in royal officials actually encouraging the peasantry to challenge seigneurial dues and perquisites. Something of the sort appears to have taken place in Burgundy in the 1760s and 1770s. What this implies is that some of the intendants had come themselves to recognise that 'privilege' posed an obstacle to effective and enlightened government. They were influenced by public opinion to be sure, but at the same time they set out to nourish the desire for reform that a crisis of state would precipitate in the winter of 1786–7. But in neither sense were they simply the tools of local interests. These intendants represented a reform constituency in their own right, albeit one unsure of its role in a new political order.

That new political order began to unfold in the spring of 1787. With the establishment or, to be more precise, the extension of Provincial, *élection* and Municipal Assemblies to nearly all the *pays d'élections*, it became apparent that a dramatic change in the nature of Bourbon government was in prospect. François Furet has quite rightly observed that 'absolute monarchy died, in theory and in practice, in the year when its intendants were made to share their responsibilities with elected assemblies'.[19] Diligent agents of absolutism who had striven for decades to consolidate their powers of *tutelle*, the intendants were nonplussed. No amount of rhetoric and elaborate obeisance to the authority of the intendant in the founding deeds of the Provincial Assemblies could disguise the fact that an alternative chain of command was being set up (see below pp. 142–6). With provincial and even Court nobles jostling for membership of the new bodies, and with parish priests and seigneurs accorded automatic membership of the Municipal Assemblies, it seemed like the final revenge of 'jurisdictional' over 'ministerial' power. A defeat inflicted by the monarchy upon itself! When the intendants were called upon to open formally the Provincial Assemblies in the summer of 1787 most put on a brave face. Some even welcomed the opportunity to pursue reform by a different route. But in many regions the intendants and the subdelegates waged a subterranean war of attrition against these rival sources of authority which would only be resolved by the complete collapse of the institutions of Bourbon absolutism some two years later.

2   Society

All states evolve social myths in order to explain how they came into being and managed to survive in an often hostile environment. As denizens of a dynastic state, French men and women would have been familiar with the image of the 'body politic' with a monarch forming the 'head', clergy and nobility figured as the 'arms' and the toiling masses performing the role of 'legs'. The early seventeenth-century jurist Loyseau expressed this concept in terms of three 'orders' or 'estates', each buttressed by law and united in a common bond of loyalty to the sovereign.[1] These orders have been described aptly as 'transparent envelopes'[2] for, on closer inspection, they dissolve into a multitude of pullulating corporate interests. 'All of your subjects', the Parlement of Paris informed Louis XVI,

are divided into as many different corps as there are different estates in the realm: the Clergy, the Nobility, the sovereign courts, the officers attached to these tribunals, the universities, the academies, the companies of finance and of commerce; all present and existing throughout the State, these corps may be regarded as the links in a great chain of which the first is in the hands of Your Majesty, as chief and sovereign administrator of all that constitutes the corps of the Nation.[3]

At least, that was the theory. Even as the Parlement extolled the virtues of a society rooted in a natural equilibrium of orders and estates, other observers were drawing attention to the less than harmonious reality. Auget de Montyon, as we have seen, had concluded that corporate diversity tended to hinder rather than enhance the power of the crown. Turgot, likewise, remained unmoved by the vision of a 'great chain of being' formulated by defenders of 'jurisdictional' authority. He perceived instead 'a society composed of several different orders having no real unity and of a people who have few social ties'. In the place of unity, he found strife: a 'perpetual war of competing interests'.[4] This was Auget's diagnosis confirmed. For the physiocrats the lack of social ties simply pointed to the fundamental defect in the corporative vision. It failed to take account of socio-economic realities. How could social harmony prevail when the common interests of property owners were arbitrarily separated by an outdated framework of juridically defined orders?

We shall see shortly how far these criticisms can be justified. But it helps first to analyse the society of the late *ancien régime* in terms of individuals, and individual functions. Thanks to a buoyant birthrate the population of France was nudging 28 million as the monarchy embarked upon its final spasm of reform. The great majority of these individuals lived in the countryside: urban France accounted for around 20 per cent of the total, a proportion that had scarcely altered since the start of the century. Not all country dwellers were cultivators, however. Village society habitually included priests, craft workers, servants and beggars, and might also include petty nobles, non-noble landowners and the purveyors of services such as millers, blacksmiths and retail traders. But cultivators formed the biggest occupational group, those whom contemporaries and historians, subsequently, have referred to as 'peasants' or the 'peasantry'. Somewhere between 82 and 87 per cent of the rural population can be labelled thus. Gradations of economic well-being and social esteem within the peasant estate varied almost to infinity, although an obvious distinction to draw is that between those with access to land (either owned or rented) and those without. On this hypothesis, *abbé* Expilly concluded that 60 per cent of the agricultural labour force were landless.[5] The calculation seems reasonable provided that it is borne in mind that many wage workers also tilled gardens or tiny plots of land on their own account. Similarly, village artisans often doubled up as part-time cultivators.

Agricultural wage labour usually went hand-in-hand with large-scale cereal farming. As such it was symptomatic of the highly polarised social structure found typically in the *pays de grande culture*, that is to say the belt around Paris as well as to the north and east of the capital. Here much of the land would be cultivated by big tenant farmers acting for noble and ecclesiastical owners. A class of independent peasant cultivators controlling enough land for their families' needs came next in the pecking order, followed by a mass of plot farmers whose scattered holdings provided neither full-time occupation nor a regular daily supply of bread. To judge from the plentiful literature on rural social structure in this part of France, a typical village of several hundred inhabitants would contain two or three substantial tenants, a handful of self-sufficient farmers, perhaps a score of plot holders and anything from twenty to fifty families living off wage labour and craft activities. Elsewhere – in the Centre, the West and above all the South – differentiation within the peasant estate was less pronounced. These were very largely regions of *petite culture* where low soil fertility and stagnant urban demand discouraged land engrossment. In the Auvergne nearly all peasant households had preserved a stake in the land, although here too the threshold of self-sufficiency remained beyond the reach of the vast majority. In the South-West the large sharecropper replaced the tenant-farmer at the fulcrum of village society. And behind the sharecropper stood the landowner, whether noble or bourgeois. Neither sharecroppers nor resident landowners could be found in the villages of the northern plains.

While the evolution of rural society is now fairly well understood, the urban history of the *ancien régime* presents something of a problem. Despite a century of vigorous growth on numerous fronts, the distribution of population between country and town remained constant or nearly so. Yet there *is* a sense in which the urban experience impinged on more lives than ever before; for, although the percentage of town dwellers remained modest, the number of towns in which they dwelt was extraordinarily high. Moreover, urban pretensions and urban culture generally expanded in the eighteenth century to a degree unparalleled. The proliferation of academies, reading societies, masonic lodges and even post offices (see below pp. 75–8) testifies to the trend. In any case the impression of lethargy conveyed by crude percentages is slightly misleading. Many small administrative centres, reliant upon the ebb and flow of judicial business through their courts, failed to grow, it is true. But the great ports, inland manufacturing cities and frontier towns all expanded vigorously. Marseille staged a dramatic recovery from the plague visitation of 1721 and boasted a little over 100,000 inhabitants on the eve of the Revolution, although Lyon retained its rank as the second city of the kingdom by adding 50,000 to a preexisting population of 100,000 in the course of the century. During the same period Bordeaux, Nantes and Nîmes nearly doubled in size (to 105,000, 80,000 and 40,000 respectively), while Brest, Le Havre, Rouen, Nancy, Strasbourg and Besançon all registered substantial increases in population. Paris stood alone, of course, with approximately 620,000 citizens in 1789 (and nearly 510,000 at the start of the century). By the end of the *ancien régime* the kingdom contained some 200 towns of between 5,000 and 10,000 inhabitants and nearly 100 with a population in excess. Apart from the capital, however, only two cities surpassed the 100,000 threshold.

The dynamism and social complexity of the great port cities owed nearly everything to the expanding horizons of maritime commerce (see below pp. 97–100). They looked outwards – not inwards – and the wealth generated by trade with the Levant and the colonies sustained

affluent lifestyles and a highly developed service sector. The slave
captains and colonial importers of Nantes, for instance, kept busy a craft
economy subdivided into dozens of guilds and corporations. By
contrast, the bulk of small inland towns lived symbiotically on the needs
and the resources of the surrounding countryside. They supplied a few
basic services – usually of a judicial or spiritual character – and were
instantly vulnerable to alterations in the pattern of demand. The
relocation of an important court, the decline of a seigneurial jurisdiction,
an amalgamation of ecclesiastical institutions, or even a change in the
habits of the local nobility, could spell disaster. The fragility of such
towns was displayed for all to see during the first winter of the
Revolution when the work to redraw the administrative and ecclesiastical
map of France began in earnest. The ubiquity of small centres of
population living parasitically on the backs of the peasantry goes some
way towards explaining the stagnant profile of urban growth across the
century. Fragility of a different sort afflicted manufacturing towns whose
products were susceptible to international competition and changes in
taste or fashion. Lyon, for instance, looked neither overseas nor to its
immediate hinterland for the source of its prosperity. With half the
population dependent in some way upon the weaving of silk thread, the
city fathers looked instead to the Court and central government for
support and protective tariffs.

Most French men and women lived in the country, then, and in
conditions of unremitting physical toil. But what of those whose wealth,
upbringing or occupation emancipated them from the soil and the loom?
This elite of perhaps 2 million individuals can be divided unequally into
three groups: the clergy, the nobility and the bourgeoisie. By the blurred
standards of the *ancien régime,* the clergy formed a sharply defined
occupational group. Parish priests totalled around 39,000 on the eve of
the Revolution, and they were assisted by 20,500 curates. The non-
parish clergy, consisting of prelates and priests carrying out teaching
duties or charitable functions, can be numbered at another 5,000 or so,
to whom should be added the unbeneficed, 'odd job' clergymen
common in a number of dioceses. Contemplative vocations had declined
sharply in the course of the century; nevertheless, a contingent of 37,000
nuns and 23,000 monks occupied several thousand religious houses.
The First Estate therefore embraced only a tiny percentage fraction of
the nation, but its physical and institutional presence was quite
formidable. The church owned approximately one tenth of the land
surface of the kingdom and collected 120 million *livres* in tithes. Land
rents and tithes combined to produce an annual income of around a
quarter of a billion *livres,* all of which was technically exempt from

taxation. Discretionary donations (the *don gratuit*) had eroded this principle somewhat by the end of the *ancien régime*. Even so, the church still only paid income tax at an equivalent rate of 0.00064 per cent annually.[6]

Critics of the church espied priests everywhere. In fact the *philosophes* imagined that they were dealing with a 'party' of some 500,000 strong. The reality was more sobering as we have seen. Moreover, if Colbert's calculations can be relied upon, the ranks of the clergy had thinned considerably in the course of the eighteenth century. From an estimated average density of 12 per thousand head of population in 1667, the clerical presence had diminished to 4.5 per thousand on the eve of the Revolution.[7] It is true that such figures fail to match the common perception of a numerous and meddlesome clergy and the explanation partly lies in the uneven distribution of the resources of the church. Many small towns were stiff with priests, indeed they were ecclesiastical towns to all intents and purposes. In the South, Saint-Papoul, Senez and Vabres were all episcopal seats, yet none could muster more than 1,000 inhabitants. Bayeux in the North constituted an altogether more substantial town that could boast five law courts as well as a bishopric. Even so, clerics (parish clergy, lay sisters and religious) still made up 6 per cent of the population.

Unlike the clergy, the nobility had long ceased to resemble an occupational group and are best described as a category defined by status. But since that status lacked clarity in law (notwithstanding the notion of a Second Estate), estimates of noble numbers have tended to vary significantly. Perhaps the safest estimate is that reached by Guy Chaussinand-Nogaret[8] on the basis of those attending the specifically noble electoral assemblies established for the purpose of selecting deputies to the Estates General. According to this source, between 110,000 and 120,000 individuals – or 25,000 families – possessed incontrovertible nobility in 1789. To put it another way, roughly 0.4 per cent of the population could legitimately claim noble status, a proportion comparable to that of the clergy. And like the clergy, the nobility exercised power and influence on a scale quite disproportionate to their numerical strength. Between one quarter and one third of cultivated land, most of the forests and seigneurial jurisdiction over much of what remained belonged to the nobility. They also monopolised the highest offices of state and of the judiciary. Most prelates, indeed, were noble, as were all holders of commissions in the army. Finally, titled families enjoyed important fiscal immunities.

The question of privilege, whether fiscal or honorific, raises important issues concerning the structuring of the noble elite and its relations with wealthy commoners. These will be explored in the pages that follow. Suffice it to say at this stage that the so-called Second Estate was riven by internal tensions. Moreover, the juridical definition of those individuals comprising the Second Estate and the popular apprehension of what passed for noble coincided only approximately. Broadly speaking, contemporary opinion acknowledged four species of nobleman: the courtier, the lineage noble, the ennobled bourgeois and for want of a better word the 'phoney'. Courtier families were those whose eligible sons and daughters had been presented at Court. They were wealthy, illustrious and invisible, in the sense that they spent most of their time in Versailles. Families of ancient lineage traced back their noble pedigree over centuries as the sobriquet *noblesse de race* implied. Some were very wealthy and aspired to the honours of the Court, but the majority simply 'lived nobly' in provincial obscurity, dividing their time between their estates and the winter pleasures of the neighbouring town. Most *anoblis* had risen from the Third Estate by the simple expedient of purchasing an office conferring immediate or eventual nobility. Usually this implied an ascension through the senior courts and tribunals of the kingdom, hence the phrase *noblesse de robe*. Their numbers were legion and their pedigrees correspondingly short. Fabricated nobility consisted of aping noble lifestyle in the hope and expectation that contemporaries would in due course grant the coveted status. The practice was widespread among landowning families of the Third Estate who had withdrawn from direct cultivation of their estates in order to live off rent (the rural bourgeoisie). Add the purchase of a seigneurie or two, and the discreet introduction of the particle, and such families soon covered their social tracks. The hardest part was to win exemption from the principal tax on commoners, the *taille*; hence the appeal of office-holding.

A simple subtraction of social entities leaves us with the bourgeoisie. According to the time-honoured taxonomies of *ancien-régime* jurisprudence they did not exist; perhaps they could be identified among the plethora of interests lumped together in the Third Estate, but that is all. Yet it is certain that the bourgeoisie did exist and that contemporaries grasped as much. Whether they existed in the form consecrated by historians of the French Revolution is another matter. At this juncture it is only necessary to resolve two questions: who were they and how many of them were there? Georges Lefebvre,[9] who spent more time pondering these issues than most historians, proposed a multi-tier classification which located the financiers, farmers-general, shipowners, manufacturers and larger merchants at the helm and shopkeepers, booksellers, postmasters, apothecaries, minor medical practitioners and a few substantial workshop owners at the base. In between and in order of esteem he placed the office-holders who staffed the courts and the higher reaches of the administration, and the liberal professions (doctors, attorneys, land agents, surveyors, etc.). The fifth group was largely free floating and consisted of a loose milieu of writers, journalists, artists, musicians, singers and actors. To these categories must be added a non-occupational species: the rentier. Families living purely from agricultural rents, from annuities or from government stock might reside either in the towns or in the countryside. In the former case they were bourgeois in the original sense of the term; in the latter the label bourgeois implied a non-noble family of landowners who had severed quite explicitly all physical connection with the soil. Lefebvre expanded this rural bourgeoisie to include the wealthy tenant farmers of northern villages. But this is to blur the distinction between manual and non-manual labour on which acceptance into the bourgeoisie depended.

Socially and juridically disparate, the bourgeoisie are even harder to count. In his *Tableau de la population de la France* (1780), *abbé* Expilly reckoned the office-holding bourgeoisie at 60,000 individuals and liberal professionals at 25,000. In addition, he enumerated 1,020,000 'Bourgeois, Financiers, Négociants, Marchands et Artisans'[10] which would be helpful, but for the inclusion of artisans. His corresponding enumeration of country dwellers makes no mention of village-based rentiers or professionals at all. The historian Pierre Léon has adopted a different approach based on extrapolation from known data. If it is assumed that bourgeois families constituted roughly 30 per cent of households in the more vigorous urban centres, the overall size of the bourgeoisie can be reckoned at between 70,000 and 80,000 individuals around the start of the century. Except, of course, that these figures leave out of account the rural bourgeoisie. By the end of the century, Léon therefore concludes, the urban bourgeoisie must have totalled some 2,300,000 individuals, that is 8.4 per cent of the total population compared with 3.7 per cent at the start. Unfortunately, however, the mode of calculation used to fix the end-of-century total is unreliable. A generous estimate of the urban population of France in 1789 would be 5,700,000, which yields a figure of 6.1 per cent at the end of the *ancien régime*.[11]

The urban bourgeoisie expanded, then, but it doubled not tripled as is sometimes suggested. This is still highly significant at a time when the nobility could only maintain its numbers by creaming off the upper office-holding echelons of commoners. Office-holding, as William Doyle has now made clear, continued to exert an enormous attraction.[12] Across the century between 5,000 and 7,000 incumbents together with their families entered the nobility by this route. There remains the problem of the rural bourgeoisie, of course, which defies even the most

rudimentary statistical analysis. Lefebvre mistook their social significance because resident bourgeois proprietors were a rare and inconspicuous phenomenon in the countryside of the North-East which he knew
best. They did not signify in the West either. But in the South, South-
West and above all the Midi, village bourgeois were legion by the end of
the *ancien régime*. They had profited from the financial difficulties of the
petty nobility during the early part of the century, expanded their
numbers during the 'high farming' decades, and by 1789 had come to
represent a formidable force in the parishes. Reliant upon the collecting
services which they provided, yet deeply uneasy about their leadership
role within the rural community, the old nobility treated the rural
bourgeoisie with suspicious disdain. The marquis de Mirabeau *père*
denounced them as a 'malicious and harmful race which it would be
advisable to purge from the face of society.'[13]

Does such contempt also betray an awareness of economic vulner-
ability among the old elite? Estimates of bourgeois wealth suffer from the
same ambiguities as bedevil attempts to count heads. In view of the
historiographical confusion surrounding the role of bourgeoisie, it is
worth emphasising that they possessed a substantial slice of the land as
well as considerable investments in venal offices and *rentes*. This
'proprietary' wealth probably accounted for 80 per cent of total private
wealth by the end of the *ancien régime* and of course all social groups
aspired to share in it. The bourgeoisie may have owned one fifth of the
cultivable land surface; they certainly owned much of the vast capital
invested in offices, and they systematically bought government stock and
private *rentes* (annuities payable in return for a fixed sum), although on
what scale we cannot tell. The wealth generated by commerce, banking
and industry tended to accumulate overwhelmingly in their hands.
Bourgeois domination of the booming maritime economy was nearly
total, and it is probable that bourgeois investment in extractive industry
outpaced that of the nobility as well. Most inland trade was short range
and conducted by individuals whose hold on bourgeois status was
tenuous at best. But the fruits of trade were, as we shall see, nearly
always laundered into assets carrying greater social consequence.
Bourgeois wealth was growing, then, but so was that of many estates of
the nation. In the prevailing economic conditions (see below pp. 82–
100), it would be surprising if this were not the case. Was the
bourgeoisie's wealth expanding faster than that of other social groups?
Here is a more difficult question to answer. Insofar as the massive profits
piled up in the colonial trade filtered out into the domestic economy, a
whole stratum of the bourgeoisie was increasing its economic leverage.
The rural bourgeoisie, too, were busily practising highly lucrative

methods of capital accumulation (land engrossment, rent collecting, money lending, etc.), while the majority of placements in offices were definitely gaining in value. But bourgeois wealth was an unstable commodity. As William Doyle has pointed out, it was constantly siphoned into the Second Estate through the mechanism of ennoblement.[14] No doubt the bourgeoisie were rising, both in terms of numbers and disposable wealth, as the century drew to a climax. But it would be wrong to conclude thereby that the nobility were a class in decline.

Privilege

The ingredient missing from this recipe description of *ancien-régime* society is privilege. For privilege served to define relations between the component parts of the body politic. But what was privilege? The *Encyclopédie méthodique: jurisprudence* published in 1786 offered the following explanation: 'distinctions, whether useful or honorific, which are enjoyed by certain members of society and denied to others'.[15] As befits a dictionary entry, the definition was couched in neutral terms. Nonetheless, privilege (literally meaning 'private laws') had become a divisive issue by the end of the *ancien régime*. How this happened and how the monarchy managed to tie itself in knots on the subject is crucial to an understanding of the transition from a hierarchic to a meritocratic society.

At the highest level privilege attached to whole provinces. All Bretons knew that they enjoyed certain 'privileges, immunities and franchises': the terms are virtually interchangeable. These had been guaranteed in the contracts of marriage between Anne, daughter of the last duke, and Charles VIII, closely followed by Louis XII. Consisting primarily of an exemption from the *taille* and the royal salt tax (*gabelle*), they were widely regarded as inalienable and intrinsic to the 'constitution' of the province. On the north-eastern marches of the kingdom similar enclaves of privilege existed. Deeds of unification signed in 1659 exempted the province of the Artois from the *taille*, the *gabelle* and the excise duties known as *aides*; and Walloon Flanders had likewise obtained favourable treatment as the price for its annexation. The Walloons escaped both the salt and the tobacco monopoly, and paid to the crown a nominal subsidy in lieu of the *taille*. Many other provinces enjoyed concessions of a less determinate and irrevocable character: part exemption from the salt levy, perhaps, or the right to compound for payment of the major direct taxes. These concessions were also extended to individual towns. Neither Paris, nor Bordeaux, nor Rouen paid the *taille*, although the monarchy was skilled at tapping urban wealth by other means. The burghers of Lectoure in Gascony proudly informed the authorities that their immunities could be traced back to 1368, the moment when their ancestors had given the signal to rise against the English. In gratitude King Charles V had confirmed their privileges and granted exemption from taxation. Nevertheless, they admitted, the town had been paying an annual 'subsidy' into the royal exchequeur since 1654.[16] Not for nothing has privilege been dubbed a 'surrogate for constitutionalism';[17] after all, when most ordinary French men and women paused to think about their rights and freedoms, it was these tangible benefits that sprang to mind. On hearing reports of the great 'sacrifices' voted on 4 August 1789, the first 'constitutional' thoughts of the Breton peasantry were for the preservation of their 'franchises et privileges'.[18]

Privilege was also attached to individuals by virtue of their member-ship of corporate bodies and estates. Seigneurs, for instance, enjoyed a broad spectrum of lucrative and honorific privileges ranging from the right to tax vassals and operate courts to rights of precedence and symbolic display. The rights of the clergy were not dissimilar, while commoners purchasing offices in the magistrature obtained *ipso facto* relief from the *taille*. Sometimes it proved possible for them to escape direct taxation merely by moving from the countryside to the town. A list of corporate bodies enjoying privileges of one sort or another would be a long one indeed. In addition to the personnel of the *parlements* and the *bailliage*, *sénéchaussée* and *présidial* courts, all excise men and employees of the General Farm enjoyed important exemptions, as did officers in the *élections*, *bureaux des finances*, *greniers à sel* and *prévôté* tribunals. Incumbents of the Royal Household and those of the Princes of the Blood were lightly taxed, and so were the mayors and aldermen of many town councils after the office creation spree of the early eighteenth century. However, members of the Second Estate benefited most from the system of privilege. Indeed, the possession of privileges had come to define the order for want of an alternative raison d'être. Nobles of all degrees could not be impressed for the militia, nor for road-building (*corvée*), nor to furnish billets for troops on the move. As seigneurs they enjoyed the prerogatives already mentioned, and the concept of honour precluded any significant liability to 'commoner' taxes. Hence they were largely exempt from the *taille*, entirely free of the *gabelle* and subject to the *capitation* and *vingtième* taxes only in an attenuated form.

What of the cost of privilege? The honorific and ceremonial denominators of privileged status cannot be quantified, but should not be overlooked for all that. When the Parlement of Paris described the various corps and estates as being linked together in a great chain, it clearly regarded privilege as a lubricant of the body politic. But such an idealisation is to be expected from a company which was one of the principal beneficiaries of the system. A more likely proposition is that privilege had begun to irritate the social fabric of the *ancien régime*. To be sure this erosion of respect for the 'society of orders' was patchy and piecemeal. While the lesser robe bourgeoisie smarted under what one writer termed a 'cascade of scorn', successful merchants were petitioning for admission to the ranks of the privileged. But doubts about the structuring of society became more widespread in the 1770s and 1780s, fostered in part by the monarchy itself. This was the mood caught by the Provincial Assemblies in 1787. Having listed the myriad categories of exemption, the Assembly at Tours asked plaintively: 'would it not be possible to restrict them?'[19] Distinctions based on merit and service were upheld, but venal privilege stood squarely in the dock.

Lucrative or pecuniary privilege weighed heavily, both on individuals and on the nation as whole. For most purposes it may be understood as conferring the benefit of partial or total exemption from taxation. Privilege of this type was palpable and prized highly, but in order to grasp its social and economic significance we must start with a brief description of the tax system. By the end of the *ancien régime* most French men and women were paying a variety of indirect and direct taxes. Indirect taxation took the form of levies charged on items of every day consumption (the *aides*) and goods entering towns (the *octrois*), or crossing the multiple internal and external frontiers (the *traites*) (see map 9(b)). Many different articles were taxed, ranging from iron, leather, soap, firewood and alcohol, to salt and tobacco. The *gabelle* or salt levy was especially lucrative since it forced consumers to purchase large quantities of the product from government warehouses and at extortionate prices. All these taxes were farmed out to contractors (the General Farm) who paid the monarchy a fixed sum per annum in return for the collecting rights. In addition, revenue was raised from leasing out a stamp duty on notarial deeds and *ad valorem* taxes on property transactions and venal offices. Over the century the total revenue from these sources rose to represent 65 per cent of fiscal yield by 1788. In part this merely reflected the upward trend of commodity prices, but it also denoted a tacit recognition within the administrative hierarchy that direct taxes were difficult to assess accurately and riddled with exemptions and abuses. On the other hand, it could be argued that sales and consumption taxes fell heaviest upon the urban consumer, thereby justifying to some degree the exemptions which many of the larger towns enjoyed. Such a calculation would not be entirely gratuitous, for there is evidence to show that the government did try to keep in mind the total

yield of taxation from a given region. In 1772 the intendant of
Montauban reported that direct taxation took one third of incomes in
his *généralité*, but, he added, the inhabitants were not liable to the *aides*
and were in large measure exempt from the *gabelle*.[20]

Three direct taxes existed at the end of the *ancien régime*: the *taille*, the
vingtièmes and the *capitation*. The royal *taille* was a permanent quota tax
dating back to the early fifteenth century. Each year the king-in-council
fixed upon a sum to be raised which was then divided up between the
généralités, *élections* and parishes. It brought in around 65 million *livres*
per annum on the eve of the Revolution. In much of the kingdom the
taille was deemed to be *personnelle*, that is it was assessed against the
presumed wealth of individual commoners. But in the *pays d'états*, in the
Dauphiné, and throughout much of the South-West it was described as
being *réelle*. This meant that it was assessed on land which was classified
as either 'commoner' or 'noble'. In Languedoc, for instance, roughly 10
per cent of land was 'noble' and therefore exempt. The *vingtièmes*, by
contrast, had a more recent and chequered history. The first *vingtième*
was established in 1750 as a temporary measure to meet the debts of
state, but on the outbreak of the Seven Years War in 1756 a second
vingtième was introduced. In 1771, after a great deal of manoeuvring, the
first *vingtième* became a permanent tax and the second was prolonged
until 1781. In the meantime, however, a third *vingtième* had been
created, in 1760, despite vigorous opposition from the sovereign courts.
It lapsed after four years, but was reintroduced in 1782 on the
understanding that it would remain in force for the duration of the
American War and three years beyond.

The *vingtièmes* were supposed to be a proportional tax applicable to all
(net) income whether it derived from the land, from office-holding, from
seigneurial perquisites, from commerce or from industry. But the yield
from these latter sources was low and in consequence the *vingtièmes*
became a tax on land to all intents and purposes. In 1784 Necker
reckoned that it brought in 76.5 million *livres* of which 74 million
derived from land income. For commoners the three *vingtièmes* can be
likened to a 15 per cent surcharge on the *taille*. The whole point of the
new tax was that it did not apply solely to commoners, however. The
vingtièmes purported to tax incomes not individuals, thereby closing off
the escape routes employed by the privileged and challenging the very
essence of *ancien-régime* society. Moreover, its potential was unlimited in
the sense that the government did not prescribe the yield in advance. In
practice, though, the spirited resistance of the *parlements* and the *pays
d'états*, together with the monarchy's own equivocations on the subject
of privilege, ensured that matters worked out rather differently. Deterred

by the costs of fiscal attrition, the crown agreed instead to lump sum payments (*abonnements*) of the *vingtièmes* from the Provincial Estates. By 1788, indeed, this facility had even been extended to some of the Provincial Assemblies (see above p. 39). A long list of exemptions developed, too. This motley collection included the Jesuits, Swiss residents, army and navy officers, postmasters, excise men and numerous office-holders. On the other hand ministers tried, at intervals, to retrieve the situation. Terray declared his intention to collect the *vingtièmes* tax more rigorously in 1771 and Necker established a procedure for verifying tax returns, much to the annoyance of the Parlement of Paris. But Necker's innovations were mostly repudiated by his successor, Joly de Fleury, and the central thrust of fiscal reform was lost.

Even though a substantial proportion of national wealth remained undeclared, the expedient of the *vingtièmes* was the closest the old monarchy came to universality of taxation. The Revolutionaries acknowledged as much when they adopted it as the model for the *contribution foncière*. By contrast, the *capitation* was a rough and ready tax indeed. In theory it resembled a general and graduated impost inasmuch as all social categories save for the clergy were included. Princes, ministers and financiers headed the table of ranks with a liability of 2,000 *livres* per annum, whereas day labourers and soldiers forming the bottom tier were obliged to pay 1 *livre* apiece. But that was in 1695 when the levy was first introduced. Within a very few years it had metamorphosed into a quota tax that was simply allocated to the *généralités* along with the *taille*. And like the *taille*, the *capitation* became a tax upon the weak and the vulnerable: the affluent evaded it by employing the usual strategems of self-assessment, nepotism and the acquisition of exempting office. Turgot admitted the truth when he remarked in 1767 that the *capitation* paid by the nobility was exceedingly modest. For ordinary taxpayers the spectacle of wealthy individuals soliciting favours from complaisant intendants was doubly vexing since every concession tended to increase the burden shouldered by the rest of the community. The *capitation*, like the *taille* was 'solidaire' and took no account of short-term fluctuations in the number of taxpayers. When the biggest landowner of the village of Naves in the Rouergue bought himself an exempting office, the 100 *livres* he had paid in *capitation* was simply transferred to the rest of the parish. In the village of Sainte-Croix, meanwhile, the well-to-do contrived to evade the *capitation* by spending half the year in the neighbouring town.[21] Such cases were legion and they offered a powerful incitement to disaffection with the regime of fiscally enshrined privilege.

A tax which fits neither of the categories outlined above was the *corvée*. The royal *corvée* evolved informally during the early decades of the eighteenth century as a means of repairing and extending the highways. Men and women, their vehicles, draught animals and tools were requisitioned by the intendants to work on the roads in what amounted to a form of labour service. Clerics, nobles together with their servants, town dwellers and several other categories were exempt, with the result that the burden fell mainly on the peasantry. As such it was deeply resented, especially when intendants chose to summon the parishes at harvest time. Speaking on behalf of the physiocrats, Dupont denounced the *corvée* as 'one of the most pernicious inventions that ever emanated from the administrative mind'.[22] As doubts about the economic wisdom of using forced labour to maintain the roads started to surface in the 1760s, a number of intendants began to toy with schemes to convert the *corvée* into a monetary tax. Foremost among the reformers was Turgot who not only devised an alternative method of funding road works, but actually put it into effect while intendant of the Limousin. The rooted objection to all such schemes of commutation, however, was that they spread the burden to social categories that had hitherto enjoyed exemption from labour service. This was why Turgot's ministerial edict of 1776 provoked such bitter opposition (see below pp. 110–11). In effect he proposed to convert the *corvée* into a surcharge upon the *vingtièmes*. A few months later Turgot resigned and the edict was revoked. Nevertheless, the impetus for reform persisted at the provincial level and by 1787 compulsory labour service on the highways had become a thing of the past in large areas of the kingdom. But the costs of the operation were now loaded on to payers of the *taille*.

So much for the tax system, then. Even from this rather formal description, it is possible to reach an estimate of the differential benefits and burdens conferred by the possession of fiscal privilege. To start with whole provinces sheltered behind a rampart of institutionalised privilege. Brittany, Artois, Walloon Flanders, Languedoc, the Cambrésis, the duchy of Burgundy – in short the *pays d'états* generally – were significantly undertaxed. Auget de Montyon, who had a better understanding of administrative matters than most government officials, reckoned that the *pays d'états* paid around 50 per cent less tax than the *pays d'élections* and he cited figures which largely backed up his claim.[23] This was the reality behind exemptions from the *taille* and the *gabelle* and the right of *abonnement* for the *vingtièmes*. However, the *pays d'états* contained a further layer of pecuniary privilege which was replicated, more dramatically, in the country at large. Breton nobles exploited their control of the Estates to ensure that the principal burden of provincial and royal taxes fell upon the Breton peasantry and bourgeoisie. Similarly, Burgundian seigneurs contrived to off-load the bulk of their province's liabilities on to country dwellers. So, whereas all Bretons or Burgundians were in a sense privileged, some were more privileged than others.

The point is important, for it is easy to lose sight of the fundamentally divisive and onerous character of *ancien-régime* privilege. 'Because privilege could take so many different forms,' remarks Betty Behrens, 'and because it penetrated into so many spheres of social, political and economic life, everyone, apart from those with no fixed domicile or occupation, can be said to have been privileged in some degree, since all belonged to one or more groups with special rights.'[24] Contemporaries who had to deal with the effects of privilege on a day-to-day basis would not have been so sanguine. The evidence of noble exemption from the *taille* and the *corvée* was there for all to see. When, in the midst of the debate on the *corvée*, the Keeper of the Seals, Miromesnil, presumed to claim that the so-called privileged orders enjoyed no real advantage over payers of the *taille*, Turgot responded by itemising in great detail the pecuniary benefits attaching to membership of the nobility. Anecdotal evidence leaves little room for doubt on this score either: two examples will suffice. Following the introduction of the *vingtième* tax, President Ségur of the Bordeaux Parlement successfully petitioned the keeper of the seals to have his tax liability reduced from 32,000 *livres* to 4,000 *livres*. Several decades later the duc d'Orléans freely admitted to the use of similar tactics. Commenting upon the decision of the Assembly of Notables to endorse Calonne's proposal to set up Provincial Assemblies, he remarked to the marquis de Bouillé: 'Do you know, Monsieur, this pleasantry is going to cost me at least 300,000 *livres* of income.' 'How so, my lord?', rejoined the marquis, to which the duke replied 'because I do a deal with the intendants and pay more or less what I please. But the Provincial Assemblies will make me pay with the utmost rigour.'[25]

It is true, of course, that fiscal privilege extended far beyond the confines of the nobility. The constant recycling of ennobling offices enabled ever more bourgeois to enter the ranks of the partly tax exempt. In 1788 the *élection* assembly of Saint-Flour complained that king's secretaryships were changing hands so fast ('there are some in this district which have been sold and resold four times in the short space of five or six years'[26]) that municipalities were finding it difficult to keep tax rolls up to date. Meanwhile, a buoyant market in non-ennobling offices was producing a similar inflationary effect. Nearly half of the 1,715 names appearing on the tax roll of the town of Montargis in 1789 were described as being in possession of some form of immunity. How far these individuals enjoyed complete fiscal exemption is difficult to judge, but if a recent estimate that between 2 and 3 per cent of adult males owned offices can be relied upon, the ramifications of privilege were broad indeed.[27] Necker described the consequential loss of revenue as 'a veritable injury to the rest of the nation'.[28] Whether the elimination of fiscal privilege would have made much difference to the parlous state of royal finances is another question, however.

In any case, privilege both facilitated and impeded the monarchy. The sale of offices provided much needed income, loans could be raised on the superior credit-worthiness of institutions such as the Provincial Estates, and the attractions of privileged status helped to staff an expanding bureaucracy. The system could also be used to accommodate the impatient elites who might otherwise have channelled their energies in more troublesome directions. On the other hand, many of the most tangible and desirable forms of privilege served to erode the tax base of the kingdom, and the sale of offices tended to diminish central government control over many vital functions of state. In brief, the mechanisms of privilege could be operated to the short-term advantage of 'ministerial' power, but in the longer term they worked to the advantage of those bodies exercising 'jurisdictional' authority. Whenever the crown sought to discipline the Parlement of Paris by sending it into exile, for instance, the administration of justice always became the first casualty. Would ministers have responded differently to privilege had they enjoyed greater freedom of manocuvre? The question is largely speculative since opportunities for unconstrained experimentation occurred infrequently. Nonetheless, it is interesting to note that in the case of Corsica Choiseul instructed his agents to set up Provincial Estates, a move which necessitated the incorporation of the Corsican nobility. On the other hand, it was agreed from the start that the land tax would be based solely on ability to pay with no exemptions.

However, Corsica was not France. In the 'old world' of entrenched privilege, the monarchy could not behave thus. Before Calonne's great project, the best hope for fiscal reform lay in Terray's revision of the *vingtièmes* which Necker continued. But Necker was brought down by a cabal of *parlementaires* and was confined, henceforth, to issuing warnings about the dangers of fiscal privilege from the sidelines. Instead, ministers chose the easier course of short-term advantage. In 1786 yet another batch of offices (this time of auctioneers) was put on the market. The public reaction to this fraudulent manipulation of the 'society of orders' is difficult to gauge since the arguments for and against venality drew little comment from pamphleteers. Nevertheless, it is certain that the issue of privilege was not raised for the first time in the autumn of 1788. Discussions at parish level, among the victims of fiscal and seigneurial privilege, had been going on for decades. Necker, meanwhile, sensitised the educated public to the structural weaknesses of the tax system in his best-selling book *De l'administration des finances de la France* (1785). Then, in 1787, the Provincial Assemblies caused the whole subject to reverberate around the political arena.

Towards a unified elite?

As privilege ramified, that sense of design which had informed the 'society of orders' was lost. The attributes of each corps and estate of the nation became blurred to the point where even contemporaries ceased to use the customary judicial categories. Historians have followed this cue and posited explanations of the breakdown of absolute monarchy in terms of modern social theory. The *ancien régime* fell foul of a conflict of classes pitting the bourgeoisie against the nobility. Or else it played host to an emerging class of landowning notables whose precarious unity was rudely shattered by an ill-judged attempt to reimpose the 'society of orders'. Or maybe the transition to constitutional monarchy owed more to a general diffusion of ideas unlinked to the dynamics of either class or order. The strengths and weaknesses of these arguments will be tested in the pages that follow. But our point of entry should properly be the theory of a single, undifferentiated elite which has dominated Revolutionary historiography in recent years.

According to Guy Chaussinand-Nogaret, one of the first historians to challenge the axiom of class conflict, *ancien-régime* elites were engaged upon a process of social regrouping. On the eve of the Revolution a distinct noble estate had ceased to exist for all practical purposes: 'bourgeois and noble elites were intermingling in all directions'.[29] All that remained was for the Revolutionary legislators to acknowledge the fact formally. In place of the juridical polarities of the 'society of orders', a new social divide – indeed a veritable chasm – was opening whose determinants were wealth, education and leisure. On all of these counts the bourgeoisie shared more in common with the nobility than with the hefty peasant and artisan battalions of its own order, the Third Estate. It is significant that Chaussinand-Nogaret first formulated this idea in the context of a history of elites between 1700 and 1848, for the synthetic quality of his interpretation owes much to hindsight. Reading history backwards from the vantage point of the censitary regimes of the early nineteenth century tends to magnify the trend towards elite formation. Nevertheless, there are strong arguments for convergence which do not depend upon a long-term perspective.

Clearly, the land formed the common bedrock of bourgeois and noble economic strength. As a capital investment the return was low, but at least it was reliable, and in any case what counted most was the social return. The land conferred respectability: without rents it was virtually impossible to 'live nobly'. In consequence, the acquisition of land and the rights thereof featured prominently in the familial strategy of nearly every bourgeois dynasty. More often than not, indeed, the overriding objective was to convert commercial wealth into landed wealth as rapidly as possible. Concomitant with this process was investment in offices and the trappings of seigneurialism. Landownership, office-holding and seigneurial status each served to blur the distinction between the bourgeoisie and the nobility. Ambitious families, like the Ayrals, would naturally seek to combine all three. On the eve of the Revolution the Chevalier d'Ayral described how his great-grandfather, a non-inheriting younger son, had quit his native province for a small town in Gascony where he had set up in business as a cloth merchant. The business prospered, he married and in due course procured for his son both an office and a wealthy bride. Having advanced in the world despite such unpromising beginnings, 'he thought it demeaning to remain in commerce',[30] and bought considerable estates in the neighbourhood, to which he retired. His son (our chronicler's grandfather), meanwhile, had a numerous progeny and the first-born male received all the grooming that education could bestow. This was the Chevalier's father who proceeded to buy a seigneurial property. Aged forty and calling himself the baron de Sérignac, he cast around for a rich match. The eventual bride supplied the final ingredient in this saga of social transformation, for her dowry included the ennobling office of treasurer in the *bureau des finances* of Montauban.

The success of the Ayrals demonstrates the social fluidity of eighteenth-century France. Wealth, status and breeding could always subvert the ramshackle categories of the 'society of orders'. The Revolution may have denied them the ultimate possession of fully matured noble status, but the overall trajectory of the family is unmistakable. They were predestined to enter the nineteenth century's 'notable' class. But can the Ayrals stand duty for the totality of the *ancien-régime* bourgeoisie? And how were such families regarded by those whose nobility, if not illustrious, was covered by a decent veneer of age?

The prevalence in certain parts of the country of a rural bourgeoisie living comfortably from rents scarcely requires further demonstration. Simulated 'noble living' had marked out the plateau from which the Ayrals launched their assault on noble status. Office-holding, as we have seen, helped to lubricate that ascent. But venality of office should not be regarded as an instant recipe for ennoblement. Of an estimated 80,000 offices in circulation[31] by the end of the *ancien régime*, very few conferred nobility on their owners, either directly or indirectly. According to Necker around 4,000 carried such a privilege. If we allow for a degree of turnover, this means that between 5,000 and 7,000 individuals, together with their families, contrived to enter the nobility from this direction in the course of the century. In reality, though, the majority of the offices put up for sale by the monarchy were quite minor and scarcely conferred bourgeois status, let alone a passport into the nobility. For instance, it was alleged in 1791 that there existed 30,000 offices of wigmaker alone. In between the extremes could be found a hard core of officers serving in the *bailliage* and *sénéchaussée* courts and the provincial administrative and financial bureaucracy. From this milieu were recruited many of the deputies of the Revolutionary legislatures which attaches a certain interest to their hopes and fears. Their best hope, it seems, was to trade upwards as rapidly as possible since the office of *conseiller* in the *présidial* court of Rodez, for example, cut little ice with the local nobility. At such levels, office-holding was more likely to have been a recipe for social frustration than social advancement.

The purchase of fiefs by commoners had been permitted since the Middle Ages and it provided the most cost-effective means of narrowing the social space between bourgeois and nobles. Many a bourgeois, or even peasant, dynasty founded its fortune by farming the dues and monopoly rights of an absentee seigneur. This wealth would then be used to buy the fief and supplant the seigneur altogether. In the *élection* of Issoire nearly two-thirds of the fifty-two lay seigneuries were put up for sale between 1700 and 1789.[32] Indeed, some were sold twice. Most ended up in the hands of the resident bourgeoisie. A similar picture obtained in the Rouergue: from 1750 or thereabouts an enriched bourgeoisie began to buy up offices and fiefs in large numbers and by 1789 more than half the seigneuries of the province were held by commoners.[33] But law and social custom still tended to mark out an intricate pattern of distinction between two groups. Ambitious bourgeois who bought up fiefs and land that was classified as noble were required to pay a special tax (*franc-fief*) equivalent to the annual income of such properties every twenty years. Far from decaying in the face of new social realities, this obligation was intensified in the two decades before the Revolution. Similarly, the lineage nobility grew increasingly restless at the sight of upwardly mobile bourgeois clambering into the Second Estate via the ladders of office-holding and seigneurial substitution. In their *cahier* the nobility of the *sénéchaussée* of Rodez strenuously demanded an end to the process of ennoblement.

Bourgeois convergence upon the trappings of noble status is not to be disputed, then. But nor can there be much doubt that this pressure was resented and, when the opportunity arose, resisted. What of a co-mingling of the nobility with the bourgeoisie? Guy Chaussinand-Nogaret detects a two-way process which a recent historian has summarised as follows: 'the prominent contributions of nobles to capitalist ventures and the strong presence of bourgeois on the land show that from the point of view of economic function, the two groups were a single class'.[34] It is true that the conflictual model of social relations tends to play down the extent of noble involvement in the developing commercial capitalism of the *ancien régime*. Indeed, it is sometimes suggested that the nobility constituted an elite in decline, unable to adjust to either the ideas or the productive forces of the new century. The researches of Chaussinand-Nogaret have conjured up a radically different picture which is built around the image of the thrusting and entrepreneurial nobleman committed to the principles of liberal individualism.[35] Local studies certainly provide some support for this reassessment: in Toulouse, for instance, the *parlementaire* nobility were far removed from the rentier stereotype. Many were major players in the regional grain market, and significant noble involvement in commercial enterprise can be detected in Bordeaux and Rennes as well.

But such involvement was patchy; the big grain producers of the Toulouse hinterland cannot stand proxy for the nobility as a whole. What Chaussinand-Nogaret is describing is an elite within an elite whose liquid wealth, business acumen and cultural sophistication set them apart, not only from the bulk of the nobility, but from the non-entrepreneurial mass of the bourgeoisie as well. Abundant local studies underline this point. Most provincial nobles lived almost exclusively on the product of their leases and the perquisites of seigneurial jurisdiction, supplemented, to be sure, with money lending and intermittent specula-tion in foodstuffs at the neighbouring market. Absentee magnates behaved no differently, except that they could tap into the spoils system of the Court. The duc de Saulx-Tavanes rack-rented his vassals and showed little interest in land improvement or capitalist investment of profits.[36] While more nuanced, a long-range study of the barony of Pont-Saint-Pierre in Normandy reaches a similar conclusion. The Roncherolles progressively abandoned the practice of feudal lordship, but proved incapable of the scale of adjustment required to exploit fully a buoyant market economy.[37]

Noble investment in extractive industry is often mentioned in this connection. According to Chaussinand-Nogaret 'all the most important mining and metallurgical enterprises' of the last two decades of the *ancien régime* had noble backers.[38] But we should be wary of concluding therefrom that the nobility were the pioneers of industrial capitalism, having forged an alliance with the 'grande bourgeoisie'. To start with, noble ironmasters like the Dietrich or the d'Anthès – that is to say families which combined large-scale industrial activity with landowning – were exceedingly rare. And second, it seems that noble involvement in mining, in particular, was scarcely conducive to long-term investment. Seigneurs tended to regard coal, or for that matter ironstone, as a product of the land like any other. Defined thus, these resources were to be 'cropped' rather than exploited in a systematic and capital-intensive fashion. The clash between the Maréchal de Castries, feudal overlord of the county of Alès, and Pierre-François Tubeuf who in 1773 obtained a concession to mine the Alès coal seams neatly illustrates the rival conceptions of how to extract wealth from the soil. Tubeuf can be regarded as a prototype bourgeois entrepreneur and his attempts to begin the deep mining of coal were blocked at every turn by aristocratic and provincial vested interests.[39]

Tubeuf was ruined and saddled with huge bills for damages and legal costs just a matter of months before the opening of the Estates General. In 1791 he emigrated to the United States of America. His tribulations serve as a reminder of the gulf separating the high aristocracy from that parallel elite of shipowners, merchant manufacturers and budding industrialists: those for whom Turgot had already coined the term 'capitalistes'.[40] Though they might ape the manners and the lifestyle of the aristocracy, though they might solicit favours and concessions from government, they lived and worked in a world far removed from the proprietary values of the *ancien régime*. Nowhere was this more apparent than in Marseille[41] where an immensely powerful and self-confident community of 800 merchants had succeeded in stamping a distinctive commercial culture upon the city. These *négociants* had risen above and beyond the system of honours employed to domesticate commercial elites in other parts of the kingdom. If anything, the city's noble families emulated the values of the merchant community rather than vice versa. Instead, the critical line of socio-cultural division lay at one remove: between the mercantile bourgeoisie and the fief-owning, conservative and impoverished nobility of inland Provence. Their struggle to reconstitute the Estates of Provence on the old socially exclusive model embittered relations with the port city's merchant elite and helped to launch the Revolution throughout the South-East.

The proposition that *ancien-régime* France witnessed the emergence of a single, plutocratic elite fails to withstand scrutiny. By 1789 the 'society of orders' had not been blurred into oblivion and nor had privilege ceased to divide. But the counter-proposition of a palpable and potentially explosive rift between a class of nobles and a class of bourgeois commoners fares little better either. While the interpretive trend of recent historiography has been to emphasise an 'intermingling' or fusion of elites, detailed case-study research obstinately refuses to come up with evidence that will resolve the argument. If our description of the multiple categories of bourgeois corresponds even approximately to contemporary perceptions, it seems unlikely that a collective sense of identity could have existed at the end of the *ancien régime*. That is to say, a class consciousness constructed on the base of socio-economic function. What did a *conseiller* serving in a minor *bailliage* court, a village bourgeois 'living nobly' and a Marseille soap manufacturer share in common? This does not preclude the possibility of a politically constructed sense of identity, of course; a possibility that would begin to materialise in 1787.

At least the nobility possessed a formal, juridical unity. Yet incorporation offered no protection from the social and cultural fluidity of the age. On the eve of the Revolution it is probable that the Second Estate had never been more riven with tensions: between rich and poor, conservative and liberal, the noble and the ennobled. Obscure provincial squires railed against the great titled dynasts who were able to obtain rapid advancement in the army for their sons with effortless ease. Impecunious and vulnerable to the least erosion of fiscal and honorific privilege, they regarded liberal debate about seigneurialism and fiscal reform as not far short of treason. Illustrious, and even not so illustrious, families meanwhile reacted to the continuing recruitment of bourgeois office-holders into the noble estate with emotions varying from distaste to extreme resentment. The frustrations harboured on this latter issue only became fully apparent when the monarchy signalled its intention to begin root-and-branch reform in 1787. From the Franche-Comté, the Dauphiné, Provence, Flanders and Guyenne came news of clashes between lineage and robe nobles. The 'new Nobles', reported Lafayette following the inaugural session of the Provincial Assembly of the Auvergne, were opposed by the Third Estate and the 'Ancient Noblesse' alike.[42] Over the next two years the articulations within the noble estate became ever more pronounced, but it was the business of drawing up *cahiers* and electing deputies that projected the conflicting aspirations of nobles large and small, new and old on to a broader canvas.

If neither a fusionist nor a conflictual schematisation does justice to the sheer complexity of *ancien-régime* social structure, we are left with a conceptual void. The best way to fill it is to abandon any notion of smooth-edged elites locked in one-dimensional confrontation. By the reign of Louis XVI the ordering of society was in disarray: honour was no longer a foolproof guide to rank, nor yet was wealth. Confusion resulted and it took the outward form of a series of parallel hierarchies, often overlapping at the base and with no clear sense of preeminence at the top. This state of affairs would obtain until politics came to the rescue and defined categories which everyone could understand and identify with, or against.

The challenge of public opinion

The social and the intellectual history of the late *ancien régime* are closely related, but in recent years it has become fashionable among scholars to treat the two subjects independently. A sense of frustration at the rigid terms in which the debate on the social origins of the Revolution has been conducted is no doubt partly responsible for this divergence. While social history has marked time, intellectual history has been reinvigorated by application of the techniques of discourse analysis. According to the practitioners of this new history of ideas, it is the power of language that needs to be recognised. Language not only describes, it helps to fashion social reality; and this basic cipher in which the assumptions and values of a society are encoded can be discovered in texts which are taken to be emblematic of the age under study.[43] At the very least this approach has the merit of contemporaneity, for in the eighteenth century the educated public held a similar notion of the power of ideas. The optimism of the Enlightenment drew its inspiration from this source. The study of language – its uses and abuses – will also be of benefit when we come to explore the substitution during the period immediately prior to the Revolution of sharp political categories for the blurred social realities of the *ancien régime*. However, the danger attendant upon discourse analysis is that it can lead to the relegation of social history, that is to say to the study of texts rather than the people who used them. Public opinion, the subject of this section, certainly became a force in its own right towards the end of the *ancien régime*; an invisible player in reformist politics. But it is important not to lose sight of the fact that public opinion was a sociologically complex phenomenon articulated by real people whose 'language' cannot be neatly encapsulated in a selection of texts.

Literacy, literate culture and opportunities for literate expression expanded in the eighteenth century. Basic literacy is difficult to measure accurately unless we use a rough and ready measure such as the ability to sign the marriage register. On this evidence, 29 per cent of men and 14 per cent of women possessed the rudiments of literacy in the period 1686–90 compared with 47 per cent of males and 27 per cent of females a century later.[44] Such aggregate figures mask considerable discrepancies, however. The North-East of France was decidely more literate than the West, the Centre and the South. In fact, a straight line could be drawn across the country from Saint-Malo to Geneva in order to demarcate the two zones. By the end of the *ancien régime* more than two men in three (71 per cent) and nearly half the population of adult females (44 per cent) living to the north of this line could write their names, whereas less than one man in three (27 per cent) and one woman in ten (12 per cent) could do so among those living to the west and south. Other data confirm this pattern and when taken together they bespeak a profound cultural isolation from the French language subsisting throughout the West and in large parts of the South. In 1773 virtually every parish in the diocese of Reims boasted a school, compared with one in five parishes of the future department of the Haute-Garonne.[45]

However, literacy was also determined by social factors and it would be quite wrong to suppose that two-thirds of the country formed a cultural desert. Most urban populations, even in the South, could understand French, although artisans in Toulouse, Rodez or Agen would not normally employ the language in everyday speech. Elites everywhere, be they urban or rural, could speak and read French, although they too might participate in the vernacular, patois-based culture of their region on occasion. In the South-West the parish clergy sometimes preached and catechised in the vernacular for the benefit of parishioners, and lawyers, writ servers, stewards and the like also performed the role of cultural intermediaries. The great reservoir of illiteracy lay in the villages, among agricultural households, however. The oral culture of southern peasants posed a formidable barrier to French-based intercourse as the Revolutionaries would eventually discover. As for written culture, whether French or patois, it scarcely circulated beyond the confines of market towns. In the North and East, by contrast, peasant illiteracy was retreating steadily. Agricultural wage workers in the villages of Champagne signed the marriage registers with ever increasing frequency as the century proceeded, while male *laboureurs* can be regarded as more or less 100 per cent literate by the end of the *ancien régime*. Detailed research evidence bears out this trend. In the Norman barony of Pont-Saint-Pierre studied by Jonathan Dewald,[46] the eighteenth century witnessed a dramatic increase in village literacy. Moreover, it was accompanied by a development no less significant: the acquisition of books by an elite of prosperous peasant farmers.

Indeed, the demand for books was perhaps the most potent expression of widening cultural horizons. Probate records show clearly that enhanced literacy was expanding the categories of the book-buying public to include craftsmen, shopkeepers and even domestic servants, as well as yeomen farmers. At the start of the century printed matter featured among the personal effects of 30 per cent of Paris servants and 13 per cent of journeymen, compared with 40 per cent and 35 per cent respectively some eighty years later.[47] The capital was not unusual in this respect; inventories of personal effects reveal a similar trend in other towns and cities. The average size of private libraries was increasing, too; whether those of the clergy, the nobility or the bourgeoisie. But private libraries merely signal the changing cultural priorities of the intelligentsia; the newly literate classes honed their tastes in public reading rooms (*cabinets de lecture*) where, for a fee, a wide range of literature could be browsed or borrowed. The poor, meanwhile, relied on pedlars and petty open-air retailers for a supply of printed ephemera consisting of scandal sheets, sensations and lampoons. Theirs was scarcely a diet likely to sustain new ways of thinking. But, as Roger Chartier points out, the widening of institutional access to sources of information provides some measure of 'the hunger for reading matter that tormented even the humblest city dwellers'.[48]

If the market-place – in the broadest sense – was expanding, it was also changing. Voltaire captured one aspect of this process in typical sardonic fashion: the French nation, he remarked, 'having had enough of verse, tragedies, comedies, operas, romances ... and theological debates about grace and convulsions turned at last to discoursing on corn ... useful things were written on the subject of agriculture; everyone read them save for the farmers'.[49] His observation was made in the 1750s when educated opinion seemed poised at a cross-roads unsure of which way to turn. Behind lay decades of religious feuding between 'sacerdotals' and Jansenists; ahead lay paths beckoning towards religious and economic freedom in the shape of toleration and the doctrine of physiocracy. With the benefit of hindsight Auget de Montyon detected this parting of the ways, too. Among jottings penned ostensibly in the 1780s we find the following assessment: 'in the last forty to fifty years a great revolution in the human mind has taken place which is nowhere more perceptible than in France'. The range and volume of intellectual enquiry has expanded, he continued, obscurantism is in retreat, prose has replaced verse and high-minded moralising is now the order of the day.[50] The secular emphasis of this 'enlightenment' among the educated was widely remarked upon; indeed, it was a pan-European phenomenon of the 1760s and 1770s. In 1762 the Parlement of Toulouse had ordered the torture and execution of Jean Calas, a protestant merchant, on the suspicion that he had murdered one of his sons to prevent him from converting to catholicism. This miscarriage of justice caused an outcry among educated men and women whose complacent belief in the power of reason to overcome fanaticism it profoundly shocked. Within three years the verdict was reversed and the Calas family rehabilitated. Philosophically inspired toleration had taken a grip on the minds of provincial elites and it soon began to infuse many forms of public religious practice. By 1777 members of one of Toulouse's religious fraternities had stopped marching in processions unshod. It no longer seemed rational to risk injury in the pursuit of spiritual consolation.[51]

The Calas case is interesting, for it serves to remind us that public opinion was not a seamless whole. Opinion formers like Voltaire and, for want of a better term, the *philosophes* did not of necessity march in step with provincial elites. As for village- and street-level opinion, it was often frankly out of step. The debates over toleration or grain-trade regulation left the masses unmoved: Voltaire might denounce bigotry as a social evil, but ordinary catholics and protestants continued to view one another with profound distrust. The sectarian tribalism of the early years of the Revolution in towns such as Montauban and Nîmes would demonstrate a different, and perhaps truer, face of public opinion. Men of letters were aware of these ambiguities, of course, and they took care to define the burgeoning force of public opinion in a way which minimised them. For Condorcet, in common with most of the pre-Revolutionary generation of *philosophes*, public opinion was not 'popular', that is to say it did not equate with the opinion of the greatest number. The views of the masses were nothing more than a collection of fickle prejudices, whereas public opinion was, in the words of Roger Chartier, 'necessarily stable, unified, and founded on reason'.[52] The conceptual integrity which intellectual historians attach to the notion of public opinion therefore has some basis in the conventions of *ancien-régime* intellectual life. Highly educated men (and women) discussed a narrow range of issues in a manner which they deemed to be both consistent and rational. Collectively they elevated public opinion into a censuring body or 'tribunal' to use the image that became a common-place in the 1770s and 1780s. But we still need to know more about the raw material from which this tribunal was fashioned.

The lower institutional embodiments of the new 'public sphere'[53] for debate and discussion have already been mentioned. These were the *cabinets de lecture*, the subscription libraries, the cafés and the coffee houses that proliferated in Paris and the larger towns from mid-century. They provided reading-matter, conviviality and instant news and views, although Arthur Young thought them inferior to their counterparts in England. Travelling through France in the summer of 1789 he found newspapers hard to come by, with medium-sized towns like Moulins and Le Puy completely lacking in this essential commodity.[54] But at the higher and more sedentary level of academies, literary and agricultural societies, and masonic lodges the 'republic of letters' did have a more substantial appearance. Apart from a handful of ancient foundations, the provincial academies were chiefly a product of the first half of the eighteenth century. By 1760 such bodies were operating in nearly all parts of the kingdom and they supplied provincial elites with their first introduction to Enlightenment sociability. One petitioner likened their role to that of 'flaming torches putting the murk of ignorance to flight'.[55] More prosaically, they gathered together the learned and the leisured to act as a kind of gratuitous advisory council to the intendants and subdelegates, much as philosophers were said to wait at the knee of princes. Daniel Roche[56] has calculated that academicians numbered no more than 2,500 on the eve of the Revolution (and perhaps 6,000 in total during the period 1660–1789). A tiny elite, then, but one which mobilised a vast store of literate energy through the institution of essay prize competitions. These opportunities for intellectual display multiplied twelvefold in the course of the century. Rousseau's *Discourse on Inequality* was written for just such an occasion in 1754.

The impulse to form academies was soon joined by others, to produce a notable thickening of the circuits of intellectual discussion in the 1760s and 1770s. Henri Bertin's enthusiasm for agriculture while in charge of the Contrôle Général between 1759 and 1763 resulted in a rash of agricultural societies. Over a score had sprouted by the end of the *ancien régime*, although many overlapped with the academies both in terms of membership and activities. Again, they were intended to function as beacons spreading 'lumières' among a benighted peasantry. A process known as 'emulation' would encourage good practice and root out the bad. To this end the agricultural society of Limoges founded an experimental farm on which all the latest theories and technologies could be demonstrated. Turgot, whose doubts about the philosophical approach to agrarian reform were shared by many intendants, had it closed down. The money saved was allocated to planting trees along the highways and to modifying the *corvées*.[57] Practical reforms were unlikely ever to have issued from the agricultural societies or, for that matter, from the academies; but what these bodies did manage was to stir up the turgid intellectual atmosphere of the provinces. By a system of regular mutual correspondence, they helped to fashion the idea of public opinion as an independent and invariable force, a kind of critical community above and beyond the constraints of time and space.

The rapid adoption of the masonic model of sociability enormously extended the range of that critical community. Scottish and English masonry first crossed the Channel in the 1720s, initially confining its appeal to *émigré* circles and the international trading elites of the great port cities. But the lodge system offered to satisfy a convivial urge which at that time enjoyed precious few outlets outside the forum of the family. As a result masonry expanded dramatically in the 1750s, notwithstanding the intermittent anathemas of the papacy. In the 1760s the movement experienced organisational and disciplinary difficulties which caused it to mark time for a decade, but a fresh period of headlong growth ensued in the early 1770s. That growth peaked in the mid-1780s when the masonic network appears to have reached saturation point. Lodges by now existed in towns of all shapes and sizes, for masonry was essentially an urban cultural phenomenon. But the urban pretension stretched far down the scale as we know: in 1789 lodges could be found in eighty-one towns with populations of under 2,000. At its height the movement may have counted as many as 50,000 adherents grouped in 600 lodges, not to mention a small female membership in 'attached' lodges.[58]

The sheer size of freemasonry begs some obvious questions about the scope and character of public opinion at the end of the *ancien régime*. According to Daniel Roche the provincial academicians comprised a masculine elite drawn from all three orders of state. On the basis of an exhaustive analysis he concluded that 43 per cent emanated from the Third Estate, 37 per cent from the nobility and 20 per cent from the church.[59] Such figures are aggregates, of course, and can give little indication of the social texture of individual academies; nonetheless, they do suggest that it would be unwise to characterise the Enlightenment as an exclusively bourgeois current of ideas. On this evidence the structure of public opinion might be described as transcending distinctions of order or class. However, a closer scrutiny of Roche's data does lend a degree of support to the traditional interpretation. Some academies were indeed dominated by the bourgeoisie: in Villefranche-sur-Saône, Lyon, Marseille, Clermont and Bordeaux the Third Estate expanded its bridgehead as the century proceeded. As for the noble presence in the academies, it was confined almost entirely to the urban segment of the Second Estate. Rural gentlemen remained outside the institutional circuits of the Enlightenment, and therefore largely untouched by the movement of ideas.

Perhaps the academies are not the best foundation from which to mount a sociological critique of what passed for public opinion at the end of the *ancien régime*,. For, as Roche admits, they came to epitomise an older and stuffier approach to the dissemination of ideas. The same is true of the agricultural societies which were mostly in the doldrums by the 1780s in any case. By contrast the masonic lodges brought a youthful vigour to the business of intellectual and cultural exchange. In those cities and towns where academies and lodges existed side by side, the latter were noticeably more mixed in character. Masons pledged themselves to ignore the trifling distinctions of civil society and while their democratic sociability was not without limits, it is nonetheless true that the lodges were recruited overwhelmingly from the Third Estate. For the first time, large numbers of merchants, shopkeepers and even craftsmen won admission to the 'republic of letters'. In the Paris lodges, for instance, nearly 30 per cent of Third Estate recruits were drawn from the milieux of wholesale commerce and manufacturing, the trades and retailing.

But can masonry be counted a constituent element of public opinion? Is it likely that the 'republic of letters' had become 50,000 strong by the end of the *ancien régime*? Roche favours a conservative estimate of between 13,000 and 15,000 based on more stringent definitions. This is for what he terms 'la classe culturelle',[60] an entity that the eighteenth-century architects of stylised public opinion would have had no difficulty in recognising. Yet it would be rash to exclude masonry from a 'public space' that was expanding by great leaps and bounds as the *ancien régime* drew to a close. Small-town freemasonry scarcely operated at the leading edge of the Enlightenment, but it helped to stir from torpor elites for whom interminable quarrels over precedence had hitherto provided the only intellectual exercise. Above all, it helped to put into social circulation the language of rights and claims that gave public opinion its resonance in the country at large.

This new language of universals ('nation', 'liberty', 'citizen', 'patriot', etc.) is associated indissolubly with the Revolution. But historians have traced the process of semantic and conceptual renewal back to the 1750s, if not earlier. The Jansenists and their *parlementaire* allies employed recognisably constitutional language during the controversy over the refusal of sacraments. It was used initially for religious purposes, of course, but once the Jesuits had been defeated the impetus of Jansenist thought became largely secular. Chancellor Maupeou's 1771 coup against the *parlements* revealed the Jansenists for what they had become: a 'patriot' party of resistance to the 'despotic' policies of the crown. In fact, Maupeou's high-handedness seems to have accelerated the evolution of the new political vocabulary among broad swathes of educated opinion. The highly localised concept of the 'nation' discussed briefly in chapter 1 (see above pp. 13–14) was now juxtaposed with the notion of the 'nation' implying a communion of peoples emancipated from the clogging effects of institutionalised privilege. In similar fashion the word 'liberties', used customarily to describe the powers and rights of specific individuals or groups, began to acquire a secondary and singular meaning which expanded its scope to the undifferentiated nation as a whole. With the 'society of orders' thus subverted, the logical next step could only be the assertion that the nation was sovereign. In which case the king had to become 'the first minister and agent of the sovereign'.[61]

Such ideas would not have echoed loudly in the country at large, however. Even within the perimeter of what passed for public opinion, there was no unanimity as to the constitutional way ahead. Old ideas and attitudes that had sustained the monarchy for centuries were eroding remorselessly in the 1770s and 1780s, but there existed no blueprint of the 'declaration of the rights of man' ready and waiting in the wings. The new language of political debate was not yet a language, properly speaking. Instead it consisted of slogans and catchphrases whose meaning was far from agreed. The social configuration of intellectual debate remained fluid, too. After the passions stirred by Maupeou's attempted 'revolution' (for that is how contemporaries regarded it), *parlementaire* rhetoric lost its stridency for a decade or so. In the meantime ministers showed no compunction about appropriating some of the new slogans for their own use, for it should not be forgotten that the absolute monarchy was a leading player in the assault on sectional privilege. But government officials never felt entirely at ease in this treacherous semantic minefield. In 1781 Governor Marbeuf instructed the deputies of the province of Ajaccio to refrain from using the phrase 'the Corsican nation' and others like it in their petitions: 'you should use the terms *Etat de Corse* or *pays de Corse* and avoid that of *Nation* in all circumstances'.[62] But this ban did not extend to ministers of the crown. When, in March 1787, Calonne tried to outmanoeuvre the assembled Notables by appealing to the opinion of the nation-at-large (see below p. 117) the tactic exploded in his face.

3   Economy

The eighteenth century was a period of prosperity, certainly when compared with the final decades of Louis XIV's reign. As material well-being improved, the threat, if not the fear, of famine receded. Between 1728 and 1789 the average price of a loaf of bread doubled and more on just four occasions, whereas price spirals of this magnitude occurred nine times between 1661 and 1715. For whatever reason, nationwide 'subsistence crises' were becoming rarer, and this perception was reflected in the bullish confidence of landowners as they clamoured for an end to controls over the grain trade. For the 'never had it so good' possessing classes of the 1750s and 1760s, France stood poised on the threshold of an age of plenty. With an expanding population, untapped agricultural potential and a vigorous merchant marine, she would shortly outstrip her powerful rival across the Channel. All that was needed was an enlightened government committed to removal of the institutional fetters on agriculture, industry and trade. Such, at least, was the view of France's homegrown political economists – the physiocrats – as they measured the sinews of the nation from the vantage point of the relatively uncomplicated mid-century decades.

Yet, historians have been less sanguine about the performance of the French economy in the eighteenth century. The perception of growth and prosperity is not to be challenged, perhaps, but it should certainly be qualified. Growth and prosperity for whom? While tenant farmers converted agricultural surpluses into hard cash, manual workers appear to have lost the battle with price inflation. Real wages slumped, implying a drop in standards of living or, at the very least, a surfeit of toil for the majority. And in any case the reality of growth and prosperity was extremely patchy and spasmodic as this chapter will demonstrate. After rich pickings in the 1760s and early 1770s, many tenant farmers fell victim to the combination of raised rents and sagging commodity prices in the 1780s. Merchant clothiers and their diasporas of spinners and weavers were also highly vulnerable to fluctuations in demand, for woollens and silks especially. Even overseas traders whose profit margins seemed rock solid were showing ominous signs of commercial fragility as the *ancien régime* drew to a close.

All this and much more is known to specialists, but it scarcely adds up to a consensual vision of the state of the economy on the eve of the Revolution. The search for 'origins' divides economic historians no less than other scholars. Those of the optimist school lay stress on the continuing buoyancy of the French economy at the end of the *ancien régime*. To be sure, France experienced a short-term 'subsistence crisis' of classic proportions in 1788–9 and to this limited extent a causal link may be said to have existed between economic hardship and the outbreak of Revolution. But this was no more than a blip in an ascendant curve of material well-being. Notwithstanding seasonal difficulties in the primary economy, the France of Louis XVI continued to forge ahead in the direction of a mobile, consumerist society patterned on the English model. The pessimists construe the available evidence rather differently. Taken together, the indicators reveal an economy caught up in a structural crisis traceable to the 1770s, if not earlier. The undoubted growth of the first half of the century had run into blockages of a largely institutional character. As a result it ceased: France in the 1780s was marking time while England prepared for rapid growth. It has even been suggested that the country went into reverse as agricultural and industrial production tailed off, while population pressure continued to intensify.[1]

The arguments presented in this chapter invite a broadly pessimistic assessment of economic conditions following the boom decades of the mid-century. Nevertheless, it should be acknowledged at the outset that both positions contain more than a hint of teleological reasoning. Behind the pessimists' arguments lies the Marxist paradigm of a society caught in the throes of a transition to capitalism, whereas the optimists make no secret of the fact that they believe the Revolution to have been the primary cause of France's economic retardation in the nineteenth century.[2] Fortunately, the question of whether or not the Revolution broke France's economic momentum is not at issue here. This should make it easier to marshal dispassionately the evidence pertaining to economic performance in the eighteenth century. But in this field, all serious enquiries must begin with Labrousse.

Over a long lifetime of research, Ernest Labrousse produced the most scientific and still the most satisfying account of the movements of the French economy in the eighteenth century. Even historians who would question his wider interpretation of the origins of the Revolution (he remained a firm adherent of the political Left) admit the reliability and cogency of his quantitative approach. Such criticisms as have been raised against his methodology have tended to come from economists rather than historians. Labrousse published his findings in two big books[3] in the 1930s and 1940s, but a mature and more accessible version can be found in the multi-volume *Histoire économique et sociale de la France*[4] which appeared in 1970. In these works he directs our attention firmly towards the agrarian economy on the argument that activity in the primary sector acted as the motor for the whole system. Demand factors play the determining role in his model of the *ancien-régime* economy and with enormous dexterity he constructs a number of price series which give us a broad impression of performance over time. According to Labrousse the economy entered a phase of sustained growth in the 1730s which can be measured in terms of an across-the-board rise in commodity prices. Indeed, prices would continue to rise until the early years of the Restoration. On a shopping basket of agricultural products (corn, meat, wine, beans, etc.), the weighted rise was something like 60 per cent between 1726–41 and 1771–89. Cereal grains rose faster still, as did meat and firewood.[5]

The overall trend is unmistakable, then. But closer analysis reveals three 'intercyclic' movements which add significantly to our understanding of the crisis from which the Revolution emerged. Between 1726 and 1763 prices rose in a gentle but regular profile, apart from a climatic hiccough between 1747 and 1750. Then, on the morrow of the Seven Years War, a phase of accelerating price increases intervened to produce the high farming decades of good harvests matched by high prices. This happy conjunction began to break up from the mid-1770s as prices reached a plateau (to use Labrousse's term), and seasonal swings became more pronounced. If overall prices scarcely sagged, the secular trend was certainly braked for the next fifteen years or so. Indeed, in many regions, grain prices actually fell for a time in the late 1770s and early 1780s, while viticulture succumbed to a serious crisis of overproduction in 1781. Not until 1785–6 did cereal and vine growers begin to see prices moving in their favour once more. Nevertheless, it is the duration of this third spasm that retains our attention. It signalled the onset of a general malaise that spread beyond the confines of the agrarian economy.

Labrousse's analysis of the rhythms of the eighteenth-century economy is a piece of vintage research which no historian bent on exploring the transition from *ancien régime* to Revolution can afford to ignore. His rigorously quantitative approach relaunched the study of economic history and commended him to the founding fathers of the Annales School. It is therefore fitting that his analysis should provide the framework for that quintessentially Annaliste synthesis, the *Histoire économique et sociale de la France*. Yet Labrousse shares some of the weaknesses as well as the strengths of the Annales historians. His focus upon the deep structures of the agrarian economy tends to relegate to a secondary role all non-agricultural economic activity, whether practised in the towns or in the countryside. No doubt the well-being of the primary sector did determine to a very large degree the fortunes of the textile industry. The production of cheap cottons and woollens was heavily dependent on purchasing power within the domestic market. As the intendant of the *généralité* of Rouen remarked, 'bread prices are the barometer of the workshops, they fall idle when bread is too dear'.[6] But not all textile manufacture was sensitive to the price of domestic foodstuffs, and it is likely that the link between the towns and the vicissitudes of the agrarian economy was far more complex than Labrousse implies. As for the great port cities, they tended to respond to the rhythms of overseas trade. Harvest failure and price spirals might cause temporary hardship, but the effects of overextended credit, commercial treaties, or war were to be feared much more.

Another consequence of the refocusing of French economic history performed by Labrousse and the Annales historians has been the relegation of institutional factors. With harvest data, price series and demography combining to provide all the answers, few scholars bother nowadays to weigh institutional factors in the balance. Yet, it is one of the contentions of this chapter that tolls, taxes, internal customs frontiers, institutionalised privilege and government interventionism generally, not to mention skill levels and entrepreneurship in trade and industry, played a significant role in determining economic outcomes. The deregulation of manufactures and commerce in the 1750s and 1760s could have long-term repercussions, as James Thomson[7] has demonstrated in an exemplary study of the Languedoc cloth industry. Equally the persistence of internal customs zones until the very end of the *ancien régime* tended to fragment markets and slow down the economic pulse of the nation. For government, they represented a handy source of revenue, but for manufacturers and traders transit duties simply made their goods harder to sell. Is it surprising that French industrialists should continue to operate within a cycle of profit-taking and retirement? Entrepreneurs of the calibre of the ironmaster, Pierre Babaud de la Chaussade,[8] who bought their way into the system of privilege in order to turn it to commercial advantage were comparatively rare.

Agriculture

Agricultural activities occupied the bulk of the population as well as feeding and clothing them. In this sense Labrousse is surely correct to identify agriculture as the motor of the pre-industrial economy. Agriculture, moreover, was one of the success stories of the eighteenth century. During this period the population of France increased by 33 per cent, yet the frequency of lethal 'subsistence crises' diminished. How this was achieved can be explained in a number of ways. The traditional accounts lay stress upon the unchanging character of the French countryside. According to Pierre Goubert,[9] agriculture evolved at a snail's pace and always within a context that militated against new techniques and more specialised forms of husbandry. On this hypothesis a century's growth was accommodated inside existing structures, typically by adjusting land-use to demographic pressures. If more mouths needed feeding, more land would be ploughed up: a simple expedient that did little violence to established habits, providing always that the land supply remained elastic.

That growth did occur is undeniable, although specialists disagree in their estimations. Jean-Claude Toutain[10] calculates that agricultural production rose by 60 per cent across the century, but this figure is disputed by Joseph Goy and Emmanuel Le Roy Ladurie[11] on the basis of evidence drawn from tithe yields. Most economic historians would find the latter team's calculation of a net rise of between 25 and 40 per cent more credible. Still, it seems likely that the production of foodstuffs kept pace with population, if only at the aggregate level. In reality, of course, matters were not this simple, for the productive capacity of *ancien-régime* agriculture was not evenly distributed. Nor was it realised in an even fashion across the century. After the misery and land abandonments marking the final decades of Louis XIV's reign, production climbed sharply as Toutain's statistics indicate. But these 'gains' betray an exercise in catching up as the cereal economy returned to the productive levels of Colbert's time. Conversely, it seems likely that agricultural production had begun to falter in the closing years of the *ancien régime*, even as population pressures continued to mount.

Production increases achieved by putting more land under the plough should not be confused with productivity increases achieved by means of new crops, enhanced yields or a reduction of labour inputs. It is on this distinction that the case for viewing French agriculture in a less stationary light turns. Some new food crops (maize, the potato) were introduced, it is true, and experimentation with fodder substitutes for stock was widespread and continuous. But yield levels of the major bread grains advanced little, if at all, across the century, and for all the talk of seed-drills and threshing machines husbandry remained a low technology and labour-intensive industry. What was the point of speeding up such operations as sowing, haying and harvesting if the villages were bulging with willing hands who would otherwise be thrown out of work? At the end of the *ancien régime* the old economy still seemed capable of delivering the goods: full-blown agricultural revolution was not in prospect.

Does this mean that we can endorse Goubert's picture of a nearly static and introverted agricultural sector? Not entirely, for the resilience of peasant-based agriculture lay precisely in its capacity to absorb incremental change. Consider again the question of agricultural production. The bulk was consumed on the spot, but a proportion – perhaps 30 per cent – was marketed either directly or through the mechanism of surplus extraction. Now market opportunities were expanding, particularly in the vicinity of the towns and cities, and they brought in their wake shifts in attitude, vocation, occasionally even shifts in the pattern of activities within the countryside. These changes were most noticeable in the hinterland of Paris. A traveller quitting the capital in the late eighteenth century would have passed through a thick belt of kitchen gardens from which the fallow had been abolished long since thanks to the abundant supplies of manure. Emerging on to the plains of the Ile-de-France, he would have encountered a landscape dotted with large grain farms. It was these farms that kept Paris supplied with wheat, oats and straw for urban stables. If a recent study of the Chartier dynasty of tenant farmers can be used as a guide, such farms represented the leading edge of highly capitalised, commercial agriculture at the end of the *ancien régime*.[12] Anything up to 70 per cent of their gross cereal production was destined for the market. Big tenants like François Chartier (1696–1760) brought no new technology to bear on their activities, nor did they succeed in lifting wheat yields to a significant degree; they were above all efficient farmers who managed relatively compact holdings well equipped with draught animals while keeping a tight rein on labour costs.

Such was the pull of Paris, that the Ile-de-France had developed the characteristics of a special economic zone which distinguished it even from the adjacent wheat-growing plains. But that pull was starting to be felt further afield, too. The Limousin, the Charolais and parts of Normandy all supplied the capital with fatstock, and there were clear signs that this regional vocation was strengthening on the eve of the Revolution. In the Charolais and the Brionnais, for example, arable land was being converted for use as pasture. Shorter-range specialisations no doubt developed on the perimeter of many towns and cities; the problem lies in separating the newer patterns of economic activity from those which had existed for centuries. It is important to remember, after all, that the pull of urban markets was still weak and uneven in this period. Often it was the search for a fodder substitute that prompted the first faltering steps towards a more outward-looking style of agriculture. In the Haut Poitou peasant cultivators switched sainfoin from the back garden into mid-field as a market for the crop began to develop in the neighbouring town of Poitiers. Meanwhile, further south in the sprawling province of Languedoc, an agricultural transition of much broader dimensions was taking place. Possessing good access to the cities and ports of the South-West, Upper Languedoc veered towards grain production whereas the populations of the Mediterranean plain found a vocation in olives, vines and proto-industrial textile manufacture.

Normandy permits an interesting case study of expanding commercial opportunities, for, by the late eighteenth century, the province was in the grip of three powerful solvents of traditional relationships. Stock raising for the Paris meat markets was, as already noted, highly developed in grazing districts (Cotentin, Bessin), while a booming cereal agriculture had grown up in the Pays de Caux to the north of Rouen. Widespread planting of fodder crops pushed back the fallow and enabled farmers nearly to double the quantity of stock they could feed. Supplies of manure rose in proportion and so, in consequence, did yields. According to Guy Lemarchand,[13] a productivity breakthrough in the order of 40 to 45 per cent was achieved on Norman grain farms in the sixty or so years before the Revolution. Proto-industrial spinning and weaving of cotton thread for the merchants of Rouen completed this commercialisation of the rural economy. As many as 300,000 cottagers appear to have been involved in the manufacturing process, many on a full-time basis. In Normandy, at least, textile manufacture was fast becoming a rural activity in its own right, alongside but distinct from agriculture. Yet all these steps away from traditional polyculture brought vulnerabilities in their wake. After 1775 cereal prices fell back, although the value of fatstock and dairy products continued to rise. But then two years of drought, in 1785 and 1786, nearly wiped out the livestock industry and brought cattle merchants close to default on their contracts with the city of Paris. Nearly simultaneously, demand for cheap cotton fabrics began to contract, thereby relaying the crisis to a vast rural proletariat of spinners and weavers.

What conclusions can be drawn from this spotty picture of market-led modernisation? Clearly, there is a danger in applying Pierre Goubert's model of the *ancien-régime* agrarian economy too rigorously, if only because much new research has come to light since the publication of the *Histoire économique et sociale de la France*. The 'histoire immobile'[14] thesis beloved of scholars of the 1960s and 1970s contains many traps for the unwary. Clearly, too, there is a difficulty in the notion of incremental change, for, in absorbing successive incremental changes, the rural economy might be totally transformed from within. Normandy would appear to be a case in point. Nevertheless, it is important to keep matters in perspective and to avoid crude juxtapositions of mobility and immobility, innovation and tradition. Eighteenth-century France contained several agricultural economies, each proceeding according to its own rhythms of development. In the zones falling within the provisioning 'crowns' of the city of Paris, the pulse of the rural economy was quickening unmistakably and the same was true, to a lesser degree, in the littoral zones of the Garonne and the Mediterranean seaboard. But an enormous subsistence sector remained and it was to be found in the interior of the country. Here the pace of life was slow, the agricultural infrastructure fragile, and market contact short range and spasmodic. In this vast region yields were low and irregular and mostly consumed on the spot. Surpluses had to be coaxed on to the market, or forcibly extracted from cultivators who needed ready money for the payment of taxes. Needless to say, this subsistence sector acted as a brake on the performance of the economy as a whole.

In an age when 70 per cent of agricultural production was consumed on the farm, how could it be otherwise? Peasants who were striving to attain the ideal of household sufficiency provided a weak domestic market for goods of any description. And in any case, a fully integrated market did not yet exist – not even for bread grains and wine. Despite undoubted improvements to road and river communications in the course of the eighteenth century, the interconnecting grain market scarcely stretched beyond the boundaries of the *pays de grande culture*. Even then it was subjected to unremitting institutional and geographical stress. Barges laden with wheat for the capital averaged twelve days to mount the Seine from Rouen and absorbed the energies of many men and horses. Overland movement was quicker, but twice as expensive. In the open-field countryside of the North-East such costs could be absorbed, up to a point, but the land transportation of bulky goods over greater distances became prohibitive. The Provincial Assembly of the Auvergne complained in 1787 that excise duties quadrupled the price of wine despatched from Clermont to Paris. Owing to the vagaries of the customs system, it was often cheaper to move goods for export than to shift them from province to province for domestic consumption. Indeed, in the southern highlands, it could be prohibitive even to move foodstuffs from parish to parish.

These realities invite a degree of caution as scholars start to probe the legacy of economic thinking enshrined within the 'histoire immobile' thesis. Labrousse and the Annales historians tended to visualise *ancien-régime* France as an assortment of virtually self-contained regional and local markets. This view still has much to recommend it providing we bear several qualifications in mind. First of all, the nodal role of Paris in the economic infrastructure of the north-eastern provinces should be recognised. Secondly, we must allow for the 'quickening' effect of transportation improvements. For all the continuing natural and man-made obstacles, agricultural production circulated better by the end of the century than it had done at the start. Third, and finally, the temptation to comprehend market activity and auto-sufficiency in mutually exclusive terms should be resisted. There existed, in reality, a complex hierarchy of markets ranging from nationwide circuits for the production and distribution of high-quality textiles, to intensely local entrepots for the satisfaction of day-to-day needs. This could result in the phenomenon of overlap: long-range circuits of commercial exchange (lace-making, ironmongery, etc.) embedded in neo-subsistence regional economies.

Industry

Industry and commerce were not sharply differentiated in *ancien-régime* terminology. In fact, the word 'commerce' was often used to describe all forms of manufacturing, as well as trading and banking activities. At least this had the merit of capturing the reality of industry before 'industrialisation': a predominantly rural occupation structured by itinerant merchants who would supply cottagers with the raw materials and then return to collect the finished products. On the other hand, the fluid boundary between industry and commerce makes it difficult to establish a set of trends across the century. According to the team of quantitative historians headed by Jean Marczewski, gross artisanal and industrial production multiplied by a factor of 4.5 between 1701–10 and 1781–90.[15] Even if this computation is overly generous, as some specialists believe, it remains true that French industry fairly rocketed in the eighteenth century. Booming textile manufacture accounted for the bulk of the growth, or so it would seem, for textiles made up around 50 per cent of this production in terms of value. Other sectors – ironmongery, metals, coal – were secondary by comparison. Cottage textile manufacture tended to develop in tandem with the agrarian economy as has already been noted, and it is instructive to trace its profile of growth. Production surged between 1730 and 1750, only to ease off over the next two decades in marked contrast to the continued buoyancy of agricultural prices. Then, from 1770 or thereabouts, the older woollen and linen-based industries entered a stagnant period which would be followed by a sharp contraction of output in the years immediately preceding the Revolution. However, it would be simplistic to measure the performance of the industrial economy by the yardstick of cloth production alone. After 1750 newer industries (cotton, coal, iron, glass, chemicals) emerged which served to replace the declining growth potential of the old staples.

Let us look at some of these industries in more detail. Most regions of the country could boast a woollen cloth-making activity of some description, whether one that specialised in heavy, high-value fabrics or rough serges, and overall the industry grew by a respectable margin (between 61 and 76 per cent).[16] Nevertheless, the trend lay firmly in the direction of a regrouping around more profitable centres of manufacture in the North-East. The Lower Languedoc industry, which had boomed throughout the first half of the eighteenth century, went into a protracted decline from the 1750s. In some measure this reflected a switch to silk which started to challenge the driving role of woollens in the regional economy, but institutional factors seem also to have played a part. The cloth towns of Louviers and Elbeuf in Normandy as well as Clermont-de-Lodève in Languedoc all experienced difficulty in coming to terms with government economic policy shifts in the 1750s and 1760s. Linens – another old textile industry – coped rather better with production expanding at an estimated 1.5 to 2 per cent per annum.[17] But growth was patchy and figures indicate another industry in the process of regrouping. Activity in the ancient centres of linen manufacture in Brittany and the Choletais had begun to slow, whereas production was booming in the Norman *bocage*, in the Cambrésis and on the outskirts of Grenoble in the Dauphiné. In the West the size of the industry was further eroded by the spring droughts of the mid-1780s which seriously depressed the supply of flax.

Local climatic conditions placed no restraint on the cotton textile industry, however. From modest beginnings around Rouen in the late seventeenth century, it entered a phase of sustained growth (3.8 per cent per annum) in the 1730s which was only curtailed in the years immediately preceding the Revolution.[18] The demand for cheap cotton garments, and increasingly for printed cotton fabrics, was such that 30 million pounds (weight) of Levantine cotton was being imported annually by mid-century. Following the lifting of the ban on colour printing in 1759, manufactories mushroomed in many towns. Over 170 have been counted, located in every corner of the country, but the best known was Oberkampf's factory at Jouy-en-Josas near Paris. By the end of the *ancien régime* this modern, water-powered plant employed 800 hands in the colour printing of calico fabrics. The silk industry remained emphatically small scale in organisation, but it, too, enjoyed boom conditions for much of the century. Increasingly, production concentrated in the South-East, within a triangle bounded by Lyon, Nîmes and Grenoble. Output from the Dauphiné quadrupled between 1730 and 1767, while the number of looms in the vicinity of Nîmes increased on average by 5.7 per cent per annum in the last six decades of the *ancien régime*.[19] However, all other centres were overshadowed by the city of Lyon where the fortunes of the silk industry affected half of the population either directly or indirectly. At the peak of its prosperity in the early 1770s, the city contained some 14,000 looms and over one third of artisans were classed as weavers.

Like the textile sector, the heavy industries remained dispersed and technologically rudimentary at the end of the *ancien régime*. Yet this did not preclude a significant expansion across the century. Coal production seems to have tripled between 1750 and 1789 to reach at least 600,000 *tonnes* per annum, although this total still fell short of the actual demand which had to be made up with imports.[20] Progress was hindered by artisanal modes of extraction and jurisdictional disputes between seigneurs and entrepreneurs over ownership of the subsoil. Not until the close of the *ancien régime* were there signs that a modern coal industry was taking shape. By 1789 the Anzin mining company had 4,000 workers on its books and was extracting 300,000 *tonnes* of coal each year from the Valenciennes basin. Extreme dispersion allied to a proto-industrial style of production also characterised the iron industry. Nevertheless, output of pig iron rose from 40,000 *tonnes* to around 135,000 *tonnes* between 1740 and 1789, that is to say a level well in excess of English production at this time.[21] The frailty of France's iron industry lay rather in overreliance on charcoal for fuel, an expensive and diminishing resource. When Spain banned charcoal exports in 1769, the ore mines and forges in the Pyrenees quickly started to run down.

All the industries described above were organised on proto-industrial lines for the most part. The concentration of manufacturing activity on one site was unusual and only likely to be found in brewing, tanning, glass making, and smelting and forging. Technological advances in the dyeing and printing of cotton fabrics and wall papers would necessitate a concentration of this industry in due course as well. But for practical purposes, the bulk of industrial activity in the eighteenth century took place in cottages and workshops. The typical 'industrialist' was in fact an entrepreneur, like the lace merchant of Villiers-le-Bel who would travel to Paris to buy thread which would then be distributed to lace makers in a thirty kilometre radius of villages.[22] Sometime later, he would return to collect the finished products and sell them to retailers back on the rue Saint-Denis in Paris. Most of the industrial expansion achieved in the course of the eighteenth century occurred within flexible and informal arrangements such as these. But growth within a traditional framework inevitably brought new pressures to bear on the rural economy. Long before Controller-General Turgot attempted to abolish the guilds, craft industry had spread from the towns into the countryside. Indeed, the government had encouraged merchants to seek out a cheaper, if less skilled, labour force in the villages with an edict breaching guild controls on textile manufacture in 1762. As a consequence, in several parts of the country the balance of the rural economy began to alter.

The shift was most noticeable in the hinterland of the big cotton and woollen centres of Normandy and the north-eastern provinces. The growth of a wage-dependent workforce of spinners and weavers in the villages around Rouen has already been mentioned. As Jonathan Dewald[23] remarks in his long-term study of the barony of Pont-Saint-Pierre in Upper Normandy, expanding opportunities for outworking simply delivered the final *coup de grâce* to the old agricultural economy. A similar transition was taking place on the Picardy plain between Beauvais and Amiens, and in Champagne to the east. Three-quarters of the weavers in that province were to be found in a broad halo of villages encircling the town of Reims. But the logic of proto-industrialisation found its fullest expression further to the north in the frontier provinces of Flanders, Hainaut and the Cambrésis. Here, the rapid advance of outworking during the second half of the eighteenth century produced a durable realignment of the rural economy, detectable in a reorganisation of physical space and the development of new, interregional relationships. Cottage industry concentrated in a densely populated middle zone, almost to the exclusion of other types of economic activity, while food and dairy products were supplied from the grain lands of Avesnes to the south-east and the pastoral district of Bergues to the north-west. It hardly needs saying that proto-industrialisation on this scale catered not for local needs, but national and even international markets.

However, the market economy was not a natural mechanism subject solely to the laws of supply and demand. It depended on government, that is to say a host of institutional factors ranging from the monarch and his councillors, the tax farmers, urban oligarchs and the multiple privileged bodies forming the estates and orders of the nation. Chief among these hurdles, from an industrialist's or merchant's point of view, were taxes, tolls and customs duties on the movement and sale of goods. Indirect taxes and internal customs duties can be grouped together, for they amounted to the same thing and were leased out by the crown to a company of financiers in return for regular, lump sum payments into the exchequer. These 'farmers' maintained a complex system of tax and customs 'walls' that intersected the kingdom and encircled cities and towns. The internal customs posed the greatest obstacle to the activities of industrialists and traders, for they divided the country into three main zones (see map 9) which were policed by a plethora of busybodying officials. Not counting external frontier check points, there existed over two and a half thousand customs posts at the end of the *ancien régime*, and a measure of the efficiency of their operations can be found in the near fourfold increase in customs revenue between 1715 and 1788.[24]

Receipts also rose in keeping with the volume expansion of industry and internal trade. Yet it is worth spelling out the logistics for anyone wishing to shift merchandise across customs zones, whether by road or river. Goods travelling downstream from Gray on the Saône to Arles on the Rhône were liable for six different customs duties, not to mention thirty river tolls. Thus iron produced in the Franche-Comté cost about 35 per cent of its value to transport to Marseille. Similarly, the overland movement of merchandise from Brittany to Provence was burdened by a requirement for hauliers to make eight customs declarations, halt for eight inspections and assessments, and finally to pay seven different duties. No wonder it was claimed during the Anglo-French trade negotiations of 1786 that British merchants would still be able to compete in nearly the whole of the French domestic market, even after meeting a 12 per cent import duty. As a contemporary observer remarked:

It costs from 10 per cent to 12 per cent to send silk gauze, cotton cloth and velveteen from Lyon to Brittany, and it costs as much to send Flemish products into the interior of the kingdom. Woollen goods manufactured in Lille pay $7\frac{1}{2}$ per cent at the bureau of Péronne alone. The cloth of Languedoc arrives in Paris and in Brittany only after having paid 15 per cent or 16 per cent in duties, and expenses.[25]

In view of the failure of all attempts to reform the system (see below p. 114), manufacturers had little choice but to pay up, or to smuggle their goods past the customs posts. The rewards of smuggling could be high, but so were the risks since discovery entailed seizure and a hefty fine. Alternatively, well-connected industrialists might try to beat the system on its own terms. Thus Pierre Babaud de la Chaussade, the timber merchant and forge owner, petitioned ministers in order to obtain free passage for his anchors down the river Loire on the ground that they were strategic materials of war. He even used his privileged status as an ennobled office-holder to try and procure for his workmen

Map 9 Internal customs zones

(a) *Gabelle*

grande gabelle: average price of salt in 1780=58 *livres* per *minot* approx.

petite gabelle: average price of salt in 1780=29 *livres* per *minot* approx.

pays de salines/gabelle de Rethel: average price of salt in 1780=24 *livres* per *minot* approx.

pays de quart-bouillon: average price of salt in 1780=13 *livres* per *minot* approx.

pays rédimés des gabelles: average price of salt in 1780=9 *livres* per *minot* approx.

exempt regions: free trade, no taxes hence average price of salt in 1780=5 *livres* per *minot* approx.

Sources: G. Cabourdin and G. Viard, *Lexique historique de la France d'Ancien Régime* (Paris, 1978), pp. 148–50; G. T. Matthews, *The Royal General Farms in Eighteenth-Century France* (New York, 1958), pp. 88–116.

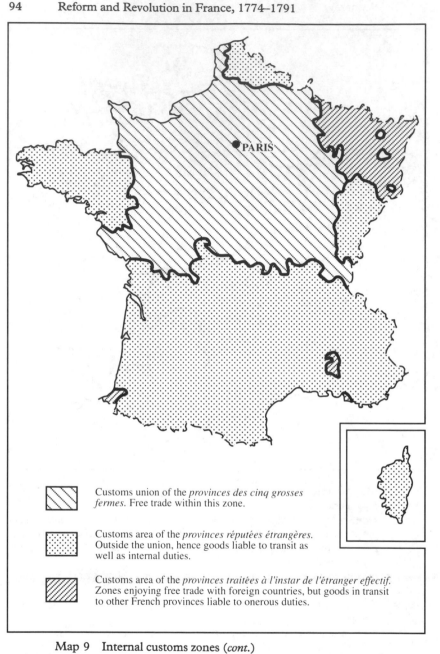

Customs union of the *provinces des cinq grosses fermes*. Free trade within this zone.

Customs area of the *provinces réputées étrangères*. Outside the union, hence goods liable to transit as well as internal duties.

Customs area of the *provinces traitées à l'instar de l'étranger effectif*. Zones enjoying free trade with foreign countries, but goods in transit to other French provinces liable to onerous duties.

Map 9   Internal customs zones (*cont.*)
(b) *Traites*
Sources: Bosher, *The Single Duty Project*; Matthews, *The Royal General Farms*, pp. 134–8.

exemption from militia service and the *corvée*. Ministers were not blind
to the economic consequences of fiscal policies, of course, but where the
prerogatives of the General Farm and the *pays d'états* were concerned a
perpetual shortage of ready cash left them with little room for
manoeuvre. Instead, they preferred to focus on more vulnerable
sectional interests. Private owners of road and river tolls (*péages*), for
instance, were quietly picked off one by one. By 1789 more than two-
thirds of the 5,688 tolls subsisting at the start of Louis XV's reign had
been extinguished.[26]

The mid-century shift in government thinking about how best to
harness the productive capacities of the nation provides a final context
for assessing the performance of the industrial economy. Deregulation
of industry and of the grain trade were major accomplishments of the
1750s and 1760s, although it is worth noting that the comparable shift in
thinking about the problems of agriculture produced, not laissez-faire,
but creeping interventionism. Industry was to be set to rights by
unshackling it from Colbertian controls, whereas agriculture required
outside help if it were to escape from a stop–start cycle of growth.
Commercially minded farmers would be assisted by the free circulation
of cereals, even as their subsistence-oriented neighbours were cajoled
with measures curtailing common rights and enclosing common land.
But how did manufacturing industry weather the transition to free-for-
all conditions?

The faltering growth of the textile sector in the 1750s and 1760s
raises the possibility of a connection between performance, both
quantitative and qualitative, and liberalisation. In short, the possibility
that a further cluster of institutional factors may have hindered the
smooth functioning of the industrial economy. The abandonment of
strict controls over the production and marketing of cloth encouraged
a mass of would-be entrepreneurs to enter the industry whose
experience of textile manufacture was negligible. Concomitantly a
long-established and highly skilled elite of clothiers withdrew, reluctant
to remain in an industry which had lost its familiar framework.
Naturally they took their capital and business contacts with them,
and, like the Ayral dynasty[27] discussed earlier, invested instead in land
and offices. Thus the customary cycle of development in a pre-
industrial society was intensified and exacerbated by administrative
interventionism conceived originally as a means of boosting the
nation's trading and manufacturing capacity. This argument has been
put most persuasively by James Thomson[28] in a monograph study of
the cloth-making town of Clermont-de-Lodève. It cuts across the
grain of most recent writing on French economic history in defending

the importance of non-quantitative institutional factors – bureaucratic meddling, entrepreneurship, social mores and the like. Whether the argument can be applied more generally must await further research. Yet it is certain that the crisis in Languedoc's cloth industry reflected more than simply the dislocation of the Levant trade occasioned by the Seven Years War. Its origins were social as well as economic.

Trade

Commerce boomed in the eighteenth century and by 1780 France had emerged as a world-class trading nation. However, the components of this prosperity are poorly understood, as is the relationship between commercial expansion and the performance of the economy as a whole. External trade achieved the best results, with shipments to and from the colonies out-performing all other sectors. But external (in practice, overseas) trade accounted for no more than one third of the total volume of commercial transactions in these years. Most trade was inland and, unlike colonial cargoes, largely unrecorded.

Nevertheless much can be inferred from the preceding discussion, for industry and commerce were interlocking activities. Moreover tax, toll and customs receipts all testify to enhanced consumption and a quickening in the circuits of exchange. The number of vehicles stopped by the Prince of Monaco's toll collectors at Valence all but tripled between 1750 and 1788, while the incidence and importance of fairs seems to have been rising rather than falling. Turnover at the Beaucaire fair, situated on the Rhône at a strategic regional intersection, increased threefold in the last four decades of the *ancien régime*. In a matter of days transactions worth 41 million *livres* (equivalent to around 10 per cent of the annual value of overseas trade) were concluded.[29] Arthur Young was caught up in the preparations for this fair as he travelled through Languedoc in 1787 and made a note that it 'fills the whole country with business and motion'.[30] Decades of steady investment in viticulture were having the same effect, for wines and brandies were preeminently market commodities with interregional, indeed international, outlets. As the industrial fortunes of Clermont's clothiers began to ebb, the townspeople rediscovered the merits of agriculture. By the 1780s wine had become their principal crop. In similar fashion, the brandy distillers of Cognac and La Rochelle showed considerable enterprise in establishing ever widening markets for their wares.

However, the racing pulse of commerce and consumerism should not pass unchecked. Many exchange circuits dwindled in the 1770s and 1780s as large sectors of the economy headed into recession. Even the

Beaucaire fair seems to have passed its peak by the late 1780s, and for all his fulsome comments Young was no less struck by the emptiness of roads in other parts of the country. The Clermontais may have found an alternative outlet for their energies, but most textile *bourgs* hit by crumbling markets, administrative and fiscal pressures simply sank towards commercial oblivion. No less important, we should make allowance for the silences in the record: the myriad agricultural parishes quite untouched by industrial and commercial activity. Only on rare occasions do we hear their voices – in the municipal reports of 1788 or the *cahiers* of the following year. But they form a chorus: 'There is no commerce or industry or any manufactures in the parish.'[31]

France's external trade consisted of exports, imports and reexports, nearly all of which moved by sea. Indeed, even domestic merchants would sometimes use the sea lanes to move goods from the north to the south of the country, and vice versa. Save in times of war, shipping was safe, secure and above all cheap. There were no customs stations on the high seas. The four great river and sea ports of Le Havre, Nantes, Bordeaux and Marseille handled the bulk of this commerce and the registers kept by the port officials enable us to evaluate the activities of merchants plying overseas with some degree of precision. Overall, the value of external trade at current prices appears to have quintupled between 1716–20 and 1784–8. Allowing that prices probably doubled, it seems likely, therefore, that the volume at least doubled in this period. This implies that France's overseas commerce was growing at roughly 2.5 per cent a year.[32] As with agricultural production, however, trade did not expand in an even and continuous fashion. The first half of the century witnessed dynamic growth (perhaps 3 per cent per annum) as the country accelerated out of the stagnation marking the final years of Louis XIV's reign. But the post-1750 decades were much less buoyant (growth of perhaps 1 per cent per annum), a fact underscored by the rising curve of imports at the expense of exports.

But this was the global picture, it must be emphasised. The jewel in the crown lay in France's trade with her Caribbean colonies, the islands of Guadaloupe, Martinique and Saint-Domingue. This sector expanded tenfold and with no immediate sign of a downturn after 1750.[33] By the end of the *ancien régime*, two ships were leaving French ports every day for the Caribbean in a trade which had doubled its contribution to the total volume of external commerce since the start of the century. Sugar, coffee, cotton and indigo were the major items of exchange, in return for which French ships brought flour, textiles, wines and brandies and, for those vessels engaged in the 'triangular' trade, slaves. Much of the colonial produce was not destined for the home market, however.

Rather, it was reexported to the countries of northern Europe, and eastwards, down the Mediterranean to Italy and Turkey. La Rochelle, one of the lesser ports of the Atlantic seaboard, reexported nearly all the colonial products entering its harbour and it has been calculated that, by the 1770s and 1780s, reexports accounted for one third of France's total export trade. This busy recycling of colonial products proved highly lucrative: shipowners could expect a return of anything up to 10 or 12 per cent per annum at a time when investment in land yielded scarcely 3 per cent and shareholders in the Anzin mines were getting 7 per cent at most.[34]

With the exception of a small but expanding commerce with the Indies late on in the century, all other trade routes were fairly subdued. The widespread expectation that France would derive a commercial advantage from aiding the American colonists in their struggle against Britain failed to materialise. With evident satisfaction, the British ambassador to France informed his superiors in July 1784 that no American vessels had been seen in Bordeaux harbour since the preceding November.[35] France and Britain were trading rivals rather than partners, and each country took care to seal off its domestic and colonial markets from the other by means of hefty tariffs. Not until the signing of the Eden Treaty in 1786 did this situation alter. In the meantime smuggling remained the principal form of economic intercourse between the two nations. Trade with the Levant (Turkey and the eastern Mediterranean) was channelled through the port of Marseille and served to vivify a broad swathe of Provence and Lower Languedoc, as we have seen. Any interruption, whether caused by English competition or turmoil in the Ottoman Empire, produced immediate knock-on effects within the textile industry. In fact the weavers and merchant manufacturers of Languedoc were vulnerable on two fronts, for they also relied heavily on the export of mass-produced silks to Spain and the Spanish American colonies. Yet in 1778 the Spanish government began to squeeze foreign exports out of its markets by means of tariffs. Only the north European trade route continued to show evidence of stamina into the last quarter of the eighteenth century. From the Baltic, France drew wheat and naval stores in a profitable exchange for wine and colonial reexports.

France's stature as a trading nation should not be underestimated. By the end of the *ancien régime*, she had overtaken all her rivals with the exception of Great Britain. And even on this front she seemed to be catching up. To judge from the English pattern of economic development, she appeared to be preparing for industrial take-off. Yet her commercial strength was built on frail foundations which suggests that the English model may not be applicable after all. If we take figures for the export of manufactured goods as broadly indicative of the extent to which trade drove the dynamo of industrialisation, the position of France is revealing. Between 1715 and 1787 the percentage of manufactured articles (essentially fabrics) in the total volume of French exports scarcely altered, whereas the quantity of manufactured imports, again measured in percentage terms, rose significantly. Britain, by contrast, mainly imported raw materials and by the 1780s her exports consisted overwhelmingly of manufactured goods.

The implication is that France's external and domestic economies were not well integrated. Foreign trade certainly acted to stimulate growth in the maritime provinces, but these coastal enclaves remained poorly connected with the interior of the country. Thus the booming commerce of Bordeaux exerted a powerful attractive effect on agriculture and industry throughout the Garonne basin. Flour millers in the Montalbanais and the Agenais, rope and sail makers at Tonneins, glass bottle manufacturers in Libourne and Bazas, and vine growers in the Médoc all relied heavily on the continuing prosperity of the Atlantic trade routes. So did the cluster of colonial processing industries (sugar refineries, distilleries, tobacco factories, tanneries) which had sprung up on the outskirts of Bordeaux. Yet the 'reach' of these diverse circuits of exchange soon faltered as the ground began to rise to the east and the rivers ceased to be navigable. A voyager crossing the waist of France from Bordeaux to Rodez, a small town in the central highlands, at the end of the *ancien régime* would have found himself moving from a maritime to a mulepack economy in the space of a few days.

Servicing overseas commerce provided some localised stimulus to domestic industry and trade, then. But it must be questioned whether trade and merchant capitalism alone could have shifted the French economy on to a new footing. The key mining and metallurgical industries remained scattered, undercapitalised and technologically backward. On the eve of the Revolution France still imported a significant proportion of her coal requirements. Buoyant imports of colonial goods scarcely betokened a dynamic consumer sector either. Domestic demand for such products was fairly weak: around two-thirds of the sugar and one third of the coffee entering the country was reexported. This recycling of colonial wares around the markets of Europe could be highly lucrative, of course, and no doubt the profits were redeployed to some degree as well. Merchant capital from Nantes and Bordeaux certainly assisted the expansion of the silk industry in Lyon. On the whole, though, specialists question whether much commercial capital was siphoned into industrial ventures;

indeed, whether the profits generated by overseas trade entered the capital flows of the domestic economy at all. In a painstaking study of the colonial trade, Jean Tarrade concludes with a vision of 'dual economies'[36] operating in parallel but largely independently of each other. A thriving international commerce offers no sure indication of industrial preparedness, then. Yet the pacemaker role which Labrousse attributes to the rural economy is no less problematic. In this scenario it seems inherently unlikely that the great ports such as Marseille and Bordeaux (and perhaps the inland cities, too) responded solely to the stimuli of agricultural prices and incomes.

Downturn

All historians are agreed that the French economy eventually took a downturn after decades of growth and prosperity. To this extent, the existence of some kind of socio-economic crisis of the *ancien régime* would appear to be common ground. In reality, though, scholars are probably as far apart as they ever have been on this vexing issue. Was the economic crisis profoundly structural; the product of conjunctural events; or purely meteorological? Labrousse formulated the most complex account of the crisis in the sequel to his study of price and wage movements across the eighteenth century.[37] It still enjoys widespread support and is buttressed by numerous regional monographs.[38] The objection can be made, however, that Labrousse's structural diagnosis of the ills besetting Bourbon France is overly deterministic, indeed teleological. Many historians would accept the outlines of his analysis, while insisting that a long-term economic malaise was not, in itself, a sufficient cause for the breakdown of the *ancien régime*.

Nevertheless, this view can be challenged on more fundamental grounds. We might start from the proposition of growth and ask whether conjunctural rather than structural factors caused its curtailment. This is the line pressed by Jean Marczewski[39] and his team and it results in an emphasis on the mid-1780s (rather than the 1770s) as the moment when the growth curve finally ran out of momentum. The economic crisis is thus telescoped and made a tributary of short-term institutional and climatic factors. Others assert that a more radical pruning is warranted. They argue, in effect, that the economic crisis can be confined to the meteorological phenomena that produced a bad harvest in 1788, followed by a bad winter in 1788–9. All of these interpretations contain trenchant arguments and it will be the task of this section to sort them into a meaningful synthesis.

The onset of Labrousse's cyclical crisis is a little fuzzy. Between 1770 and 1778 grain prices stopped rising and in many regions started to fall back. Presumably this eased the pressure on consumers for a time, but it plunged tenant farmers into a scissors crisis of high rents and low prices. The source of these difficulties lay in the high farming decades of the 1750s and 1760s during which period the relationship between rents and prices had shifted decisively in favour of cultivators. As agricultural prices climbed, anyone with a surplus to trade in the market-place made immediate cash gains, whereas landlords and institutional proprietors were inhibited by contract from making equivalent adjustments to the terms of their leases. Most leases only ran for three, six or at most nine years, it is true, but all parties were slow to digest the significance of the trend. Thus, tenants of the royal farms adjoining the park of Versailles faced no significant rent rises between 1745 and 1770; similarly in Upper Normandy rents remained stable until 1768 or thereabouts. However, the trend towards ever increasing cereal prices petered out in the 1770s, just as rents began to spiral in a compensatory surge. The fat years for the tenant farmer were replaced by the 'golden age' of the landed proprietor. Aided by buoyant demand for farms, landlords exacted a high price for the opportunities they had let slip in the 1750s and 1760s. Stewards of the royal demesne pushed rents sharply upwards in the 1770s and 1780s, and equivalent pressures were felt as far afield as Normandy, Brittany and the Auvergne. Overall that segment of the peasantry reliant on rentals for access to land emerged as net losers. Labrousse reckons the agricultural commodity price rise at around two-thirds, as we have seen, whereas leases doubled between 1730–9 and 1780–9.

A distressed middling peasantry occupy an important place in the structural diagnosis of the late *ancien-régime* crisis, then. Caught in the scissors trap, weakened by the wine glut, vulnerable to cattle pest, they were living precariously by the later 1780s. While Calonne tried to rally support within the Assembly of Notables with a smug reminder of 'the revolution which has caused income from land virtually to double over the past twenty years',[40] the Provincial Assembly of Lower Normandy was warning of the difficulties ahead for tenant farmers as prices started to fall away.[41] In comparison with the difficulties facing poorer peasants these problems were minor, however. For the key to Labrousse's immiseration thesis is to be found among plot holders, agricultural labourers and industrial wage workers. As demographic pressure intensified a number of phenomena made an appearance: subdivision of farms, trespass into state and private forests, tillage of the commons and wastes, and the random grazing of stock. In short, the tell-tale symptoms of proletarianisation became more pronounced at the lower end of the agricultural labour force. These developments have all been well documented, especially in the provinces of the East and the North-East which were experiencing headlong population growth. In the Artois, for instance, the bottom-most tier of self-sufficient peasants came under great pressure as holdings were divided in response to a 39 per cent increase in population between 1750 and 1790.[42] Subdivision, in turn, created the conditions for engrossment – a form of anti-social behaviour in which wealthy farmers bought up the assets of their less solvent neighbours. In 1789 the *cahiers de doléances* of the open-field villages would frequently carry complaints about activities of this sort.

Pauperisation was not confined to the grain land of the North and North-East, though. It seems to have been widespread, save perhaps in the Massif Central where the land supply remained elastic and isolation preserved local industries from the vagaries of the wider market. In Brittany and the Norman *bocage* the repeated failure of the cider apple harvest had, by 1787, pushed many small holders to the brink of destitution. The droughts of the mid-1780s dealt a similar body blow to day labourers who relied on small patches planted with flax in order to make ends meet. In fact, the rapid downward spiral of the cottage textile industry provides the third element of the crisis as perceived by Labrousse. Between 1787 and 1789 national cloth production dropped by half, with a corresponding fall in proto-industrial employment opportunities. No doubt this was partly a reflection of competition as English manufactured goods invaded the domestic market following the signing of an Anglo-French commercial treaty in 1786. But it is intrinsic to Labrousse's reasoning that the textile industry responded primarily to demand factors, in this instance the diminished purchasing power of hard-pressed country dwellers. Subsequent research has certainly confirmed the fact that difficulties in the textile sector pre-dated the implementation of the trade treaty. Production of cotton fabrics in the *généralité* of Rouen peaked in 1770 and began to fall sharply from 1785. Output of worsted cloth from the Pays de Caux began a nose-dive in 1785, too, whereas the dislocation of the Montauban textile industry occurred earlier, apparently in response to the loss of Spanish markets. On the other hand, cloth production in and around the towns of Mazamet and Sedan continued to expand, while trade in the *cadis* of Saint-Geniez-d'Olt only slackened when new duties ('la marque et du plomb') were introduced in 1787.

What all this suggests is that Labrousse goes to considerable lengths to produce a seamless interpretation of the crisis of the *ancien régime*. Yet, while the individual components of his argument carry conviction, the mode of assemblage leaves something to be desired. The downturn in textile production, for instance, clearly stemmed from more than the collapse of domestic demand. His analysis also alludes to a factor which is not stressed sufficiently – by any of the parties to the debate – namely the disruptive impact of abnormal weather conditions in the years *preceding* the climatic disaster of 1788–9. Recent research advances by climatologists have made possible for the first time a synoptic view of conditions during the last decade of the *ancien régime*. Their findings are unambiguous and coincide with the field evidence: the agricultural year 1781–2 marked a turning-point. After a run of fine summers which had generated bountiful cereal and grape harvests, weather conditions over western Europe entered a cycle of extreme instability. A wet and tardy spring in 1782 produced a poor harvest, only to be followed by another in 1783 which climatologists have linked to volcanic dust in the upper atmosphere. This haze depressed temperatures in a broad band of latitudes and it may have been responsible for the severe winter of 1783–4. Benjamin Franklin, living at that time in Passy near Paris, certainly drew this conclusion.[43] The next scourge to afflict the European landmass was drought. After a chilly spring and summer, a prolonged period of meagre rainfall ensued from the autumn of 1784. This dryness turned into drought as high pressure systems repeatedly blocked westerly airflows during the late winter and spring of 1785. The cereal harvest was short in consequence. A milder version of the same pattern prevailed in 1786, but at last a respite from climatic adversity materialised in the shape of a bumper harvest in 1787.

Harvest shortfall was an all too frequent hazard of *ancien-régime* France. But grain kept well, and those with sufficient means would stockpile in order to even out the peaks and troughs. Surpluses from the 1787 harvest would be used in this fashion to attenuate the hardships of 1788–9. However, the combination of winter cold followed by spring drought posed a more serious threat for it weakened the several sinews of the rural economy – agriculture, stock raising and cottage industry – all at once. These knock-on effects all came into play as a consequence of the 1785 drought. They are worth looking at closely, for it seems to have been at this point, rather than 1788–9, that the agrarian downturn really began.

From early February until the end of July not a drop of rain fell in Brittany. Travelling through the Artois in May, John Adams reported: 'the Country is a heap of Ashes. Grass is scarcely to be seen and all sorts of Grain is short, thin, pale and feeble while the Flax is quite dead.' Cattle and sheep, he added, 'stalk about the fields like Droves of

Walking Skeletons'.[44] Another of Thomas Jefferson's correspondents transmitted a similar account from Bordeaux. Indeed, there is a wealth of contemporary reportage to indicate that three-quarters of the kingdom lay in the grip of drought by the spring of 1785. The first fear to be expressed was for the hay harvest and with good reason. Officials from as far afield as Upper Guyenne and the Bourbonnais announced a 50 per cent shortfall compared with the previous year. In Burgundy it was 25 per cent down, in Champagne between 25 and 16 per cent; elsewhere terms like 'ruined' and 'destroyed' sprang to mind.[45] As a result, hay prices rocketed in a movement reminiscent of the very worst swings in cereal prices.

The immediate focus of concern was stock, for animals performed multiple roles in the pre-industrial economy. They pulled ploughs, fertilised the soil with their dung, furnished hides and wool for yarn, and supplied the towns with meat, milk and butter. On the other hand, they consumed large quantities of fodder which, in the conditions of the eighteenth century, derived primarily from natural pasture. The situation was most acute in Brittany which had already suffered a significant stock loss as a result of the cold winter of 1783–4. More losses of yearlings occurred during the winter following, whereupon overwintered animals immediately encountered the fodder famine of 1785. The effect of this combination of mishaps was little short of disastrous: over one third of stock died on the hoof or was slaughtered and the whole economy of the province experienced a severe setback. Bertrand de Molleville, the intendant, successfully petitioned to have lifted the ban on grazing in royal forests, and he intervened to eke out hay supplies.[46] But these measures could only be palliatives, for the drought had wiped out flax plantings and had caused grain prices to surge as well. Ramifications of the crisis spread in all directions. Fears were expressed for tax receipts, extra funds had to be found for poor relief, farmers cut back on wage labour, even coastal shipping was affected. Lack of fodder served to slow down the transportation of salt to the ports of southern Brittany.

By the summer of 1785 this combination of drought and dearth had enveloped much of rural France. And it tended to exacerbate those structural weaknesses in the rural economy which Labrousse has identified. Hard-pressed tenant farmers defaulted on their leases. Visiting his estates near Blois in July, the wealthy tax farmer and chemist, Antoine Lavoisier,[47] was shocked to learn that two of his tenants had gone bust. He had little choice but to receive what remained of their harvests and to seek out workmen prepared to take on the autumn sowings. But the fragile household budgets of agricultural labourers had been hard hit, too; especially those dependent on cash supplements from textile outworking, apple and pear orchards, or kitchen gardens. Bertrand de Molleville was anticipating the next stage in the crisis when he urged the merchants of Nantes and Saint-Malo to import flax as well as hay and oats.[48] It started to rain again – in the Paris region at least – on 20 July. Yet the repercussions of the drought would continue to reverberate. Stock could not be replaced overnight, and supplies of fatstock, in particular, remained seriously disturbed. The Provincial Assembly of Lower Normandy estimated that it would require fifteen years to restore the pastoral economy of the Cotentin and Bessin regions.[49]

This remark was made in 1787, in gloomy recognition of the damage caused by yet another spell of dry weather in 1786. Occurring at the end of a decade of sagging wheat and grain prices, these droughts severely tested the rural economy. For Labrousse they provided further, unshakable evidence of a generalised socio-economic crisis of the *ancien régime*. Construed from a different perspective, such phenomena take on a different meaning, though. They become symptoms of a conjunctural downturn in an economy which had nothing much wrong with it, at least not before the mid-1780s. But an emphasis on growth necessarily involves a widening of the frame of reference to include commerce and perhaps industry as well. Overseas trade, and the colonial trade in particular, remained buoyant until the end, and even beyond the end of the *ancien régime*. On the eve of the Revolution, the ports of Marseille and Bordeaux had never been busier. No sign here of a generalised crisis, which has prompted one historian to throw off the mantle of Labrousse completely with the verdict that 'the French economy was dynamic during the reign of Louis XVI'.[50] Such arguments carry an implicit, sometimes even an explicit judgement on the role of the Revolution in arresting economic growth, of course. But they also beg an important question of more direct relevance to the concerns of this chapter. Can the rhythms of overseas commerce serve as a meter of the performance of the economy as a whole? It seems unlikely, for the 1780s witnessed the stark juxtaposition of an expanding maritime economy with an internal, landlocked economy which had become sluggish and was now starting to falter. Marseillais and Bordelais may indeed have been riding a wave of prosperity, but their counterparts in Lille were having to cope with a mounting toll of bankruptcies which had been rising, moreover, since the 1770s.

The final act in this saga of dual economies is not in dispute. In 1788–9 the putative structural downturn entered a resolutely meteorological phase. Once again the initial hardship was caused by a long spring drought and scorching winds which stunted developing grain crops.

Then, as the harvest for 1788 approached, violent storms beat down the corn in many regions. The most serious of these occurred on 13 July as an active cold front pushed eastwards leaving a seventy mile swathe of destruction across the best grain fields of France. Massive hailstones smashed everything in their path, prompting the British ambassador to report from Paris that 'it is certain that a Country of at least thirty leagues in circumference is entirely laid waste'.[51] As alms collections for those injured by the hail got under way (Jefferson made a donation of 72 *livres*[52]), the true proportions of that year's climatic disasters began to dawn. If the harvest had not been universally catastrophic, the fact remained that a shortfall was reported from twenty-seven *généralités* out of thirty-four. And in districts affected by storm damage, the yield from both vines and cereals was negligible. Stocks held over from the 1787 harvest now took on critical importance, but Brienne's edict of June 1787 permitting the export of grain had diminished the supplies normally retained for release on the domestic market. The government responded by buying in grain on a massive scale and at an eventual cost of some 70 million *livres*, and in September the royal Council provisionally suspended the freedom to export cereals and flour. Yet none of these measures served to prevent a rapid and sustained increase in prices.

Then the winter of 1788–9 intervened. The cold was exceptional and a thick layer of ice on road and river brought the economic life of the nation to a virtual standstill. By 8 January 1789, according to the Royal Agricultural Society, Paris had been frost-bound for fifty-seven days in a row.[53] André-Hubert Dameras, a peasant farmer in the Champagne, noted in his diary that all the wine and cider in his cellars had frozen.[54] In the South olive trees, mulberry bushes and even chestnut orchards perished. The thaw came a few days later. But with it came flood, destruction and untold misery for millions living on or near the banks of rivers and streams. Ice-floes smashed boats down the length of the Loire, bridges and mills were swept away, low-lying fields were inundated. As bread prices continued to climb, beggars and vagabonds took to the roads in alarming numbers, mingling with the unemployed of the towns. In March the first reports of popular disturbances reached officials in many parts of the country. But by now a very different mobilisation was under way, launched by the publication of instructions for the holding of an Estates General.

4   Reformers and the reform constituency

The 'big bang' theory of the French Revolution's origins renders discussion of reformers and reform initiatives largely irrelevant. If 1789 marked a clear break with the past, the *ancien régime* need only be mentioned in order to chronicle its abuses. Yet it was not always thus. An older, and no less respectable, generation of historians tended to explore the phenomenon of the Revolution on a broader canvas, anxious lest points of comparison and links between regimes should escape notice. Leo Gershoy's[1] influential textbook survey of 'enlightened despotism' can be considered a monument to this approach as can Alfred Cobban's three-volume *History of Modern France*,[2] first published in 1957 and constantly reprinted ever since. For Cobban there could be no question of neatly stowing the tangled threads of French history; like Gershoy he dubbed the three decades prior to the Revolution 'The Age of Reform'. Indeed, he went further and described the Revolution as 'a fall of snow on blossoming trees'.[3] This chapter provides little support for that last remark. But it does offer a picture of the climactic years of the *ancien régime* which undermines many of the slogans peddled by the Revolutionaries and repeated uncritically by historians ever since. As will be seen, Cobban's focus on 'The Age of Reform' is not misplaced, provided always that the failures as well as the successes are kept in mind. The corollary to this reformist activity is an argument about the mechanics of passage from one regime to another, specifically the transition from administrative to constitutional monarchy. If late *ancien-régime* France can be likened to an 'on-going building site for enlightened reform' as François Furet[4] has suggested, it is important to know at what point the workmen considered that they were constructing anew, as opposed to refurbishing the old. And who were the architects? This chapter looks closely at the role of the monarch, his ministers, permanent officials and field agents in the belief that the essential momentum for reform came from with the Bourbon state machine.

Reform and revolution are not the same thing, although the former often serves as the prelude to the latter as Tocqueville pointed out.[5]

Before 1789 reform proposals – whatever their source – tended to be legitimated by reference to past practice. Thus Lamoignon's eleventh-hour restructuring of the judiciary in May 1788 was motivated by the need to continue and to perfect the court reforms introduced by Henry II in 1551. Yet this traditional notion of reform, implying the re-forming or re-balancing of ancient institutions, no longer corresponded to actual usage of the term by the end of the *ancien régime*. Reformers of all stripes would continue to express their arguments in terms of legal and historical precedents, but the real justification lay elsewhere – in guarded references to natural law, to utilitarian ethics, to humanitarianism and to Bourbon raison d'état. Lamoignon might wrap his proposals in the soothing language of judicial continuity, but the fact remained that they marked a fundamental break with the past. By 1789 that break had already occurred in many walks of life. What the early revolutionaries did was to repackage the reforms, employing a universalistic language of rights which explicitly repudiated the mantle of the past.

As the chief source of reform initiatives, the monarchy experienced the dilemma of what species of reform to promote more acutely than any other body in the state. This was understandable for the task which Louis-Auguste inherited from his grandfather, Louis XV, was to uphold the power and prestige of Bourbon absolutism at home and abroad. Now, it was not certain, and became progressively less certain, that this objective could be achieved by means of traditional reforms alone. Already, in the 1760s and early 1770s, Louis XV's ministers had started to break the mould of customary political practice. On the other hand, the brusque adoption of innovative reforms tended to produce resistance and cries of despotism from the parties most affected. No single episode demonstrated this dilemma more starkly than Chancellor Maupeou's reassertion of royal authority vis-à-vis the Parlement of Paris in 1771, which resulted in the exile of its members and the truncation of its powers and jurisdiction. When the lesser *parlements* protested, they were subject to similar treatment and several were abolished outright. Contemporaries viewed this rending of the constitutional fabric of the state as a 'revolution', no less, but for the king it was a reform made necessary by the magistrates' encroachment upon his legislative prerogative. Maupeou planned to press further his advantage with a systematic restructuring of the judicial system, but that really would have seemed 'despotic' and the king demurred. Nevertheless, Louis XVI was sufficiently discomfited by the treatment meted out to the *parlementaires*, that he reversed Maupeou's measures on his accession in 1774. In the eyes of the public the damage was done, however. Henceforward, each and every attempt at reform would be scrutinised minutely for evidence of despotic intent. If bodies such as the *parlements* could be obliterated in the name of so-called reform, what protection could ordinary French men and women expect from the overweening power of the crown?

Reform ministers

By the time Louis XVI came to the throne, ministerial attempts at reform had been underway for a decade and more. Controller-General Laverdy (1763–68) had responded to the mounting clamour of the physiocrats with a thorough liberalisation of the grain trade, and he had initiated a farreaching experiment in municipal self-government which replaced venal office-holders with elected officials. Terray, who held the post of controller-general from 1769 to 1774, repaired the finances and procured for his royal master a fiscal breathing space, while Maupeou engineered the defeat of the *parlements* as we have noted. The narrative history of these reforms will be explored below; for the time being it is more important to identify the architects of reform at the several levels of royal government, and the objectives which they had in view. According to the theory of absolute monarchy, only the king was positioned in such a way as to know the needs of state. For he alone was a public person, and he brooked no rivals in the business of defining the parameters of reform. This was the theory which Louis XV sought to uphold in the so-called *séance de la flagellation* of 1766 when the *parlements* were sharply rebuked for using their judicial remonstrances to make themselves a focus of public attention. Yet it was plain that the reality no longer corresponded to this theory, not even during the reign of Louis XV.

Despite his youth and lack of political experience in 1774, Louis XVI quickly mastered the functional aspects of kingship. As a recent biography makes clear, it was the ceremonial exercise of power which he performed badly.[6] He understood the business of public finance and never shrank from the need for reform, on the principle that reform would serve to maintain the viability of absolute monarchy. Nothing remarkable in this perhaps, but Louis also displayed a readiness to harness innovative reform to the business of government. This set him apart from some of his ministers and not a few of his privileged subjects whose continued well-being depended on a more restrictive approach to the task of refurbishing the machinery of state. Controller-General Calonne's attempt to persuade an Assembly of Notables to ratify a comprehensive package of reforms signalled the high water-mark of the king's policies. The loss of Calonne and the refusal of the Notables to come to terms threw everything into disarray. The reform impulse did not come to an end; indeed, it entered a new phase, but Louis' stamina ebbed. Instead, the king switched his energies to the hunt once more and turned away from public affairs.

But this retreat took place in the spring of 1787. Having resolved to dispense with the principal architects of his grandfather's reforms (Terray and Maupeou), Louis began his reign by appointing to the post of controller-general a man whom he judged to be a reliable auxiliary in the enterprise of reequipping and modernising the absolute monarchy. Anne Robert Jacques Turgot had established an impressive record as a reforming intendant in the *généralité* of Limoges. However, he was also reputed to be a systemiser owing to close links with the *philosophes*, notably Condorcet and Dupont – the man who had coined the term 'physiocracy'. Louis, whose reforming urge borrowed little from the Enlightenment, set any doubts he may have felt about his new minister to one side and was right to do so. Turgot rapidly demonstrated that he was perfectly capable of fulfilling the role allotted to him. The clash over the Six Edicts of 1776 is instructive in this respect, for it clarified the position of several of the major players in the drama of reforming absolutism, positions that would be taken up repeatedly in the years ahead.

The reform proposals which Turgot drew up for discussion in council at the start of that year contained several items that were already the subject of legislation. However, the objects most obviously fixed in the minister's sights were the *corvée* and the guilds. The scheme to replace the *corvée* with a monetary tax was in the pipeline, but the assault on the guilds caused quite a stir. The proposal, reported the British ambassador, is 'to abolish all the *corps de métiers* throughout the kingdom and to have all trades quite free as they are in our towns as have no corporations'.[7] It was primarily on these two issues that the debate was joined. Louis' reaction is interesting and consistent with the view that depicts him as a staunch reformer, until 1787 at least. He took the various memoranda away to read and after several days emerged to give Turgot as much backing as he could muster. Predictably, the chief opponent of thorough-going reform turned out to be Miromesnil whom the king had unwisely placed at the head of the judiciary following the removal of Maupeou. Miromesnil was a former senior magistrate in the Parlement of Rouen and a determined defender of 'jurisdictional' authority. His was a conservative vision of absolute monarchy according to which the king ruled in partnership with the sovereign courts and the privileged orders. Worse, Miromesnil had retained close links with the *parlements* and was prepared to use them in order to block royal legislation. Indubitably, Louis had cause to regret his elevation of Miromesnil, for as a minister he became, in the words of the king's recent biographer, 'the biggest single obstacle to reform'.[8]

There can be no doubt that Turgot's Edicts did pose a challenge to the old static image of absolute monarchy. That was the point. Commutation of the *corvée* would distribute its load over all owners of land irrespective of status. Destruction of the guilds would erode the substance of privilege further and gnaw at the corporatist heart of the *ancien régime*. When Miromesnil tried to mount a defence of privilege, Turgot spelled out brutally the economic cost to the rest of the nation. But, in sensing the implication of Turgot's reforms, Miromesnil was on firmer ground. He seems to have understood that an operation to unstitch a part of the fabric of the *ancien régime* might easily cause the whole to unravel. Already there was talk of a general redemption of feudal dues, and in ministerial circles it was known that Turgot was working on schemes to curtail tax farming, to eradicate customs barriers and to harmonise weights and measures.

Besides, there was a tension in Turgot's political philosophy which stemmed, in part at least, from the intellectual company which he kept. Neither his mentors (Quesnay, the marquis de Mirabeau), nor his collaborators (Condorcet, Dupont) could see much of a role for absolute monarchy with its elaborate corporate structures. The 'rule of nature' required that the institutions of the state be designed to very different specifications. Turgot seems to have admitted as much in conversation with the *abbé* de Véri several years after his fall from power.[9] Contemplating the efforts of his successor, Jacques Necker, to set up consultative assemblies in the provinces, he was moved to reflect on his own schemes for local government reform which Dupont had roughed out in the form of a *Mémoire sur les municipalités* (see above p. 28). Appointed as the king's man, he is reported as saying, his line of duty was unambiguous: to uphold and promote the royal conception of reforming absolutism. Left to his devices as a private citizen, however, he would have welcomed the setting up of Provincial Assemblies, notwithstanding the curbs they would inevitably have placed on the exercise of royal authority. Was Turgot, therefore, a closet constitutional monarchist? Perhaps, but his interest in Necker's experiment with Provincial Assemblies should not be misinterpreted. In Turgot's view, Necker's approach to local government reform was more likely to entrench the power of the privileged elites. The physiocrats hoped rather to use assemblies to build a more streamlined, administrative style of monarchy.

Among contemporaries, Necker's claim to fame as the preeminent reform statesman of the *ancien régime* rested upon the *Compte rendu* of 1781 which brought his first ministry to a rapid and untimely end. In fact his reforming credentials were already well attested by that date, but it is convenient to begin with the *Compte rendu* because the episode sheds a good deal of light on Necker's conception of his role. Jacques Necker was a banker and a foreigner whose understanding of the world owed little to the charmed circles of Bourbon absolutism. As a banker he had learned to appreciate the value of public confidence; as a politician he found his role model in the aristocratic constitutionalism practised across the Channel; that, allied to a certain reflexive respect for the patrician politics of his Genevan homeland. The budgetary statement known as the *Compte rendu* should be regarded, therefore, as an attempt to introduce an English-style system of public accounting. Necker doubtless had in mind the image of the first lord of the treasury who would each year take Parliament through every item of income and expenditure. Whether or not the *Compte rendu* was accurate is unimportant; the point to note is that it was unconstitutional. The Bourbon monarchs had come round to recognising the force of public opinion it is true. But this was to give a status and an extension to the public interest which crossed all bounds. Within weeks, 100,000 copies of the *Compte rendu* had been sold. Vergennes, the long-serving foreign secretary, warned the king that Necker's enthusiasm for alien political models had caused him to lose sight of the founding principle of Bourbon absolutism: 'the monarch speaks; all others belong to the people and obey'.[10]

In reality, of course, Necker was not trying to harness the people to the business of government. He was addressing a constituency consisting of the intelligentsia, elite members of the Third Estate and the liberally inclined provincial nobility whose role in the state had suffered at the hands of both the intendants and the *parlements*. At the top this constituency embraced 'Whig' aristocrats like the marquis de Castries and the marquis de Ségur whom Necker brought in to the ministry as, respectively, secretaries of state for the Navy and for War, while at the base it included the petty noble and the non-noble landowners, reforming prelates and urban dignitaries who were to staff the new Provincial Assemblies. As Keith Baker surmises, the attraction of these bodies lay in their confidence-building potential.[11] Docile, non-venal bodies of public-spirited men, they would become the perfect allies of reforming monarchy. The *parlements*, even the intendants, would have to yield in the face of his new chain of command. All these advantages, and many more, were sketched out in a confidential memorandum which Necker submitted to the king in 1778. Needless to say, the new policy attracted immediate hostility from both the *parlements* and the established agents of government in the provinces. Only two Provincial Assemblies ever took office, although two others reached an advanced stage of planning (see below pp. 149–50). The king's commitment to the scheme was never in doubt; what blew the reform off course was the controversy over the *Compte rendu* and the leaking of Necker's unguarded memorandum on the subject.

Both the Provincial Assembly of the Berry and its counterpart in the Haute-Guienne survived Necker's resignation which is more than can be said for most of his reforms. Nevertheless, there is reason to believe that the king and his Finance Minister were thinking at cross purposes. Louis looked forward to the creation of a tier of administrative bodies which would streamline absolute monarchy, whereas Necker plainly did not. The king had been led to expect an administrative reform which in the fullness of time could be relied upon to produce a counter-weight to the power of the *parlements* and the Provincial Estates. But Necker had ideas with a wider frame of reference which included the regeneration of public life. Whether his aim was to set up 'modern deliberative bodies',[12] as one biographer suggests, is difficult to determine, for what Necker wanted while in power and what he favoured while out of office were not necessarily one and the same. Nevertheless, he clearly grasped that the government, as currently constituted, lacked credibility. The way to build confidence was to establish institutions which could convey the king's will, but which could also make 'representations' on behalf of the wider constituency of tax-payers. In the event, the two prototype Assemblies did just that. They evolved in a direction compatible with liberal constitutional monarchy, albeit of a decidedly aristocratic hue. Among the first to be discomfited by this development were the intendants who were understandably confused as to the role assigned to them.

Necker's public and highly controversial efforts to realign the monarchy were merely the visible tip of his reform programme. No less controversial for being largely invisible to those outside Court circles were his attempts at retrenchment and cost-cutting. Such measures were largely intrinsic to the job of controller-general and would scarcely register as significant deeds were it not for the fact that they were accompanied by major structural reforms. Necker's role in helping to professionalise and to bureaucratise the royal accounting system should not be underestimated. 'System' is perhaps too strong a word to describe the ways in which revenue was collected and disbursed: before the Revolution there was no such thing as a central treasury. Instead, there existed 'a vast network of separate *caisses*, each holding a deposit of government funds'.[13] Those *caisses*, moreover, were managed by private accountants who were office-holders and therefore quite distinct from the salaried employees of the Contrôle Général. Necker's restructuring of the financial administration aimed to root out the venal accountants and to replace them with docile permanent secretaries, while at the same time reducing the number of independent *caisses*. The various Royal Households, which were widely considered to rank among the most profligate departments of state, were brought under financial control, as was the payment of pensions to courtiers. The following year – 1777 – the lax administration of the Royal Domain came under scrutiny with the result that salaried officials were brought in to run it in place of Court favourites. However, the biggest upheaval concerned the General Farm whose lease to collect indirect taxes fell due for renewal in 1780. To judge from his subsequent writings, Necker planned to abolish internal customs zones and to mount a thorough reform of the hated *gabelle* tax on salt. In the event, he managed only to detach the drinks tax (*aides*) from the General Farm, although its lease was renegotiated on terms far more favourable to the government. The machinery of direct tax collection offered less scope for reform for the major state levies, unlike consumption taxes, were not farmed out. Here, the problem, as Necker perceived it, was a loss of control stemming from venality of office. In consequence he abolished forty-eight posts of 'general receiver' of direct taxes and replaced them with a corps of twelve salaried officials who would henceforward remit receipts into a central exchequer. A logical solution, perhaps, but one which ignored the fact that the general receivers performed a lending function – enabling government to anticipate tax revenue.

Necker's exit from the Contrôle Général in the spring of 1781 brought a decade of restructuring within the departments of state to a halt. The trend towards professionalisation and enhanced treasury control would resume when Loménie de Brienne became principal minister in 1787. It would culminate during the Revolution, assisted by continuities of personnel as well as policies across the political watershed. Nevertheless, in the short term, Necker's administrative reforms were not merely abandoned but reversed, just as Turgot's had been before him. This is important for it serves to remind us that there was no simple bureaucratic solution to the old monarchy's problems, even allowing that Court politics and the ministerial merry-go-round made matters very much worse. The fact remains that the institutional structures of the *ancien régime* had ended up forming an interlocking whole. Reform of venality in government office – to take only the most obvious example – inevitably threw into turmoil the circuits of credit on which the crown traditionally relied.

Charles Alexandre de Calonne who was called to the Contrôle Général in 1783 seemed to understand this. At least, he arrived in office with no plans to 'rationalise', preferring rather to manage a ramshackle system than to sort out its inconsistencies. His background was provincial and socially questionable, inasmuch as he hailed from recent noble stock. On the other hand, there could be no doubt about his attachment to the administrative concept of absolute monarchy: as a young crown lawyer he helped to draft the uncompromising speech of 1766 in which Louis XV put down the pretensions of the Parlement of Paris. Calonne was no friend of the magistrates in the sovereign courts, then, yet nor did he favour the Neckerite approach to reform. While intendant of Valenciennes, he had joined in the hue-and-cry against a proliferation of the Provincial Assemblies, and once in ministerial office he used his authority to curb the powers conferred on the new bodies. Far from building up support by broadening the base of the political nation, Calonne resorted to entirely traditional means of exuding confidence: pay-offs, pensions and lavish public spending.

Circumstance, and circumstance alone, made Calonne a reformer. In 1785 relations within the ministry and between the ministry and the Parlement of Paris (hitherto mediated by the Keeper of the Seals, Miromesnil) began to break up. Calonne's spendthrift days were drawing to a close and in December of that year the Parlement only agreed to register another loan with extreme reluctance. In fact, the judges had to be summoned to Versailles for a royal reprimand. Calonne knew that he would never again obtain consent for loans by such means, and it was to overcome this political deadlock that an Assembly of Notables would eventually be called. In the meantime, Calonne spent most of 1786 drafting memoranda and discussing them with the monarch. Once again, Louis found himself invited to give the go-ahead for radical surgery in order to restore absolute monarchy to its ancestral vigour. He rose to the occasion manfully. As for Calonne, he assembled a package of reforms which revealed a talent for scrambling together the ideas of others. Necker's Provincial Assemblies were now to be established in all the *pays d'élections*, albeit on a model borrowed from Turgot and Dupont. While the yield of the *taille* would be frozen, a general land tax (first proposed by Terray) would replace the *vingtièmes*, the third of which was about to expire. A cadastral survey of land holdings (echoes here of Bertin) would eradicate anomalies and ensure that everyone paid according to his means. As for the proposal to remove controls on the grain trade, its legislative pedigree can be traced back to Laverdy; and the commutation of the *corvée* carried unmistakable echoes of Turgot's 1776 reform. Ever the pragmatist, Calonne planned to increase revenue by means of an extra indirect tax on legal documents (stamp duty), while rolling back the customs barriers in order to boost commercial activity. This was a project which had been in the ministerial pipeline for decades.

Whatever the provenance of these ideas, there can be no doubt that they signalled a significant alteration to the structures of absolute monarchy. The only doubt concerns Calonne himself. Of course, in the late autumn of 1786, he could not have known how the Assembly of Notables would seize on his proposals. And besides, he had the backing of the monarch and of Vergennes. Miromesnil, the advocate of *parlementaire* interests, and Castries and Breteuil, the defenders of traditional aristocratic monarchy, were, by contrast, hostile. Were they able to see – as Calonne and his supporters could not – that fiscal and administrative reform on this scale was likely to jeopardise the established social hierarchy? Or were they simply motivated by sectional interests, blissfully unaware of the forces that a defence of fiscal privilege would bring into play?

For, indeed, the failure of Calonne's high-risk strategy threw everything into the melting pot. Even before the Notables had gathered in Versailles, informed sources were describing the impending event as the convocation of a 'national assembly'.[14] In the absence of indications to the contrary, public opinion naturally assumed that the monarch had finally decided to act upon the schemes which Turgot and Necker had outlined in the 1770s. But the Assembly of Notables was not a truly national assembly, far from it. Yet nor was it a puppet assembly which could be relied upon to rubber stamp the minister's proposals. Having resolved upon a signal break with the past in the fiscal domain, Louis nonetheless insisted that the composition of the Notables should conform to precedent. This implied an antique body redolent of the old constitution of France, rather than the new constitution in the making: 144 dignitaries, very few of whom were drawn from the Third Estate or representative of commoner interests. All the senior magistrates of the *parlements* were included, as were the plenipotentiaries of the Provincial Estates, but town councils were grossly underrepresented and neither of the two subsisting Provincial Assemblies was permitted to send an envoy. Thus constituted the forum appeared better calculated to place obstacles in the path of reform than to expedite the king's business.

The church stood to lose most from the plan to introduce a land tax, since it enjoyed exemption from state taxation and had long concealed the true scale of its wealth. Not surprisingly, therefore,

Calonne's proposals drew heavy fire from the fourteen prelates numbered among the Notables. The leader of this opposition was Etienne Charles Loménie de Brienne, the sixty-year-old archbishop of Toulouse. Loménie de Brienne already enjoyed a formidable reputation as a reforming ecclesiastic stemming from his role in the Commission des Réguliers (see below pp. 129–30) which had been founded in 1766 to tidy up and reorganise the monastic orders. The cadet son of a family which specialised in producing state secretaries, he entered the church for want of a better career and made no secret of his lack of calling. As a young man he had developed a sympathy for the ideas of the *philosophes* and he counted Turgot among his personal friends. Later on in life this identity of outlook was reined in somewhat as Brienne manoeuvred for advancement. Nevertheless, the reformist cast of mind marked everything he turned his hand to, whether as an administrator in the Estates of Languedoc, as a *rapporteur* of the committee of enquiry into the regular clergy, or as a minister of the crown. For the moment when twenty years of unstinted administrative ambition would be rewarded with ministerial office was fast approaching.

In March 1787 the solution to the crisis of *parlementaire* intransigence – which was the Assembly of Notables – became a source of crisis in turn. The crucial decision on the land tax had been deferred and Calonne's attempts to retrieve the situation, which included the disclosure that Necker's *Compte rendu* was in error, only made matters worse. Louis continued to support his principal minister, but from an isolated and desperately vulnerable position. When an attempt to outflank the Notables with a public statement (*avertissement*) castigating their self-interested defence of privilege failed to evoke a response from the nation at large, Calonne's strategy crumbled. Unwilling to abandon the reform project, the king's first thought was to dismiss Miromesnil and Breteuil who were Calonne's principal opponents within the ministry. But the queen intervened to rescue Breteuil and to join the chorus for a change of controller-general. In the end both Miromesnil and Calonne were dismissed – to make way for Lamoignon to take over as Keeper of the Seals and Brienne as Finance Minister.

For a period of sixteen months, starting in May 1787, Brienne headed the last great reform ministry of the *ancien régime*. It was a period of urgent and energetic renovation of the fabric of state which issued in a spate of reforms affecting the army, the navy, the machinery of central government and the administration of the Royal Domain. More than a century of official intolerance of protestants was overturned, and Calonne's proposals for the deregulation of the grain trade, the commutation of the *corvée* and the extension of the Provincial Assemblies were all converted into law. Yet, these achievements pass largely unrecognised owing to a persistent tendency among historians to dub these months the period of the 'Pre-Revolution'. Contemporaries, who lacked the benefit of hindsight, construed the situation rather differently. The advent of Brienne caused all the closet reformers to emerge from the woodwork, as though the episode of the Notables had broken the spell of absolute monarchy. Few observers – as yet – could tell what the monarchy would become, but change was in the air and many people sensed it. Only Louis was gloomy at the prospects for the future, perhaps because *he* sensed that the historic opportunity to construct a streamlined absolute monarchy, the task he had pursued since his accession, had passed with the loss of Calonne.

Not long after Brienne's appointment as principal minister, the aristocratic Navy and War Ministers, Castries and Ségur, resigned, which enabled Brienne to build a ministry with unusual cohesion and unity of purpose. His brother, the comte de Brienne, took over the War department, while Malesherbes was recalled to office as minister without portfolio. Malesherbes was not of much use when it came to getting things done but he had a long track record as a thinker and reformer, having broached the subject of Provincial Assemblies with the king as early as 1775. Instead, the task of practical reform fell to Brienne himself and to Lamoignon. Brienne deserves more credit than he usually receives from historians, for he stood apart from the common run of reformers in his attachment to the concept of liberal monarchy. In the recent verdict of John Hardman, he initiated a 'bold and experimental phase of royal policy-making'[15] which sought to fashion Calonne's scheme for Provincial Assemblies into a viable constitutional alternative to absolute monarchy. Already, while a Notable, he had welcomed the idea that the electoral principle should be employed as the means of recruitment to these bodies. Having become the chief minister, he took the opportunity to rework the reform in such a way as to enhance its liberal representative character. In place of the physiocrat insistence that control of the Assemblies be confined to substantial landowners, he substituted a taxpayer franchise.

In the meantime, however, voices had been raised in support of the idea of calling an Estates General. They were heard first in the Assembly of Notables which was fast becoming a sounding board for the notion of 'no taxation without representation'. The king responded by disbanding them in late May; but in July 1787 the Parlement of Paris publicly signalled its assent to the idea, declaring that it was not competent to endorse an extension of stamp duty or any other royal tax. In the months that followed, calls for an Estates General swelled to become a veritable hue-and-cry. Brienne resisted this turn of events as long as he was able; not because he hoped to salvage absolute monarchy, but because he wanted to get the Provincial Assemblies up and running. Here was a model for a transition to liberal, representative monarchy based on institutions which were already partly elective and which would be fully elective by 1791. If anything resembling an Estates General were still required by that date, its members could be chosen from within the regularly elected constituency of the Provincial, District and Municipal Assemblies. This strategy, which placed ministers ahead of public opinion for once, was enthusiastically supported by Malesherbes. In a memorandum drawn up for the king in July 1788, he outlined how the Provincial Assemblies would elect a 'national assembly' of undifferentiated deputies who would represent the whole nation as opposed to individual estates or orders.[16] Thus, at the very moment when looming bankruptcy overtook the ministry, Brienne and Malesherbes prepared to cross the last frontier of absolute monarchy.

Chrétien-François de Lamoignon was the third party in this reforming triumvirate. Unlike his cousin Malesherbes, his bent lay more in the direction of the nuts and bolts of reform than grand theory. A senior figure in the Parlement of Paris, he had devoted his entire career to the task of reforming criminal procedure. This task he pursued with such determination that serious dissension erupted within the Parlement in 1783–4, requiring the intervention of Miromesnil, the Keeper of the Seals, to restore peace. Nevertheless, the episode signalled Lamoignon's credentials as a reformer to the king, and also to Calonne. His credentials as a politician are less easy to fathom. John Hardman dubs him 'the last true servant of the old monarchy',[17] but he started off his public career as an energetic defender of the Parlement at the time of the Maupeou coup. Indeed, he was sent into exile for his pains. Certainly, Lamoignon was not a reformer cut in the mould of Brienne and Malesherbes, for his conception of the functions of government betrayed few traces of liberalism. His conception of the role of the Parlement must also have altered over time, for appointment to the headship of the judiciary in place of Miromesnil revealed him to be a king's man through and through. If any doubts as to the necessity of separating administrative and judicial functions within the state continued to linger, they were scotched by the behaviour of the *parlements* in the summer and autumn of 1787. Lamoignon's May Edicts revamping the courts proved to be the last attempt by a minister of the crown to uphold the principles of reforming absolutism. Failure cost Lamoignon everything; his reputation, his career and even his life.

Bureaucrats

Office-bound professionals who drafted memoranda and communicated by means of decisions taken in committee were the necessary accompaniments of administrative monarchy. They provided the thread of continuity linking the efforts of successive ministers, and they helped to concert the activities of the intendants, that is to say the agents of government in the country at large. Whether sedentary in Versailles or Paris, or fixed in the provinces, the role of these men should not be underestimated. Often they intervened actively to stimulate reform, and by their actions they helped to promote and to disseminate that climate of expectancy so characteristic of the final decades of the *ancien régime*. This reformism cannot be neatly equated with the ideas of the Enlightenment which remained fuzzy or contradictory when applied to the realm of practical politics. Rather it bespoke a cast of mind obsessed with a vision of the well-ordered state. Efficiency, or what administrative documents of the period described as 'le bien du service',[18] was to be the objective of reform. But in the meantime bureaucrats were forced to acknowledge that the Bourbon state was a hybrid in which professionals competed with courtiers, judicial power overlapped with administrative power, and whole areas of national life – the clergy, the *parlements*, the Provincial Estates – were still a law unto themselves.

Necker, the complete outsider, did more than any other controller-general to shake up the subaltern echelons of royal officialdom. Whether his attack on venality and decentralised accounting procedures actually produced cost savings and greater efficiency is open to dispute, but it certainly enabled him to move like-minded officials into positions of influence. His employment of *premiers commis* to carry out functions hitherto performed by venal *intendants des finances* is a case in point. These low-born salaried officials became his most trusted executive assistants, and on returning to office in August 1788 he immediately reinstated them. Indeed, the careers of some of the *premiers commis* spanned the entire epoch of reform from Turgot to Napoleon. Not untypical was Marie-François d'Ailly who began his career as a senior civil servant in the tax department of the Contrôle Général in 1772. A childhood friend of Turgot, he became one of the closest advisers of that minister, working alongside the *intendant des finances*, Henri d'Ormesson, on the project to establish a land tax, and subsequently on schemes to improve the yield of the *vingtièmes*.[19] The arrival of Necker signalled the eclipse of the *intendants des finances* and gave effective control over the tax department to d'Ailly which he retained until 1782. Contemporary opinion regarded this breach in the wall of venality as nothing less than a 'revolution' which bore comparison with the reforms undertaken in the magistrature and the army. Necker, it was suggested, wanted nothing better than to surround himself with revocable slaves. Not surprisingly, perhaps, d'Ailly chose to follow Necker into retirement. But his administrative career was far from over. In 1787 he was chosen as chief attorney for the Third Estate in the newly established Provincial Assembly of the Ile-de-France, and the following year returned with Necker to the Contrôle Général. Elected subsequently to the Estates General as the commoner representative of a Norman *bailliage*, the Revolution launched him on yet another career as a deputy, a department administrator and finally as a senator.

Men like d'Ailly spanned regimes effortlessly. As the technicians of administrative monarchy, their skills were in heavy demand. As faceless servitors excluded by birth from the spoils system of the *ancien régime*, they carried no unwelcome political baggage either. Their more exalted collaborators in the business of servicing the monarchy – the tax farmers, general receivers, *intendants des finances*, even the provincial intendants – found the change of regime more difficult to negotiate. In d'Ailly's own department of the Contrôle Général, the Lefèvre d'Ormesson family[20] passed the office of *intendant des finances* from father to son until Necker abolished it in 1777. After a brief and unhappy spell as the minister in charge of finances, Henri d'Ormesson abandoned public life and in due course settled down to write his memoirs instead. However, it is important to emphasise at this juncture that 'privilege' and 'reform' were not of necessity antithetical. Venal officials such as the d'Ormesson could be every bit as enthusiastic about reform as salaried servants of state. Marie d'Ormesson, the second generation holder of the intendant's office in the tax department, was a distinguished campaigner for agricultural reform. Between 1763 and 1773 he coaxed successive ministers into tabling legislation to promote enclosures, to divide up the commons and to curtail collective rights such as gleaning. As for his son, Henri d'Ormesson, we know that he worked alongside d'Ailly on Turgot's fiscal reforms and the paperwork which he accumulated on the land tax was retrieved for use over a decade later by Calonne. The paperwork on Provincial Assemblies, originally collected by Necker's officials, also made its way into Calonne's files. Henri d'Ormesson's parting contribution to the reform lobby took the form of a memorandum drafted in 1783 while he headed the Contrôle Général. In it he identified the year 1787 as a potential turning-point in the fortunes of the monarchy. With the General Farm's lease of indirect taxes due to run out simultaneously with the expiry of the third *vingtième*, an opportunity for a thorough reappraisal of the fiscal system would present itself. D'Ormesson's suggestion that the appraisal should begin at once produced a ripple of indignation among all those involved in tax farming and led to a rapid exit from the ministry.

Possession of hereditary privilege was not inimical to the concept of reform, then; at least not among the robe nobility. Dynasties like the Lefèvre d'Ormesson or the Trudaine who, from father to son, ran the bridges and highways department were fired with a vision of state service. To be sure, they were also venal office-holders who enjoyed the usual run of privileges and exemptions, and this was to cost them dear in 1789. But before 1789 it is more appropriate to think of them as part of the solution to the difficulties confronting the monarchy than as part of the problem. The thirty-three royal intendants who administered the provinces are not to be confused with the *intendants des finances*. They were not venal officers, but professional administrators whom the controller-general moved from province to province at will. All were nobles by the closing decades of the *ancien régime* and no doubt many of them hoped in due course to become *intendants des finances*, for that was the usual career pattern. A few might even aspire to a commission of councillor of state. These stalwarts had grown up with absolute monarchy (see above pp. 28–9); indeed, they were believed to personify its most despotic tendencies. But now that the monarchy had come of age, so to speak, their role was destined to change.

At the end of the *ancien régime* all the intendants were king's men, although some of them trod a fine interpretive line in terms of what they construed to be the royal will. This is important because it used to be argued that the intendants had begun to acquire a new set of reflexes which were turning them into 'men of the provinces', that is to say vectors for the transmission of local power to the centre rather than vice versa. If such a confusion of roles did occur, it reflected rather the confusion in ministers' minds as to the direction the monarchy should take in the late 1770s and 1780s. The repercussions of this dilemma on the field agents of absolute monarchy in regions possessing powerful Provincial Estates have been explored in chapter 1. Broadly speaking, the style of royal administration was changing because the expectations of society were changing. Long gone were the days of Colbert when the intendants would enforce the *gabelle* by means of free-billeting, the galleys and the noose. Such episodes were etched into the public memory, of course, but the spirit animating government in the second half of the eighteenth century was consensus-seeking and supervisory rather than antagonistic and coercive. Auget de Montyon, a one-time intendant himself, defined the objective of public administration as being 'to procure for men the greatest possible happiness within the form of society which they have chosen to adopt'.[21] However, he admitted that the current generation of intendants continued to be blamed for the despotic tendencies of their predecessors.

Certainly they were much more closely regulated after mid-century and expected, in turn, to supervise closely the lives of their 'administrés'. This equipped energetic ministers such as Terray or Necker with quite unprecedented power to bring reform to the doorstep of ordinary town and country dwellers. The printing bills of the intendancy of Bourges are illuminating in this respect, for they bring out the scale and breadth of government interventionism by the 1780s. In a single year clerks made fifty-seven mailings (of circular letters to syndics and parish priests, of copies of laws, administrative instructions, fiscal pro-formas, etc.) in multiples ranging from 60 to 1,000; a total output of some 15,600 printed items.[22] In matters of administration the intendants, acting on behalf of central government, brooked no interference. They worked tirelessly to curb the power of seigneurs over rural communities, especially where that power was backed by sovereign courts as in Burgundy. Indeed, they would sometimes interpose themselves in disputes between villagers and their seigneurs in an effort to encourage the transfer of loyalties to an all-seeing and all-providing state. Yet, as the administrative domain expanded to embrace everything from taxation to the provision of classes for midwives, ministers sought also to refocus the responsibilities of their agents. Chief among their priorities was the disentangling of judicial from administrative authority, for the intendants often doubled as tribunals, just as the courts, both royal and seigneurial, continued to exercise considerable administrative powers. On this front the wide-ranging reform of urban oligarchies which Controller-General Laverdy initiated in 1764–5 is worth recalling. Laverdy took away from the intendants the power to audit town accounts and transferred it to the courts instead.

So, the picture of the intendants drawn by Maurice Bordes[23] which has them performing as diligent auxiliaries of reforming absolutism does not fall far short of the mark. They were men who had caught the mood of the times and who had learned to use the diluted version of the language of the Enlightenment so fashionable during the reign of Louis XVI. The language, that is to say, of fuzzy humanitarianism with its studied ambiguity on the subject of civic equality and political rights. Imagine their dismay, therefore, when Louis began to dally with ministers whose commitment to reform seemed to take priority over their attachment to the hallowed principles of absolutism (see below pp. 139–40). But this begs an important question: were any of the intendants reformers in their own right? The answer is undoubtedly yes. By commission and by their own efforts they enlarged the constituency of reform.

The activities of Turgot while royal intendant in the *généralité* of Limoges are well known. Between 1761 and 1774 he carried out a structural reform of *taille* assessment, devised a method of spreading the burdens associated with road-building (the *corvée*), and concocted a scheme to ease the anguish of militia service by the purchase of a replacement. These were all free-lance initiatives pursued with little or no governmental support, yet they were all taken up by ministers subsequently. The task of indexing the *taille* against land values took twelve years to complete and he enlisted the assistance of the parish clergy in this and many other administrative chores. The expedient would be employed by later intendants as a matter of routine. In a sense, of course, Turgot's reforms were bound to enjoy a wider audience, for, in 1774, he moved directly from the Limousin to the Contrôle Général. Yet he was not alone in seeking to nudge forward the cause of fiscal reform by demonstrating what could be achieved by perseverance at the local level. Louis-Jean and Louis-Bénigne-François Bertier were engaged upon a similar, if more exhaustive, project in the *généralité* of Paris. Between 1771 and 1789 this father and son team of royal intendants brought close to completion a massive cadastral survey which sorted arable and woodland into twenty-four categories by value. By 1787 land holdings in some 1,800 parishes had been measured up, with work continuing on the remaining 300 parishes. However, the key feature of the reform can be found in the consultative mechanisms which the Bertiers introduced. After repeated administrative verifications, the assessments were submitted to assemblies of landowners and tenant farmers for final scrutiny. Should the scrutineers find reason to doubt the original assessments, they were empowered to reopen the process of consultation with the deputies of the parishes concerned. It seems likely that this system influenced Necker's conception of Provincial Assemblies, in which the distribution of taxation by consent (of the wealthy) figured prominently. In the *généralité* of Paris the success of the reform owed much to the fact that the surveyors uncovered over 1,000 hectares of undeclared land which helped to spread the fiscal load.[24]

Reform of the *taille personnelle* attracted other intendants, too; notably Rouille d'Orfeuil who occupied the intendancy of Châlons-sur-Marne between 1764 and 1790. Longevity of tenure, not to mention the beginnings of dynasticism among state employees, provided the necessary stability for long-term projects of reconstruction. While welcoming the advent of the Provincial Assembly of the Ile-de-France, Bertier *fils* expressed deep personal regret that circumstances had not permitted him to bring the reform to term. Typical in this respect were the Chaumont de la Galaizière, another father and son team. Antoine-Martin – the father – served as chancellor to the king of Poland, in his capacity as duc de Lorraine from 1737, while the son – Antoine – took over the intendancy of Lorraine and the Barrois on a commission from Louis XV in 1766, before finishing his career as intendant of Alsace (1778–90). Both were ardent and wide-ranging reform administrators with a keen awareness of the socio-juridical anomalies that distinguished the provinces of the East. Prominent among these was the extreme subdivision of land holdings, to which the Academy of Metz drew attention in its prize essay competition for 1771. Antoine Chaumont de la Galaizière sought to solve the problem with a radical policy of land reorganisation. At the intendant's insistence, several villages in the district of Bayon were subjected to this treatment.[25] The legacy of bitterness among small holders whose fragmentary properties had been 'rationalised' was such that the Revolutionaries decided not to generalise the experiment. Land reform on such a scale entailed the harnessing together of crown agents and seigneurs in what amounted to a collective abuse of power: most intendants who were interested in agrarian matters confined their energies to exhortation instead.

The province of Lorraine fell to the French crown late (in 1766), which may explain the willingness of central government to endorse a robust approach to reform that it would not have risked elsewhere. This was certainly true in the case of Corsica. The island had been ceded to France by the Republic of Genoa in 1768 and it presented the government with a rare occasion to experiment without interference from vested interests. As writers drawn from all shades of informed opinion tirelessly advised, here was an opportunity to try out every pet project of the Enlightenment: a written constitution, representative institutions, a land tax paid in kind, judicial reform etc. To some of these proposals the ministry, led by Choiseul, turned a deaf ear. Nevertheless, initiatives which reveal to us the abiding objectives of reforming absolutism were implemented. For the purposes of justice, the island was equipped with institutions foreshadowing the changes that Maupeou would shortly introduce to mainland France. As for taxation, all exemptions were eliminated: even the lands of the clergy and the Royal Domain were brought into the fiscal net. Ministers in Versailles laid down the broad parameters of reform, but much of the detail fell to the intendant, Bertrand de Boucheporn, who spent ten fruitful years (1775–85) on the island.[26] In agreeing to Estates where votes would be taken by head rather than by order, the government signalled its flexibility on the subject of representation. Had this reform occurred a little later, it is likely that Corsica would have been endowed with a Provincial Assembly instead. Boucheporn pressed for a fully proportional system of representation within the Estates, but at this juncture ministers refused to move beyond a position whereby each order returned the same number of deputies.

Turgot, Bertier *fils*, Antoine Chaumont de la Galaizière and Bertrand de Boucheporn were all intendants who became impatient with the stop–go politics of reform. Rather than wait upon events, they pushed on with practical measures hoping to convert ministers along the way. In many respects they were men ahead of their time: advocates of some form of power sharing rather than diligent instruments of traditional absolute monarchy. It comes as no surprise, therefore, to find them involved constructively in the break up of the *ancien régime*. Turgot, to be sure, was long dead by this date. The puzzle of his political convictions was never put to the test, although Dupont, his amanuensis, made free use of Turgot's reputation during the final slide towards Revolution. Bertier pinned his colours to the mast in August 1787 when he was invited to address the body that had usurped some of his fiscal authority. Far from complaining, he saluted the Provincial Assembly and urged the idea of a fruitful partnership in the running of the province. Antoine Chaumont de la Galaizière reacted in similar vein. Late in 1786 Calonne invited him to join the 'think tank' that was assembling the documentation to be placed before the Assembly of Notables. Galaizière's agrarian expertise was employed in drafting the reform of the *corvée*. The following year, he, too, would identify strongly with the Provincial Assembly established in Alsace. Bertrand de Boucheporn left Corsica for good in 1785 having been switched to the intendancy of Pau, and from thence to Auch. From the vantage point of this much reorganised *généralité* in the South-West of France, he signalled to Calonne the need for a thorough overhaul of the practice of selling offices in local government.

Enlightened bureaucrats they may have been, but they were still intendants. As such they were king's men, associated indissolubly with the negative as well as the positive practices of absolutism. For the public the true face of monarchy bore the imprint of Lamoignon, whose inflammatory edicts the intendants were required to enforce. This police operation against the senior courts of the land tended to destroy the credibility of even the most reform-minded of intendants. Unlike the high officials of the Contrôle Général, few, if any, of them survived the transition from the old regime to the new. Of the small band of intendants whose activities we have examined, only Boucheporn made a serious effort to come to terms with constitutional monarchy. He followed the work of reconstruction (see below pp. 191–207) put in motion by the National Assembly avidly. And when the Provincial Estates of the Béarn refused to publish the new decrees, he used his residual authority to do so instead. He even stood for election to the recently created post of *procureur général syndic* in the department of the Gers. This attempt at political rehabilitation failed and he retired to the decent anonymity of Toulouse. However, his two sons had emigrated, and Boucheporn attracted mounting suspicion. Eventually he was tried on a charge of sending money abroad and, in 1794, executed.[27] Bertier *fils* ended badly, too. As the king's commissioner in charge of provisioning the troops stationed around Paris in the summer of 1789, he fell victim to mob violence without being allowed the luxury of resolving his attitude to the new regime. Antoine Chaumont de la Galaizière *fils* simply emigrated.

The reform constituency

Public opinion, it has been noted, was the invisible player in the game of reformist politics (see above pp. 75–9). But if the notion of a 'public' sits uneasily with the traditions of Bourbon absolutism, so too does that of a 'reform constituency'. Contemporaries defined public opinion in rhetorical rather than sociological terms, yet it is unlikely that anyone would have grasped the import of the phrase 'reform constituency'. What we mean by this anachronistic use of terms are the constellations of opinion, rooted in different social and professional milieux, which collectively resembled a constituency of men and women who were seeking after reform of one kind or another. Since France lacked modern representative institutions until shortly before the demise of the *ancien régime*, the 'reform constituency', like 'public opinion', remained a fluid and contingent phenomenon. Not until the final crisis of absolute monarchy – launched unwittingly by Calonne in 1787 – did the bulkheads of particularism give way and the multiple compartments of reformist sentiment start to connect. This section looks beyond individual reformers in an effort to identify the various lobbies or 'constituencies' agitating for changes to the fabric of society and the state. Some of the reforms which they procured have already been mentioned in passing, but these achievements are presented more systematically in the pages that follow.

The explosion of intellectual energy known, inadequately, as the Enlightenment scarcely requires further emphasis. Its social and cultural underpinnings have been explored already (see above pp. 72–9). What is more relevant to the current discussion is its application to public policy.

The signs of a convergence appeared first in the economic sphere under the banner of physiocracy. In this sphere, as in so many others, the 1760s proved to be the curtain-raiser decade. Having emerged from the humiliating ordeal of the Seven Years War, the government showed itself to be unusually responsive to proposals for agrarian and fiscal reform. This was just what the physiocrat writers of the 1750s and 1760s were offering: a set of concrete proposals which would expand the fiscal capacity of the state by mobilising the productive energies of agriculture. 'POOR PEASANTS, A POOR KINGDOM' wrote Quesnay with some sleight of hand as to what constituted a peasant.[28] In reality, he had in mind the large farmers whose ability to turn a profit from the land was hindered by restraints on the marketing of grain, by consumption taxes, by the vestiges of seigneurialism and by suffocating regulations enforced by the village community. Laverdy's edicts of 1763–4 scrapping centuries of controls upon the grain trade marked the first and most dramatic victory of this reform lobby. In effect, the legislation signalled that the government no longer regarded the maintenance of the food supply as being its overriding responsibility, which leaves Steven Kaplan to the conclusion that the liberal laws of 1763–4 must rank 'among the most daring and revolutionary reforms attempted in France before 1789'.[29] Certainly the physiocrats exploited their bridgehead in government to push through a whole parcel of agrarian reforms over the next decade or so, although Laverdy's liberalisation of the grain trade was terminated by Terray in the early 1770s. The ending of the boom harvests of the 1760s, growing popular unrest, and misgivings among some of the intendants all conspired to bring an end to the experiments.

The vogue for physiocracy in government revived in the later 1780s under the auspices of Calonne and would be carried over the political threshold into the early years of the Revolution. Nevertheless, it suffered from being an unduly cerebral approach to reform. A policy so firmly wedded to the interests of producers at the potential expense of consumers could not help but muddy the waters. Laverdy might well reassure the intendant of Tours[30] that the benefits of liberalisation would soon show in the payment of taxes, but consumers were taxpayers also, and traditional responsibilities towards the poor were not so easily cast to one side. Nor was it clear (to each and every intendant) that the dismantling of the rural community would improve fiscal yields. Then there is the attitude of the *parlements* to take into account. The magistrates of the sovereign courts were cautious reformers at best, and their support for the new policy may have owed more to tactical finesse than ideological conviction. Laverdy was one of their own, and besides, liberalisation seemed to offer a painless alternative to fiscal restructuring.

On the other hand, the *parlementaires* were committed to the notion of balance in the constitution and liked to posture as defenders of the common man. As landlords they stood to benefit from the unfettered freedom to export grain, and this calculation clearly influenced the Parlement of Toulouse whose members owned grain-producing estates in the nearby Lauragais. However, as jurists, they could not remain insensitive to the 'breach of trust' perpetrated on consumers. Nor could they remain indifferent as the public order implications of deregulation became apparent. For it was a fact that the liberalisation of the grain trade, whether implemented by Laverdy, by Turgot, or by Brienne, always ended in loss of life or limb and assaults on property.

An altogether more substantial constituency of reformers and consumers of reform could be found among the clergy. In this respect the church displayed few symptoms of the crisis of conscience that was to afflict it during the Revolution. No other estate responded more thoroughly to the varied stimuli of the Enlightenment. Those responses stemmed from both the elite and the rank-and-file, and it is worth looking at each in turn. The eighteenth century witnessed the rise to fame and fortune of the bishop-administrator, an urbane and cultivated species of churchman typified by Boisgelin of Aix, Champion de Cicé of Rodez, Loménie de Brienne of Toulouse and by Talleyrand – the *abbé* de Périgord and future bishop of Autun. Such men moved effortlessly among ministers and councillors of state, imbibing the ethos of administrative monarchy and spreading an ecumenical and functional vision of religion. In so doing they prepared the way for the desacralisation of the Bourbon monarchy and the secularisation of the Gallican church. Evocative of the new consensus in religious affairs was the setting up of a commission to reform and rationalise the contemplative orders. This Commission des Réguliers, as it was known, was really the handiwork of Loménie de Brienne and the duc de Choiseul, for the Holy See was not consulted. All the members were appointed by the king and no more than half of them were ecclesiastics. Plainly, monasticism was now perceived to be an administrative problem, not one susceptible to papal intervention and spiritual remedies. With men like Marie d'Ormesson and Antoine Chaumont de la Galaizière attending the sessions of the Commission, it could scarcely be otherwise.

Between 1766 and 1780 several hundred religious houses were reformed, that is to say amalgamated or closed down, and several orders were abolished outright. Although the fiction of a renovation of the contemplative life was maintained, the thrust of the Commission's work was more destructive than constructive. In this Brienne was assisted by a change of outlook among the bishops themselves. Whereas the old, pre-Enlightenment bishops were reluctant to identify communities in need of reform, the generation taking over in the 1770s were briskly utilitarian in approach. 'I do indeed have a lot of religious communities in my town' wrote the bishop of Agen in reply to Brienne's circular, 'and the abolition of many of them I would view with the greatest pleasure.'[31] What this suggests is that a rough agenda for the restructuring of the Gallican church had taken shape one and even two decades before the outbreak of the Revolution. When, in 1780, Brienne was forced to wind up the Commission des Réguliers, he managed to replace it with a similar body whose remit was to advise the government on procedures for the amalgamation and abolition of benefices. This was dangerous territory for a church increasingly worried by the prospect of a state-sponsored raid on ecclesiastical assets. It beckoned unmistakably towards nationalisation and the Civil Constitution of the Clergy.

Despite the sacrifice of Jean Calas on the altar of catholic fanaticism (see above pp. 74–5), the spirit of the age was also beckoning in the direction of toleration. *De facto* toleration of protestants had become quite widespread in the 1750s as the intendants and the courts turned a blind eye to acts of open-air or 'desert' worship. As early as 1754, indeed, Turgot proposed that protestants be granted civil recognition on terms which removed them from the jurisdiction of the catholic clergy. Admittedly, the outbreak of war with the protestant powers of Europe in 1757 set back the cause of reform for a time, and it was in this context that the flare up of passions in Toulouse occurred. Nevertheless, two connecting forces were plainly at work in the 1770s and 1780s. One was the move to lift the disabilities bearing down on non-catholics; the other was the gradual secularisation of the monarchy itself. In these respects, as in so much else, it was Turgot who set the tone. Appalled at the likely cost of Louis XVI's coronation, the chief minister tried to get the event transferred from Reims to Paris instead. A long-time supporter of toleration, he also tabled proposals to secularise the coronation oath in such a way as to exclude from the divine mission of Bourbon monarchs the obligation to exterminate all heretics within the realm. On both counts, he failed. But the king was clearly embarrassed by some of the more bloodthirsty and obscurantist duties attaching to his role as defender of the faith. The whole thrust of the streamlined version of absolute monarchy which Louis hoped to install ran counter to medieval notions of the link between throne and altar. As the objective of civil uniformity became ever more sharply defined, the importance of maintaining confessional uniformity correspondingly declined.

This process, which Jeffrey Merrick[32] has aptly dubbed the desacralising of monarchy, is revealed in tell-tale shifts of language and the piecemeal removal of disabilities on Lutherans and Jews in the 1770s and early 1780s. At the same time the government sought to control and confine the clergy's monopolistic right of recording births, marriages and deaths, as though the coincidence of catholicity and citizenship should no longer be taken for granted. In 1782, for instance, parish priests were told to refrain from speculating on the legitimacy or otherwise of newborn children when recording the facts of parentage. The Edict of Toleration of protestants which Brienne and Malesherbes pushed through the Parlement of Paris in 1787 brought this process to a natural climax. Contrary to widespread expectation, it did not confer on French Calvinists the right to worship as they pleased. Rather, it granted them some of the most important attributes of citizenship such as the right of residence, the right to go before a magistrate in order to register births, marriages and deaths, the freedom to practise a profession and so forth. This was reforming absolutism in its purest form. In pursuit of an ideal of legal and civil uniformity, the monarchy had finally abolished what the protestant pastor, Rabaut Saint Etienne, described as 'the ridiculous distinction between citizens and subjects'.[33] Protestants would continue to press a claim for religious freedom on a par with catholic citizens, but at least they could now participate in the civil life of the state. For them the symbolism of the calling of an Estates General was particularly poignant: it marked the readmission of outcasts to the polity.

The lower clergy watched these developments with misgivings, it is true. For sooner or later the role of the catholic church in the constitution of the state would have to be addressed. However, the stark clarity of the issues in 1790 should not be projected back to 1787. Before the Revolution the parish clergy tended to line up in the camp of reform. There were general as well as specific reasons for this stance. Generally speaking, priests were the most literate denizens of the countryside and as the administrative pretensions of the monarchy expanded, it was nearly inevitable that they would be sucked into the role of part-time auxiliaries to the intendants and subdelegates. Village syndics were often illiterate and parish priests, or their curates, routinely filled in forms that no one else could understand. However, priests were also men equipped with intellectual and cultural resources whom the government was happy to employ in a wider, propagandist role. The pulpit lent itself to all manner of announcements and exhortations concerning poor relief, the militia ballot, the royal *corvée* and sundry local government changes. Turgot, both as intendant and as minister, had been quick to spot the potential of the pulpit as a means of extending the 'reach' of government. The next stage was to annex the priest to the service of the state; an operation which Brienne accomplished by means of the 1787 local government reform. All members of the new Municipal Assemblies – the lowest tier – would be elected, save for parish priests and local seigneurs whose membership was automatic. In 1790 this apprenticing of the rural clergy would be exposed to public gaze when villagers all over France elected their priests as mayors.

Powerful forces beyond the control of ministers were redefining the role of the clergy in any case. Enlightenment writers depicted the parish priest as a benevolent intermediary between the government and the general population, as a species of public servant whose access to 'lumières' would progressively detach the masses from their prejudices and herd instincts. Did the priests envisage themselves in this light? By the 1780s it is arguable that increasing numbers had indeed absorbed the utilitarian and humanitarian gospel of the late Enlightenment. While Turgot was still in office, a Dauphiné priest, Henri Reymond, put forward a powerful case for consolidating the social and political role of the parish-level clergy. His book, *Droits des curés* (1776), clearly drew on the 'good pastor' model of the *philosophes*, and its timing suggests that he was conversant with the broader debate about the function of the church within a secularising monarchy. At all events, the book was widely distributed and studied, and may be accounted a significant factor in the tide of restlessness which swept through the lower clergy in the closing decade of the *ancien régime*.[34]

While the groping progress towards a post-Tridentine role model of the clergyman doubtless caused confusion and heartache in abundance, that tide of restlessness had more specific causes. The main objective of Reymond's tract was to defend the rights of ordinary priests against the ecclesiastical hierarchy and secular owners of benefices. Ever since the 1760s, the parish clergy of a number of dioceses in the East and South-East had been asserting their right to hold local 'synods' with growing determination and eloquence. Needless to say, the purpose of these strictly illegal assemblies was to discuss grievances. The inadequacy of the *portion congrue* and the burden of clerical taxation (the *décimes*) provided ample grounds for complaint, but, increasingly, the assembled priests asserted a constitutional right to approve bishops' ordinances. It was this 'institutional presbyterianism'[35] that Reymond's book sought to uphold, and the answer to his provocation came in the form of a renewal of the royal ban on assemblies of parish priests. That was in 1782, but by now the rank-and-file clergy had come to resemble a reform constituency in their own right. The unrest subsided for several years, only to flare again as the policies unveiled by Calonne and Brienne gave notice of a fundamental restructuring of absolute monarchy. From July 1788 the pent-up energy of the lower clergy poured forth in a flood of petitions and brochures articulating everything from petty local grievances to comprehensive schemes for the reform of society and the state. The cohesion and militancy of the *curés* took nearly everyone by surprise, and it ensured them a preponderant voice in the First Estate elections to the Estates General. In this respect, at least, Reymond's rousing defence of the clerical underdog could not have succeeded better.

However, it was a loaded attempt at judicial reform that finally wrecked plans to renovate the monarchy. The constituency of active support for judicial reform was not large, for even a tinkering with the machinery of justice threatened to expose several raw nerves. One was the constitutional issue implicit in the *parlements*' powers of judicial review, another was venality of office, and a third was the decadence of seigneurial courts. Both venality and seigneurialism raised awkward questions pertaining to the privatisation of judicial authority. On the other hand, the lobby for reform in this area was committed and intelligent. In addition to the crown's own agents, it comprised individual *parlementaires* like Lamoignon and Guyton de Morveau, the barristers Target and Martineau, and talented writers such as Linguet, Servan and Pétion de Villeneuve. It was also remarkably clear-sighted, for the experts found themselves in broad agreement as to what needed to be done. French law should be unified and rendered applicable to the whole of the national territory, judicial and administrative authority should be disentangled, the court system reorganised, procedure streamlined, and judicial redress made cheaper and quicker. Increasingly, reformers also advocated measures to curtail the trade in judicial offices and to diminish the competence of seigneurial assize courts, although it is less certain that these had the backing of the country at large. Nevertheless, the renovation of the judicial machinery of state proved to be one of the least arduous tasks devolved to the National Assembly, precisely because so much had been agreed, or clarified, in advance.

What could not be resolved prior to 1789 was the role of the very highest courts in the land. Did the *parlements* exist to enforce the laws of the kingdom and to receive appeals? Or did they exist in order to place obstacles in the path of 'despotism'? Ever since Chancellor Maupeou's abortive attempt to refashion the judiciary, educated Frenchmen had worried that what the government chose to call reform concealed nothing less than a bid for despotic power. This suspicion bedevilled relations between the *parlements* and ministers, and enormously complicated the task of judicial reform. As far as ministers and their agents were concerned, the issues were straightforward enough. A well-defined hierarchy of courts freed from all jurisdictional ambiguity formed part of the project of administrative monarchy. Chancellor d'Aguesseau began the work of reform in the 1730s and 1740s with a plan to strengthen the *présidial* courts and to scrap minor royal assizes (*prévôtés, vigueries*) in towns already possessing *bailliage* or *sénéchaussée* courts. He succeeded more in the latter objective than in the former, but the foundations had been laid for subsequent initiatives. In the 1750s some progress was made towards the extinction of judicial office-holding in Lorraine, a province which at that time lay beyond the jurisdiction of the *parlements* and which attracted more than the usual quota of experiments in enlightened absolutism. However, the key to a viable system of royal justice lay with the *présidiaux*, as both Maupeou and Lamoignon realised. If the competence or scope of these courts could be raised, much judicial business would start to flow in their direction. On the other hand, the *parlements* would lose many lucrative suits and might even find their role confined to hearing appeals. Therein lay the problem.

The magistrates of the sovereign courts were not by nature reformers. They were nearly all nobles steeped in the traditions of the robe and imbued with a distinctive professional esprit de corps. This is not to deny that the crisis buffeting the monarchy in the second half of the eighteenth century often produced liberal and even radical rhetoric from the benches of the courthouses.[36] But the test of *parlementaire* radicalism measures deeds, not words, and it reveals a body of men whose reflexes were conservative. The same may be said of the corps of barristers, their close professional cousins, although a distinction must be drawn between the personnel of the higher and the lower courts. The judges and lawyers of the *présidiaux, bailliages* and *sénéchaussées* were a different breed, inasmuch as they had a far smaller stake in the continuance of the *ancien régime*. Their offices carried no prospect of ennoblement, indeed some were depreciating in value; their professional careers were blocked by the *parlements'* judicial omnicompetence, and no one expected them to behave as watchdogs of the constitution. These were the men who really 'intervened' in the autumn of 1788.

The quarrels between the *parlements* and the crown over religion, taxation, the *corvée*, Provincial Assemblies and, latterly, judicial reform were spectacular and have naturally attracted a good deal of attention from historians. In view of the part played by the Parlement of Paris in forcing the hand of government during the crisis of 1787–8, the involvement of the courts in the final break up of the *ancien régime* can scarcely be questioned. But if this is common ground among scholars, a wide area of disagreement remains as to the motives of the protagonists. Should the *parlementaires* be portrayed as stout-hearted defenders of the rule of law, or, rather, as eloquent and self-interested spokesmen for the continuance of 'privilege' in all its forms? A more helpful approach might be to distinguish between causes and symptoms. After the shock of Chancellor Maupeou's dismembering of the Parlement of Paris, the actuality of rival conceptions of the state became apparent to many senior figures in public life. All the subsequent clashes between the crown and the courts betrayed an awareness of that fact. Increasingly, the monarchy was seeking to extend its supervisory activities into spheres hitherto untouched or regarded as out of bounds to the secular power. The set-piece explosions of *parlementaire* anger which greeted these encroachments usually focused upon a perceived abuse of 'ministerial' authority, but it should not be forgotten that the intendants were also busily enlarging their powers of *tutelle*. However, an important qualification to this scenario must be borne in mind. The growth of administrative monarchy was not an even and continuous process, and nor were reformist policies confined to those ministers imbued with a statist vision of the way ahead. Laverdy, for instance, took over the Contrôle Général following a successful legal career in the Parlement of Paris. He initiated the first experiment in grain trade liberalisation as we have seen, not to mention an important reform of urban oligarchies (see above pp. 27–8). Yet he remained a jurist in outlook whose conception of the state caused unease among the intendants.

No doubt Laverdy would have argued that acknowledgement of the monarchy's right to tax and to administer implied acknowledgement of the corresponding right of the courts to provide judicial redress, not least in cases involving the alleged abuse of administrative power. In practice, however, the defence of 'jurisdictional' authority mounted by the *parlements* in the 1770s and 1780s encompassed rather more than this. As the monarch progressively weakened the 'society of orders', it became a defence of the status quo. For Louis XVI and his ministers, the rule of law meant the power to command execution of the royal warrant in every corner of the kingdom. For the magistrates of the sovereign courts it meant just the opposite: the preservation of legal diversity and social particularism. Thus Louis might issue an edict to emancipate his crown land vassals from the last vestiges of serfdom, but it remained inoperable unless endorsed by the *parlements* whose angle of vision was frequently at odds with that of the monarch. In the Franche-Comté the Parlement of Besançon held back both the 1779 edict abolishing *mainmorte* in the Royal Domain and the 1787 Edict of Toleration. The Royal Council put up with this situation until 1788 when the confrontation over Lamoignon's judicial reforms at last provided a chance to browbeat the magistrates into recording 'the edicts, rulings and declarations which for the past ten years the Parlement has refused to register'.[37] Few courts were as candid in their defence of the status quo as that of Besançon, but all, without exception, found their reason for being in an organic conception of society – a conception which they believed the monarchy was preparing to subvert.

This fear became manifest in the late winter of 1787–8 when reports started to circulate that the Keeper of the Seals, Lamoignon, was planning to implement a Maupeou-style reform of the judiciary. When it was unveiled in the form of six royal edicts on 8 May, the reform proved to be largely consistent with the schemes discussed by writers and government officials over many years. Lamoignon announced his intention to unite the common law by amalgamating the various Customs, to reform legal training and to uproot a number of the tribunals dispensing 'extraordinary' justice; that is to say the *bureaux des finances*, the *élections*, the excise courts and some others. Their properly judicial responsibilities would be taken over by the mainstream courts, while their administrative competence would be transferred to the Provincial Estates and the Provincial Assemblies. As for the judicial powers of seigneurs, Lamoignon acknowledged the difficulties inherent in tampering with the rights of fief-owners, but then proceeded to place so many restrictions on the exercise of these rights that he sounded the death-knell of seigneurial courts to all intents and purposes. Farreaching as they were, however, none of these changes threatened serious upset. The real challenge of Lamoignon's reform package lay in the proposal to establish forty-seven *grand bailliage* courts and a plenary court (*cour plénière*). The *grands bailliages* were plainly intended to become the principal judicial bodies of the kingdom, for they were equipped with appellate jurisdiction over all criminal suits save those involving ecclesiastics and nobles, together with civil competence to the value of 20,000 *livres*. This wiped out the judicial livelihood of the *parlements* at a stroke. As for their quasi-constitutional powers of registration, they would be transferred to a new body known as the *cour plénière*. And in order to counter the tendency of the *parlements* to stall royal legislation on the ground that it conflicted with the traditions of this or that province, the *cour plénière* would be entrusted henceforth with the scrutiny of all laws which the monarch wished to have enforced across the length and breadth of the kingdom.

This was reform on a grand scale, careful wording of the legislation to emphasise continuities notwithstanding. Marcel Marion described the May Edicts as the most thorough and the most audacious reform initiative ever undertaken by an *ancien-régime* minister.[38] Similar sentiments were expressed at the time by the band of writers gathered around

Lamoignon. Everyone realised that the fate of the reform depended on how it was received by public opinion. Condorcet rushed into print in order to claim the 'liberal' middle ground with a reminder of the blessings which the Brienne ministry had bestowed upon the nation: the Provincial Assemblies, the destruction of the *corvée*, the freeing of the grain trade, civil toleration for protestants and now reform of the criminal law. 'Is this the moment to level accusations of despotism?', he asked rhetorically.[39] But Lamoignon knew perfectly well that appeals of this sort would not sway opinion on their own. Indeed, it is far from certain that he saw himself as a liberal reformer. Rather he counted on the older tactic of divide and rule, for his measures cleverly exploited the fault line between the higher and the lower courts. With the *parlements* relegated to a largely ornamental role, the judicial load would now be borne by selected *présidial* courts – henceforward upgraded to *grand-bailliage* status. And as an incentive, personal nobility (convertible to hereditary nobility after twenty-five or thirty years) would be available to judges entering the new bodies. Furthermore, as officers of the *grands bailliages*, they would enjoy immunity from prosecution by vengeful *parlements*. In a similar fashion the reform played upon the frustrations and ambitions of the ordinary *sénéchaussée* judiciary, for they were offered the prospect of elevation to *présidial* rank which carried a much enhanced competence to judge civil suits. In the scramble for places and honours, Lamoignon expected that sense of professional loyalty which had sustained the *parlements* in the past to give way.

The failure of his strategy and the subsequent collapse of the ministry forms part of a larger story which it is not the purpose of this chapter to relate. But one final point does deserve to be made. Lamoignon's audacious and ill-timed decision to gamble the fate of absolute monarchy on a root-and-branch reform of the judiciary forced the sovereign courts to define their position as never before. Summoned to Versailles on 8 May 1788 to hear the enforced registration of the edicts, the magistrates of the Parlement of Paris riposted with a quintessential statement of the doctrine which the reforms of Louis XVI's reign were designed to undermine. 'The Coronation Oath unites all France with its sovereign', the judges informed the monarch:

but the king does not reign with equal title over the provinces. In Normandy, Brittany, Gascony, Languedoc, Provence, Dauphiné, Alsace, Burgundy, Franche-Comté ... different conditions regulate the obedience of each province. In Béarn, the first article of the Custom is an oath by the king to respect local privileges. This oath is renewed each reign before the deputies of the province by the king in person ... The will of the king, if it be justly exercised, must, therefore, vary from province to province.[40]

This was no idle piece of rhetoric, but a cry from the heart. In the months that followed it was taken up in Grenoble, in Besançon, in Rennes and in Rouen. 'Rash innovators', complained the Norman *parlementaires*, 'have dared to advance the fatal project of bringing everything into a system of *unity*.'[41] Such schemes, they continued, would serve only to destroy the 'society of orders', whatever their progenitors might say to the contrary. Herein lay the basic dilemma of reform-minded absolute monarchy: how to win an argument against 'privilege' when the defenders of 'privilege' could claim with a grain of truth that it benefited large sections of the community. In the summer of 1788 the monarchy lost the argument amid a deafening roar of 'despotism'. But the tensions within the 'society of orders' which Lamoignon and others had sedulously cultivated were not far beneath the surface. Sovereignty of the people would shortly establish a new source of authority against which it was difficult to argue. This body – known to history as the National Assembly – inherited the reform agenda of the old monarchy and wasted no time in enforcing its political will.

5   Towards 'a truly national representation', 1787–1789

The year 1787 saw the debate on the constitution of France begin in earnest. Accordingly, historians usually refer to the events taking place between the first meeting of the Notables and the summoning of the Estates General as the 'Pre-Revolution'. Or else they label this period the 'aristocratic revolt'. There are two objections to such a manner of thinking and they are worth stating at the outset. First, the labels determine the process of change in a way that none of the participants in the drama of reforming absolutism could possibly have comprehended. In a book whose objective is to explore the dynamics of transition from reform to revolution, it is important to resist the temptation to close off options. Second, neither term is satisfactory from a descriptive point of view. No doubt these years witnessed a resurgence of aristocratic political ambition, just as they witnessed a *parlementaire* resistance which displayed several of the characteristics of a revolt. But it is safer to keep these partners in the anti-ministerial alliance well marked. As the most recent student of the magistrates has observed, the Parisian and the provincial *parlementaires* were scarcely paladins of the aristocracy.[1] Nor should we make the mistake of supposing that the resistance offered to ministers stemmed solely from sections of the elite. From the middle of 1788 ordinary town and country dwellers entered the debate, often to the dismay of nobles, magistrates and bourgeois professionals who preferred to concentrate upon a very different game of politics.

Representation – how to embody it both institutionally and socially – was the big issue exercising Frenchmen during these years. Ever since Calonne's opening speech to the Notables had put power-sharing back on the agenda of government, educated minds had been puzzling over the country's constitutional history. Could Provincial Assemblies provide the stimulus that would lead to the replacement of the worn-out fabric of absolute monarchy from within? A large contingent of the intelligentsia clearly thought so, not least the *abbé* Morellet who was privy to Brienne's innermost thoughts on the subject of constitutional reform. In a steady flow of letters to the English aristocrat Lord

Shelburne, he estimated the chances of the Provincial Assemblies taking root. 'We are in a very interesting moment of crisis for our constitution', he reported after the clash with the Parlement of Paris on 19 November 1787 over the plans for fresh loans; nevertheless he expressed confidence that the Assemblies would supply the germ of 'a truly national representation sooner or later'.[2] But first the clutter of old ideas had to be cleared out of the way.

In the realm of pure theory matters could not have been simpler, for the monarch represented the kingdom in his person. According to the doctrine of absolute monarchy, society enjoyed no independent existence and therefore no right of representation. However, the Bourbon monarchs were relative latecomers on the constitutional scene, and never succeeded in obliterating antecedent traditions of representation. These were vested in bodies such as the *parlements*, the Provincial Estates and municipal oligarchies. Indeed, monarchs had come to rely on such bodies even though they curtailed royal sovereignty. They helped to raise taxes, to secure loans and they performed numerous administrative tasks which the crown's bureaucracy was not strong enough to handle on its own. So society *was* represented, despite the juridical fictions of absolute monarchy. But how exactly? The *Encyclopédie* defined the representatives of a nation as 'chosen citizens who, under a temperate government, are entrusted by society to speak in its name'.[3] However, this proto-liberal definition confused wish with reality. In the 1750s, when the volumes of the *Encyclopédie* started to appear, representation was corporative and virtual rather than individual and proportionate. Almost nowhere in French public life were 'citizens' chosen to give free expression to the interests of society and to participate in the conduct of affairs. On the contrary, the power of representation was normally vested in a collectivity, transmitted from one generation to the next by inherited right, and confined to the stylised expression of 'observations', 'remonstrances' or grievances. In the words of Russell Major, representatives were 'more proctors holding the power of attorney for the community'[4] than elected deputies in the modern sense. Thus the provost of the merchants of Lyon could declare quite properly in 1789 that the municipal body was 'the *représentant né* of the universality of citizens, defender of the rights and property of the city whose titles are all under its guard'.[5]

Such remarks seem to invite the conclusion that the old monarchy was incapable of evolving a modern representative system. François Furet (see above p. 2) certainly inclines to this view which has been advanced most forcefully by Patrice Gueniffey in his study of the implementation of representative theory in the Revolutionary Assemblies.[6] The turning-point was reached on 17 June 1789 when the newly proclaimed National Assembly unambiguously transferred sovereignty to the nation (alias 'society'). In the process, it is alleged, the old ideas of representation based on corporate bodies – in this instance orders – were repudiated in favour of a concept of representation rooted in individuals. This interpretation of the cycle of events that culminated in the calling of an Estates General has the merit that it preserves the status of the year 1789 as a dramatic moment of political discontinuity. However, it is one of the tasks of this chapter to offer more in the nature of a transformist reading of constitutional developments. By 1789 the monarchy had several times experimented with reforms that involved alterations to the established pattern of representation. To be sure, vested interests usually contrived to stifle these initiatives after a short span of time. But even aborted experiments left a mark on public opinion, and it would be unwise to assume that the political education of French men and women all took place during the final, frantic months of the *ancien régime*.

Experimentation with elective municipal councils can be traced back to Laverdy's period in office (see above pp. 27–8). In a bid to break up local oligarchies and widen the constituency of support for the central government, the minister procured two edicts in 1764 and 1765 which terminated the sale of municipal offices and instituted a regular system of elections for the appointment of mayors, aldermen and town councillors. If anything, the reform worked too well for the following year it proved necessary to issue a royal Declaration restricting the scale of the artisan franchise. The legislation also tended to curtail the power of the intendants, as we have noted, and in 1771 Controller-General Terray put government policy into reverse. Nevertheless, the initiative was not forgotten; on the contrary it became a key item on the reformist agenda. In 1789 a number of towns and *bourgs* would call for the reactivation of Laverdy's edicts in their *cahiers de doléances*. The same may be said of Necker's experimentation with Provincial Administrations between 1778 and 1781. Here was an opportunity to bypass established representative bodies by defining and incorporating a constituency of property owners. He hesitated to obliterate distinctions of order in the new bodies and showed no sustained interest in making membership elective. On the other hand, he signalled the drift of ideas on the subject of representation by doubling the effectives of the Third Estate. In 1787 first Calonne and then Brienne would build on these foundations. Indeed, Brienne planned to construct 'a truly national representation' from the raw material of his Municipal, *élection* and Provincial Assemblies if time and the state of royal finances permitted. The king's decision to call an Estates General before 1792, uttered in front of the assembled Parlement on 19 November, was therefore most unwelcome.

Assemblies versus estates

That same month the Provincial Assemblies met in plenary session for the first time. Altogether, some seventeen *généralités* were affected by the reform; nineteen if we count Necker's surviving creations in the Berry and the Haute-Guienne. Ministers had hoped to establish Assemblies in all twenty-six *généralités* of the *pays d'élections*, but the Parlements of Besançon and Bordeaux refused to sanction the edict, and difficulties arose in the Dauphiné as well (see below pp. 149–50). Nevertheless, this was an impressive legislative achievement by eighteenth-century standards. Employing a mixture of manoeuvre and timely concession, the ministers had succeeded in getting on to the statute book one of the key items in Calonne's package of reforms. Particularly gratifying to the Assemblies was an instruction published a few days before the opening session which curtailed somewhat the supervisory powers of the intendants. It seemed to promise well, for the obstructionism of the king's commissioners had marred the functioning of Necker's original Provincial Administrations. Auget de Montyon, whose writings convey to us the outlook of an enlightened servant of absolute monarchy, expressed surprise that the draft legislation did not include the proviso that the Provincial Assemblies could only deliberate in the presence of the intendants. He feared the cumulative impact of dozens of Assemblies, all corresponding with one another and exchanging printed *procès-verbaux*. He also anticipated that the new bodies might evolve into bastions of the provincial nobility, an anxiety shared by some of the *parlements*. Both judgements would be borne out by events, in part at least, for the Assemblies did start to circulate printed accounts of their transactions. In the process they helped to expand and to 'nationalise' the arena of political debate almost a year before the historic awakening of the Third Estate. As for the provincial nobility, they widely interpreted the forming of Assemblies as a heaven-sent opportunity to make a comeback. The fact that their reentry to politics would occur at the expense of the intendants only made it more satisfying. As the duc de Praslin put it in a correspondence with the comte de Serrant concerning the Provincial Assembly to be established in Anjou, 'we are going to get fat on the remains of the intendant'.[7]

The royal agent in question was M. J.-B. N. d'Aine, intendant of Tours. Like the ex-intendant Auget de Montyon, he viewed the new departure in government thinking with profound misgivings for it appeared to restore power to those groups whose subjection had been the *sine qua non* of absolute monarchy: political prelates and provincial nobles in alliance with Court grandees. However, alongside such sceptics should be ranked men like Bertier *fils* and Chaumont de la Galaizière *fils* whose reactions were positive and even enthusiastic as we have noted (see above p.126). Where was the political risk if it was understood, from the outset, that the Assemblies could only be summoned on the express instructions of the king? This was the tenor of debate within the royal Councils as the framing legislation was drawn up in the early autumn of 1787. In the event, it seems that roughly half of the intendants indicated acceptance of the new bodies, provided administrative know-how and cooperated in the demarcation of responsibilities. The remainder were more or less hostile, notwithstanding the government's attempt to salve the injured pride of its agents with elaborate rituals for the opening and the closing of the Assemblies' sessions. In the Touraine, d'Aine refused point blank to part with any of his fiscal powers.

The focus quickly switched from the plenary meetings of the Provincial Assemblies in any case, for none of them lasted for more than a month and they were all over by Christmas. By the following autumn the political debate had moved on and Necker decided not to summon them, pretexting the imminent reconvening of the Notables. Instead, the fate of the reform devolved upon the permanent committees (*commissions intermédiaires*) which the members had appointed before dispersing. These executive bodies remained in useful existence right across the political watershed from November 1787 until the Revolutionary local government structure was finally completed in the late spring of 1790 (see below p. 194). They were seconded, intermittently, by the District or *élection* Assemblies (plenary sessions held in 1787 and 1788), and by Municipal Assemblies. In Brienne's thinking the Municipal Assemblies were to act as a reservoir of public-spirited individuals which would serve to 'top up' the higher echelons of his administrative edifice. Within a few years the whole system would be elective in such a way as to render otiose calls for an assembly of Estates, or so he hoped. Almost accidentally, however, the Municipal Assemblies ended up playing a larger and more independent role in the transition from administrative to constitutional monarchy. They were established from September 1787 onwards by a process of election which prefigured, in several respects, the representational practice of the National Assembly. Over the next two years they wielded an expanding array of official and unofficial powers until they were replaced early in 1790 by municipalities summoned into existence by Revolutionary decree (see below pp. 195–6). But by that date the presence of elected officials in the parishes had acted to undermine the regime in three important respects.

To start with the hybrid species of representation which Brienne had devised for the Municipal Assemblies had the effect of transmitting the gathering debate over privilege to the grass-roots. Criticism of Calonne's original plan for a franchise based solely on proprietors irrespective of juridical estate (the 'physiocratic option') had forced Brienne to tack. Instead, he applied to the lowest tier of Assemblies a taxpaying franchise (the 'neo-liberal option') moderated by the inclusion – ex officio – of the parish priest and the local seigneur (see above pp. 41–2). This satisfied no one: neither the physiocrat lobby whose definition of citizenship was strictly proprietary and therefore excluded non-landowning taxpayers, nor the privileged for whom the gesture towards a status-based mode of representation was purely token, nor the intendants for reasons we shall see. The privileged, that is to say clerics, nobles and village bourgeois who had bought offices or seigneuries, disliked an arrangement which failed to offer sufficient guarantees of social hierarchy. For it soon became apparent that in the absence of the seigneur, the titular headship of the Municipal Assembly would fall to the elected syndic. Thus a low-born and perhaps semi-literate official could find himself in charge of a municipal body containing ordinarily elected members who might be wealthy and even noble landowners. Such an eventuality would offend against natural hierarchy, not to mention the 'distinction of orders', observed one of the comte de Serrant's correspondents.[8] It seems likely that a number of the clergy were unimpressed by Brienne's fig-leaf attempt to disguise the introduction of a neo-liberal system of representation, too. The parish priest of La Chapelle-du-Genêt recorded in his book of sermons the receipt of a circular from the controller-general explaining the procedures for presiding over Municipal Assemblies, adding that in his opinion this honour 'ought to belong to the local seigneur or his representative if he is a noble, or to the parson in their absence, and not to the syndic as has been suggested'.[9]

So provincial elites were generally well satisfied with the working of the Provincial and District Assemblies, but they soon discovered that Brienne's edict carried a sting in its tail. Indeed, the more perspicacious commentators quickly grasped the implications of the neo-liberal model of representation pioneered in the Municipal Assemblies. Within a few years the electoral mechanism would steadily promote the 'low-born' members of these bodies until they peopled the District and ultimately the Provincial Assemblies as well. A foretaste of what lay in store was already apparent in some localities by late 1788 as the new village councils took over responsibility for the apportionment of taxes. At Pliboux in Poitou councillors reduced the tax assessments of eighty wage earners and raised those of the well-to-do. The syndic of Ambillou in the province of Anjou tried to mount a similar operation, but was blocked by tenant farmers who had got themselves elected to the Assembly and who categorically refused to redistribute the tax load.[10]

The second symptom of confusion was intrinsic to the enterprise of administrative reform. Calonne and then Brienne determined that it was necessary to alter the pattern of local government in the *pays d'élections*. But this was bound to produce a short-term weakening of royal authority before it could be reconstituted on fresh foundations. In the event the reform gave rise to a dual-power situation across large swathes of the country, and at a critical moment in the fortunes of the monarchy. Even with the best will in the world, it proved difficult to disentangle those responsibilities to be exercised henceforth by the Assemblies and those to be retained by the intendants. But goodwill was signally lacking in a number of *généralités*, as we have noted. The problem was most acute at village level, for the reform established an elected syndic in every parish who owed allegiance to the executive commissions of the higher Assemblies. What it failed to acknowledge was the prior existence in every parish of an appointed syndic owing a duty of administrative loyalty to the subdelegate and the intendant. Ministers appear to have assumed that the incumbent syndics would be elected, more or less automatically, to the new post; at any rate they were categoric that only an elected syndic could represent henceforth the interests of the community.

Plainly, this was not how many intendants viewed the matter. From Poitou, Anjou, Touraine, the Orléanais, the Ile-de-France, Champagne, Picardy, the Lyonnais came complaints that parish government was hindered by intractable conflicts between old and new authorities. 'In the smallest as in the largest parishes of this province', reported the members of the District Assembly of Châteauneuf to the Anjou interim commission, 'two syndics have been nominated; one goes by the name of syndic of Monsieur the Intendant, the other by that of the Municipality'.[11] The first received orders from the intendant and the subdelegates, while the second took orders and instructions from the Assemblies. It was the same story in the Orléanais, to judge from a complaint addressed to Necker towards the end of 1788. The executive commission instanced rivalry 'between the old regime syndics and those of the Municipalities' and warned that the 'two types of syndic, [each] proclaiming different authorities, left the country dweller in a state of uncertainty as to what he should fear, or expect, from the one or the other'.[12] What was at stake, as everyone agreed, was the prompt payment of taxes. For important tax distributing and collecting powers had been devolved on to the Assemblies. With evident dismay, the officers of the Provincial Assembly of the Orléanais reported at the height of the judicial insurgency against the Lamoignon edicts that the usual seasonal tax-raising instructions had not been sent out to the parishes. Apparently the intendant took the view that it was no longer his responsibility. This was the kind of breakdown in communication which the government could ill afford as the storm clouds gathered over the absolute monarchy. Squabbles over social precedence, fiscal score settling and a perceptible loss of administrative direction at the grass-roots all contributed to the more widespread phenomenon of dissolving loyalties as Brienne's reform ministry struggled to keep control of the situation.

The counterpoint to this process was the emergence of a new power elite whose loyalties could be commanded by the absolute monarchy no longer. Only time would tell whether the allegiance of this group would coalesce around the idea of Assemblies, that of Estates, or something else. Here, too, the Municipal Assemblies played a crucial role, for they provided a training ground for the future cadres of the peasant revolution. Louis Simon, weaver and part-time dairy farmer and wine trader, was fairly typical of the milieu which the reform brought to prominence. In his memoirs he describes how the parson and the seigneur of his village near La Flèche jointly entreated him to stand for the office of syndic. A man of firm character was needed, he was told, for 'terrible doings in the affairs of government were in the offing'.[13] Simon had little choice but to agree, and he goes on to relate how he drew up the community's *cahier de doléances* which was duly scrutinised by his sponsors, the parish priest and the abbess of the convent. The following year, on 15 February 1790, he performed his final duties as syndic only to be swiftly chosen as the first mayor of the commune. Thereafter a long civic career beckoned which lasted until 1818. Louis Simon's experience was not unusual: in the neighbouring *sénéchaussée* of Baugé over half of the delegates carrying *cahiers* to the meeting of the Third Estate held elective office in the Municipal Assemblies. At the meeting of the *bailliage* of Amboise in the province of Touraine the proportion was over two-thirds.

This political apprenticeship operated even more powerfully in the higher reaches. Pierre Renouvin who long ago wrote the only full-length study of the Provincial Assemblies reckoned on the basis of a rough count that over thirty of the executive officers of the senior Assemblies went on to sit in the Estates General.[14] Such a figure represents about a fifth of the individuals chosen in 1787 to staff the *commissions intermédiaires*, and more detailed research would probably increase the proportion. Indeed, the Assemblies experiment helped to launch a number of spectacular careers, albeit ones confined largely to the more moderate, constitutional phase of the Revolution. Among the Third, Mounier, Dupont de Nemours and Thouret all rose from the ranks of the Assemblies. Thouret had served as procurator for the commoner members of the Provincial Assembly of Upper Normandy and had been deeply involved in the organisation of the Municipal Assemblies. He would call on this experience some two years later, having become the prime mover in the Constitution Committee of the National Assembly. In similar fashion the noble deputy Heurtaut de Lamerville used his position in the Agriculture Committee to rework the case for agricultural reform which he had first formulated while a member of the Provincial Assembly of the Berry. Prelates like Champion de Cicé, archbishop of Bordeaux, and Anne-Louis-Henri de la Fare, archbishop of Nancy, also carved brief parliamentary careers for themselves having acquired a taste for administration while presiding over Provincial Assemblies. Even Sieyès, still an unknown priest in 1787, had begun his public career as a rank-and-file member of the Orléanais Assembly.

However, the manifest progress towards a system of Assemblies scarcely monopolised the debate on representation. Over one third of France could legitimately claim to be represented by Provincial Estates (see above pp. 20–1). To be sure, these Estates did not 'represent' their provinces in the sense in which Brienne and liberal reformers understood the term. Nevertheless, there persisted a deep-rooted conviction that bodies antedating the establishment of absolute monarchy were more 'constitutional'. After all, the Estates met at preordained intervals with little or no interference from ministers of the crown, and they enjoyed the right of consent to taxation; that is to say the power to negotiate the level and to carry out the collection thereof. Even when in the ascendant, Brienne and his ministers were never able to overcome entirely the objection that the Provincial Assemblies provided a camouflage for continuing rule by the intendants. In this respect the promulgation of Lamoignon's judicial and constitutional reforms in the spring of 1788 marked a turning-point. They produced a ripple of indignation across the kingdom which was closely followed by a provincial backlash as corporate bodies strove to define what exactly was so repugnant about the edicts. The substantial rallying behind the idea of a commonwealth of Estates can be dated from this moment. However, it is helpful first to explore the origins of the movement in favour of Provincial Estates which antedated the reflex triggered by Lamoignon's initiative.

Although none of the texts laid before the Assembly of Notables indicated any intention to extend local government reform to the *pays d'états*, it was inevitable that the proposals would be debated across the length and breadth of the realm. As a result, two sorts of pressure began to build. Certain parts of the kingdom 'remembered' that they had once possessed Estates and began to agitate for their restoration, while provinces whose Estates had survived the depredations of Bourbon absolutism began to experience calls for the modernisation of these bodies along the lines laid down for the Provincial Assemblies. That is to say, a fuller representation of the nobility and the bourgeoisie, and voting 'by head'. The call for Provincial Estates came loudest from four peripheral regions which had never been fully incorporated within the administrative structures of the monarchy: Hainaut, Provence, Franche-Comté and the Dauphiné.

The composite frontier *généralité* of Valenciennes, which embraced the French portion of the province of the Hainaut, had no settled administrative history and Brienne was persuaded that it would be inappropriate to establish a Provincial Assembly in this region. Instead, he allowed an advisory assembly to convene in November 1787 which put forward a proposal for Estates in which the privileged orders would enjoy a built-in majority. This the government accepted in April 1788, even though it offered the Third Estate a smaller representation than they would have obtained had the Provincial Assemblies edict been applied to the province. In Provence, by contrast, the constitutional precedents were much less blurred. The old Estates had been a fortress of the fief-owning nobility and restoration implied the complete subjugation of the urban bourgeoisie, not to mention nobles of more recent lineage. In these circumstances the spokesmen of the Third Estate would have preferred to retain the hybrid arrangements in force since 1639 (see above pp. 36–7), or to have imported a version of the Assemblies reform. However, if neither of these options proved feasible, they were prepared to campaign for the return of the Estates in a revamped form. Brienne, who seems to have believed that content mattered more than labels, tried to respond to these multiple pressures. On 1 October 1787 the government announced that the Estates of Provence would be allowed to reconvene, but only on condition that they reformed themselves in a manner consistent with the constitutional changes taking place elsewhere in the kingdom. Subsequent instructions made it clear that the nobility should reconsider its representation, reconsider also the size of its contribution to the provincial tax burden, and that Third Estate delegates should equal in number those of the privileged orders. Accordingly, on the last day of 1787, the Estates reconvened in Aix.

The Franche-Comté was initially included in the remit for Provincial Assemblies. However, the notoriously unbridled Parlement of Besançon refused to register the enabling legislation; this despite Brienne's inclusion of a 'sweetener' clause dangling the prospect of a revival of the Estates. As far as the magistrates were concerned, it was a question of the Provincial Estates or nothing at all. Nevertheless, the campaign to restore the historic rights and privileges of the province did not gather significant momentum until the following year when the Parlement was coerced into acceptance of a huge backlog of reform legislation, before being sent into exile along with so many others. By the time Lamoignon fell from power, a complete change of policy was under way and it worked to the advantage of those clamouring for a rampart of Estates against future acts of 'ministerial despotism'. But if everyone by now agreed that it was time to recall the Franche-Comté Estates, sharp differences had emerged on the subject of representation. Ancient precedent restricted access to fief-owning nobles and commoners drawn from a small number of privileged towns and territories as in Provence, and a large gathering of nobles insisted on 1 October 1788 that there were no grounds for altering this state of affairs. Not so, declared the spokesmen of the Third, and they promptly organised a demonstration of solidarity grouping town councils around the theme of free elections and double representation. Overwhelmed with petitions and counter-petitions, ministers finally chose the course of action offering the prospect of least resistance. An order-in-council of 1 November announced that the Estates of the Franche-Comté would reassemble in accordance with ancient protocol on the 26th of the month, but with a mandate to put their house in order. This task was doomed from the start. For the Estates, as constituted, adequately represented neither *anobli* families nor the urban bourgeoisie. As for the rural parishes and the lower clergy, they were left almost completely out of account. By mid-December negotiations had broken down and the Third rallied behind the demand for a modified version of the Dauphiné constitution instead. Shortly afterwards the government suspended the experiment.

The Dauphiné model was on everyone's lips by the end of that year. But in order to understand the factors in play we need to go back to the start of the cycle, that is to say to Necker's pioneering attempt to broaden the bases of representation. The Parlement of Grenoble had several times called for the restoration of the province's Estates in the 1760s and 1770s. Usually the calls betrayed a game of cat and mouse with the royal intendant rather than a heartfelt desire to reinstate the political power of the local nobility. Nevertheless, they were renewed in 1778 which no doubt appeared a propitious moment to propose constitutional change, for Necker had just unveiled plans to set up a Provincial Administration in the Berry. Envoys despatched to Versailles from Grenoble soon discovered that ministers were in no mood to license a wholesale revival of Estates. In these years only Corsica obtained institutions of this type, as we have seen (above p. 65). However, Necker was persuaded to include the province in his plans for bodies which would be known as Provincial Administrations or Provincial Assemblies. A royal *arrêt* to that effect was promulgated in April 1779. Yet the sixty-member Provincial Administration of the Dauphiné never came into being, largely because it proved impossible to reconcile the long-established traditions of precedence and corporate representation in a former *pays d'états* with the format prescribed for the new bodies. These difficulties, coupled with the ambivalent attitude of the *parlementaires* themselves, would resurface when the issue came to the boil again in 1787.

Initially the Parlement of Grenoble welcomed reports emanating from the Notables that Assemblies were on the agenda of government once more. Or to be precise, a substantial faction of magistrates did so. When Brienne submitted the enabling legislation in the summer of 1787 it was registered. Yet magistrates were clearly worried: by the expense of the operation and by the fear that they might be creating a rod for their own backs. On the other hand their original option – restored Estates – scarcely offered a better guarantee of preserving their political hegemony in the province. Also ministers were making soothing noises. In a letter designed to rally the courage of pro-government supporters within the *parlement*, Marshal Ségur explained that the king regarded the Provincial Assemblies and the Provincial Estates as separate issues: 'the establishment of such Assemblies does not cancel out the possibility of convening these Estates [of the Dauphiné]'.[15] Why not give the reform a chance to demonstrate its potential, was the gist of his advice. For a regime of Assemblies might prove preferable to one of Estates.

Ségur's gloss on government policy was accommodating, perhaps too much so. A month or so later he resigned from the War Ministry once it became apparent that Brienne had a mandate to act as prime minister. As for Brienne, his objectives were clear. The best chance for the regeneration of the kingdom lay with the Provincial Assemblies, for only they were capable of achieving the wider form of representation on which he had set his sights. Therefore, lone calls for the reinstatement of highly idiosyncratic Provincial Estates had to be discouraged lest they trigger a chain reaction. That was in the summer of 1787, of course; a year later provincial particularism had ignited and Brienne had little choice but to open the constitutional debate to all comers. That chain reaction started in the Dauphiné, although no one could have foretold the fact at the time. On 1 October the Provincial Assembly finally convened in Grenoble, but within a few days the *parlement* intervened to paralyse its activities to all intents and purposes. Objecting that the Assembly was little more than a puppet in the hands of the intendant, the magistrates called instead for the return of the Estates. Indeed, they had already submitted to ministers advice on how the province's constitution might be refashioned in order to cater for just such an eventuality. But by now the whole reform project was in danger of getting bogged down and ministers were no longer interested in a softly-softly approach. The *parlement* had shown its true colours and so did Brienne: two of the most intransigent judges were ordered forthwith to Versailles. Throughout the winter of 1787–8 tension remained high, although the numerous supporters of the Assemblies reform in Grenoble continued their efforts to find a compromise. What ended the stalemate and ignited the fuse of the Dauphiné 'revolution' was the plan concocted by Brienne and Lamoignon to have done with *parlementaire* opposition to the policies of central government once and for all.

The four-month resistance of the provinces unleashed by attempts to enforce the May Edicts needs to be kept in perspective. It is often described as an 'aristocratic revolt' on the principle that the vast majority of judges in the sovereign courts enjoyed noble status. Yet the nobility were deeply divided in several of the major centres of resistance as we have seen. Equally, it would be inexact to describe the opposition as a 'judicial revolt' save in a narrowly technical sense. The lesser royal courts of the kingdom had little to fear from the reform and much to gain as many of their members realised. As for the personnel of the Provincial Assemblies, they took no part in the confrontation and nor, for the most part, did the ordinary people of town and country. What gave the *parlementaire* revolt its significance and helped to disguise its narrow base was the support of the leaders of the Third Estate; those talented writers, barristers, attorneys and municipal officers whose self-awareness had been heightened by the sudden quickening in the political life of the nation which the Assemblies reform had brought about. For the most part this support was tactical. As one barrister wrote within days of the promulgation of the edicts, 'there are now three parties in the realm and in Paris: Royalists, Parlementaires and Nationals. The last two are making common cause.'[16] In Grenoble the young Calvinist advocate, Antoine Barnave, was instrumental in forging that alliance. He joined in the condemnation of the still-born Provincial Assembly and in June 1788 issued a stirring call for the nation to rally around its *parlements*.

And indeed, events in Grenoble set the pace for the revolt. When, on 7 June, troops sought to distribute orders exiling the *parlementaires*, spectacular riots broke out. Having been bombarded with bricks and tiles from the rooftops, the soldiers of the garrison were instructed to withdraw in order to avert further bloodshed. A few days later the magistrates also withdrew, under cover of darkness and no doubt embarrassed at the way in which their political struggle had spilled onto the streets. Nevertheless, their retreat proved largely notional, for the 'Day of the Tiles' achieved a much more important feat of concentrating the energies of all three orders around a programme demanding the restoration of the Dauphiné Estates and the prompt calling of an Estates General. At a meeting in Vizille near Grenoble on 21–2 July a large number of delegates endorsed this programme and the parameters for future constitutional debate were carefully set out. Those present signalled their intention to campaign not only for the particular rights of Dauphinois, but those of 'all Frenchmen',[17] namely double representation for the Third Estate in the forthcoming Estates General, free elections, voting by head and recognition of the power of consent to taxation by the assembled representatives of the 'nation'. For the moment the tensions within this less than perfect assembly of the three orders of the province were pushed to the background.

By the middle of the summer of 1788, it must have been apparent to Brienne that his plans to regenerate the *pays d'élections* through the medium of Provincial Assemblies were unravelling fast. On 2 August the government relented and agreed that a plenary meeting should be held in the town of Romans in order to prepare the way for the reconvening of the Dauphiné Estates. The five-hundred-odd deputies to the Romans assembly gathered in auspicious circumstances. The news of Lamoignon's dismissal and the final collapse of the Reform Ministry reached the province on 18 September and within a few days the king had authorised the restoration of the *parlements*. When the magistrates reentered Grenoble they found the political atmosphere greatly altered. All eyes were now focused on the discussions taking place in Romans. There the debates on how to reconstruct the ancient representation of the province blurred insensibly into the wider issues of constitutional reform. Despite the best efforts of Mounier, Barnave and other Vizille 'veterans', long-standing tensions came out into the open, too. That is to say rivalries between towns, between town and country, and power conflicts between upper and lower clergy and between lineage and more recent nobles (as in Provence and the Franche-Comté). These issues carried greater import now that the deputies gathered in Romans were claiming the right to determine the mode of election to the Estates

General. The government endorsed most of the proposals emanating from Romans in late October, although the insistence that the province's Estates be permitted to act as an electoral college caused grave misgivings. At any event, the Estates of the Dauphiné were duly summoned to meet – after a lapse of 160 years – on 1 December 1788. Reinforced by the addition of a number of other electors, this body proceeded to nominate the patriot party leaders – Mounier, Barnave, the comte de Morges, the comte de Virieu, etc. – as its representatives in the Estates General.

The assemblies held in Vizille and Romans which culminated in the recall of the Provincial Estates turned the Dauphiné into the pacemaker for constitutional change at both the provincial and the national level. Indeed, the Dauphiné patriots showed Frenchmen across the realm how they might 'scale up' their expectations of reform. This is why events in the south-eastern corner of the kingdom have been examined in such detail. It should not be forgotten, however, that the provincial backlash against Lamoignon's edicts had several epicentres. When the first president of the Parlement of Grenoble returned from exile at the head of a triumphant company of magistrates, he was presented with a banner embroidered on one side with the arms of Provence, the Dauphiné and the Béarn. The symbolism was unmistakable for Provence had recovered her principal freedoms unaided roughly a year earlier, whereas the Parlement of Pau in the Béarn had blatantly defied ministers by continuing to meet publicly after receipt of the edicts. Their courage had been fuelled by an insurrection of the populace angered at the suspension of judicial services, it is true. Nevertheless, the attitude of the magistrates remained obdurate throughout the summer despite attempts by ministers to patch up a compromise. Eventually they were hauled to Versailles for reprimand, while the townspeople of Pau were subdued with troops.

Only in Brittany did a movement of resistance develop which was comparable in its energy to that of the Dauphiné. However, the energy expended by the Parlement of Rennes found its source in the nobility rather than the Third Estate for Brittany was the most distinctive of the *pays d'états*, both in terms of its history and the degree of control which the aristocracy exerted over the institutions of provincial government (see above pp. 35–6). In its early stages, therefore, the Breton resistance bore all the hallmarks of an 'aristocratic revolt'. After all, Lamoignon's multi-pronged attack on seigneurial justice, on the competence of the *parlements* and on the legal diversity of the provinces as enshrined in the Customs seemed calculated to antagonise fief-holding and *parlementaire* nobles in equal measure. As in Grenoble and Pau, the confrontation began with a refusal of the magistrates of Rennes to take exile as an answer to their grievances. Egged on by boisterous crowds they continued to meet in public session, and when an unconvincing military intervention failed to give the royal authorities the upper hand, it was the intendant, Bertrand de Molleville, who took the road to exile instead. But in the meantime hundreds of non-*parlementaire* nobles had mobilised in defence of the magistrates. However, the king refused to receive the envoys of assemblies lacking any legal status and even imprisoned some of them in the Bastille. This inflammatory deed galvanised the *parlementaires* into further acts of defiance, but they, in turn, engendered no sign of weakening in Versailles. Not until 30 July 1788 did Louis consent to meet a delegation from the province, and he used the opportunity to emphasise that the proper channel for communication was the Provincial Estates whose biennial session fell due at the end of the year.

At this juncture the Breton nobility took a leaf from the Dauphiné book of constitutional practice and tried to broaden the base of their opposition to include the clergy and the Third Estate. The clergy, it appears, were not unsympathetic, but the Breton bourgeoisie showed little desire to become the junior partners in an anti-ministerial alliance which, in contrast to the shining example of the Dauphiné, was still rooted in the politics of privilege. Besides, prospects of preferment in the three *grands bailliages* and fifteen *présidial* courts to be established in the wake of the reforms weighed heavily. By the time a rudimentary 'popular front' had been constructed, that is to say by the late summer of 1788, the focus of the debate had moved elsewhere in any case, for Brienne and the whole Reform Ministry were in the process of packing their bags. Instead, the object of political calculation became the forthcoming assembly of the Provincial Estates, and it would soon become apparent that none of the alignments that had characterised the province over the previous five months was likely to endure much longer. With the constitutional regeneration of the entire kingdom now in the offing, the noble leaders of the Estates had no intention of yielding primacy to their erstwhile comrades in the *parlement*; meanwhile the Third had started to emerge as a completely autonomous political force. Commoner dissatisfaction at the way in which the Breton Estates distributed the province's tax load had simmered throughout the 1780s as we have seen (above p. 36). However, since the Third's representation was confined to the deputies of forty-one privileged towns, the situation appeared irremediable. Or at least, it did until the dramatic news from the Dauphiné transformed the expectations of literate commoners across the length and breadth of the kingdom.

As the date for the scheduled meeting of the Estates approached, the professional and commercial bourgeoisie of Rennes, Nantes, Quimper and many other towns emerged from the shadows to pursue their own game of pressure politics. Encouraged from behind the scenes by the agents of central government, they demanded wider representation for the Third Estate, voting by head and a fairer distribution of taxation. But in the short term, their efforts were concentrated on winning the support of the 'official', urban representatives of the Third. This was accomplished by municipal 'revolutions' which either ousted or diluted the old oligarchies in the course of November and December 1788. Thus, by the time the Estates opened for business on 29 December, the Breton patriots were highly organised and, from an urban perspective, firmly united. On the other hand, they lacked significant liberal noble support which might have cleared the way towards a compromise as happened in the Dauphiné. Instead of compromise, the Estates provided a forum for overt conflict. Incensed by Necker's decision to allow the Third Estate a double representation in the forthcoming Estates General, the nobles brought business to a halt and the government responded by suspending the sessions. A month's delay was announced so that tempers could cool, but, if anything, the gulf between the parties widened during the interim. Necker came under intense pressure to intervene and finally consented to a tripling of the urban representation of the Third, whereupon the nobility tried to outflank their bourgeois tormentors by stirring up the populace of Rennes and canvassing support among the peasantry. By March it was clear that an impasse had been reached, for completion of the king's business required the Estates to reassemble, yet neither side could agree on the format of representation. As to the wider question of how the province should be represented in the Estates General, it simply added to the climate of antagonism. Necker tried to accommodate the warring parties by announcing, on 16 March 1789, that the privileged orders of Brittany would assemble separately in order to choose their deputies, whereas the Third would abide by the procedures laid down for the rest of the country. Not so, protested the nobility, insisting to the last that the deputies of all three orders could only be elected in a regularly constituted session of the Provincial Estates.

The struggle to reclaim or refurbish representative institutions gripped the whole of France by the autumn of 1788. Events in the Dauphiné sent out a clarion call to the restless urban intelligentsia of the Third Estate. But equally, events in Provence, the Franche-Comté and Brittany signalled the difficulties that lay ahead. Brienne's decision to stake the future of the monarchy on a nationwide scheme for Provincial,

District and Municipal Assemblies had let the genie of representation out of the bottle. The challenge was now to find ways of controlling the use of a concept which had slipped loose of its traditional moorings. Once the historical and legal fixity of representation had been cast aside, every argument in favour of the enfranchisement of this or that social group became vulnerable to another. Thus the 'rights' of nobles raised those of *anoblis*, the 'rights' of prelates those of ordinary clergymen, and the 'rights' of well-to-do members of the Third Estate those of peasants and workmen. Of course, Brienne had hoped to avoid these difficulties by circumnavigating the old hierarchies entrenched in the Provincial Estates. His Assemblies reform offered an alternative benchmark against which to align representational theory. But the king's expedient decision in November 1787 to promise a future meeting of the Estates General undercut his ministers' efforts, for it set public opinion on a different track. Nevertheless, the Assemblies succeeded in building a constituency of support for the crown during the winter of 1787–8. Indeed, they might have achieved more had the reform not been derailed by the storm of protest that greeted Lamoignon's edicts. As magistrates up and down the land stoked the embers of provincial particularism, the Assemblies experiment went into partial eclipse. In the statement of surrender of 8 August 1788 the government declared that the promised meeting of the Estates General would be brought forward to 1 May 1789, adding that it would also be necessary to assemble the Provincial Estates 'wherever they existed and to re-establish them in certain provinces where they had been discontinued'.[18]

Necker and the preparations for the Estates General

The return of Jacques Necker to full ministerial office on 27 August created the opportunity for a fresh start. Within a few days Lamoignon, whom the chargé d'affaires at the British Embassy described as 'the most obnoxious person in the kingdom',[19] followed Brienne into retirement. With the king's support, or at least his grumpy compliance, Necker was master in the house. Once the cash-flow crisis which forced Brienne's departure had eased, he was left with considerable room for manoeuvre. How would he use it? By yielding on the contentious issue of the *cour plénière* (see above pp. 136–7), he could probably have saved the judicial essence of Lamoignon's reforms. After all, the so-called revolt of the provinces had generated more sound than fury and the new courts had actually taken root in large areas over which the Parlements of Paris and Toulouse claimed jurisdiction. Equally, he could have intervened in the developing debate on the Estates General in order to direct it into channels of the government's choosing. A royal declaration uttered on 5 July had positively invited public discussion of how this antique body might be renovated so as to bring it into line with modern conditions. In fact, Necker did neither of these things. He failed to extract concessions from the Parlement of Paris prior to its reinstatement, and he squandered an opportunity to build political bridges to the Third Estate. The only decisive action he took concerned the economy, although his foresight in this sphere should not be underestimated. With a harvest year of exceptional dearth beckoning, he revoked Brienne's edict of June 1787 which had permitted the unlimited export of grain from the kingdom, and readied monies for the purchase of supplies abroad.

Historians have interpreted Necker's 'wait and see' approach to the pressing political issues of the day in various ways. Was this masterly inactivity designed to produce an exhausting and inconclusive public debate which would effectively neutralise the Estates General as a vehicle of opposition to the crown? If so, contemporaries mistook the policy for a sign of weakness and indecision. The plaudits that had greeted his return to the ministry soon gave way to doubt, for on 11 September the British Embassy noted that the public had started to wonder whether Necker had any instant remedies up his sleeve after all. The departure of Lamoignon and the recall of the Parlement of Paris revived confidence somewhat, but the following month his popularity rating began to slip once more. An alternative view shared by many historians is that Necker was simply coasting during these critical months. In charge of a caretaker ministry with no mandate to press ahead with root-and-branch reform, he preferred to keep decision-making to the minimum and to pass on the task of national regeneration to the Estates General. This description would certainly fit his handling of the Brittany imbroglio which was irresolute in the extreme. It also fits Necker's own estimate of the situation, albeit one proffered many years later. According to his memoir *De la Révolution française* (1797), the maxim guiding his political conduct was to act only from necessity while giving the appearance of spontaneity.[20]

Nevertheless, Necker had ideas of his own, obligations incurred during his earlier spell in office, and no doubt scores to settle, too. Also he found himself at the centre of a political vortex which demanded ministerial intervention whether he wished it or not. His innermost ideas on the Estates General are not easy to fathom. Jean Egret[21] believes that Necker, unlike Brienne, did support the calling of an Estates General as both desirable and necessary, but a more recent biographer is sceptical. According to Robert Harris,[22] Necker would have preferred a constitutional body which borrowed from Anglo-American precedents, namely a bicameral legislature consisting of an upper house of peers and a lower house recruited from among the Provincial Assemblies. Such an arrangement would certainly have been more consistent with the trends of his first ministry. For it was Necker who had cultivated the ministerial ambitions of the high aristocracy and pioneered the quest for an alternative mode of representation in the provinces. The approved model for the latter was now ready and waiting in the form of the Provincial Assemblies; the problem lay in the fact that it was being outflanked by the drift of events. Whilst acknowledging the political impossibility of detaching public opinion from the long-promised meeting of the Estates General, Necker seems initially to have envisaged a continuing role for the Provincial Assemblies. On 5 September he despatched a circular letter to the interim commissions announcing his return to office and offering assurances of continued support.[23] However, his stance shifted in the weeks that followed. For by mid-October the government had decided to abandon plans for the second plenary session of the Provincial Assemblies scheduled to take place in November. Either Necker genuinely supposed that time was too short to reconvene the Provincial Assemblies, a second Assembly of Notables (due to meet on 6 November) and the Estates General (proposed for January 1789), or he had simply given way in the face of an irresistible tide favouring Provincial Estates. It is certainly true that the pressure on ministers to license a wholesale reestablishment of Provincial Estates increased markedly in October and November. According to the usually well-informed author of the *Correspondance secrète*, 'it is affirmed that it is M. Necker's intention to engage the king to grant Provincial Estates to all the provinces of the kingdom'.[24] Yet the same author did not draw from this intelligence the conclusion that the Assemblies experiment was therefore dead and buried. Many Frenchmen continued to envisage a constitutional regeneration which featured both Provincial Estates and Provincial Assemblies.

In the absence of a firm lead from government, the Parlement of Paris supplied the political void. With a statement tacked on to the registration of the king's decision to call the Estates General, the magistrates indicated that the meeting should take place 'in accordance with the forms employed in 1614'. Public opinion hesitated for a moment, for contemporaries were less familiar with the constitutional niceties of the seventeenth century than historians have become subsequently. But within a few days the message sank home. The magistrates were proposing to harness the regeneration of the kingdom to precedents established 174 years earlier when the Estates General had last assembled. Ostensibly their intention was to inhibit the power of the crown, but the more immediate consequence was to preempt any possibility of free elections, doubled representation for the Third and voting by head. The outcry was all the more indignant for the fact that these very issues had been vigorously debated at the regional and the local level over the previous twenty-one months. Indeed, thanks to the Provincial Assemblies experiment, there had come into being the rudiments of a consensus in this area. Now everything was thrown into jeopardy. Already sorely tested in Provence, the Franche-Comté and in Brittany, the anti-ministerial alliance succumbed never to recover. In its place there emerged a fully-fledged patriot party consisting of elite members of the Third Estate, liberal nobles and parish priests.

Necker's tardy response to the constitutional free-for-all was to fall back on Calonne's expedient and to organise another Assembly of Notables. Reluctant to intervene himself, he was nonetheless angered by the attempt of the Parlement of Paris to corner the debate and keen to demonstrate that matters were still open-ended. There could be no doubt about this in any case, for the printing presses were working overtime in response to a veritable eruption of Third Estate loquacity on the subject of reform. Moreover, these 'political publications',[25] as the British ambassador described them in December, no longer confined their comments to the constitutional issue, but raised questions relating to fiscal and even seigneurial privilege as well. This slippage affected the country at large, too. More and more provinces were petitioning for the recovery of their Provincial Estates, sometimes with the active support of the permanent officials of the Provincial Assemblies. And behind every ritualised request for a Dauphiné style reform, the stirrings of deeper forces could be detected. Petitioners called for the removal of exemptions, the equalisation of fiscal burdens, tax-based electoral laws and the reorganisation of seigneurial justice. Bit by bit, the various reform agendas mooted since the start of 1787 were being brought into focus. But who would give up what, and when, remained unclear as long as the Estates General lacked definition. Nobody, not even the Dauphinois, were prepared to sacrifice their collective and individual privileges until everyone else did so – on the altar of the Nation.

The second Assembly of the Notables was clearly intended to provide that definition, notwithstanding Necker's airy display of political agnosticism when he opened the sessions on 6 November. The membership was largely unaltered, apart from the inclusion of several presidents of Provincial Assemblies and changes necessitated by deaths. As for the task, it consisted of providing answers to a long list of questions pertaining to the organisation of the Estates General. In view of the shortness of time it was by now agreed that the Estates would not convene until May after all. The questions appeared simple enough: what should be the numerical composition of the Estates General? To whom should the letters of summons be addressed? What electoral constituencies should be adopted? What electoral qualifications? What instructions should accompany the deputies? And so forth. Yet each of those mentioned, and many of the others besides, was loaded with social and political implications which a body of well-to-do, indeed privileged, individuals could not help but view with alarm. Only one committee voted (narrowly) in favour of doubling the Third's representatives, and overall the proposal was resoundingly defeated. Voting by head attracted little support either. As to the question of electoral constituencies, the Notables declared in favour of the *bailliages* and *sénéchaussées*, but turned down the suggestion that representation be proportional to their population. Among so many negatives their acceptance of complete fiscal equality scarcely attracted any attention. It had been promised before and, in any case, the debate had moved on.

Indeed, it was the rapid movement and radicalisation of opinion that so perturbed the Notables. As the bright hope of political reformation acquired the shadow of social subversion, the high clergy and nobility retreated to their bunkers. There they started to draft a warning to the king listing the perils of his situation, but were forbidden to issue it in the name of the Notables. Instead a memorandum was handed to the king signed by five of the Princes of the Blood. In no uncertain terms they declared that the limits of reforming monarchy had been well and truly reached. One more step would plunge the state into revolution. Both Louis and Necker had now reached a turning-point, and on 12 December the deliberations of the Notables were brought to a conclusion. Even by Necker's standards, decision-taking had become unavoidable. After days of intense discussion with his ministers, the king resolved to grant double representation to the Third Estate. Necker's support, it seems, was less than wholehearted although no one outside a small circle was aware of it at the time. At any event, on 27 December 1788, a proclamation headed 'Result of the King's Council' informed the public that elections to the Estates General would take place in the *bailliage/sénéchaussée* constituencies with seats adjusted to population, that over 1,000 deputies would be called and that the Third Estate would enjoy a representation matching that of the other two orders combined. An accompanying report by Necker explained that none of these decisions affected the question of voting (by head or order?) within the Estates General which remained open, but that it was the sincere wish of the king to rule henceforth as a constitutional monarch.

Ice and heavy snow hampered the transmission of the news. For many nobles quitting Paris in the expectation that Provincial Estates would shortly reconvene, the tidings they bore were gloomy in the extreme. The squires of Brittany greeted the decision to expand the voting strength of the Third Estate with cries of betrayal as we have noted. Yet the pamphleteers and tacticians of the patriot party savoured a rare moment of triumph. Necker's decision (for that is how it was seen) triggered widespread rejoicing and was followed by a fresh avalanche of tracts and pamphlets which subjected the prerogatives of the nobility and the upper clergy to minute and hostile examination. For something had happened to the debate: the polite discussion of the rights and wrongs of 'privilege' which had begun in 1787 under the aegis of the Provincial Assemblies had finally burst into the open. 'Public debate', remarked the Swiss journalist Mallet du Pan, 'has changed. Now the king, despotism, the constitution are merely secondary: it is war between the Third Estate and the two other orders.'[26] The echo to this sentiment was provided by a priest, the *abbé* Sieyès, at the turn of the year. In a pamphlet resoundingly entitled *What is the Third Estate?* he declared that the 'nation' now bestirring itself contained no room for privileged groups and local particularisms. Therefore, if the nobility and the clergy wished to enter the new polity they should relinquish their corporate rights without delay. Was this war? Not yet perhaps. Sieyès' estimate of the civic capacity of the nobility was exceptionally harsh. Many educated observers continued to believe that assemblies of noblemen would mandate their deputies to make the necessary sacrifices. Nor was it strictly true to assert that constitutional issues had slipped out of the limelight. There remained the problem of orders: that is to say how the sessions of the Estates General should be organised and votes taken. If no agreement could be reached on this issue, the doubling of the Third's delegation made little political sense.

But first it was necessary to assemble the orders, draft lists of grievances and choose the deputies. To this end the government published, on 24 January 1789, a set of electoral regulations. Accompanied by detailed notes and instructions, the document ran to twenty-two pages and somewhere in the region of 100,000 copies were printed. Secular clergy were granted the right to vote directly for their representatives as were all nobles, whether or not they owned fiefs, provided always that their noble status had fully matured. By contrast, the regulations applying to contemplatives, regular canons and unbene-ficed clergy generally only permitted an indirect mode of representation. The same was true for the Third Estate, of course, whose unwieldy size and distribution necessitated highly complex voting arrangements. In principle, all resident taxpaying males aged twenty-five and over were enfranchised. Thus the elections to the Estates General can be said to have inaugurated a decade of intense electoral activity with a provision amounting to universal suffrage for adult males. However, the vast majority of commoners were only ever invited to vote in 'primary' assemblies of their parish or urban guild. The choosing of the deputies took place within electoral colleges made up of delegates from the lower assemblies. This introduced one, two, and sometimes even three stages to the process of consultation. As for the decision to employ the judicial *bailliages* and *sénéchaussées* as the basic electoral constituency, it proved difficult to adhere to rigorously. Boundaries were ill defined, *bailliages* varied enormously in size, and some parishes found themselves in a geographical limbo. Even the notion of the parish could give rise to ambiguity in certain parts of the country, for it was not always equivalent to the fiscal community. However, the symmetry envisaged in December's royal Council decision faltered most obviously with regard to the larger cities and certain of the *pays d'états*. In several major urban centres, including Paris, Lyon, Rouen and Strasbourg, special arrangements had to be made, while in the Dauphiné, the Béarn and Navarre the government grudgingly allowed the elections to be conducted by the Provincial Estates. The Breton and the Provençal Estates might also have clung on to this privilege, had it not been for the bitter feuding in their midst. Elsewhere the pretensions of corporate bodies to play a role in the electoral process were firmly rebuffed.

By and large, however, all three orders of Frenchmen completed the rituals preparatory to the convening of the Estates General within the *bailliage* or *sénéchaussée* constituencies, or their subdivisions. Perhaps as many as 4 or 5 million adult males participated, of whom some 105,000 attended *bailliage* assemblies in order to cast votes for the candidates.[27] The spectacle was not lost on contemporaries. 'All the world here is occupied in electioneering, in chusing or being chosen',[28] reported Thomas Jefferson from Paris, while the British ambassador marvelled at the fact that the Princes of the Blood would sit in the Estates by virtue of an election and not by right. More prosaically, the peasant André-Hubert Dameras jotted down the news that 'today, 20 February, two men in each parish were nominated in order to go to Châlons and choose the deputies for the new government: they are Simon Demeaux and Eloy Carlier who were appointed at the church door'.[29] Little mention of anything resembling an election here; merely a reference to the age-old practice of assembling the community after the Sunday service. This is important, for it urges caution in construing the character of the events now unfolding. In spite of the ample definitions of eligibility enshrined in the January electoral statutes, it is difficult to agree with François Furet that they foreshadowed 'a modern and democratic type of system'.[30] In reality, the committee of Notables and royal bureaucrats who had drafted the statutes produced a hybrid document mixing progressive and regressive features. The attempt to produce a uniform set of regulations, if not completely successful, betrayed the full thrust of reforming absolutism, as did the rather timid efforts to adapt ancient institutions to a mode of representation reflecting numbers rather than status. But the minutiae of deliberating and voting in parish and guild assemblies were almost entirely drawn from the past. In a final display of 'jurisdictional' authority, peasants and workmen were instructed to gather under the eye of the local judge, whether seigneurial or royal, or that of an urban magistrate. The precedents established for the purposes of the Municipal Assemblies reform received no official recognition, despite the fact that Brienne had confirmed just a year earlier that the municipal syndic was the only legally empowered representative of the village community.

In fact, the first task confronting Frenchmen in the late winter of 1789 was not to elect their representatives, but to list their grievances and hopes for change. Every properly constituted electoral assembly possessed the right to draw up a *cahier de doléances* and, of course, nearly every such body availed itself of the facility. Since the regulations anticipated the creation of five different types of deliberative body ranging from *bailliage* assemblies of the clergy and the nobility to craft meetings in the towns, and parish deliberations in the countryside, the quantity of such documents was enormous. After all, the parishes of the kingdom numbered nearly 40,000. In practice, however, it was never intended that all these *cahiers* be presented to the Estates General for action. The vast majority were to be subsumed into a hardcore of 615 composite or 'general' *cahiers* containing the distilled anxieties of each order for each *bailliage*.[31] Most of these documents have survived, together with many thousands of 'preliminary' *cahiers*. They represent a precious, if sometimes confusing, source of information on the hopes and fears that gripped the subjects of Louis XVI in the weeks preceding the meeting of the Estates General.

'It is being said that we shan't have monks any more as there are at Laval-Roy and La Piscine; nor tithe, nor seigneurial law. Everyone is saying that it is a good thing; we'll have the right to go hunting, to kill hares.'[32] This is how Dameras interpreted events from the station of a village near Châlons-sur-Marne. Whether these unbridled thoughts found expression in the parish *cahier de doléances* is another matter, for the presence of the local judge or attorney as recording officer tended to curb tongues. Nevertheless, it is broadly true that the village assemblies confined their discussions to local issues, and more especially to local burdens stemming from the incidence of the state's direct and indirect taxes, and of the seigneurial regime. Calculations based on a sample of *cahiers* have shown that 45.8 per cent of the grievances expressed by villagers relate to burdens experienced in their daily lives, whereas the general *cahiers* of the Third Estate restricted remarks of this nature to 24.4 per cent of their subject-matter. As for the nobility, articulation of burdens is confined to 18.5 per cent of their grievances.[33] On the other hand, the language of the parish *cahiers* remained firmly traditional; voices calling for change can be heard, but signposts indicating the direction which the assembled Nation should take are far and few between.

Instead, the rhetoric of change is to be found in the general *cahiers*, and most notably those of the Third Estate. Elaborate schemes of constitutional renewal, suffused with Enlightenment jargon, keep company with de rigueur calls for the erection of Provincial Estates 'on the Dauphiné model', for taxation by consent on an even-handed basis, and for root-and-branch judicial reform. Nearly every composite *cahier* of the Third Estate demanded that the Estates General count votes by head, too, whereas those of the nobility displayed profound differences on this crucial issue. A mere 8.2 per cent declared unambiguously in favour of this mode of voting, whereas 41.0 per cent insisted that votes must on all accounts be reckoned by order.[34] At least the months of attrition directed against pecuniary privileges had persuaded most nobles of the wisdom of retreating from this position. All but a handful of their *cahiers* signalled a desire to enter Sieyès' redefined polity shorn of personal fiscal distinctions. However, this convergence did not extend to the trappings of seigneurialism from which many nobles continued to derive tangible benefits. If anything, alarm over this issue was mounting as a severe winter of agrarian distress threatened to spill into overt acts of anti-seigneurial violence (see below pp. 170–3). While nearly two-thirds of the general *cahiers* of the Third Estate demanded an end to feudal dues, most noble assemblies seem to have decided that the best tactic was to avoid the subject altogether. Only 30.0 per cent raised the issue, in order either to condemn or to uphold seigneurial rights in roughly equal proportions.[35]

The clergy's *cahiers* tended to display a dualist character. No doubt this reflected the bitter rivalries pitting the lower clergy against the prelates and canons in a number of *bailliage* and *sénéchaussée* assemblies, but it also expressed the ambivalence of many parish priests in trying to come to terms with the social and intellectual pressures of the eighteenth century. On the key issues there was an impressive degree of consensus and goodwill. Nearly all ecclesiastics acknowledged the need for a constitutional restructuring of the kingdom which would bring to an end the fiscal immunities enjoyed by the church. Clergymen would pay pro rata taxes like everyone else. On the manner of voting in the Estates General, the clerical *cahiers* were more reserved, although nearly two-thirds indicated that 'par tête' deliberation would be acceptable in certain circumstances, if not all.[36] Unlike a large proportion of the nobility, the clergy's deputies did not arrive in Versailles determined to resist any merging of the orders. However, the radical instincts of the lower clergy found expression mainly in economic and political demands pertaining to the internal organisation of the First Estate. There was a general lament about the inadequacy of the *portion congrue*, the scandal of 'useless benefices' and the need to make better provision for old and sickly incumbents. Allied to these grievances we find calls for a democratisation of church structures along the lines first proposed by Henri Reymond (see above p. 132). Yet clergymen were also worried by the 'licence' of the century; that is to say the patchy enforcement of press censorship, the failure to observe Sundays and feast days, and the slackening bond between church and state as evidenced in the decision to rehabilitate French Calvinists. This reflex of conservatism should not be underestimated. It helps to explain the rapid cooling of enthusiasm among the parish-based clergy once the Revolution began in earnest.

Democratic in appearance, the electoral process proved to be much less so in practice. At village level the regulations envisaged an initial meeting for the reading aloud of the government's circulars. This was open to all comers and would be followed no more than eight days later by a more closely defined deliberative assembly whose task was to compile a list of grievances and to choose delegates who would bear it to the whole *bailliage* assembly of the Third Estate. However, it seems likely that this process was telescoped in many localities, if only for reasons of timing. Likely, too, that in numerous parishes the electors were chosen in a constituency of something less than the totality of taxpaying household heads, if rather more than the old *conseil politique* or inner council of the village. In the *sénéchaussée* of Nantes, for example, the participation rate varied from a modest 12 to 20 per cent of households, which nonetheless represented a scaling up of the parish councils (*généraux*) of between two and five times.[37] Elsewhere, and especially in Normandy and Upper Languedoc, the turn-out was higher. But everywhere the end result was the same: a more or less democratically constructed village assembly chose local worthies and well-to-do farmers to carry their *cahiers* to the neighbouring town or *bailliage* seat. Once there, these rustic electors were almost invariably outmanoeuvred and at length outvoted by resident members of the professional bourgeoisie who packed the relevant committees and controlled the selection of deputies. However, they usually took care to incorporate some of the grievances of country people in the 'general' *cahiers*.

The situation was little different for the working population of the cities and large towns. Indirect voting, or the imposition of tax qualifications, or both restraints acting in combination, served to defeat a nominally democratic franchise. The ordinary people of Paris were kept at bay with a stiff 6 *livres* tax threshold, with the result that only a handful of artisans and retailers were chosen as electors. In the port city of Toulon everyone paid some sort of tax and was therefore qualified to vote, but the municipal officers arbitrarily excluded journeymen and the bulk of dockyard workers from the preliminary electoral assembly. A few days later a riot triggered by steeply rising bread prices and a simmering sense of injustice brought electoral operations to a standstill. None of these barriers disturbed the pattern of Second Estate voting, however. The vast majority of noblemen were able to participate directly in the choosing of their deputies from within *bailliage* constituencies. Nonetheless, the process produced some surprises for those who were apt to confuse the liberal instincts of a minority of urban and Court aristocrats, with the sentiments of the order as a whole. Three days after the opening of the Estates General, Thomas Jefferson informed a correspondent that 'the Noblesse on coming together shew they are not as much reformed in their principles as we had hoped they would be'.[38] Direct voting within democratic assemblies displayed the French nobility in its true colours, therefore. And the same may be said of the electoral assemblies of the First Estate. They destroyed for ever the illusion that bishops enjoyed the natural respect and submission of the rank-and-file clergy. Two-thirds of the deputies chosen to represent the interests of the church in Versailles were parish priests.

Representation by riot

The determination of ordinary workmen in Toulon to enforce their newly discovered rights with acts of violence recalls to mind the missing ingredient in the transition from administrative to constitutional monarchy. Throughout 1787 and for much of 1788, town and country dwellers had been spectators to the duel between reform ministers and the so-called privileged orders. Even Lamoignon's overturning of the judiciary had produced little more than isolated ripples of popular discontent. The government, which had ordered intendants back to their provinces and placed troops on standby, was mightily relieved. In the end Brienne sounded the retreat not because of mounting popular violence, but because of a run on the treasury. Yet this could not last. Despite the nearly unanimous wish of all parties for a peaceful outcome to the conflict, politics could not be confined indefinitely to the courthouse and drawing room. And besides the bleak economic outlook of the past few years was about to take a dramatic turn for the worse.

The loss of momentum evident in most sectors of the French economy by the late 1770s has been explored already (see above pp. 100–6). It is now necessary to introduce the social dimension of this malaise, for there is a tendency among historians to narrate the events leading up to the outbreak of revolution as though popular discontent were contingent solely on harvest failure or seminal moments such as the taking of the Bastille. In reality, collective protest, whether violent or non-violent in character, was both intrinsic to the *ancien régime*, and contingent upon the revolutionary process itself. Each must be looked at and the best way to appreciate the continuities is to start with the closing gestational decades of the old monarchy. In a provocative article Emmanuel Le Roy Ladurie[39] once drew attention to the docility of eighteenth-century rural society compared with the tumult and rebellion of the preceding century. The comparison is a little misleading and his explanation hinges upon estimates of the real weight of taxation which are inconclusive to say the least. Nevertheless, this comparative approach has been fruitful in other respects. Social historians have been forced to clarify definitions of popular protest, to work out criteria for measurement, and, of course, a great deal of research has been undertaken subsequently.

As a result we have come to realise that rising social tensions should not be measured solely in terms of set-piece rebellions. Town and country dwellers practised all manner of foot-dragging and non-compliance techniques which fell well short of the dangerous and irrevocable expedient of outright insurrection. One of the most favoured 'weapons of the weak' was litigation, for as the bureaucratisation of village life advanced peasant communities discovered that they could win court cases as well as lose them. Is this to be construed as evidence of docility or sophistication? But overt actions of collective protest (known to contemporaries as riots, 'emotions', 'troubles', *attroupements*) by no means ceased at the turn of the century. On the contrary, they displayed growing signs of sophistication and maturity. An ongoing research project has already collected data on around 4,500 crowd actions which occurred between 1661 and the opening of the Estates General in 1789.[40] Preliminary analysis of this information suggests some interesting conclusions. To start with the overwhelming majority of disturbances were rural in character and they clustered in an unmistakable temporal pattern. Presented graphically, these findings reveal sharp spikes of activity in the years of harvest dearth and climatic disaster (1709–10; 1723, 1725; 1754, etc.). However, the underlying trend during the early part of the century is stable. Yet from the 1760s a distinct escalation of social agitation occurred, expressed as a rising curve from 1765 until the onset of revolution with peaks in 1775 and 1789. In the later 1770s the rate of disturbances ebbed somewhat (while still remaining above the levels registered in the 1760s), only to accelerate once more in the later 1780s. Furthermore, this reflex of unrest during the final decades of the old regime seems to have been general and not confined to specific provinces and districts. In contrast to the chronological distribution of collective protest, analysis of the accumulated data in terms of content is still rather sketchy. However, it is clear that the majority of incidents were small-scale crowd actions impelled by food shortages and fiscal grievances. Youth or peer group actions appear to have been on the increase whereas the mobilising potential of religion was on the decline, before 1789 at any rate. As for crowd actions directed against seigneurs and tithe-collectors, they were certainly increasing in the period under discussion, but not in any linear fashion. Even in the 1780s the excrescences of the seigneurial regime were not the principal target or preoccupation of villagers.

Here we have some useful lines of enquiry, then. The mobilisations of 1789 did not emerge out of thin air. Nor, in all likelihood, were they totally inexperienced in terms of organisation and objectives. Subsistence disorders remained paramount to the very end of the *ancien régime*, yet anti-tax struggles had not ebbed as was once supposed (they had merely changed their form). Finally the animus against seigneurial power and privilege was growing, but even during the years immediately prior to the Revolution it proved a secondary rallying-cry at best. Something must have happened to push it into the foreground. Most of these hypotheses can be confirmed by turning to another set of data compiled by John Markoff and a team of American social scientists.[41] Markoff's data base consists of some 4,700 rigorously defined crowd actions[42] which took place in the countryside from the summer of 1788 until the summer of 1793. Most of the conclusions he draws fall beyond the confines of this chapter, but it is interesting to note that he too endorses the value of the longitudinal approach for a proper understanding of the mobilisations of the Revolutionary era. Before 1789 the temperature in the French countryside was already rising, but it was further inflamed – and focused – by specific events in the Revolutionary process. Figure 1 makes this point eloquently. It extends the trend

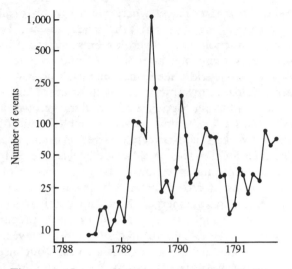

Figure 1   Insurrectionary events (1788–91, by month) (based on
4,689 events)
Source: Markoff, *The Abolition of Feudalism*

already observed and highlights the frequently ignored fact that the
movements of country dwellers started *before* the political crisis which
supposedly brought them into play. From August 1788 peasants, and for
that matter townspeople, were on a mobile footing in response, not to
Lamoignon's edicts, but the state of the harvest.

Food shortgages often served to trigger mobilisations that quickly
developed a more ideological character and it is worth considering them
in more detail. The worst disorder that Louis XVI ever had to face while
ruling as an absolute monarch was the so-called Flour War. For several
weeks in April and May 1775 the government all but lost control of the
provinces adjacent to the capital and even of the streets of Paris itself.
Poor harvests in 1770, 1772 and 1774 had caused grain and bread prices
to move sharply upwards, and Turgot's ill-timed decision to lift controls
on the grain trade merely fuelled the widespread conviction that
unknown parties were hoarding, hiding or exporting foodstuffs in order
to starve the people. Apart from the scale of the rioting, none of this was
especially unusual. What was unusual, however, was the behaviour of
the crowds for, mingled with the customary attacks on officials, pillage
of bakeries, public acts of price-fixing in the market-places and so forth,
were indications of a more informed grasp of the potential of crowd
action. Cynthia Bouton,[43] who has analysed the patterns of subsistence
violence more closely than anyone hitherto, detects a shift in the locus of

crowd actions from the market-place (where grain was on display for distribution) to the barn of the big farmer, the monastery and even the château (the site of production). Moreover, it seems that the Flour War witnessed the first really significant attempts to 'splice on' to the old tradition of market invasions and price fixing, the newer practice of farm and château-visiting. This, in turn, fits neatly with what we know of the demographic pressures afflicting country dwellers in the grain-producing belt around Paris. In the 1770s and 1780s roaming bands of wage labourers, village outworkers and underemployed artisans became a veritable social menace in the wheat fields, and it was precisely these categories that came to prominence during the disturbances of 1775. Some of the key features of crowd actions during the Revolutionary climacteric were beginning to emerge, then. If we follow Bouton's reasoning, it seems that a more rural and a more male practice was developing which involved the seizure of grain before it ever got to market. This shift brought to bear an anti-seigneurial (but also anti-monastic and anti-prosperous peasant) animus.[44]

Signs that a comparable splicing of elite and plebeian concerns was making progress first became evident in the South-East. A short time after the 'day of the tiles' in Grenoble, the subdelegate of Crest at the southern extremity of the Dauphiné announced a general effervescence in the surrounding villages. 'It is strange', he reported, 'to hear peasants of the roughest appearance assert that if it is right to pay taxes to cover the needs of state, it is no less right that the monarch should give account to his people of the use to which he has put these taxes.'[45] Although he did not say so, there was also mounting criticism of the seigneurial regime. This tension threatened to undermine the tactical alliance which the urban leaders of the Third Estate had forged with liberal nobles and parlementaires, not least because the magistrates numbered in their midst some of the most notorious exploiters of seigneurial dues. When the revived Estates of the Dauphiné convened in December 1788, the deputies of the Third pointedly refused to guarantee the integrity of seigneurial property rights. Indeed, by the late winter and early spring of 1789 it was clear that the running was being made from below. After a 45 per cent increase in grain prices since the preceding harvest, the month of March was punctuated with riots in Crest and Grenoble. Meanwhile, rural communities were petitioning with a growing sense of urgency for the ending of harvest dues.

In the Franche-Comté the articulation between town and country was not as well developed. Anti-seigneurial tinder existed in abundance for this was the province of mainmorte[46] and parlementaire obstructionism par excellence, but the fusing of political agendas was impeded by the isolation of the urban fraction of the Third Estate. Instead, the petitioning for the abolition of *mainmorte* and the Third's campaign to ensure adequate representation in the event of the restoration of the Provincial Estates ran along parallel tracks. Not until December 1788 was there a flicker of support from peasant communities for the wider objectives of the robe bourgeoisie. This rapprochement firmed at the start of the New Year as the *parlement*, the fief-owning nobility and the upper clergy all protested the royal decision to double the deputation of the Third Estate, but it still retained a distinct anti-seigneurial undertow. The detonation finally occurred in March, as in the Dauphiné. Famished crowds pillaged several bakeries in Besançon as well as ransacking the mansions of two notorious defenders of aristocratic privilege. 'We have had an appalling riot', reported a citizen of Besançon, 'which seems to have been undertaken more for the purpose of attacking certain of the magistrates than for hunting out corn which they did not have.'[47]

Clearly, food riots had become a cover, as well as a training ground, for collective action of a more ideological character. Both in the Dauphiné and the Franche-Comté the tensions generated by provincial politics had brought elite and plebeian reform agendas into rough alignment, albeit on a variable time-scale. How much more would the irruption of national politics in the form of assemblies to list grievances and choose representatives achieve? One final example will suffice. The clamour for the return of the Estates of Provence began early as we have seen. It resulted in an inaugural session held in January 1788 at a time when much of the rest of the country was still engrossed in the Provincial Assemblies experiment. However, the task of rebalancing the membership of this antique body ran into insurmountable difficulties. Much of the Third Estate, whether urban or rural, the non-enfeoffed nobility and the lesser clergy remained grossly underrepresented, and little progress was made towards addressing tax injustices either. For the time being, though, the common struggle against Lamoignon's edicts served to disguise these divisions. The turning-point came in the autumn of 1788 as the frustrated bourgeoisie of Provence donned the mantle of the nation, and an unbridgeable fault line developed between the fief-owning and *parlementaire* nobles. With the second session of the Estates scheduled for January 1789, the province slipped into political as well as economic crisis.

In an uncharacteristic display of firmness, Necker cut short the dispute in March. He announced that the province would choose its representatives to the Estates General within *sénéchaussées*, in common with much of the rest of the kingdom. But that still left a rising tide of

Third Estate (and to a lesser extent clerical) anger directed at the much abused 'constitution' of Provence. As an expression of regionalist ambition, all parties to the struggle had rallied behind this catchphrase the year before. By the early months of 1789, however, it had become abundantly obvious that the 'constitution' invoked by the fief-owning nobility was an inflexible feudal construct offering little comfort to the mass of the Third Estate and the clergy. 'Constitution is a fine word, but very disheartening for the people', as one pamphlet put it.[48] Instead, the leaders of the Third started to mobilise opinions in the towns and villages around the themes of fiscal and seigneurial privilege. The intendant of the province warned Necker that plans were being laid to withhold the next instalment of local taxes. Fortunately, the major royal subsidies had been voted before the suspension of the Estates in late January, but this was still a high-risk strategy in view of the mounting evidence of economic distress.

The authorities first started to receive reports of hungry people gathering in a menacing fashion at the turn of the year. These were quickly followed by news that women, in particular, were preventing traders from moving grain out of the villages, while large crowds of peasants were intimidating alleged hoarders at other pressure points in the provisioning network. By March 1789, in consequence, the province stood on a critical threshold. With the summoning of primary electoral assemblies towards the end of that month, the economic and the political crises fused. In the towns food shortages triggered most of the riots, whereas anti-seigneurial disturbances were more typical of the *bourgs*. However, the distinction has limited value, for the rioters tended simply to focus on whichever source of authority could be held responsible for their plight. In the cities municipal oligarchs and big grain merchants controlled the food supply, but in smaller centres the key role was often played by local seigneurs. At Solliès, for instance, the crowd attacked the banal mills of the marquis de Forbin, followed by the house of his agent. There it might have ended, but the Solliès peasantry had received word of the disturbances in Toulon on 23–4 March when workmen had protested their exclusion from the electoral assembly. As a result they vented their anger upon the symbolic as well as the economic instruments of seigneurial power: the château was ransacked from top to bottom, coats of arms torn down and the authority of the seigneurial assize court repudiated.[49]

This admixture of the economic, the anti-seigneurial and the frankly political typified the disturbances that rocked Provence in the early spring of 1789. According to Monique Cubells over three-quarters of the fifty-two riots known to have broken out in the province between

March and June of that year can be grouped in one or more of these categories.[50] In several instances the assembling of electors and the drafting of *cahiers de doléances* were sufficient, on their own, to trigger civil unrest. The case of Toulon has been mentioned already, and Marseille succumbed to repeated bouts of economic and political agitation as well. On 4 April the crowd coerced the city's electoral assembly into nominating Mirabeau as a deputy for the Third Estate. But even where the chronology of unrest indicates no direct link, it is safe to assume that the ongoing preparations for the meeting of the Estates General enormously magnified the range and the stamina of the discontent. After all, the violence reached a climax during the final week of March (twenty-nine riots), when the majority of Provençaux were pondering what to put in their *cahiers de doléances*. 'It is the peasant and guild assemblies that have done the damage', reported the intendant, 'they have been a constant source of fear and worry.'[51] As for the *cahiers*, they gave expression to what was fast becoming the new battle-ground for proto-revolutionary action. Recrimination against seigneurial obligations headed the list of grievances (87.7 per cent of the 187 documents surviving).[52] Where Provence led, other provinces would follow.

The politicisation of the masses, like that of the elites of French society was a drawn-out process. It did not proceed evenly, nor was it preordained. To be sure a steady seepage of change was redefining the polity, even at the grass-roots, but the decisive shifts occurred in great lurches which transformed the reactive politics of particularism into a proactive politics of claims lodged in the name of a wider social entity. These shifts are not difficult to identify: the calling together of the Notables in February 1787, the novel experience of consultative Assemblies later that same year, Lamoignon's last-ditch attempt to retrieve absolute monarchy from the clutches of 'jurisdictional' power, and Brienne's dramatic surrender in the summer of 1788 were all events which suddenly and irrevocably altered the political landscape. As new definitions of the polity were kindled in men's minds, the old language in which corporative rights had been articulated hitherto, struggled to keep up. Notions of the 'constitution' and of the 'nation' could be expanded and recycled, or so it seemed in the spring of 1789. But what of 'orders' and 'estates'? These were concrete entities with deep institutional roots which could not be eradicated overnight. Besides the king had just summoned an 'Estates General', not an 'Assembly General', which many took to be a step backwards not forwards. The ambiguity was compounded in the country at large, too, for the landscape was still littered with the debris of Brienne's reformist vision. What future lay in store for the Municipal, District and Provincial

Assemblies now that the green shoots of Provincial Estates were breaking the surface? Most of the *cahiers* resolved the tensions inherent in competing reform projects by calling for Estates. But the transaction implied that the 'best practice' of the Assemblies would be grafted onto the older root-stock. In effect, Frenchmen signalled cautious support for the resurrection of Provincial Estates provided that a purgative dose of liberal representation theory was administered at the same time. Yet even this synthesis left a fundamental question unanswered, for neither the Provincial Assemblies nor the exemplar Estates of the Dauphiné had cut the umbilical of *ancien-régime* society: the distinction of orders. Thus, as the so-called Pre-Revolution drew to a close, it was still by no means clear what kind of revolution lay in the offing.

6   The National Assembly, 1789–1791

The calling of an Estates General to meet in Versailles on 5 May 1789 did not mark a break with the past. On the contrary, it represented the revenge of the past on a decade of spasmodic attempts to promote root-and-branch reform from above. Brienne was hostile to the idea, as we have seen, and Necker was scarcely enthusiastic. Yet this same body gave birth to the National Assembly and a system of government known as constitutional monarchy. Both of these developments would serve to redirect the course of French history. However, it is unlikely that the deputies assembling in Versailles grasped the role that they were about to play: men make history without knowing what history they make. In 1789 men, and women, of very different backgrounds took steps which decisively altered the shape of the polity. On 17 June an impatient Third Estate laid claim to the authority of the nation and with extraordinary audacity declared illegal taxes not sanctioned by the National Assembly. On 14 July the people of Paris diminished the monarchy in a more physical sense. Then on 4 August the deputies voted – in some disarray it is true – to put an end to 'privilege', a decision that would entail major institutional reforms. Finally, in the autumn of that momentous year, the balance of power within the kingdom was tilted irrevocably in favour of the legislative body. Having been deprived of the right to make laws, Louis XVI also lost the power to block legislation (vote of a suspensive veto on 15 September). After the March to Versailles on 5 October, he would also be deprived of his freedom of movement. Brought back to Paris, Louis XVI would spend the rest of his reign in daily contact with his former subjects.

Yet the crisp narrative which historians construct from the events of 1789 can easily mislead. Contemporaries were by no means as clear-sighted about the forces in play. In fact, it required a heavy dose of myth-making to establish the credentials of 1789 as the 'year one' of Revolution. This involved the parallel invention of the concept of the 'old regime' in order to highlight the ambitions and achievements of the National Assembly. But many educated observers would have been perfectly well aware that the 'achievements' of the nation dated back to 1787 at least. For it was the Calonne/Brienne local government reform that gave the first unambiguous signal that the monarchy was preparing to abandon the practice of absolutism. Indeed, some writers dubbed this development the start of a 'new regime' (even a 'revolution') at the time. To be sure, the relinquishment of kingly prerogatives did not signify an immediate advance towards constitutional monarchy. Even in 1789 the majority of deputies was decidedly hazy on constitutional issues. In all probability the resort to a National Assembly claiming sovereign authority was a reflection not of premeditation, but of the organisational paralysis gripping the Estates General for the first six weeks of its existence.

The Monarchiens, it is true, had a clearer idea of what they wanted to achieve on the constitutional front. They sought to dilute the authority of the National Assembly and to enhance the king's executive power by granting him an absolute veto over ordinary legislation. But their proposals were defeated overwhelmingly, which suggests that the deputies knew what they did *not* want, even if they found the nitty-gritty of constitution-making an uphill task. In the event, it took a further two years of discussion and negotiation before a document could be placed before the monarch for his endorsement. The promulgation of this constitution on 14 September 1791 brought the political cycle which had started in 1787 to an end. To all intents and purposes the transition from absolute to constitutional monarchy was now complete. With the election of a Legislative Assembly, France finally emerged from the shadow of the old regime, its structures substantially remodelled. The process was far from painless, as this chapter will demonstrate. For, despite the myth of 4 August, the parameters of the nation could not be redefined overnight. Pockets of resistance abounded and ordinary people continued to invoke the Estates General rather than the National Assembly (and in neo-feudal terms), long after the innovative Declaration of 17 June. Over time these hesitations would be soothed away, of course, thanks in no small measure to the tact and forbearance of the deputies themselves. The real challenge to national consensus would come later in the spring and summer of 1791 – when they were confronted with the dilemma of non-juring priests and emigrant noblemen. Characteristically, the Assembly preferred to hand over to its successor the unpleasant task of amputating these members from the body politic.

Redefining the nation

The decision of Louis XVI to boost the representation of the Third in the forthcoming Estates General seemed to acknowledge that the nation, as understood hitherto, was in need of some redefinition. But the studied refusal of Necker to declare in favour of voting by head introduced a fatal ambiguity to the proceedings. It implied that the umbilical of the *ancien régime* had not after all been cut. To be sure, the concept of a society juridically divided into orders had come under sustained attack. And there was by now a broad measure of agreement that personal fiscal exemptions could no longer be tolerated. But did this admission place the entire tripartite structure of privilege in jeopardy? Did it, moreover, imply the concomitant destruction of urban and provincial immunities? To judge from the general *cahiers*, the position of the Third Estate was clear: near unanimous opposition to voting by order. Yet this chorus may only be telling us that the deputies of the Third would oppose the political device of separate assembly which threatened to strangle the Estates General at birth. In fact, there are good grounds for supposing that the Third Estate was not campaigning for a total remodelling of society in the spring of 1789. That came later, in the summer, as the old regime started to crumble from below as well as above. The parliamentary session of 4–5 August is rightly viewed as a crucial stage in the progress towards a new, undifferentiated nation. However, the process was more prolonged and contentious than is often allowed, for the death-blow to the 'society of orders' was not delivered until 19–20 June 1790 when the Assembly voted to abolish noble titles and chivalric orders. These decrees caused dismay even in some deputies of the Third, which serves to remind us that the new nation remained a fragile and controversial entity for many months after its formal promulgation on the night of 4–5 August.

However, the first task was to achieve the *political* unification of the nation. In the absence of a common forum for debate among the deputies, the first move in this direction should have come either from Necker or from the king himself. In the event leadership came from neither, and it fell to the Third Estate to make the running by breaking the mould of *ancien-régime* politics. Necker's inactivity (after the opening session of the Estates General) seems to have stemmed from his obsession with English parliamentary procedure; besides, he harboured the hope that the Estates would somehow evolve of their own accord into a legislature consisting of upper and lower houses. The views of Louis XVI are harder to fathom, although one thing is certain: he no longer sought to rule as an absolute monarch. On the contrary, he expressed sympathy for the Third in their vain attempts to secure voting by head. Even the Declaration of the National Assembly did not unduly perturb him, although the impromptu oath sworn in the covered tennis court on 20 June caused greater misgivings. In any case, planning was already under way for a royal initiative designed to break the deadlock in the Estates General. The summoning of the deputies to a *séance royale* was Necker's idea, for the minister now thought the time ripe to intervene. But the optimum moment had passed. Having established their credentials as representatives of the nation only days earlier, it is probable that the Third Estate would have looked askance at even the most conciliatory of speeches from the throne. In the event, when the much redrafted speech was finally delivered on 23 June, it was not especially conciliatory. Necker's influence was plainly on the wane, while the queen had succumbed to the conservative entreaties of the comte d'Artois.

Although Louis indicated his willingness to rule henceforth as a constitutional monarch, he went out of his way to defend the rights of the nobility and balked at the opportunity to make a resolute declaration in favour of voting by head. The members of the Estates were enjoined to deliberate in common session, but only for purposes of mutual interest to all three orders. The Third reacted badly to the speech, as is well known. What Mirabeau and company objected to was less the reaffirmation of noble prerogatives than the signal failure to force the issue of voting. For, if we follow the reasoning of Michael Fitzsimmons, there was no serious intent to obliterate distinctions of order at this stage. With or without a royal summons a trickle of clerical and noble deputies had started to join the Third Estate in any case, and every attempt was made to accommodate their separate character. Thus, when a number of parish priests crossed over on 13 June, they were not subsumed into the common mass of deputies, but 'maintained their separate identity as an order and were seated in a place designated for the clergy'.[1] Even when the king finally instructed the clergy and the nobility to unite with the National Assembly, the etiquette of 'orders' was preserved. With the political impediment to an effective representative body removed, there appeared to be no further need for social levelling. Arthur Young captured the mood in his diary entry for 27 June: 'the whole business now seems over, and the revolution complete'.[2]

But all was to change in July and August as the focus of events switched from Versailles to Paris and the provinces. For one thing, the spirit of fraternity in the National Assembly did not extend to the country at large. Nor did it move the Court. While the leaders of the Third Estate might have agreed to confine the debate to the fiscal and political ramifications of privilege, ordinary townspeople and country dwellers were far more concerned about day-to-day burdens; that is to say customs and excise duties, the salt tax, the tithe and the manifold irritants of seigneurialism. At this level the complex political balancing act attempted by Louis XVI in the *séance royale* was largely irrelevant. Instead there existed concrete grievances and a vague, almost millennial, hope that conditions might at last be about to improve. A peasant woman whom Arthur Young encountered on the road to Metz summed up the situation as she understood it: 'it was said, at present, that *something was to be done by some great folks for such poor ones, but she did not know who nor how*, but God send us better, *car les tailles et les droits nous écrasent*'.[3]

The most concrete grievances in late June/early July were economic, for the harvest crisis had entered its final paroxysm. After a pause in May during which all eyes were fixed upon the Estates General, unrest began to build afresh. Fears for the new harvest, kindled in part by the preparations of tithe proctors and seigneurial bailiffs, provoked widespread anxiety among a famished population. On 4 July the subdelegate of Ploërmel in Brittany reported that local peasants had given notice that they would resist any attempt to collect the tithe that year. After all, they declared, a plea for tithe relief had been incorporated in their *cahiers*, therefore it must have been granted. The fishermen of Collioure at the other extremity of the kingdom reasoned in identical fashion. This expectant confusion of wish and fulfilment proved a powerful incitement to revolt once the remaining constraints were removed in the aftermath of the Paris insurrection.

The trigger that made possible the consummation of a full-scale revolution took the form of a potent, if poorly founded, belief that the Court was plotting to overturn the National Assembly. On the face of it, this conclusion seemed warranted. Ever since the *séance royale*, conservative voices had been uppermost in the royal Council and the decision to call in large bodies of troops and to encamp them in the vicinity of Paris prompted fears that they would be used for offensive purposes. The long-rumoured dismissal of Necker, together with three like-minded ministers, on 11 July added substance to those fears. On the other hand, the in-coming ministry headed by the baron de Breteuil did little, if anything, to organise a showdown with the National Assembly. In all probability Breteuil was seeking a negotiated settlement with the deputies who, after a little browbeating, could be induced to accept the programme outlined in the *séance royale*.[4] Of course, the Parisians did not see Necker's dismissal and precipitate departure from Versailles in this light at all, and after clashes with soldiers encamped in the Champ de Mars a wholesale insurrection ensued. This uprising caught the ministry and the monarch completely unprepared, which is ultimately the best argument against the conspiracy thesis. When the royal Council convened to take stock of the situation, Louis was advised to flee to Metz. He refused, but his brother Artois, cousin Condé, Breteuil and several other Court families headed for the border.

Among the fleeing courtiers, only the comte d'Artois had consistently favoured a military solution to the crisis precipitated by the Third Estate's assumption of the mantle of the nation. Nevertheless, it is easy to see why belief in an aristocratic conspiracy was so swiftly and firmly embedded in popular consciousness. Troops *had* been put on a mobile footing (for whatever reason), and now carriages full of nobles were rumbling through the villages in the direction of the frontiers. At any event, the incidence of urban and rural unrest sharply escalated in the second half of July. The destruction of customs posts had started in Paris on the 12th as a reflex response to the news of Necker's dismissal and the high price of bread, and the onslaught soon spread to other towns. Meanwhile, the bureaucracy established by the Farmers General to police the salt monopoly came under unbearable strain. Most of the toll stations positioned along the landward frontiers of Brittany and Lower Poitou were overturned as vast crowds migrated into this tax exempt zone in order to purchase salt at free market prices. According to one source, the Breton town of Fougères daily received between 3,000 and 4,000 visitors from adjacent provinces. Each one arrived with a sack, a packhorse or a cart with which to carry off the precious commodity. By mid-September Normandy and Maine had been provisioned with enough salt to last three or four years. In Picardy and the provinces of the North-East, though, it was the officials responsible for collecting duties on drink, tobacco, soap, etc. (the *aides*) who bore the brunt of popular anger.

The most violent disturbances occurred in the countryside proper, however. And here a pronounced, even increasing, anti-seigneurial animus was evident (see figure 2). To all appearances the controlled and circumspect hostility to seigneurialism expressed in the parish *cahiers* just four months earlier was giving way to a more explicit articulation of grievances now that the arena for political debate had significantly widened. At least, the timing of the *jacqueries* that enveloped large areas of the kingdom in the summer of 1789 seems to suggest as much. Agrarian revolt in Alsace, the Franche-Comté and the *bocage* country of Normandy burst forth a matter of days after the taking of the Bastille in Paris. By the end of July the Maconnais and the Dauphiné had risen, too. Often the towns performed the role of relay stations, spreading hope (and fear) into the surrounding countryside, while consummating their own 'municipal' revolutions. In Normandy disturbances in Caen and Argentan led the way; in Alsace rioting in Strasbourg and Colmar. It

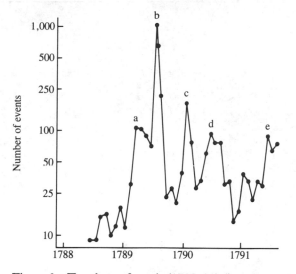

Figure 2   Typology of revolt (1788–91) (based on 4,689 events)
a Subsistence 68%; anti-seigneurial 28%
b Panics 41%; anti-seigneurial 30%
c Religious 27%; anti-seigneurial 87%
d Subsistence 24%; religious 32%; anti-seigneurial 62%
e Anti-seigneurial 69%
Source: Markoff, *The Abolition of Feudalism*

could be argued, indeed, that the revolts facilitated a rare moment of
complicity between ordinary town and country dwellers, and no doubt
this was the prospect that so alarmed the deputies assembled in
Versailles. When tensions simmering in the Dauphiné since the spring
exploded in an orgy of anti-seigneurial violence on 28 July, the common
people of Grenoble made no secret of their sympathy for the insurgents
and acted to hinder the deployment of troops and the militia.

Endemic fear, culminating in the Great Fear of 20 July – 6 August,
served to strengthen the momentary alliance between town and country.
In all some seven epicentres of panic have been identified by scholars[5]
(see map 10). The rapid transmission across the kingdom of wild stories
featuring armies of 'brigands' (in the pay of the aristocracy?) speaks
volumes for the volatility of opinion during the anarchic summer of
1789. In effect, the Great Fear set up a parallel call-to-arms which
extended or replicated *jacqueries* that were already under way. The
precise causal sequence is hard to disentangle, but only in the
Maconnais and the Dauphiné is there evidence which suggests that
currents of Fear actually helped to trigger the uprisings. Identification of

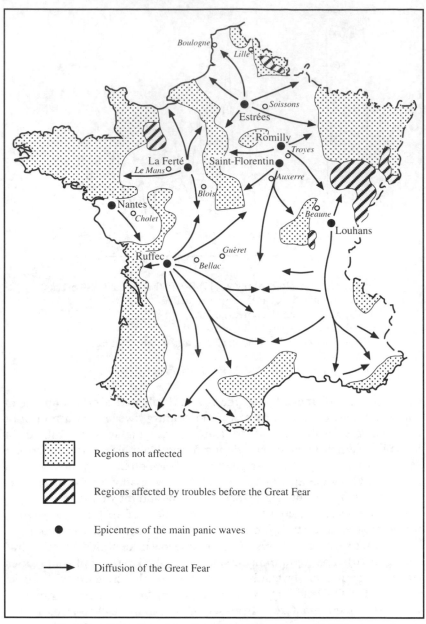

Regions not affected

Regions affected by troubles before the Great Fear

● Epicentres of the main panic waves

→ Diffusion of the Great Fear

Map 10   Diffusion of the Great Fear (July–August 1789)
Source: M. Vovelle, *The Fall of the French Monarchy* (Cambridge, 1984),
p. 109.

the perceived enemy is no less problematic, for historians at least. The word 'brigands' carried many resonances: it could mean aristocratic plotters, troops of vagabonds, even riotous peasants, depending on the social and geographical context. Town bourgeois feared pillage, peasants feared destruction of their crops, while alarm at the mischievous designs of aristocrats fleeing Versailles gripped all parties to a greater or lesser degree.

The Assembly could not help but regard this unscripted enlargement of the Revolution with dismay. After all, it was still trying to digest the consequences flowing from its own genteel uprising of 17 June. Not until 4 July was the first voice vote taken, and the discouragingly large number of clerical and noble deputies who refused to participate seemed to indicate that the business of redefining the nation was far from complete. Matters improved the following week when the deputies voted to relabel themselves the 'National Constituent Assembly', and the decision was also taken to revoke the binding mandates that hindered deliberation in common. At this point the ministerial crisis supervened, followed by the revolt of Paris. But no sooner had order been restored in the capital and its environs by General Lafayette, the new constable of France, than worrying reports began to come in from the provinces. Far from expressing the sovereign will of the nation, the deputies suddenly found themselves presiding over an impending social collapse. This is the context that produced the celebrated 'give away' decrees of the night of 4–5 August. Contemporaries drew attention to the spirit of self-sacrifice that pervaded the proceedings (as have historians subsequently). But there can be little doubt that the dominant sentiment was one of fear.

Throughout the second half of July the deputies were bombarded with alarmist news from their constituents. As John Markoff[6] has demonstrated quantitatively, the reverberations reached a crescendo on or around 28 July and remained at a high level for the next week or so (see figure 3). If we allow for a postal delay in the receipt of reports at Versailles, the sense of social emergency would not have started to ease until the second week of August. Facts such as these go a long way towards an explanation of the timing and hasty, even over hasty, acceptance by the deputies of the swingeing reforms proposed during the evening session of 4 August. That morning had dawned with most of the Dauphiné deputies huddled together reading letters from home. The despatches all urged swift action, for 'the disorders already committed are less frightening than those that some are trying to commit'.[7] Indeed, the province would eventually record a tally of nine châteaux burned, forty-three pillaged and the archives of thirteen others destroyed.

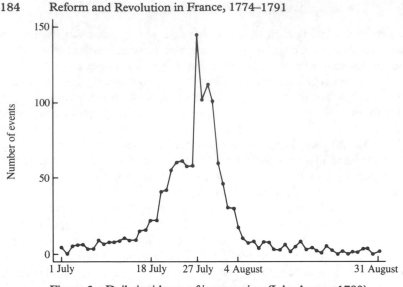

Figure 3   Daily incidence of insurrection (July–August 1789)
Source: Markoff, *The Abolition of Feudalism*

Equally, deputies whose home regions were not yet prey to unrest were becoming alarmed. Jean-Baptiste Ponçet-Delpech representing the Third Estate of Montauban reported to his constituents the tide of lawlessness engulfing the country on the 3rd, while François Ménard de la Groye, a deputy from Le Mans, made similar remarks in a private letter the following day. It seems likely that both men owed their information to the Assembly's new Correspondence Committee which had started to analyse and to disseminate the news coming in from the provinces.

When the evening session began several speakers made abundantly clear how much was at stake. Dressed reputedly in a peasant's smock, Le Guen de Kerangal told the Assembly in no uncertain terms that the social chaos now threatening could have been avoided if the deputies had moved sooner to curtail the seigneurial regime. Act now for there is not a moment to lose, was the gist of his speech. Even the intervention by the duc d'Aiguillon, who had hoped to mastermind an orderly 'sacrifice' of aristocratic privilege, showed a keen understanding of socio-political realities. Depicted frequently as an act of unstinting altruism, the duke's call for an end to feudalism actually incorporated a highly conservative estimate for the commutation of seigneurial dues. On this proposal fief-owners would have been handsomely rewarded for their 'generosity'.

Nevertheless, the troubled landscape of that first summer of Revolution does not explain entirely the scale of the changes agreed on the night of 4–5 August. For not only did the deputies pronounce the destruction of feudalism (*sic*), they went on to tear large holes in the institutional fabric of the *ancien régime*. Personal servitude, manorial courts, exclusive hunting rights, venal office-holding, corporate and provincial privilege, ecclesiastical pluralism, the tithe and much else besides was thrown onto the bonfire. Apart from fear, what forces had been called into play? Many accounts stress a pervasive atmosphere of reconciliation and fraternity as deputies vied to repudiate privileges and prescriptive rights that the *cahiers de doléances* had deemed non-negotiable only months before. According to Michael Fitzsimmons, the night's activities kindled a wave of emotion which he terms a spirit of 'sublimity of the nation'.[8] In place of the sectional loyalties that had hampered the work of the National Assembly hitherto, there emerged a unity of vision and purpose that would make possible the rebuilding of France on new foundations.

To be sure, a mood of euphoria was much in evidence as the debate unfolded in a way that no one had predicted. But so, too, was a mood of calculation, trimming and even spite as speakers intervened to ensure that everybody shared in the costs of the operation. Many deputies, particularly clergymen and members drawn from the *pays d'états*, indulged in real heart searching as well. Repentance after the event (it took a further week for the August decrees to be drafted in final form) was not an uncommon reaction either. After all, the pressure of external events subsided sharply from mid-August onwards. The Spanish ambassador to France – admittedly a partial witness – reported reactions of 'stupefaction' and 'horror' among the nobility and the clergy, concluding that it would be more apt to describe the transaction as 'the night of despair than the night of patriotism'.[9] This cautions against too ready an acceptance of the 'sublimity of the nation' thesis, for as we shall see the politics of national regeneration were not placed on a new footing overnight. The king, for one, was not impressed. At the end of their marathon session, the deputies hailed Louis XVI as the 'regenerator of French liberty', but this was gratuitous for there exists no firm evidence that he was ever consulted about what was being decided. When invited to sanction and promulgate the decrees, he procrastinated. All in all, an interpretation based on contingency makes the best sense of the Assembly's behaviour at this juncture. Thomas Jefferson came closest to the mark with his comment to John Jay on 5 August that 'this will stop the burning of châteaux, and tranquilize the country more than all the addresses they could send them'.[10]

What the decrees of 4–11 August 1789 *had* done was demonstrate the interactive quality of the new politics. Henceforward the pace and direction of change would be determined by a dialogue between legislators and many different constituencies. For country dwellers the direction, if not the pace, of public policy was broadly welcome, but corporate bodies cocooned in centuries of privilege viewed the latest developments with some alarm. Ever since the opening of the Estates General the issue of provincial privilege had preyed on the minds of the deputies. For the aim of fiscal parity as between the orders could not be dissociated from the larger question of the pecuniary exemptions and privileges enjoyed by some parts of the country, but not others (see above pp. 58–64). Moreover, the question of provincial privilege tended to confuse the political argument as conducted hitherto, since the Third Estate also benefited from these immunities. Any tinkering with the status of the *pays d'états* was likely, therefore, to produce a class of 'fiscal victims', without ensuring any immediate relief for the heavily taxed population of the *pays d'élections*. Such considerations clearly weighed on the minds of many who participated in the fateful session of 4–5 August. And sure enough, reports soon began to come back to Versailles that all was not sweetness and light.

In early September Fernan Nuñez, the Spanish ambassador, relayed the news that most of the provinces had 'acquiesced or appeared to acquiesce' in the decisions.[11] As far as he could tell only the Béarn, the Roussillon, the Cambrésis, the Hainaut and the Artois had openly declared against the August decrees. But in the weeks and months that followed the list lengthened to include Brittany and Burgundy among the *pays d'états*, Alsace, the Auvergne, Poitou and Quercy. There were also rumblings of discontent in the Dauphiné and Provence – the two pacesetter provinces in 1788 – and several smaller 'pays' of the South-West. As for privileged corporations, the Parlements of Paris, Toulouse, Bordeaux, Besançon, Metz, Rennes and Rouen made no attempt to disguise their dismay at the turn of events. Nor did the *chambre des comptes* of Dijon, while in Languedoc a *Déclaration de l'ordre de la noblesse* formally protested moves to disfigure and dismember the province. In short, it seems that the project to transform Alsatians, Bretons, Burgundians, Provençaux into Frenchmen, that had lurched on to the agenda on the evening of 4 August, was initially little more than a statement of intent. The *ancien régime*, after all, had put down deep roots which would make necessary a period of compromise and co-existence before the task of national regeneration could be completed. But let us look at this process in more detail.

The debates of 4–5 August 1789 left Jean de Turckheim of Strasbourg in a difficult position. For he and his Third Estate colleague, Etienne-Joseph-Francçois Schwendt, had arrived in Versailles pledged to uphold the special customs regime enjoyed by the province of Alsace, together with all the privileges granted in the capitulation of 1681. The following morning they reported in a mood of deep unease: 'those of us who had managed to stay cool and collected during this exceptional session imagined they were privy to a beautiful dream driven by passion for a hypothetical public good. But the next day the illusion was shattered in the light of reason. Alsace was called to the bar: your deputies were placed in considerable embarrassment.' They went on to assure their constituents that the sacrifices made were subject to approval. Nevertheless, they warned, 'the city of Strasbourg can escape the national will, the common law, only with the greatest difficulty.'[12] In fact Turckheim's enthusiasm for revolution cooled rapidly thereafter and he resigned his seat in October. Relieved of the responsibilities of office, he put into words what his compatriots were thinking: 'you wanted reforms and not a revolution; you were keen to retain your privileges, not to swop them for alien customs and modes of organisation'.[13] Only when the municipal elections of February 1790 brought Dietrich to power as mayor of Strasbourg, would Alsace start to return to the national fold.

Bretons, likewise, had good reason to look askance at messengers bearing gifts from Versailles. In common with Alsace, the old duchy enjoyed tangible tax, customs and judicial privileges, some of which dated back to the late fifteenth century. Accordingly, the deputies of the various Breton constituencies found themselves in an awkward position indeed when invited to slough off all vestiges of the past on 4 August and subsequent days. In the event they temporised like so many representatives of the *pays d'états*. That is to say they signalled a conditional assent to the wishes of the 'nation' (who could do otherwise?), while hastily organising a referendum among their constituents. Interestingly, the documents generated by this consultative exercise have survived in a few instances, and notably in the *sénéchaussée* of Nantes. They provide a snap-shot opportunity to examine the dynamics of opinion formation at a less sublime level.

Early in September the seneschal of Nantes received a message requesting him to organise a general convocation of the parishes for later that month. This was to reuse the machinery for the drafting of the *cahiers* and the preliminary elections to the Estates General to all intents and purposes. In all a total of 141 parishes responded and on 30 September their delegates met in a general assembly at Nantes. Despite a vigorous propaganda effort mounted by the *patriote* bourgeoisie of the city, no more than 50 per cent of the country delegates could be persuaded to grant their deputies unlimited power to continue the work of renovation begun on 4 August. Around 37 per cent stolidly refused to surrender the 'liberties' of Brittany, while 13 per cent conditionally endorsed the August decrees provided always that the *gabelle* or salt tax was not introduced to the province. At best, this amounted to a hesitant mandate in favour of the nation as now defined. Even the citizenry of Nantes, like those of Strasbourg, indicated less than whole-hearted confidence in the future. Seventeen corporate bodies (including the barristers, the attorneys and the bailiffs attached to the *chambre des comptes*, and eleven craft guilds) voted for the province, whereas thirty-five 'companies, corps and corporations' opted for the nation.[14]

All of the parish assemblies acknowledged that something momentous had happened even if several continued to employ the nomenclature of the *ancien régime*, referring to the Estates General rather than the National Assembly. While noting the difference from their previous assembly on 5 April the villagers of Goulaine Basse declared on 27 September that, notwithstanding the change of political climate, they saw no reason to modify their *doléances*. The privileges of Brittany formed part of a contract that could not be altered unilaterally. But the word 'privilege' was becoming embarrassing and most Bretons (on this evidence) wanted negotiation rather than confrontation. The inhabitants of Sainte-Luce sought to compliment the National Assembly, while translating their resistance to the *taille* and the *gabelle* into a language which they hoped the deputies might understand: 'the franchises of this province are not by any means a privilege; rather an ancient form of property confirmed by the treaties uniting Brittany to France'.[15] And lest the point be missed, they quoted the last article of the newly voted Declaration of the Rights of Man which endorsed the 'inviolable and sacred' status of property under the new order. So treaty terms remained sacrosanct, and so did the property of the church and enfeoffed nobility? Not necessarily; the villagers of Conquereuil who had earlier stigmatised the burdens of the feudal regime, happily endorsed the anti-seigneurial legislation of 4–11 August, while refusing to budge on the issue of provincial privilege. But an expedient acceptance that Bretons should not stand alone now that all around were changing their opinions is perhaps the dominant message of these documents. The parishioners of La Chapelle Glain started off their meeting with a unanimous resolution to stand firm behind the ramparts of their province, yet doubts set in as the discussion developed. In the end they decided to empower their delegate to adopt the majority viewpoint, whatever that might prove to be.

This was wise. Most of the towns of Brittany were ardently patriotic and it is possible, even likely, that the National Assembly attracted greater groundswell support elsewhere in the province. In the *sénéchaussée* of Ploërmel, for instance, the question of Breton 'freedoms' seems not to have generated much heat. Besides, few, if any, of the other deputies representing *pays d'états* were prepared to make a stand. Those of Provence moved swiftly to defuse tension between the new nation in the making and the revivified constitution of Provence that they were pledged to obtain. Once the deputies had ensured the acquiescence of commissioners despatched by the communities, this project became little more than a pipe dream. Even so, it is worth stressing that the fusion of allegiances that the August legislation was designed to achieve was not a foregone conclusion. Provençaux, like Bretons, retained a powerful sense of separate identity. Indeed, they were taught from childhood that their country was a state apart and one which had only been attached to France by a treaty between equals. Despite the blandishments of their delegates, a hard core of Provençal communities firmly refused to renounce privileges dating back to the fifteenth century.

Regionalist sentiment remained potent in Burgundy, too. Here a tradition of administration by Provincial Estates – unbroken since 1543 – posed problems of institutional as well as psychological transition which would not be quickly overcome (see below pp. 193–4). Yet traditionalism and inertia were not the only forces to be reckoned with as the deputies strove to convert the vision of 4 August into a manageable political reality. The old monarchy's administrative reforms had stirred hopes and ambitions in regions hitherto regarded as composing the nucleus of the kingdom. After all, the king had signalled support *both* for a system of regional government based on Provincial Assemblies and for one based on Provincial Estates (the latter in the *séance royale*). It remained to be seen how, and whether, such bodies could be fitted in to the newly defined nation. The case of the Dauphiné is worth recalling in this respect. For, having retrieved the right to hold annual Estates in 1788 after a lapse of 160 years, there was naturally some reluctance to forfeit this 'privilege' in the name of the wider community only a year or so later. But the attempt to reconvene the Estates for November 1789 appeared presumptuous enough, and when the National Assembly learned that representatives would be called by 'order' its irritation knew no bounds. Merely allowing the provinces to organise assemblies during this critical period of transition seemed foolhardy, and despite the protests of the Monarchiens the deputies moved swiftly to outlaw any kind of assembly that acknowledged the principle of orders.

The dissidence of companies and corporate bodies was dealt with in similar fashion. On 3 November the *parlements* were 'buried alive', to use Mirabeau's striking phrase. That is to say, they were kept on permanent summer vacation until such time as they could be replaced with a fresh system of courts. This decision produced both squeals of anger and acts of defiance: with studied insolence the *parlementaires* of Toulouse questioned the authority of 'the deputies of the *bailliages*',[16] while their counterparts in Metz and Rennes went further and challenged the legitimacy of decrees emanating from the Assembly. The deputies responded calmly and firmly which suggests a growing confidence in their role as national arbiters. No doubt the attitude of the country at large helped to boost that confidence, for, at the least sign of resistance from privileged interests, the towns rushed sustaining addresses to Versailles. Thus the towns (and many villages) of the Dauphiné signalled their opposition to the scheme to reconvene the Estates, while the burghers of Metz and Rennes reproved the behaviour of their *parlements*. The immediate reaction of the Assembly was to summon the dissident *parlementaires* to Paris for a public dressing down, but, on a surety provided by the patriots of Metz, the deputies relented. Nevertheless, all eleven judges of the *chambre des vacations* of the Rennes Parlement were called to account. On 8 January 1790, in a session heavy with symbolism, the judges were kept waiting before being admitted to the bar of the Assembly in an atmosphere of utter silence. Unnerved, the president sought shelter in the privileges of Brittany which, it was claimed, could only be altered by consent of the Estates.

Stern silence and public censure were the preferred weapons of a body not yet entirely convinced of its sovereignty. For the mission to redraw and rebuild the nation did not emerge, phoenix-like, from the ashes of the *ancien régime* on the night of 4–5 August 1789. Nor, for that matter, did the National Assembly inherit the absolutist habits of the old monarchy, as some historians have argued.[17] Such habits had been discontinued before the Revolution broke. Indeed, the funereal appearance before the Assembly of the Rennes magistrates triggered a two-day debate which exposed continuing divisions among the deputies on the issue of sovereignty. Now that the task of renovating the structures of the state looked likely to take longer than anyone had anticipated, some deputies argued that ancient constitutions like that of Brittany should be allowed to subsist on an interim basis. In which case the plea of the Rennes *parlementaires* was not without foundation.

But that was in January 1790, by which time the influence of those deputies drawn from the most conservative wing of the old First and Second Estates had reached its zenith (see below p. 213). Thereafter the balance of power within the Assembly tilted as the commoners became better organised and more confident of the support of public opinion. Indeed, the spring brought signs of a separation in the ranks of the patriots, distancing the early heroes of the Revolution (Bailly, Lafayette, etc.) from a more tough-minded bunch of deputies grouped around the Lameth brothers and Barnave. This was the context which made possible a final rupturing of the delicate umbilical linking the new France to the 'society of orders' of the *ancien régime*. On 19 June 1790 the deputies voted to obliterate the distinction between political and honorific privilege with a decree abolishing hereditary nobility and all the titles and perquisites attached thereto. In tones of evident approval the non-noble member for Le Mans, François Ménard de la Groye, reported the 'ending ever more of this vain and tiresome prejudice which by attributing distinctions to the hazard of birth separates what is called noble blood from what passes for commoner blood'.[18] More thoughtful minds than Ménard's were deeply disturbed by the decree, however. 'Equality of condition is desired', remarked a Toulouse barrister on learning the news, 'I do not know where it will end. I do not think it can result in anything good. Subordination is necessary otherwise we will fall into anarchy.'[19] Nobles, for their part, were stunned by a turn of events which few had anticipated and which would now force a radical reappraisal of their role in the polity. Ferrières, the ever sensible deputy for the *sénéchaussée* of Saumur, simply told his wife to stop writing to him as 'Monsieur le Marquis', adding that she should have the arms of the family covered with a prudent coat of whitewash.[20] But the decree produced seething resentment in several parts of the kingdom and a perceptible drift from the national fold. When forty noblemen of the Puisaye signed a letter of protest, their action served only to ignite a vigorous anti-seigneurial movement throughout the region.

Rebuilding the nation

Despite the confusion and loss of momentum at the start of the Estates General, the task confronting the deputies in the early summer of 1789 still looked relatively straightforward. They were to draw up a constitution and present it to the monarch for his signature. This would take months rather than weeks; nevertheless, everyone expected to be home by the end of the year. The Paris revolt, followed by insurrection in the provinces, placed that timetable in serious jeopardy. But what really lengthened the agenda were the promises made on 4–5 August. Thereby, the National Assembly committed itself to a legislative programme that would take two years and more to complete. In the process the business of drafting a constitution got bogged down as properly constitutional and administrative laws became hopelessly intertwined. Seeking to tidy up their handiwork in September 1791, the exhausted deputies would acknowledge that theirs had been a transitional regime. Now that the nation had been redrawn and rebuilt on fresh foundations, the period of turmoil would surely come to an end. But what were these foundations in which the deputies placed so much confidence? How new were the institutions erected on them? And how would the deputies negotiate the complex legacy of administrative monarchy?

It makes sense to take the last question first, for there is a commonplace assumption that the summer's unrest plunged the country into a power vacuum. Whereupon new institutions, staffed by a new personnel equipped with a new political mentality, sprang into existence. In fact, this was rarely, if ever, the case. Even in Paris during the long weekend of 11–14 July, the power vacuum was of a few hours' duration at most. Many of the major towns experienced municipal 'revolutions' either in July or August, it is true. But these tended to recycle familiar (bourgeois) faces in the shape of committees that were often content to share executive authority with preexisting institutions. For the apparatus of royal power did not wither overnight. Indeed, much of it continued to function, albeit in a subdued fashion, pending decisions by the deputies as to how they wished to reconstruct the kingdom.

The intendants were the most hated agents of administrative monarchy and many of them fled. After all the fate of Bertier *fils*, intendant of Paris, at the hands of an irate crowd which associated him with the concentration of troops around the capital was no incitement to linger. Yet the bureaux of the intendancies often continued to transact business throughout the autumn and winter. Amelot de Chaillou, intendant of Dijon, retreated to Paris, but left his staff with instructions to carry on with their work as best they could. Esmangart of Lille also did his utmost to maintain administrative continuity. In January 1790 his officials forwarded to all communities the Municipal Law of 14 December 1789, that is to say the first fruits of the Assembly's reform labours. At Tours, too, the wheels of the government's bureaucracy continued to turn, albeit at reduced speed. Denis-Nicolas Genty, the subdelegate-general, kept up a running correspondence with his absent chief which sheds precious light on the distribution of powers during this period of transition. Everyone was still turning up for work, he assured the intendant in mid-October, but the load had diminished, not least because the 'permanent committee' of Tours had taken over responsibility for provisioning the city. Relief at having got rid of this chore was nonetheless mixed with sadness at the diminished status of the intendancy. It had become little more than a clearing-house, he reported on 25 November, for the dissemination of the decrees of the National Assembly.

Aged seventy and with a proven record of nearly fifty years in government offices, Genty was worried about his future. For the executive arm of absolute monarchy had no future, he concluded: 'by the time the Estates General separate there will no longer remain any traces of the intendancies'.[21] His best guess, proffered in October 1789, was that the Provincial Assemblies would now take over the business of administration in the provinces, in tandem with a new hierarchy of courts which would be entrusted with the judicial powers of the intendants. Others were thinking along similar lines, and from July until October it looked as though the Provincial Assemblies might stage a political comeback. In a sense they had never ceased to function, for, although Necker had put the annual plenary sessions of the Assemblies on hold in November 1788, their executive steering committees (*commissions intermédiaires*) continued to meet. Also, no one had bothered to discontinue the experiment with Municipal Assemblies. At any rate, while the deputies cast around for a suitable model of local government reform, these bodies, like the expiring intendancies, kept some of the basic functions of government intact. In the Lyonnais, for instance, the *commission intermédiaire* took over the patriotic duty of ensuring that the rural population continued to pay taxes, while its counterpart in Lorraine attempted to dispel the confusion surrounding the legislation of 4–11 August. A printed circular dated 18 December 1789 tried delicately to point out that the statement 'the National Assembly destroys in its entirety the feudal regime'[22] should not be taken at face value. Equally, the Municipal Assemblies elected in the late summer of 1787 continued to function in many localities. Indeed, they had important new responsibilities thrust upon them: policing the grain trade, assessing the harvest and enforcing martial law, to name just a few.

A third source of power resided in the Provincial Estates, or to be more accurate in the powerful executive organs that had developed to maintain continuity between sessions. The National Assembly viewed these bodies with suspicion as we have seen. In fact it abolished the Estates of Brittany on 5 November and instructed the *commission intermédiaire* to wind up its affairs by 31 December 1789. But there were difficulties in this manner of proceeding, for it threatened to leave large areas of the kingdom without any government whatsoever. Also the deputies were hampered by the reluctance of the king's ministers to take executive action to liquidate institutions which the monarchy had relied upon in order to raise revenue. The case of Burgundy is eloquent in this regard. Here the Estates had last met in 1787 and since they were not due to reassemble until 1790, the day-to-day running of the province fell to the Elus (see above p. 36). The immediate consequence of the

Revolution was to enhance their power. For, in the absence of the intendant and the Parlement of Dijon (in recess), the Elus would represent the only properly constituted source of authority until the Department administrations were elected in May–June 1790. As such they continued to handle the ongoing business of the old regime (mainly public works), mixed up with the incoming business of the new. There were the tax rolls for 1790 to be got ready, the *contribution patriotique*, and the special levy on the privileged to cover the last six months of 1789. No mean task for a body of men who had vigorously resisted equality of taxation in 1787.

After a tussle over accounts and paperwork with the new authorities, the Elus eventually stopped working in the summer of 1790. Even so, the archives of the Estates were not finally handed over until April 1791. The Provincial Assemblies stepped down with more dignity, between June and September 1790, whereas the Municipal Assemblies all ceased functioning just as soon as the Revolutionary municipalities were elected in February and March of that year. For many of these bodies, of course, the act of dissolution was a moment of joyful communion. When presenting its accounts to the newly elected officials of the Rhône-et-Loire department on 30 June 1790, the executive of the Lyonnais Assembly expressed its satisfaction in no uncertain terms: 'Messieurs, we are handing over to you the service vested in the Provincial Assembly by the edict of June 1787. This body was, in many respects, the precursor to the fully constitutional administrative bodies bestowed on a nation restored to liberty by the decrees of the legislature and the sanction of the best of kings.'[23]

What finally turned the deputies against the Provincial Assemblies was the realisation that general acquiescence in the decrees abolishing corporate privilege could not be taken for granted. Already, in September, they had voted decisively against the establishment of a two-chamber legislature. This put paid to residual notions, traceable to Brienne, that the Assemblies might provide the political reservoir for a Senate. Now, the news reaching Paris in November that several *parlements* and local Estates were unenthusiastic about the new concept of the nation persuaded the deputies that the retention of any institution that might sustain provincial loyalties was too big a risk to take. Genty captured this transition well in his correspondence with the expatriated intendant of Tours. On 25 November he reported on 'the current plan to remove all vestiges of the former constitution and administration. The kingdom will no longer be divided into provinces, the very names of which are abolished, but into eighty departments of roughly equal area.'[24] This was a momentous decision indeed. For it brought to a conclusion both the venerable centralising traditions of Bourbon absolutism and the more recent experiment with consultative bodies (Assemblies and Estates).

The first phase of the new infrastructure plan consisted of drawing boundaries on a map of France and of identifying future capitals and central places. Showing remarkable energy, the deputies completed the bulk of this task in under three months. Edmund Burke mockingly remarked that the exercise required no great legislative talent, 'nothing more than an accurate land surveyor, with his chain, sight and theodolite',[25] but this was far from the case. Changing the status quo of centuries triggered unimaginable numbers of local rivalries. The Assembly's Constitution Committee, which was in charge of the operation, found itself besieged by petitioners from all over the country. Notwithstanding these pressures, a definitive list of eighty-three departments was ready for promulgation by mid-January 1790. The following month the question of labels was settled. Nature was pressed into service in order to disguise historic origins and more recent urban rivalries. Thus the department of the Aveyron (alias the province of the Rouergue, alias the hinterland of the towns of Rodez, Villefranche and Millau) was named after the most inconspicuous river running through its territory.

The second phase of the operation began in earnest in February 1790 and continued to the end of June. This was to give administrative life to the new territorial divisions in place of the intendancies, Estates and *commissions intermédiaires* whose existence was now drawing to a close. Even before the issue of the departments had been settled, the deputies had agreed on the necessity for at least two subdivisions: one at the base and one at an intermediate level. Most towns already possessed municipal institutions of some description, and after much discussion it was decided that every 'town, *bourg*, parish or community'[26] should enjoy the right to manage its affairs as well. This base unit eventually became known as the 'commune', whereas the principal intermediate division of the department was labelled the 'district'. The deputies also defined a constituency which they dubbed the 'canton'. It grouped together a number of communes, but for electoral and judicial rather than administrative purposes. By the spring of 1790, therefore, the new department of the Aveyron which had hitherto been ruled from Montauban (seat of the intendancy) and Villefranche-de-Rouergue (seat of the Provincial Administration of Haute-Guienne) was subdivided territorially into nine districts, eighty-one cantons and 684 communes. More to the point, each commune boasted an elected municipality, while separate administrations would shortly be voted into being in the district seats, and a department administration in the capital, Rodez.

The impact of these changes should not be underestimated. Not least because the territorial restructuring of the civil administration provided a template for the restructuring of the judiciary and the church. In the north and north-east of the kingdom, particularly, the redrawing of boundaries paid scant attention to the administrative geography of the old regime. Burgundy, for instance, was completely dismembered as was the Ile-de-France. No wonder one of the first official acts of the Yonne department authorised a local entrepreneur to remove the pillar marking the border between Burgundy and France and to sell it off. The costs of the operation to the towns could be no less damaging. For the claims of around 800 administrative and ecclesiastical centres had somehow to be reconciled with the fact that the new order made available only 444 department and district seats. The number of bishoprics alone dropped from 136 to 83 in the course of 1790. Nevertheless, it is easy to be dazzled by the spectacle of change and to miss the threads of continuity in consequence. Some smaller provinces contrived to pilot their way through the wreckage of the *ancien régime*; the case of the Rouergue has been mentioned. And even larger entities such as Brittany, Languedoc and Provence managed to handle the challenge to their integrity with remarkable aplomb – testimony perhaps to the committee skills of their deputies. The sleight of hand performed by the National Assembly in decreeing the establishment of elective municipalities should not pass unnoticed either. For quasi-representative Municipal Assemblies already existed in large parts of the kingdom, as we know. Even the electoral *cens* which the constituents devised to curb the excesses of popular sovereignty had its forerunner in Brienne's edicts. As the king is alleged to have commented on inspecting the text of the new Municipal Law: 'it is an improvement on our proposals'.[27]

What founding principles guided the deputies in their work of reconstruction? As François Furet rightly observes, the final product represented a compromise between rationalism and empiricism, between a desire for uniformity and a commitment to local autonomy.[28] The more hairbrained schemes for a geometrical division of territory, or perhaps one proportional to population, soon had to be given up, if only because they ignored the economic and social weight of the cities. Instead, the Assembly tempered its zeal for uniformity in the knowledge that the remodelling of the kingdom must secure the immediate political objectives of the Revolution. These were three in number: decentralisation (in order to destroy the threat of a resurgence of monarchical absolutism); dismemberment (in order to curb provincialism); and accountability (in order to give institutional root to the nation as now defined). Within these parameters the deputies seem to have mandated their Constitution Committee to produce a blueprint that did no more violence to historic boundaries, ecological imperatives and local habits than was strictly necessary. The weak link in the chain turned out to be the district administrations, and before the year was out there was talk of abolishing them. By contrast, the new municipalities put down sturdy roots. Of all the institutions founded by the National Assembly, they did most to convert the new ethos of the nation into a reality (see below p. 222).

Reform of the judiciary, of jurisdictions and of jurisprudence had been discussed for decades. First Maupeou and then Lamoignon had pushed through major programmes of restructuring (see above pp. 136–8), before being jettisoned by Louis XVI. The problem as with so many of the reform intentions of the old monarchy, was that it touched on too many raw nerves. Only pamphlet writers could afford to tackle the theme of judicial restructuring in a vacuum. For royal bureaucrats the subject raised thorny issues of constitutional propriety and financial management. There was also the disincentive that public opinion tended to rally behind beleaguered courts in the belief that 'reform' sought to eradicate 'jurisdictional power' so as to advance the cause of 'ministerial despotism'. All of this was to change in 1789. The unedifying spectacle of the Parlement of Paris urging the king to adopt a hard line during the *séance royale*, the decisions to abolish venality and seigneurial justice taken in August, and the decree of 3 November effectively suspending the judicial functions of the sovereign courts created a window of opportunity. And if that was not enough, the malevolent obstructionism of some companies of magistrates provided proof that the entire edifice needed to be rebuilt from scratch.

Yet this summary tends to abbreviate and to simplify the shifts of opinion on the subject of reform. Once again, we must listen to what was being said in the provinces as well as Versailles and Paris. The first intimations that a sharp break with the past was in prospect came on 17 August 1789 when the deputy Bergasse presented the first thoughts of the Constitution Committee on how criminal and civil jurisdiction might be organised under the new order. These reveal a vision of institutional uniformity and, in embryo, a hierarchy of courts in which the *parlements* no longer play a significant role. Over the following months this vision was brought into alignment with the territorial redrawing of the kingdom for administrative purposes, with the result that in late December the Committee confirmed its intention to use the departments, districts and cantons as rungs in a new ladder of law courts. However, provincial opinion remained out of step with these developments. Many observers appear to have expected a return to Lamoignon's style of reform. After all, his *grands bailliages* had been welcomed in several parts of the kingdom, notwithstanding *parlementaire* hostility. 'When the question of the new organisation of courts comes up', wrote the *patriotes* of Brest to their deputies on 9 November, 'you must be sure to solicit for Brest a *présidial* and a *consulat*.'[29]

The distance travelled in the sixteen months since Lamoignon had been hounded from office finally became apparent on 24 March when the National Assembly decided, by an overwhelming vote, 'to reconstruct the entire judicial order'.[30] Henceforward, justice would be dispensed at three levels: by criminal courts distributed on the basis of one per department; by civil courts operating in each and every district division; and by justices of the peace whose constituency was confined to the canton. Appellate jurisdiction would be exercised by a single high court (*tribunal de cassation*) whose powers of intervention were mainly procedural. The symmetry of this new 'judicial order' is perhaps its most arresting feature, for, in truth, only the institution of the *juge de paix* marked a complete break with the past. The real departure lay in the principles upon which the structure was built. The privatised justice of seigneurs had been outlawed on 4–5 August 1789, and special courts (for taxes, to enforce the salt monopoly, forest code, etc.) would follow in short order. But these changes had been foreshadowed in Lamoignon's edicts; the major innovation lay in the deputies' determination to eradicate venality in the judiciary. Henceforth all judges would be elected (like the new administrative personnel) by their fellow citizens, and for a fixed term. Since court judges could no longer rely on fees paid by litigants, they would also be salaried. For defendants and plaintiffs, the changes offered the prospect of cheaper, more accessible justice and, in criminal cases, trial by jury. Some attempt was even made to disentangle 'police' from law enforcement, thereby clarifying, if not entirely resolving, the confusion of powers under which the *ancien-régime* courts had operated.

Despite general agreement on the framework for the new courts, the task of putting the structure in place took longer than anyone anticipated. Most of the paving legislation was on the statute book by late August 1790, having been delayed by parliamentary discussion of appeals and disputes over the physical location of judges and law courts. But the first elections did not take place until November, and most justices of the peace and district tribunals did not open for business until the start of the following year. As for the departmental criminal courts, they only came into being in early 1792, several months after the deputies of the first Assembly had dispersed. In these circumstances it was fortunate that the village-level seigneurial courts continued to operate, despite the anathemas pronounced against them on the night of 4–5 August. Most appear to have disbanded in the final months of 1790, although the administrators of the department of Maine-et-Loire complained that seigneurial personnel were still holding audiences in the spring of 1791. More widespread was the view that the reform had achieved a laudable improvement in judicial provision at the grass-roots, while diluting significantly the facilities for redress available to city dwellers. As the date for the election of district judges approached, a correspondent of Barnave writing from Grenoble expostulated, 'how in all reason can it be imagined that, in two weeks' time, five judges and four deputies will replace three sovereign courts, five or six royal seats of justice, nearly one hundred inferior courts, and a legion of assorted magistrates!'[31] Grenoble had lost a *parlement*, a *chambre des comptes* and a *cour des aides*. Montpellier, by contrast, forfeited a *cour des aides* and a *présidial* consisting of twenty-eight office-holders, in return for a humble district court. Yet, despite this evidence of institutional rupture, it is interesting to note some threads of continuity. Three of the five judges elected to staff the district court of Montpellier were former magistrates of the *cour des aides*, and the new body contrived to inherit the furniture of the outgoing *présidial*.

Reconstruction of the Gallican church started adventitiously on the night of 4–5 August with a proposal to commute the tithe and a move to surrender *casuel* fees. Only the latter had been clearly foreshadowed in the *cahiers*, but the debates that followed brought to the surface a rich vein of anti-clericalism uniting the deputies of the Second and Third Estates. Rapidly, the questioning of the tithe shifted towards outright abolition, while on 7 August a noble deputy uttered for the first time the suggestion that financial collapse could be averted by means of a loan secured on the possessions of the church. After all, the church was a bloated corporation whose wealth lay beyond the fence erected around private property in the Declaration of the Rights of Man. But the point at issue was not so much wealth as power, for the catholic church enjoyed near autonomy as a self-taxing and self-financing institution. As such, its continued existence was inimical to the dawning concept of the nation. Whether the clerical deputies grasped the implications of an uncompensated surrender of the tithe is not entirely clear, but no one could have mistaken the purpose behind the steady encroachment upon the fixed assets of the church which took place over the next couple of months. A church despoiled might yet mean a nation saved from the abyss of bankruptcy; it would certainly mean a church reduced in status and quite incapable of resisting interference by the secular power.

Ominous signs that the Assembly would not hesitate to don the reform mantle of the old monarchy if given the chance were evident from the start. Even as the fate of the tithe hung in the balance, clerical pluralism was condemned and a deputy intimated that the work of the Commission des Réguliers be carried to its logical conclusion with the requirement that all remaining monastic orders be disbanded. In fact, the blow felling religious houses was not delivered until 13 February 1790, but the reverberations it caused prompted the first serious stock-taking of the business of reconstruction. Senior prelates again called for assurances that none of the reforms would jeopardise the preeminent role of catholicism in the French state, while the laity began to reckon up the costs as well as the benefits of institutional reform. In many towns and villages the closure of monasteries and abbeys would bring only the promise of economic dislocation and grinding hardship for the poor. Anxiety over the spiritual status of the catholic church can be traced to the partial rehabilitation of French Calvinism which Brienne and Malesherbes had engineered in 1787 (see above p. 131). In this respect, the listing of freedom of conscience among the fundamental 'rights of man' was scarcely calculated to allay the fears of the clergy. The issue resurfaced in April 1790 when a Carthusian monk, Dom Gerle, tried once more to secure the future with a motion that catholicism be considered the religion of state, and the only religion entitled to hold public acts of worship. Still largely anti-clerical in outlook, the Assembly refused to be led in the direction of sectarian politics. Besides, its Ecclesiastical Committee had plans of its own for the future.

Proposals for a structural reform of the Gallican church, otherwise known as the Civil Constitution of the Clergy, were presented for discussion on 29 May. They were approved by the deputies on 12 July and submitted to the king for his sanction and official promulgation. Despite serious misgivings, Louis had agreed to perform these formalities by the end of August. Only papal endorsement remained outstanding, but the signs were none too promising. Pius VI had expressed (privately) his hostility to the doctrine of popular sovereignty and religious toleration earlier in the year, and in the meantime the Assembly had become embroiled in the politics of the papal enclave of Avignon and the Comtat which it would eventually annex. In the absence of an official response from the pope, the deputies decided to press ahead with the reform in any case. However, the bishops demurred at this attempt to force the pace, whereupon the Assembly took a fateful decision on 26 November 1790 to require all priests with pastoral responsibilities to swear an oath of loyalty to the Civil

Constitution. The pope finally declared his hostility to the programme of reform in March and April of the following year.

The proposals tabled by the Ecclesiastical Committee took the precarious position of the church since the dawn raid on its privileges to its logical conclusion. Henceforward the boundaries of the dioceses would be redrawn to match those of the departments, and the parish structure in town and country rationalised. Immediately, therefore, nearly one third of the episcopate were earmarked for redundancy and, by implication, a considerable number of parish clergy would find themselves out of a job in due course as well. In any case the ecclesiastical hierarchy was to be streamlined, that is to say confined to those occupying the three basic grades of bishop, rector and curate. This sounded the death-knell for cathedral chapters and the host of unbeneficed clergy and contemplatives. The reformed state church would be a lean institution, and one which conformed to the (secular) spirit of the nation. In consequence, all future vacancies would be filled by ballot, employing the electoral assemblies used to designate district and department administrators. Thus, popular sanction (which might include the votes of non-catholics) rather than canonical institution, became the new modus operandi. The archbishop of Aix protested that these changes failed to acknowledge the higher source of ecclesiastical authority, only to be told brutally that 'the church is part of the state. The state is not part of the church.'[32]

Most of the items on this agenda would have been familiar to the reforming monarchs of *ancien-régime* Europe. Nevertheless, the verdict of a recent historian that the Civil Constitution of the Clergy was an 'amazingly radical' piece of legislation is not misplaced.[33] Neither the desacralising thrust of Bourbon government in the 1770s and 1780s, nor the winds of change blowing through the ranks of the lower clergy suffice on their own to explain the religious policy of the National Assembly. Nor does the great awakening occasioned by the drafting of the *cahiers de doléances* shed much light. The Third Estate was certainly preoccupied with clerical discipline, the need to unblock channels of promotion and to eradicate surplice fees (the *casuel*), but the economic might of the church attracted little comment, and scarcely anyone remarked on the need for organisational reform, or for the lay election of the clergy. Instead, the policy seems to have evolved out of the set of circumstances confronting the deputies in the autumn of 1789, exacerbated, no doubt, by the descent into quasi-party politics (see below p. 213) during the late winter and spring of 1790.

Thereafter, the radical momentum driving forward church reform came from two sources. The clerical oath turned religion into a matter of police and public order in the sense that enforcement and the disciplining of recalcitrants became the dominant issue. Meanwhile, the day-to-day business of implementing the Civil Constitution was handed down to the freshly installed local authorities whose secular vehemence far surpassed that of the National Assembly. Throughout 1791 these bodies made the running; measuring up church properties for auction, organising the replacement of non-jurors and designating parishes for disestablishment. The deputies reacted uneasily, as well they might. Informed of events back in Le Mans, Ménard de la Groye remarked to his wife that 'the zeal of our administrators has carried them away, and they would have done better not to abolish such a large number of parishes'.[34] A month or so later, in June 1791, we find him worrying about the ruthless amalgamation of parishes in the surrounding country-side. 'But how can we here', he asks, 'prevent what has been jointly agreed between the directories of the District and the Department and Monseigneur the Bishop?'[35] The note of frustration aptly conveys the mounting sense of foreboding as the deputies contemplated the prospect of the nation divided over a gratuitously radical reform programme that was now threatening to come apart at the seams.

At least the decision to confiscate all the assets of the church, taken on 25 June 1790, created a financial breathing space. For it established a credible backing for a new paper currency to be known as the *assignat*. Some respite on this front was sorely needed since the events of 1789 had done nothing to resolve the balance of payments crisis confronting the monarchy. On the contrary it was growing worse as tax receipts dwindled, while expenditure started to escalate. Sooner or later the deputies would have to turn their attention towards a restructuring of state finances and the fiscal regime, just as they had set about the task of reform and reconstruction in other areas. The argument for acting sooner was social as well as economic, for the hue-and-cry against indirect taxes threatened to impede the restoration of law and order. Certain taxes (the *gabelle*, the *aides*, the *octrois*) were abolishing themselves willy nilly. Fortunately, the expedient of nationalising the property of the church was found in time to ward off financial collapse. However, the argument for acting later eventually carried the day. Designing a new tax system was bound to take time, even if the deputies could have agreed on first principles. Besides, a prompt escape from financial embarrassment was not, perhaps, in the best interests of the Revolution as a whole. Distrust of the executive, of a monarchy rejuvenated by a reliable cash-flow, remained paramount. In the event, though, the deputies were simply too busy to make quicker progress than they did. As a result a hybrid and transitional fiscal regime continued in force for most of the period of the National Assembly.

According to the carefully prepared financial statement which Brienne submitted to the king in April 1788, forecast expenditure for that year was likely to be 630m *livres*, whereas income was unlikely to exceed 472m *livres*. A crude shortfall of 158m *livres*, therefore. But analysis of these figures exposes the true extent of the problem facing the monarchy. Over 300 million or 49.3 per cent of expenditure was being earmarked each year to service the national debt (most of which was unconsolidated), compared with 28 per cent in 1751 and 39 per cent in 1775. Moreover, the composition of anticipated income was distinctly unhealthy with 46.4 per cent expected to derive from duties on the movement and consumption of goods and only 34.5 per cent from direct taxes. The energy which ministers devoted to widening and evening out the tax base in the 1770s and 1780s thus takes on a fuller significance, for it seems that *ancien-régime* France was not so much a high taxation state as one in which taxes were maldistributed.[36] However, the immediate difficulties confronting the deputies stemmed from the political and social collapse of the summer of 1789. Both direct and indirect tax receipts nosedived. For the year beginning on 1 May 1789, the latter yielded just 59m *livres* compared with 206m in 1788. Over the same period total tax receipts dropped from a (projected) 472m to 299m *livres*. Or, to define the crisis in quantitative terms, the tax 'take' expressed as a proportion of gross national product declined from around 11 per cent in 1787 and 1788 to between 2 and 3 per cent in 1790, and perhaps 5 per cent in 1791.[37] What made this situation even more alarming was the fact that expenditure commitments were rising sharply as a result of the Assembly's own reform programme. The reimbursement of venal offices would cost 780m *livres* alone, and the wage bill for local government administrators, judges and ecclesiastics put the exchequer under additional strain. Between 1790 and the end of 1791 government expenditure would more than double.

How did the deputies react? Surprisingly for men whose rhetoric demanded the total liquidation of the *ancien régime*, they set themselves firmly against a repudiation of the national debt. Perhaps the patriot party counted too many rentiers and stock-holders in its ranks. Not even a partial repudiation or a temporary suspension of interest payments was seriously contemplated. Instead, they committed themselves to refunding the unconsolidated debt and also that of the clergy, admittedly in paper money. Taxes, and above all indirect taxes, were the most pressing issue, however. For, unless the rural population could be persuaded to carry on paying, advances to the treasury from the various farms and *régies* would dry up. Every attempt was made therefore to prop up the existing financial structure, albeit purged of personal exemptions. In spite of evidence of massive non-compliance, the National Assembly declared in September 1789 that the salt tax would remain in force. Only the realisation that the violence would therefore continue indefinitely prompted its abolition in March 1790. For, as an assembly of municipal delegates held in February in the town of Pontivy pointed out, 'the removal of this monopoly is the only relief to have been enjoyed so far by country dwellers, the only one within their grasp, the one that makes them bless and defend the revolution'.[38] But this decision signalled no general retreat. Throughout 1790 the deputies reaffirmed their determination to retain the *aides* on beverages and the municipal tolls (*octrois, entrées*). The former were not abolished until March 1791, while excise duties on products entering the towns and cities finally lapsed a couple of months later. The state tobacco monopoly survived until 1791 as well.

On the whole these attempts to reverse the popular verdict of 1789 – to restore the toll booths – were not successful as we have seen. By September 1791 the old monarchy's long-nourished plan to roll back the customs posts to the national frontier had been finally achieved, though by a route that few had anticipated. The pendant to this short-term policy of clinging to established sources of revenue was an attempt to raise money from new quarters. Forms of privilege that conferred tax exemption were an obvious target. If little could be done immediately to redistribute the load as between *pays d'élections* and *pays d'états*, the inclusion of individuals enjoying personal immunities was a relatively straightforward matter. On 26 September 1789 the Assembly voted to bring all hitherto 'privilégiés' into the tax net and to assess them, moreover, for the last six months of the year. This, it was reckoned, would yield an extra 32 to 36m *livres* per annum, or roughly half the current yield of the *taille*.[39] The deputies also abolished compounding (*abonnement*), the process by which whole provinces negotiated special terms to cover their *vingtième* liabilities. A few days later a one-off income tax was invented 'to extract the fatherland from peril'. This 'patriotic contribution' fixed at 25 per cent was to be paid in instalments over the next two years. Those whose incomes fell below 400 *livres* per annum were invited simply to contribute whatever they could afford.

The trouble with all of these expedients was that they were introduced in a climate of non-compliance, and at a time when the deputies had forsworn the use of coercion and had barely begun the task of institutional renewal. With the best will in the world, the new municipalities found the compilation of supplementary tax rolls a daunting business, not least because the Assembly had decreed that taxes would henceforth be levied on property in its place of origin rather than on owners in their place of residence. Many villagers plainly expected a pro rata reduction in the liabilities of the existing taxpayers to match the receipts from formerly privileged citizens, too. After all, the interim commission of the Lyonnais Provincial Assembly unwisely announced that 'the proportional tax, to which nobles and the privileged have agreed for the last six months of this year, will be used to relieve ordinary taxpayers'.[40] But this was not at all the intention of the deputies, and a palpable sense of fiscal anti-climax, if not yet fiscal disappointment, began to develop. By mid-1790 over half of the supplementary rolls were in arrears, and in the meantime many other time-consuming fiscal chores had been devolved upon the municipalities.

Having been advised by their Finance Committee in January 1790 that it would be best not to attempt to establish 'an absolutely new and constitutional regime'[41] in matters of taxation until 1791, the deputies gladly concentrated on the existing agenda of reforms instead. Each retreat from indirect taxation was compensated for by adding an extra sum to the direct tax bill; but, of course, the compensation was illusory, for *taille* and *vingtième* payments were often being withheld as well. Not until the later summer did work on a new structure begin in earnest and it soon became apparent that the majority favoured an approach to the problem which betrayed an intellectual debt to Quesnay and the physiocrats. Henceforth consumption levies would play a minor role. Instead, the bulk of revenue would be raised by means of a land tax (*contribution foncière*), seconded by a poll or property tax (*contribution personnelle et mobilière*), and a modest tax on commercial activity (*patente*). Although the necessary legislation was not all voted in time, the changeover was scheduled for the start of 1791.

But this was easier said than done. How ought the new land tax be assessed and at what level? The duc de la Rochefoucauld, spokesman of the Tax Committee, declared that all land should be liable on a principle of 'proportional equality',[42] that is to say in proportion to its yield. However, no one knew for sure how to calculate the net revenue of the soil without first commissioning a comprehensive cadastral survey of all the land holdings in the kingdom. Experiments conducted on a small scale by the Provincial Assemblies and a handful of intendants had proved both arduous and acrimonious. Yet, such experiments had helped to produce a consensus that the land tax ought not to take more than one sixth of net income. The essential problem therefore remained one of collecting a new tax on the basis of old documentation. This was never resolved satisfactorily, at least not in the 1790s. Instead, the *contribution foncière* was determined by means of a quota and then distributed between the departments (decree of 27 May 1791). Although the most glaring discrepancies between provinces and between departments could be identified and removed, this mode of assessment resembled the system in force during the *ancien régime* and perpetuated many of its anomalies.

Intimations that a tax structure geared very largely to the product of the soil would escalate the perceived burden on land-owners began to dawn in the autumn of 1790. Nadaud, another employee of the intendancy of Tours, reported to his former boss in November that 'to judge from reports of decrees in the newspapers, taxes are likely to be very considerable and to bear down on everybody. I even fear that in place of the reduction we were led to hope for, we will suffer a very considerable increase.'[43] Clearly the deputies were worried, too, for on 24 June 1791, in the aftermath of the king's attempted flight, they issued a proclamation seeking to reassure French men and women that they were paying less tax than in the days of 'tyranny'. Had they been paying taxes at all, the burden would have been about the same. However, the more flagrant anomalies were now receiving attention. In the Cambrésis the per capita incidence of taxation rose sharply, which helps to make sense of the malevolent hostility of its Estates to the legislation of 4-11 August 1789. Likewise in Brittany where the burden of direct taxation on individuals appears nearly to have doubled. On the other hand, poor plot holders and the landless, or nearly so, do seem to have benefited. Indeed, many agricultural labourers now fell outside the tax net altogether. Lightening the overall load was probably never a realistic option, but the deputies of the National Assembly did put in place the foundations of what was to become a fairer tax system in the years ahead.

The reconstruction of local government, of the judiciary, the church and the fiscal apparatus of state was a signal achievement. It marked an undeniable break with the past. Collectively, the deputies succeeded in overcoming resistances and in rationalising inconsistencies which had stymied the reform efforts of royal bureaucrats for a generation and more. Their success can be attributed to two factors, one negative and one positive. The dwindling of royal authority from the summer of 1788 onwards created unique conditions for an alternative reform strategy, while the emergence in the spring and summer of 1789 of a potent ideology of nationhood enabled the Assembly to outbid and to neutralise hitherto powerful sectional interests. Nevertheless, it is important to avoid drawing too sharp a contrast between the old regime and the new. The legacy of reforming absolutism was not lost; often enough it was extended to those parts of the kingdom, or to those social groups, which had offered resistance in the past, and then repackaged in more appropriate wrappers. Thus we must allow for a degree of continuity within the reform project, and a significant carry-over of personnel, particularly in the higher reaches of government (see above pp. 120–1). The second point that needs emphasising is that the stewardship exercised by the National Assembly was transitional in the extreme. 'New' institutions could not be got up overnight, nor 'old' ones quickly demolished. With the result that the entire period from the launching of Calonne's reform initiative in February 1787 to the dissolution of the National Assembly in September 1791 takes on a rather makeshift quality. This, in turn, raises the question that we must tackle next. For, if the deputies finally succeeded in endowing the country with renovated institutions, did they also succeed in generating the 'new man' whose role was to make the system work?

The search for consensus

Some historians view the 'new man' of the Revolution as primarily a product of the knowledge-based culture of the Enlightenment. This socially indeterminate being believed in the power of ideas and the capacity of well-intentioned legislators to construct institutions that would answer to all human needs. Since all human needs were knowable and convergent, the task of regeneration called for little more than mechanical skills. Therefore, once the national purpose had been identified, the exercise of the general will would bring it into fruition. Expressions of doubt or dissent were unlikely to occur, and, if they did, could be safely assumed to emanate from sources extraneous to the general will. According to this line of argument, the National Assembly would adopt an uncompromising vision of its role and a style of politics to match. The search for consensus found no place in this totalising vision, for a politics of balance and compromise would serve only to acknowledge the existence of divergent interests within society.

An alternative approach might be to posit a social dimension to divergent interests; in which case the 'new man' of 1789 becomes a representative of what historians sometimes refer to as the 'revolutionary bourgeoisie'. The rationalising zeal of these sons of the Enlightenment is not diminished, but is focused instead on the class interests of the bourgeoisie. Pressed to its logical conclusion, this line of argument casts doubt upon the insistent claim of the deputies of the National Assembly that they were acting on behalf of the nation as a whole. Equally dubious would be the claim that they embodied the general will. The tax franchise which instantly diluted the rights of millions of adult males, together with economic policies based on unfettered liberalism and individualism, suggest a very different reading of the legislative achievements of the National Assembly. In this scenario, the task facing the deputies was to pilot a safe passage between the shoals of a hostile aristocracy and the uncharted seas of Rousseauian direct democracy. If the formerly privileged orders were kept on board, just about, the precarious unity of the old Third Estate was irretrievably shattered by events on the Champ de Mars as the Assembly was preparing to wind itself up.

Neither of these views seems entirely satisfactory. For it is the contention of these pages that the 'new man' of 1789 was a strictly relative phenomenon. Far from pursuing brusque 'take it or leave it' policies, the deputies generally abated any bookish tendencies towards abstract reasoning with a strong dose of common sense and political realism. The reflex of sovereign intolerance of different points of view which some historians perceive as 'scripted' into the Revolution from the outset is also difficult to substantiate. If it is seriously suggested that the Terror was prefigured between 1789 and 1791, the behaviour of the Revolutionary crowd offers more scope for prophecy than does that of the deputies. But, equally, a class-based interpretation of the work of the National Assembly provides glib rather than truly convincing answers. Reconciling the concept of a 'revolutionary bourgeoisie' with the actual make-up of those in power (a mixture of middle-class professionals, clerics and landowners) is one problem; making sense of the broadly humanitarian thrust of the policies pursued after 1789 another. In fact, the agenda of reform looks less like a concerted attempt to secure power for the bourgeoisie than a negotiated bid reflecting the priorities of the late Enlightenment and those of administrative monarchy.

Let us agree, then, that the deputies of France's first National Assembly were neither ideologues who despised consensus politics, nor bourgeois Revolutionaries seeking class hegemony. They were fairly ordinary men with tenacious local loyalties whose proficiency and credibility as politicians rarely extended beyond the confines of their home provinces. Nonetheless, they were united by education, and found themselves speaking a broadly convergent language of reform when pitched on to a higher stage. Yet still they found it difficult to stabilise the Revolution around a common set of institutions. Why? The biggest institutional challenge facing the deputies was the drafting of a constitution. The definitive version of this document was presented to the king on 3 September 1791 and the news of his acceptance of the role of constitutional monarch several days later produced a ripple of public rejoicing across the land. Nevertheless, the celebrations were less than wholehearted, for the business had thrown up a number of intractable problems. The British ambassador to France had not been alone when he predicted as early as April 1791 that 'the present constitution has no friends and cannot last'.[44]

The obvious problem was where to draw the line between the (executive) power of the monarch and the (legislative) authority of the Assembly. And, having drawn that line, how to get the various parts of the constitution to combine with minimum friction. This latter mechanical problem threatened to bedevil the operation of the new machinery of state at every level from the relations of ministers with the Assembly to the functioning of the humblest rural municipality. As early as August 1789 a group of deputies gathered around Mounier – the hero of the Dauphiné resistance – began to worry that the Revolution was slipping out of control. Ideally, these Monarchiens would have restored to Louis XVI the power to dissolve the Assembly, but failing that they wished him to retain a role in the legislative process by means of a veto. And to curb the independence of the legislature, they proposed the creation of an upper house whose composition could be influenced by the king. This strategy was reminiscent of that of Brienne, for it envisaged a partnership with the elites already risen to prominence in the Provincial Assemblies, under firm executive leadership. Indeed, a number of the Monarchiens had been confidants of the disgraced minister. What it failed to acknowledge was that the Revolution had moved on. The taking of the Bastille, agrarian insurrection, the night of 4–5 August had all happened, and the clock could not be turned back. Moreover, the proposals emanating from the Monarchien-dominated Constitution Committee placed enormous trust in the continued goodwill of the monarch. If politically unsophisticated parishes in Brittany were suspicious of the absolute veto in the belief that it would enable the privileged orders to retrieve what they had 'sacrificed' on 4–5 August, it is scarcely surprising that the deputies balked. In the end they threw out the proposal to build a bicameral legislature into the constitution, but acknowledged that Louis could not be excluded from law-making altogether. Instead, he was granted a suspensive veto applicable solely to ordinary, that is to say non-constitutional, legislation.

The deputies were probably right to harbour doubts about the goodwill of the monarch. Louis XVI had already signalled his willingness to abandon some of the most hallowed principles of Bourbon absolutism, and had defended the stance of the Third during the protracted deadlock in the Estates General. On the other hand, he seems not to have grasped the implications for his own sovereignty of the Declaration of the National Assembly on 17 June 1789. His behaviour on the occasion of the *séance royale* reveals a monarch prepared to concede some notable reforms, but not one who has made the necessary mental adjustment to a future based on power sharing. The massive extension of his own reform agenda on the night of 4–5 August, followed by the political collapse of the Monarchiens, must have come as something of a shock, therefore. The energising myth of the nation which the deputies propagated from that summer onwards probably left him cold. Besides, the movements of the royal family were greatly restricted from October onwards, and Louis could be forgiven for concluding that he had become a prisoner of his own Revolution.

Still, he went through the motions in the sincere belief that good might yet emerge from all the travails. On 4 February 1790 he visited the Assembly flanked by his ministers and gave a speech which endorsed without equivocation the work of national regeneration. To judge from the minute accounts of the episode relayed in deputies' correspondence, it created a powerful and soothing impression. This mood of detente, in Paris at least, survived until the summer when the first anniversary of the taking of the Bastille was marked with a festival on the theme of reconciliation and consensus. The king's presence inspired repeated displays of devotion, although a more critical source notes that Louis did not in fact cut a very inspiring figure and showed some reluctance to take the oath of loyalty to the nation on the specially constructed open-air altar.[45] A comment upon the pouring rain, perhaps; or was the monarch struggling with his conscience?

Even the most flexible interpretation of the concessions made at the *séance royale* could not disguise the fact that the Revolution had now travelled beyond the king's confined vision of an English-style aristocratic monarchy. Already dismayed by his virtual exclusion from law-making, Louis was further exasperated by the stealthy encroachment upon his executive powers as the committees of the National Assembly started to behave like surrogate ministries. The legislation despoiling the nobility, followed by signs that the same fate lay in store for the church, seems finally to have moved him into the camp of opposition. Certainly the king's recent biographer, John Hardman, considers that it was the inescapable obligation to sanction the clerical oath (on 26 December 1790) that set Louis on the course that would ultimately lead to the collapse of constitutional monarchy.[46] Alarmist rumours that the royal family might slip away from Paris incognito had been circulating since

June. However, the decision to flee was not taken until the turn of the year and only became all consuming in April 1791 after the monarch and his family had been prevented by a hostile crowd from making a short journey to the palace of Saint-Cloud in order to take Easter communion from a non-juring priest. But by this time Louis XVI had ceased to take any real part in the day-to-day events of the Revolution. Montmorin, the foreign secretary, reported that when he briefed the king on his position and the progress of affairs 'it was as though he was discussing matters of concern to the emperor of China'.[47]

The flight of the royal family from Paris on the night of 20–1 June 1791 exposed the fragility of the consensus which the deputies of the National Assembly had laboured to establish over the previous two years. Even if we accept that Louis had no intention of leaving the kingdom, least of all of throwing himself into the arms of foreign powers, there was no mistaking his attitude. On departing the Tuileries palace, he left behind a hand-written *Déclaration* or manifesto stating his objections to the constitution as it stood. Surprisingly, perhaps, this reads not as a plea for a return to the *ancien régime*, but as the work of a man who was still prepared to join in the task of building some kind of constitutional monarchy. But the terms had to be of his choosing and would have involved a massive strengthening of his executive authority, as well as a redistribution of legislative power. In so far as the deputies had ever contemplated a settlement on these terms, it had been rejected along with the Monarchiens in the summer of 1789.

But powerful parliamentary forces were now pushing for compromise. Most deputies on the Left shuddered at the prospect of an open-ended and increasingly radical Revolution. They realised that mistakes had been made, whether in annexing sovereignty to the Assembly alone or in pursuing intransigent ecclesiastical policies, and were prepared to modify the constitution in a direction favourable to the monarch. From a strictly parliamentary view, therefore, the attempted flight seemed much less of a disaster than it did to radical Parisian journalists or provincial patriots. In the words of Alexandre de Lameth, the 'disaster' was rather that the king had been arrested before reaching a place of safety from which to negotiate terms for a constitutional revision.[48] Consequently, the last three months of the deputies' period in office were largely devoted to the lengthy and ultimately fruitless task of reestablishing political consensus. This involved the peddling of a number of fictions (notably the 'abduction' of the monarch), and the use of martial law legislation (resulting in the so-called massacre of the Champ de Mars) against ordinary Parisians who doubted that Louis XVI could be trusted to play the role of constitutional monarch. In the end, though, it was the 250 odd 'royalist' deputies of the Extreme Right who sabotaged the operation on the logical, if dangerous, ground that they saw no advantage whatsoever in turning France into a viable constitutional monarchy. As for Louis, he resolved to accept a largely unrevised constitution whose promulgation he had no power to impede in any case. The only alternative would have been abdication.

By the spring of 1791 the defining task of the National Constituent Assembly had run into seemingly insurmountable difficulties, then. That clarity of purpose with which the deputies had embarked on the business of constitution drafting had been deflected by recurrent anxieties as to the sincerity of the monarch and by all-enveloping party strife. The health of the nation at large had started to give cause for concern, too. At the outset it had seemed quite sufficient to uproot old institutions and to install new ones in their place. No one worried unduly about the administrative viability of the new regime. But elective office-holding and decentralised decision-making were not skills learned overnight. As early as July 1790 Mirabeau warned (in his Notes to the Court) that the new administrative structures would prove unworkable. Indeed, the king felt the loss of his supervisory powers keenly and went out of his way to denounce the extreme decentralisation of local government in his valedictory *Déclaration*. He also dwelt at length upon the ecclesiastical reforms, of course. By mid-1791 it was evident that the requirement to swear an oath of allegiance had split the clergy down the middle. This was no mean achievement for legislators who had enjoyed the overwhelming support of rank-and-file clerics at the start of the Revolution. No other policy pursued by the National Assembly tarnished the image of a nation reunited to quite such a degree.

In effect, the nation so bravely proclaimed against intimidating odds in the summer of 1789 was beginning to separate into winners and losers. Towns that had done well in the competition for administrative spoils proudly asserted their patriotism; those that had not, brooded in silence. Likewise provinces whose privileges and immunities had been terminated. While the small town professional bourgeoisie rushed to exploit the opportunities for advancement beckoning in the new District administrations and tribunals, tens of thousands of employees of the General Farm, the old regime administrative courts, government offices, clerical establishments and seigneurial jurisdictions were thrown out of work. Peasants resumed the struggle with their lords which they thought they had won on the night of 4–5 August. Deprived of a say in the future by franchise restrictions, urban workers continued to practise collective bargaining by riot – against customs gates, salt tax collectors and excisemen.

Despite all the protestations of fraternity, the political animosities of 1788–9 had not been laid to rest either. Already, public opinion had received a rude shock on discovering that the urbane and flexible aristocrats of the capital were not typical of the nobility as a whole. For the noble deputies despatched by the *bailliages* seemed to have forgotten that they were supposed to form part of a 'unified elite' (see above pp. 66–72), and many harboured deep misgivings about the fluid and individualistic society which the National Assembly was bent on establishing. Even though the institutional integration of the nobility was accomplished within a year of the opening of the Estates General, suspicion lingered on both sides of the privileged/non-privileged divide. The patriot municipality of Brest, for instance, resolved to exclude nobles and senior clerics from the register of active citizens until such time as the Breton privileged orders signalled their complete submission to the decrees of the National Assembly. It is true that Brittany numbered among the provinces most resistant to the developing ethos of the nation. Nevertheless, the evidence of party affiliation among those deputies who did play a full part in the work of the Assembly is revealing in this regard. When the thorny issues raised by ecclesiastical reform started to crystallise and polarise opinions from the spring of 1790 onwards, the resultant party split tended to reproduce the social and juridical divisions of the *ancien régime*. The Right consisted very largely of deputies drawn from the two privileged orders, whereas eight out of ten members of the Jacobin Club (which formed the core of the Left) had been elected to represent the Third Estate.

But at least the nobility and the clergy remained on the stage of national politics for much of 1790, albeit defending interests which had begun to diverge from the agenda agreed in the summer of 1789. Many clergymen allowed themselves to be elected to head the new municipalities, and it was not unknown for nobles to exercise a popular mandate either. In the Aveyron the future theoretician of Counter-Revolution, the vicomte de Bonald, was chosen to preside over the Department administration. There is, therefore, some sense in describing the first twelve months of the National Assembly as the magnanimous or 'fortunate year' of the Revolution. To be sure, the country was not at peace with itself as historians once supposed, nor had consensus truly been achieved. Catholics and protestants were squaring up to one another in the South, the line army was in rebellious disarray, and sporadic attacks on châteaux were continuing.

Some fairly muted worries about Counter-Revolutionary plots had even made an appearance. Nevertheless, what distinguished 1790 was the willingness of the politicians to continue the search for consensus. That confidence that reasonable men could construct a future together ebbed dramatically in 1791. Instead of standing their parliamentary ground, the Right retreated from the fray altogether. By February perhaps 200 deputies who would normally have voted for conservative motions were no longer attending the sessions of the National Assembly. Most of the absentees were nobles and priests. This gave a technical majority to the patriots, but they were a far from cohesive force either. An Extreme Left commanding around thirty votes vigilantly guarded the distribution of powers agreed in the summer of 1789, whereas many erstwhile radicals were coming round to the view that the only secure dyke against permanent Revolution was to elevate the authority of the king. At the same time the patriots were riven by feuds, and a congenital inability to set aside small differences in order to achieve their larger goals. This could only add to the general mood of distrust and embattlement. Yet even as the horizon clouded over the deputies never altogether lost sight of the nation espied in 1789. Moves to punish or expel emigrant nobles and refractory priests were consistently defeated. The task of policing the nation in order to exclude unworthy elements would fall to the next legislature.

7   The political culture of revolution

In 1789 the political landscape of France experienced an upheaval of seismic proportions. To use the apt phrase of Isser Woloch, a new 'civic order' was in the making.[1] Indeed, the institutional aftershocks would continue throughout the 1790s and into the 1800s, far beyond the scope of this study. The new institutions were consciously designed to identify and hopefully to propagate the public virtues which the Revolutionaries intended to make their own. Liberty, equality and fraternity, to be sure, but also transparent sincerity, impartial justice and tireless devotion to the common cause. Psychologically as well as institutionally, therefore, French men and women entered a different world in 1789. Historians need no reminding of the magnitude of these changes, of course. Yet it seems fair to remark that they have experienced difficulty in finding a satisfactory framework within which to analyse the character of the new regime, now that definitions of 1789 as a straightforward 'bourgeois revolution' no longer command easy acceptance. The concept of an historically specific 'political culture' is an attempt to supply that deficiency. It embraces both the institutional restructuring of the state and the reshaping of civil society in accordance with the new norms of collective behaviour articulated in the Declaration of the Rights of Man.

But the utility of any new concept lies in its capacity to make sense of diverse phenomena. Thus, searching questions must be asked before we can proceed with the idea that the French Revolution possessed a characteristic political culture. Was the 'set of discourses and practices'[2] supposedly typifying Revolutionary politics unique to 1789 and the years that followed? Can its social determinants be ascertained? Or would it be more appropriate to portray the political culture of Revolution as a quintessential 'script' grasped by intellectuals (and intellectual historians), but by no one else? Scripted debate leaves little to chance, prompting a further question which has already received some attention in the preceding chapter. How negotiable were the politics of 1789? Should we, in other words, understand the political culture of Revolution as a set of givens which were reinforced as the decade advanced, but never seriously reassessed?

Only the most determinedly republican historian would today argue that the attitudes, expectations and practices emblematic of the Revolution sprang fully fledged from the debris of 1789. For the rediscovery of the *ancien régime* by scholars has facilitated the parallel discovery that 'Revolutionary' political culture pre-dated the Revolution in several important respects. Some of the ideas that would batter down the defences of absolute monarchy can be traced back to the rhetoric employed by the Parlement of Paris in jousts with the crown in the 1750s and 1760s. Yet, while *parlementaires* continued to employ a language of liberties rather than liberty for the most part, there can be no doubt that the monarchy's own reform agenda presumed the creation of a literate and genteel constituency for the circulation of ideas. Moreover, the infrastructure to nourish and to channel this public opinion was already in place before 1789. Academies, masonic lodges, or reading societies could be found even in small towns, as could newspapers and periodicals. Arthur Young, that omnivorous devourer of news, declared the circulation of printed matter in the French provinces to be woefully inadequate, but recent historians of the press tend rather to emphasise the ease of access to information, both censored and uncensored, by the time the *ancien régime* entered the final crisis.

Whether conjured into existence by administrative monarchy or the by-product of oppositional politics, it is at least arguable that a political culture had developed around government (the traditional 'secret du roi') by 1789. But was it proto-revolutionary? Here we need to recall to mind the highly stylised understanding of public opinion shared by contemporaries. Properly speaking, the reforms of ministers and the posturings of *parlementaires* were not aimed at the public at all. Rather they were aimed at a narrow 'political nation' of the literate and the well-to-do. These were the people whom the crown sought to take into partnership with the Provincial Assemblies experiment. It was these same individuals who raised the hue-and-cry against Lamoignon's judicial coup. Neither exercise stirred deeper passions within the body politic. By contrast, Revolutionary political culture was predicated upon a very different concept of the nation. Both spatially and socially the nation was redefined to encompass the whole of France and all of its inhabitants. In the process the antecedent 'scripts' and the institutional underpinnings of elite political discourse came under very great strain, where they did not succumb altogether. The language of the *philosophes* encountered the language of the crowd, the rhetoric of *parlementaire* resistance retreated in the face of the remorseless logic of the representative mandate, while the provincial academy was overtaken by the popular society.

At the heart of Revolutionary political culture lay a project to reconfigure the social. New men (citizens) would combine in a new social formation (the nation) and occupy a territory levelled to remove all traces of privilege (the patrie). Take the oath sworn by municipal delegates gathered in the town of Pontivy in February 1790: 'No longer Bretons or Angevins but Frenchmen and citizens of the same empire, we do solemnly renounce and abjure all our local and particular privileges as unconstitutional.'[3] For all their tinkering with the 'society of orders', the reformers of the *ancien régime* never for one moment entertained cultural and political change on this scale. Yet nor did the Revolutionaries, at least not initially. Theirs was a cumulative achievement which owed as much to contingency as forward planning. If the key values of the refashioned political culture were identified within months of the opening of the Estates General, their realisation proved a more arduous task. New institutions took time to organise, and their 'moral' influence even longer to assess. Meanwhile, Revolutionary politics remained fluid, unconstrained and, of course, unscripted. As the deputies assembled in Paris gropingly advanced towards a new regime, they were assailed constantly by local initiatives and expressions of political freedom. These had either to be commandeered and added to the expanding corpus of Revolutionary practice, or repudiated as deviant forms of behaviour. Negotiation, compromise and a measured tolerance of pluralism tended to characterise this first experiment in mass politics, therefore. The fixing of Revolutionary political culture came later, during the Terror, while the final alignment of institutions and public behaviour to produce a truly consensual political culture would only begin under the Directory.

Language and symbols

The onset of Revolution made little difference to the formal language of communication. French derivatives of English loan-words (budget, committee, the 'Commons', etc.) had appeared with increasing frequency in the 1780s, and additions to the vocabulary bank would continue throughout the 1790s, of course. Nevertheless, it is surprising that the dictionary of the Académie Française should list only 418 newly coined words by the end of the decade. However, the uses to which language was put changed a good deal during these years. Old words lost their sense completely, or acquired sinister connotations; adjectives became substantives, or were coupled into phrases describing mysterious or threatening social entities. Louis XVI was among the first to draw attention to the probable consequences of this linguistic slippage: 'I disapprove of the repeated use by the Third Estate of the expression *privileged classes*', he informed the deputies on the eve of their declaration of a National Assembly. 'Such rarely used expressions can only serve ... to nourish a spirit of antagonism.'[4]

In practice, the deputies were evolving a new language of claims to replace the servile modes of address and supplication employed hitherto. And where they pointed, the nation-at-large would follow. Petitions despatched from the provinces to Versailles, or Paris, tended to couch their requests in the self-abasing language of feudalism. They were invariably addressed to 'Our Lords and Masters' (*Nosseigneurs*) and gave voice, not to rightful claims, but humble grievances (*doléances*). However, the dramatic events of June and July triggered a cognitive chain reaction. From distant Languedoc addresses of urban origin bearing the formula 'Messieurs des Communes' began to arrive. Smaller localities played safe and stuck to the neo-feudal style, although the parishioners of Saint-Christol in the Vivarais hedged their bets with a letter beginning 'To Our Lords and Masters, Our Liberators Composing the National Assembly.'[5] Nevertheless, a perceptible shift in political outlook was under way as a linguistic analysis of items despatched in the mail to the Assembly's Feudal Committee has demonstrated. In 1789, and still in 1790, most of the communications hailed the deputies as 'Our Lords and Masters', but by 1792 the comparatively neutral formula 'Representatives' had become commonplace.[6] The appropriation of language for political purposes would be pushed further the following year when militants in the Paris Sections abandoned 'Representative' in favour of the more proximate 'Mandataire du peuple' (delegate).

However, the hegemony of language was never included in the projects of the National Assembly. After all, most French men and women tended to mangle the idiom of the old and new regimes. Only time would attach meaning to words such as 'veto', 'suffrage' and 'plurality', and until such time the titles of legislatures would be juggled more or less indiscriminately. Some country dwellers continued to refer to the Estates General two and even three years into the Revolution, if we can judge from the minutes of electoral meetings. One elector of Savenay brought the proceedings of his primary assembly to an abrupt halt with the proposal to draw up a *cahier de doléances*, and that was in August 1792. Besides, it is important to stress the pluralism of Revolutionary political culture at this stage. The obsession with linguistic purity and uniformity came later. In 1790 and

1791 the deputies' principal task was to transmit the message of regeneration without worrying unduly about the means employed. Thus the member for Bergues was given permission to arrange for a translation of the *Instruction* on the organising of municipalities for the use of his constituents. The circular would be printed with corresponding columns in French and in Flemish. The informal patriotic committees that had sprouted all over France in the wake of the Paris insurrection behaved in much the same way. Where necessary the decrees of the National Assembly should be explained in patois, advised the patriots of Brive; while the mayor of Egletons undertook both to translate the Declaration of the Rights of Man and to soften its formal, juridical diction into a tongue more easily grasped by country dwellers.

By contrast, the symbolic language of the Revolution sought to consummate the changes worked in 1789 and to render them irreversible. It was designed both to repudiate and desacralise the old order, and to solemnify and legitimise the regime now coming into being. The element of design should not be exaggerated, however. For the symbolic language of the Revolution was dynamic, spontaneous and all too frequently a product of local initiative. The most familiar symbols – the tricolour flag, the Marseillaise, the Cap of Liberty, Marianne – were all later constructions whose longevity owed much to official patronage. In 1789 and the years immediately following, the culture of freedom found expression in rather different ways: in the removal of weather-cocks from the roofs of manor houses, in the levelling of towers, the obliteration of coats of arms, liveries and honorific titles. These were all public gestures of defamation, directed at the nobility as the primary seigneurial class. The monarchy escaped frontal attack as long as the constitutional settlement survived. But the pendant to those acts of defamation was a ritual of affirmation consisting of federative pacts, fraternal banquets, solemn installation ceremonies for elected officials, festive plantings of 'liberty trees', and so forth. Reenacted across the length and breadth of the kingdom, these encounters carried a powerful emotional charge: hope for the future, but also fear lest the country slip back towards the semi-anarchy experienced during the frightening spring and summer months of 1789.

The Festival of Federation, held in Paris on the first anniversary of the taking of the Bastille, is rightly regarded as one of the most potent symbols of the early Revolution. On a vast parade ground joyfully levelled by the labours of thousands of Parisians, a communion service to constitutional monarchy was celebrated. Louis officiated from a raised dais as massed ranks of national guardsmen drawn from every town and province swore obedience to 'the Nation, the Law and the King' in that order. To his right and on a perfect level sat the president of the National Assembly: the seating arrangements, the configuration of the arena, the excited crowds chanting *Ça ira* ('Things will work out') said it all. Yet the origins of this spectacle were by no means Parisian, nor were they lacking in political ambiguity. It is worth exploring them in some detail, if only to demonstrate how the initially hybrid and undisciplined manifestations of Revolutionary political culture were brought into sharper focus.

The earliest federations were local and regional, not national. More often than not they sprang from invitations issued by towns to neighbouring centres of population to concert measures for public safety in the aftermath of the Great Fear. As such they tended to be particularist in outlook and more concerned with law and order than with the elusive concepts of liberty and fraternity. Thus the mayor of Millau, Louis de Bonald, wrote urgently to other towns and villages of the Bas Rouergue on 8 August to propose a pact of solidarity. Several days earlier Millau had found itself the point of convergence of two currents of Fear. By that autumn and winter properly regional gatherings of municipal envoys and national guardsmen had started to occur, but still it was far from clear (at least in Paris) what purposes they were designed to serve. The energy expended on federations in the South-East betrayed a lingering provincialist nostalgia which Mounier and the Monarchiens were trying to nourish, having failed to carry their views in the National Assembly. In late November several hundred national guardsmen drawn from the Dauphiné and the Vivarais assembled in the town of Bourg d'Etoile and swore to uphold the decrees of the National Assembly. But the real purpose of the meeting was to combat the attempts being made to reconvene the Provincial Estates of the Dauphiné (see above pp. 189–90). Rival federations that seem to have been called in order to rally support for the Monarchiens met in Pont-Saint-Esprit and Romans early in the New Year. Meanwhile, in Brittany, envoys from 150 localities gathered in the town of Pontivy in February 1790. Although an unalloyed patriotism was much more in evidence during the sessions of this meeting, the delegates still brooded on the continuing agrarian disorders and the failure of the National Assembly to legislate an early liquidation of the seigneurial regime.

The suspicion of political heterodoxy, combined with the very randomness of the phenomenon of federation, prompted the deputies to act. At a time when all parliamentary energies were focused on the task of converting France from a plural to a singular entity, the mushrooming of more or less patriotic organisations seeking to stitch subsidiary allegiances into the seamless cloth of the nation was unhelpful to say the least. In March the National Assembly declared its intention to organise a national Festival of Federation into which all local and regional manifestations would be henceforth subsumed. The plans were fleshed out over the next couple of months, and great care was taken to ensure that the symbolism of the event was tuned to the political needs of the moment. The nation was still a fragile concept, and it was important that every individual be involved, either personally or by proxy. Accordingly, primary assemblies of national-guard volunteers were instructed to choose by ballot representatives who would travel to Paris and participate in the Festival. On the appointed day – 14 July 1790 – church bells would ring out across the land to herald a synchronised ceremony of oath-swearing in every town and village scheduled for noon precisely.

The Festival of Federation brought a measure of discipline and coherence to popular political culture. Despite the choice of date and the hopes of its sponsors in the Paris Sections, the event did not become an opportunity to reenact the taking of the Bastille. Such symbols could not be denied, of course, but they were tucked away carefully until the summer of 1792. Instead, the Festival was billed as a celebration of the progress made *since* 1789. Its centrepiece was the oath of fidelity to the Nation and the Law: the twin absolutes of the new order to which even the power of the crown must incline. But can we be sure that the event was received by provincial Frenchmen in the spirit intended? Historians have tended to assume that the Festival did indeed produce a ripple of euphoria and transcendent unity, and yet the evidence to this effect is not conclusive. Towns and cities, it is true, organised substantial didactic pageants on the model, if not the scale, of the intended Paris celebration. This was reassuring, for signs of urban disenchantment at the direction of the Revolution had long preoccupied the deputies. The case of Strasbourg has been mentioned already, and it is worth noting here how the patriot leaders used the festivities to secure the city's return to the political fold. In the countryside enthusiasm was muted, however. Elected officials had only just taken over the running of communal affairs and were absorbed in more pressing tasks. In the department of the Haute-Vienne, for instance, half of the municipalities ignored the call to hold the prescribed *Fête*. And those that did confined their efforts to a simple oath-taking. The ideal of fraternity yielded before the more urgent need to consolidate law and order, too. As for the 'nation', it remained a construct restricted to officials and active citizens in many localities.

Elections

Nothing transmitted the message of the Revolution quite so effectively as the spectacle of an election, followed by the formal installation of officials as representatives of the people. Pierre Fillet, a well-to-do peasant farmer of Montlouis-sur-Loire, jotted down every detail of his own election as a municipal councillor. He went on to record in his journal the shopping expedition to Tours for the purchase of white, blue and red ribbon from which to make up the vivid sashes of office worn by municipal councillors. A year or so later we find an entry describing how he had sold on his sash to the next incumbent for 15 *livres*, on the condition that it would be sold back to him at the same price when he next stood for election. This flimsy, yet potent, trapping of office symbolised the presence of the Revolution at the grass-roots. It would be displayed repeatedly during the opening years of the Revolution as the deputies acted on their conviction that public accountability should become the keystone of the new order. For the 'active' citizens composing the responsible part of the nation voting became a frequent and eventually a rather tiresome civic duty. In the commune of Rancon (Haute-Vienne), for example, they were summoned no fewer than twelve times between February 1790 and December 1792.

Elections were not new, of course. Many Third Estate *cahiers* urged their adoption precisely because the gingerly experiments with elective municipalities conducted by the old monarchy had made a very favourable impression. But the reforms of Laverdy, Necker and Calonne betrayed an administrative conception of elections by and large. Only Brienne showed a wider comprehension of the potentialities of the electoral principle. Even so, the multiple extensions which the deputies of the National Assembly would give to the idea of accountability had no antecedents in the legislation of the *ancien régime*. On the other hand, the actual mechanics of voting clearly owed something to the lessons learned in 1787 when Municipal Assemblies were first introduced, and in the winter of 1788–9 when electoral statutes for the convocation of the Estates General had to be drawn up. Although conducted under very different auspices, the debates on citizenship revealed a keen under-standing of the practicalities of a censitary franchise. As for the procedures laid down for *bailliage* and *sénéchaussée* voting in 1789, they were lifted more or less en bloc and applied to the primary assemblies the following year.

However, the whole purpose of elections was now different. Or at least it was supposed to be. According to the new wisdom of Revolutionary political culture, voters were citizens possessed of rights whose choices would doubtless reflect their individuality. By contrast the elections to the Estates General had been conducted on a corporatist basis; moreover, one which appeared retrograde even by the standards of the 1780s. Collective, out-loud voting in parish or guild assemblies had been the norm, and it produced envoys with powers of attorney rather than representatives in the modern sense. The Revolutionaries retained the practice of voting within assemblies, but tried to 'individualise' the process as far as possible by requiring the electoral assembly to meet in the cantonal seat and to employ secret ballot procedures as prescribed for the Municipal Assemblies in 1787. An Instruction issued on 8 January 1790 made it clear that legislators wished to lift elections out of the rut of personalities and rivalries and thereby to lend dignity and detachment to the deliberations of the sovereign nation. 'Citizens of the countryside', it concluded, 'will surely not begrudge the slight inconvenience of a very short journey [to the cantonal seat], bearing in mind that they will obtain by this means greater independence in the exercise of their right to vote.'[7]

Whether this hybrid system of voting achieved the objectives set out by the National Assembly is doubtful. For parish-level voting remained the norm for municipal elections in any case, and it was at this level that the civic values of the new regime were supposed to take root. The existence, from 1790, of a broad primary franchise (see below p. 224) did serve to break the corporatist mould of the old 'society of orders', but in wrenching away one set of traditions, the deputies failed to install alternative structures in their place. In the absence of organised parties and declared candidatures, even the most well-intentioned voter was left politically clueless. Witness the frustrated remarks of an Alsatian patriot, published in the *Strassburgische Chronik* just weeks before the first municipal elections: 'I still do not know why I will be voting, nor what experience, abilities and talents are required. And if I knew, what would be the point? I have no knowledge of individuals and their possessions.' And he concluded: 'Would it not be possible to print a list of those qualified to stand as candidates (*éligibles*) where one might find information permitting an opinion to be formed?'[8]

This was early in 1790 when the theory of electoral democracy had scarcely been put to the test. Yet three years later a physician residing in a remote corner of the Cévennes penned a damning indictment of the reality of elections as he had witnessed it in his home canton. Far from discouraging partisan politics, cantonal voting merely raised the stakes, he observed. And how could it be otherwise, for primary assemblies brought together several hundred strangers from twenty-five and thirty leagues around. In such conditions no individual elector could possibly be acquainted with more than a handful of his fellows, which made the legal admonition to choose 'the most capable individuals' something of a joke. With no identifiable candidates, manifestoes or formal canvassing of votes, nomination might owe more to luck than to careful scrutiny. In practice, however, it was absenteeism that did the greatest damage to the project to instil a mass political culture by means of elections. Lack of experience, combined with slavish adherence to a jurisprudence inherited from the *ancien régime*, prolonged the business of declaring results beyond all measure. Many could not wait and returned home; many did not bother to come at all. 'This is so true', continued the doctor, 'that on the occasion of the renewal of the municipalities, the justices of the peace and the electors [November 1792] there were several assemblies which should have had 500 or 600 active citizens where there were not even 50.'[9]

Participation, or at least participation in those features of Revolutionary political culture that the Constituents chose to emphasise, was a problem, then. They had established a three-tier franchise which conceded political rights to French men on the basis of their tax contributions. Nevertheless, the lowest tier of active citizenship (able to vote in communal and cantonal assemblies; not able to stand for election) still embraced between 60 and 70 per cent of the adult male population.[10] By way of comparison, scarcely four Englishmen in a hundred possessed the vote at this time. The challenge, however, was to mobilise these voters. Initially, the determination of the Assembly to root the new institutions in the soil of public accountability won a large measure of support. Half and more of those listed as active citizens assembled to elect their municipal officers in February 1790 and almost as many attended cantonal primary assemblies (called in order to establish the District and Department administrations) in June and July of that year. No doubt the bafflement voiced by our Alsatian patriot was fairly common, but it did not deter large numbers from sampling the first rites of citizenship. Moreover, turn-out was highest in the countryside which suggests that the cities were not predestined to bear the torch of political radicalism. The vast electorates of the big towns proved difficult to organise and to mobilise, whereas a sense of communal solidarity helped to sustain voting in the villages and rural cantons. In the port city of Toulon rioting had destroyed all attempts to restrict the franchise, as we have seen, yet only 22 per cent of the electorate turned out to vote for the new municipality in February 1790. Not until an armature of clubs, press organs and Section assemblies had developed would the cities start to make the political running.

In the meantime the phenomenon of electoral politics hesitated and then began to contract. Attendance at the cantonal primary assemblies of June 1791 (called to elect a fresh legislature) was no more than half (23 per cent) what it had been the year before.[11] Perhaps a million active citizens responded to the summons out of a potential electorate of around four and a half million. This pattern of absenteeism was repeated in local elections, too. Not even the abolition of the active/passive distinction consequent upon the fall of the king made much difference to the trend. It was almost as though a large proportion of the adult male population had not been convinced that voting was integral to citizenship, after all. And indeed, the notion that elections were the crucial denominator of political participation would lapse altogether in 1793 and 1794. What had gone awry? There can be no doubt that the duties attaching to active citizenship were fairly arduous. It took eleven days to complete the election of the first municipality of Cherbourg, twelve days that of Caen, and a month of balloting to install those of Dijon and Lyon. Contrary to the blithe instructions issued by the National Assembly, voters did begrudge what was often a long trek to the cantonal seat, as well. Furthermore, the right to vote was not free-standing: those who wished to escape jury service, for instance, forfeited it.

However, the real problem lay elsewhere. In 1790 voting had been a meaningful novelty; by the end of 1792 it had become an objectionable chore. The determination of the National Assembly to begin the process of reconstruction from the bottom upwards was rewarded with a massive vote of confidence in the shape of the municipal ballot of February 1790. This reflected a sense of novelty, to be sure, but above all a reflex of solidarity as town and country dwellers contemplated a future bright with hope. Often villagers synthesised the best of the old with the new by electing their parish priests to commanding positions in the civil community. In the district of Civray (Haute-Vienne), for example, priests took over the mayoral office in three-quarters of rural communes. But then shadows began to appear on the face of the new regime. Overworked and unpaid, the municipalities began to stagger under the burdens placed upon them. Some, such as the obligation to transcribe into their registers each and every new law, were merely gratuitous; others, such as policing the run-down of the seigneurial regime or compiling new tax rolls, were potentially divisive. In these conditions, the dignity of elective office and the symbolism of sovereign assemblies started to look rather tawdry. However, two legislative measures did more than most to undermine the consensual mode of politics based on frequent electoral consultations. They were the linked decisions to dispose of the fixed assets of the church, and to proceed to a wholesale ecclesiastical reform. The sales of 'national property', the closure of monastic houses, redrawing of parish boundaries and enforcement of the clerical oath placed the new Department administrations, the Districts and the municipalities in an unenviable position. For the first time since 1789 elected representatives were called upon to implement policies for which there was no significant popular support. Many protested, or rather resigned in protest. Disconcerted by these developments, and conscious that the forces of the Revolution were no longer marching in step, the voters preferred to stay at home.

It is important to bear in mind that electoral participation was a skill that Frenchmen had to learn. In the weeks following the first nationwide municipal ballot, over 5,000 letters of query and complaint flooded into the offices of the Constitution Committee. No doubt time would eventually consecrate the electoral principle as an original characteristic of Revolutionary political culture, but the initial experiment was not an unqualified success. To start with, the deputies of the National Assembly determined that certain categories (women, the poor, servants, etc.) were not fit to possess the vote. It comes as no surprise, therefore, to discover that groups whose citizenship was deemed to be marginal chose alternative means of making their voices heard. Women asserted their presence in the market-place, in the bread queue and in the mutinous crowds that protested the expulsion of non-juring clergy from their livings, and the closure of 'redundant' churches. The poor kept going the guerrilla campaign against excise duties, against seigneurialism, and would spearhead the roving armies of grain pillagers in the *pays de grande culture*. But even the so-called active citizenry, for whom the constitution did provide a means of influencing the political process, showed little sustained enthusiasm for conversion into a proto-liberal constituency. Corporate habits of representation died hard, and the sight of a tricolour sash proved an unconvincing barrier to individuals bent on exercising an older and more direct understanding of their rights.

Enlarging the public sphere

The growing pretensions of public opinion, whether considered as an intellectual construct or as a social phenomenon, have been discussed in chapter 2. Plainly, the late *ancien-régime* monarchy no longer exerted total control over the dissemination and discussion of political information. Nor, in many respects, did it wish to do so. The programme of reforms from 'above' implied a quest for consent from 'below', which required, in turn, that some energy be devoted to the business of nourishing and managing public opinion. Calonne's advice to the king that he should summon an impromptu Assembly of Notables signalled a final acceptance of the logic of this relationship in the highest governing circles. But the problem which then arose was how to demarcate the public sphere in a manner consistent with the objectives of reforming absolutism. Ministers conjured into being the Provincial Assemblies, but then grew alarmed as these bodies acquired a life of their own and started to circulate copies of their proceedings. The eventual decision to allow the printing of these minutes marked a break with the practice of the old monarchy and a significant extension of the public domain. The deputies of the National Assembly would push this process a stage further. The tidy conceptualisation of public opinion familiar to eighteenth-century men of letters was revolutionised, and a vast superstructure of press, prints and political clubs was erected upon the cosy intellectual institutions of the *ancien régime*.

Newspapers, like political clubs (and elections), were quickly recognised as defining features of the new regime. However, it would be wrong to suppose that they sprang fully forged from the anvil of 1789. As two recent historians have noted, 'the "press revolution" of 1789, like so many other aspects of the French Revolution, was the culmination of a long process of development'.[12] That development included the growth of a market for uncensored periodicals, and for French-language titles printed outside France. About a dozen such newspapers circulated widely and fairly freely thanks to the efficiency of the French postal system on the eve of the Revolution. The public had also acquired a taste for pamphlet literature, increasing quantities of which were churned out during the reign of Louis XVI. However, there *is* a sense in which the press came into being at a specific moment in time. The great inflation of news media answered several calls in quick succession: Brienne's invitation to all and sundry to express their political views issued in July 1788, the desperate thirst for news in May–June 1789, the anxiety of deputies in the Estates General to stay in touch with their constituents, and the ringing endorsement of the freedom of speech and publication enshrined in the Declaration of the Rights of Man. With his usual clarity of judgement, Mirabeau was among the first to spot the integrating function that the press could now be expected to perform. 'Newspapers', he wrote in the sales prospectus for a new journal, 'establish communications that cannot fail to produce a harmony of sentiments of opinion, of plans and of action that constitutes the real public force, the true safeguard of the nation.'[13] Jean-Pierre Brissot whose career as a journalist was about to take off, had had the same intuition: by means of newspapers 'one can teach the same truth at the same moment to millions of men; through the press, they can discuss it without tumult, decide calmly and give their opinion'.[14] In short, it seemed that a new chapter in the history of the press was opening. Henceforward newspapers would play a key role in the fashioning, and channelling, of Revolutionary political culture.

The phenomenal success of constituency news sheets – exploiting the public's unquenchable appetite for accounts of the proceedings of the Estates General – was swiftly followed by a veritable explosion of the printed word in Paris itself. At the start of 1789 the capital boasted perhaps half a dozen periodical publications of a political character, yet by the end of that year over 130 new titles had appeared on the market. Pamphlet production increased by a similar order of magnitude, albeit over a longer time span. Even Arthur Young was awed by the energy which the Revolution had let loose. Following a visit to the 'pamphlet shops' of the Palais Royal in June, he noted in his diary: 'every hour produces something new. Thirteen came out today, sixteen yesterday and ninety-two last week.'[15] Political pamphlets were ephemeral almost by definition, of course, and many of the new periodical titles were not destined for a long life either. Usually they were wretchedly printed, on poor-quality paper by a single individual who doubled as author and publisher. But as fast as journals and journalists fell by the wayside, they were replaced by others. During the period in office of the National Assembly, over 400 newspaper titles were sold on the streets of Paris alone. Many appeared daily, and the majority provided purchasers with at least two issues a week. Even allowing that printers switched their activities away from book production in order to supply the new mass market for cheap political prints, the presses could not keep up. Over the decade the number of printing premises in the capital more than quadrupled.[16]

Provincial publishing was less well developed. Nevertheless, it too drew inspiration and a whole new readership from the events of 1789. Hugh Gough calculates that over 600 new titles came into being in the course of the decade.[17] Around forty-five appeared in the latter half of 1789 alone, although the main rush came later, in 1790, as the Assembly's institutional reforms began to take effect (over ninety titles). Casualties were frequent as in the case of the Paris-based press, of course, but nearly every large town and department acquired an organ of some description. In some instances, preexisting provincial journals took on a fresh lease of life, and a nomenclature more appropriate to the new order of priorities. Thus the old regionalist gazette, Les Affiches de Toulouse et du Haut-Languedoc, changed its title to the Journal Universel, et Affiches de Toulouse et du Languedoc at the end of 1789. These years also witnessed the growth of a more specialised press aimed at particular groups of provincial Frenchmen. Peasants, or more likely farmers and rural notables, were targeted by the *Feuille villageoise,* founded in the autumn of 1790. Appearing weekly over the next five years, it proved to be one of the most durable and widely disseminated press organs of the Revolutionary decade. Enterprising publishers sought out other constituencies of potential readers, too. National guardsmen, priests, public functionaries, even patois speakers were catered for. In February 1791 a news sheet printed entirely in *langue d'oc* appeared in Toulouse with the mission to explain the ideas of the Revolution to workmen who were not able to understand French.

The mission to explain, and thereby to bind together the new nation, supplied the common theme of all forms of newsprint during the early Revolution. By indicating and inculcating the values to which all men and women should aspire, the press would enlarge the public sphere and render it invulnerable to those still touting sectional interests. Thus deputies in the Estates General devised a two-way traffic in information by means of *Letters* to their constituents. As news, exhortation and advice travelled outwards from Versailles, local opinion could be realigned with national goals and reflected back to the centre. This was the task that newspapers endeavoured to perform, albeit on a grander, more formal scale. In place of the trivia of small ads and official notices that filled the columns of the old provincial *Affiches,* the Revolutionary press harped incessantly on the themes of nationhood and citizenship. Regional issues were pushed into the background in favour of a lengthy coverage of debates in the National Assembly. These, in turn, were handled in a bland and consensual manner. Only the Parisian radical press tackled debates *within* the Revolution: the veto, the restrictions placed on the franchise, the role of Lafayette, and so forth.

How much difference did this explosion of print culture make? The question is less easy to answer than it appears, for a dramatic escalation in the output of news media does not automatically denote an extended readership. Well-intentioned patriots might launch a journal in *langue d'oc,* but half of the plebeian population of Toulouse was unlettered in patois as well as French. Print runs were not especially long at this stage in the Revolution, nor were papers produced in the provinces particularly cheap. The *Journal universel* of Toulouse cost subscribers 6 *livres* and ran to 600 copies. On the other hand, we need to bear in mind the social context. Revolutionary political culture was not imbibed individually, but collectively as the prints were read out loud in clubs and on street corners by news vendors. Each issue of the *Journal universel* would be passed from hand to hand, posted up, perhaps read or commented upon publicly, thereby magnifying its circulation tenfold. Moreover, newspapers faced very little competition (except from each other). Censorship and municipal press controls had broken down, even in Paris, and in the absence of structured political parties the public remained highly receptive to the messages purveyed by the newspaper press. Political clubs would soon start to fill this void, of course, and they need to be considered next.

While the functional literacy of ordinary French men and women undoubtedly progressed in the course of the eighteenth century, it remained a very uneven phenomenon, as we have seen. Rudimentary reading and writing skills were more prevalent in the northern and eastern provinces than in the South and West, and everywhere the incidence of male literacy was higher than that of female. On the other hand the geographical distribution of cultural institutions displayed a less obvious bias, owing to the massive expansion of freemasonry in the 1770s and early 1780s. The very ubiquity of masonic lodges at the end of the *ancien régime* testifies in favour of a considerable enlargement of the public sphere. However, even masons were not ordinary folk, although they might easily be drawn from the world of commerce as well as that of the professions. The achievement of the clubs was to build on these foundations and to beckon in the direction of a truly democratic sociability. In the process they did much to define and to anchor the burgeoning political culture of the Revolution, although their role would trouble the minds of many deputies in the National Assembly. Yet another sign that at the outset of the Revolution its political culture was far from constituting a generally agreed 'text'.

The demonstrable fact that many political societies evolved from preexisting fraternities, lodges and cultural associations must not be allowed to disguise the more important point that the club movement rapidly broke away from the institutional format of the *ancien régime*. In quantitative terms some 50 academies, perhaps 100 literary societies and around 800 masonic lodges were replaced – in the space of five years – by over 6,000 political clubs.[18] The network reached maximum density in 1794, by which time possession of a Jacobin club had become a badge of loyalty to the regime rather than a vibrant expression of self-renewing political culture. Nevertheless, this physical extension of the notion of public space is impressive to behold. Virtually every department and district seat boasted a club, and such bodies could be found in 60 per cent of cantonal seats as well. Overall, the Revolutionaries succeeded in establishing the rudimentary framework for a collective political life in around 14 per cent or one in seven communes of the Republic.[19] But this was the achievement of the Montagnard-dominated Convention and its army of agents in the field. During the early years, the growth of the club movement, and the stimuli that produced it, were of more variable character.

The formal foundation for club activity was put in place in December 1789 when the National Assembly endorsed the right of (active) citizens 'to meet peacefully and without arms in specific assemblies for the purpose of drawing up addresses and petitions'.[20] Despite some unease as to whether such bodies could be woven into the seamless cloth of the nation, Sociétés des Amis de la Constitution soon began to mushroom. By the end of the first year of Revolution, societies of this type had appeared in a score of towns and cities. A year later over 300 such bodies had come into being, and by the end of 1791 over 1,000. Typically, the Societies of Friends of the Constitution were the product of local initiatives mounted by bourgeois patriots who had risen to prominence during the jousting over the Estates General. Thus the first club in Rodez emerged in May 1790 out of a series of informal meetings in which François Chabot and Louis Louchet, both future *conventionnels*, played a major role. At Bernay in Normandy, the Lindet brothers who both went on to lengthy parliamentary careers played the key role. Thomas, the senior, who had been elected to the Estates General, wrote from Paris to promote the idea of association as 'perhaps the only means of bringing home to the citizen his civil existence and the need for relations with his fellow citizens.[21] Subsequently, the town council used the opportunity presented by the Festival of Federation to inaugurate the new society.

In fact the parallel between these early societies and the federations is instructive, for they, too, flourished in a political environment that was not yet fixed or centrally directed. Whilst the vast majority of clubs intoned a vigorous, if rather unrehearsed, chorus to the constitution, a few came into being for the more or less expressed purpose of combating the dominant culture of constitutionalism. A number of towns provided fertile territory for monarchist clubs in the course of 1790, although rarely did they encounter local authorities which were prepared to tolerate a degree of political pluralism. The Society of Friends of Religion and Peace of Aix-en-Provence was banned by the municipality three weeks after its creation. An equivalent organisation in the town of Millau survived longer, protected no doubt by a District administration reluctant to implement the stipulations of the Civil Constitution of the Clergy. Nevertheless, in May 1791, it was overrun and closed down as a result of crowd action orchestrated by the rival Friends of the Constitution. Unceasing correspondence between the provincial clubs, combined with affiliation to the Paris Society of Friends of the Constitution (otherwise known as the 'Paris Jacobins'), provided a means of synchronising political outlook, of course. The imprimatur of Paris conferred legitimacy and respectability, or at least it did so until the Paris Jacobins also broke ranks under pressure of events on the Champ de Mars in July 1791. Nevertheless, it is important to bear in mind that the clubs never formed a party within the state, much less a political 'machine'. The preeminence of the Paris Jacobins was moral rather than organisational; even at the height of the Terror no more than 15 per cent of provincial clubs could claim affiliated status.[22]

But the early clubs should not be confused with the 'popular societies' spawned in large numbers under the Republic. Qualitatively, they continued to resemble gatherings of the polite and the well-to-do on the pattern of *ancien-régime* urban sociability. Members were expected to pay hefty subscriptions and they normally met in private, behind closed doors. The founding deeds of the Rodez club prescribed two meetings a week, a public session on one Sunday in each month, and a quorum of twelve. Among the initial members we find a cross-section of the legal bourgeoisie, some merchants, a smattering of priests, the town's printer and a solitary nobleman. This was not untypical. The social as opposed to the spatial enlargement of the public sphere would occur later, in 1791, although ominous signs of the exclusions to be applied to the new political culture were present almost from the beginning. Very few nobles won admission to the Societies of the Friends of the Constitution. Indeed, the Rodez club adopted a regulation reminding members not to present candidates 'suspect in their doctrines and their sentiments' as early as June 1790.[23] The patriot clergy would fall foul of this anathema several months later as clubs everywhere assumed a hawkish demeanour over the Civil Constitution and the clerical oath. But losses among the former privileged orders were more than compensated for by massive recruitment from below. Early in 1791 the Rodez Jacobins debated motions to admit 'honest artisans' without charge, and to extend the number of public sessions to one per week.[24] A similar process of social realignment occurred in Tulle where 43 per cent of club members hailed from petty trade and craft backgrounds in June 1791. This was not far short of the 58 per cent popular recruitment that would be attained in 1793–4.[25]

Of course, the seething morass of Paris clubs sits uneasily in this picture of gradual democratisation. The capital pioneered the construction of public space, and its 'anarchy' would lead to the first serious attempt to curb the club phenomenon in the dying days of the National Assembly. Between 1789 and 1794 over 100 political societies flourished and, like the Parisian press, they catered for every conceivable constituency and strand of opinion. There were clubs for deputies, for *fédérés*, for foreign patriots, for Revolutionary women, for West Indian planters and, ostensibly, for the poor. There were clubs to chorus the views of the Triumvirate, those of the Monarchiens and those of Lafayette. There were Counter-Revolutionary clubs, and republican clubs. It was these latter that disturbed the deputies most, for they operated at street level and obeyed none of the rules of the constitutional compromise. The Cordeliers club, for instance, recruited from the working-class tenement blocks of the Left Bank, admitting thereby passive citizens and even women. It specialised in harrying the municipal authorities, undermining Lafayette and in general political missionary work among the disenfranchised. Not for nothing did the club adopt the official title of 'Society of the Friends of the Rights of Man and Citizen', rather than the more usual 'Society of Friends of the Constitution'.

The Cordeliers were responsible for bringing the rift in the constitution into the open following the nocturnal departure of the king from Paris on 20–1 June 1791. Unlike the vast majority of provincial clubs, they refused to accept the National Assembly's subsequent decision to exonerate Louis of any wrongdoing. On the contrary, they helped for some time to sustain what can only be described as a street-level republican movement. The petition signed on the Champ de Mars on 17 July was a Cordelier document which, however, stopped short of calling for a republic. Nevertheless, the blood spilt on that day did considerable, if temporary, damage to the clubs and to the model of democratic sociability they had elaborated over the previous eighteen months. In September Le Chapelier, one-time radical deputy and founder member of the Paris Jacobins, moved a bill to tighten up the legal environment in which the clubs operated. They were reminded that they were no more than private associations and could neither petition nor depute on a collective basis. The Cordeliers ceased meeting for a spell, while the Paris Jacobins were nearly wiped out by a split. And for the first time since the start of the Revolution the expansion of the club network registered a loss of momentum.

The attempt to arrest the growth cycle of the clubs would prove short-lived. Nevertheless, this eleventh-hour bid to stabilise the Revolution around the constitutional compromise agreed in 1789 provides an opportunity to take stock. Festivals and elections, news sheets and political societies were all institutions which performed an integrating function. And integration, perhaps even sublimation, of plural French men and women into a singular nation became the defining task of the deputies in the National Assembly. The forging of a new consensus and its outward expression in an appropriate language of symbols and practices must count as the principal component of Revolutionary political culture, therefore. In time, it is true, a language of exclusion would develop (pivoted on constructions such as the 'émigré', the 'aristocrat', the 'suspect'). Also the objects of unanimity would change (for the 'King' read 'Republic'; for the 'Law' read the 'Public Safety'). But these complications were only glimpsed in 1791 and, in any case, they lie beyond the reach of this study.

The political culture of Revolution was formed, if not fully formed, under the National Assembly, then. However, its 'newness' will always remain problematic, if only because the impact of the language and the practices which the Revolutionaries made their own tended to be cumulative rather than instantaneous. As the decade unfolds, the conceptual clarity of the break with the *ancien régime* becomes sharper, whereas a narrower focus on the period of transition between 1787 and 1791 highlights threads of continuity as well as evidence of rupture. Nonetheless, the initial institutional continuities (a mixed constitution, incumbent monarch, elections, a censitary franchise, etc.) are ultimately less impressive than the veritable explosion of popular political consciousness that marks out these years. The National Assembly devised elaborate structures to control and to channel such energy, but would fare little better than the reform ministers of absolute monarchy when confronted with the juggernaut of public opinion. This should remind us that the construction of Revolutionary political culture was a two-way process. Even if the deputies to the Estates General had been able to agree an agenda from the outset, it is unlikely that they would have remained in sole charge of the developing debate. In practice, therefore, the political culture of the Revolution evolved as a contingent phenomenon: a product of buffeting by events and negotiation with rival forces in the public sphere.

But what of the 'new man' fashioned, supposedly, from the unpromising raw material of the *ancien régime*? The extent to which the common people thought differently about their lives and life-chances as a result of the events of 1789 is strictly imponderable. Or at least, we are forced to rely on anecdote as evidence. Arthur Young noted a profound and proud sense of worth when stumbling on some workmen busily clearing and enclosing plots of wasteland early in 1790. The poor were now the nation, he was told, and all wasteland belonged to the nation. For Louis Simon, the weaver introduced in chapter 5, the change of regime registered rather differently. What lingered in his mind were above all the cultural signs: the advent of cheap printed cottons for working women, and baggy trousers in place of gartered breeches for men. Other contemporaries remarked on the confident swing in the stride of ordinary Parisians as they marched along the pavements rather than in the gutters. These may or may not be tell-tale marks of a shift in popular apprehensions. When combined with data drawn from a later phase of the Revolution (the choice of first-names, for example), they become rather more persuasive. Whether the patterning of collective as opposed to individual behaviour owed much to the upheaval is open to doubt. Despite their best efforts, the deputies of the National Assembly failed to abolish the crowd and to replace it with forms of behaviour more in tune with the ethos of nationhood. Moreover, the deeper structures of the Revolutionary crowd resembled nothing so much as those of the pre-Revolutionary crowd. This is not to suggest that the crowd was a static formation; rather that its evolution in terms of socio-economic composition and gender stemmed from pressures beyond the immediate reach of politics.

One final question remains: did the political culture of the Revolution gestate a new political class? The answer must be a qualified 'yes'. Symbols need life to be breathed into them if they are to be effective, and so do institutions. Unquestionably, the new regime developed a civic vitality which, despite defections, required positive steps by Napoleon and his prefects in order to put it to sleep. Since not all French men were political animals, the conclusion seems inescapable that the values and the practices of the regime were nurtured and propagated by individuals who identified strongly with the reforms mooted and implemented since 1787. Whether such individuals should be described as a class is a matter of convenience; here the term is used to imply nothing more than a body of men united in service to the Revolution. What we are describing is a power elite, and one which developed strong vertical ties linking together humble municipal councillors and justices of the peace, subaltern administrators, and legislators in a common mission. Moreover, the substance of this elite augmented steadily in the years after 1789. Each administrative renewal, each change of legislature increased the pool of loyal citizens. These were men whose loyalties were not pledged to any particular sectional interest, but to the phenomenon of Revolution itself. That is to say, the force which had eradicated absolutism and feudalism and destroyed the corporate power of the aristocracy. As Pierre Fillet's municipal sash passed from hand to hand, the effectives of the new civic order would increase in proportion.

But a class of men holding political values and, increasingly, political experiences in common was bound to lack social determinacy. Pierre Fillet was a comfortable peasant farmer; Louis Simon made a living from part-time weaving, dairy farming and trading in wine. These are isolated examples, of course, but recent attempts to draw up a sociological profile of the new political class have produced similar conclusions.[26] Alongside well-to-do peasants, upwardly mobile artisans and petty traders, we find bourgeois landowners, merchant manufacturers and a substantial contingent of legal professionals. On the other hand, few employees of the old intendancies and General Farm managed to negotiate the political watershed without loss of status, and the inclusion of priests and even nobles among the cadres of the new regime was decidedly short-lived. In practice, the class that rose to prominence after 1789 lacked definable social boundaries, and to reify it as 'the revolutionary bourgeoisie' is likely to create more problems than it solves. If the ethos of the Revolution was unmistakably bourgeois, the men and women who sustained it in years of bitter division and war, as well as years of peace and fraternity, cannot be so neatly described.

Nor should the potent, and contemporary, message of 'newness' be allowed to pass without judgement. For the power elite which the Revolution would call its own had been foreshadowed in the propaganda of the physiocrats and the reforms of Laverdy, Turgot, Necker and Calonne. But what had finally mobilised the desire to participate more actively in the political life of the country was the experimental devolution of power to regional and local assemblies carried out by Brienne. Although the experiment proved short-lived, the experience did not. It put in place an elite-in-waiting, so to speak. And when the call came, these provincial notables, small-town lawyers and village syndics performed a crucial relay role in the transition from administrative to constitutional monarchy.

Conclusion

The deputies gathered for the last time on Friday, 30 September 1791. The new constitution had been promulgated a fortnight earlier and the time had come to settle outstanding debts. Sieur Lataille, the owner of the Versailles tennis court which had provided shelter for members of the old Third Estate in their hour of need was handsomely rewarded with a gratuity of 6,000 *livres*. Simultaneously, countless French men and women who had been indicted on charges of riot or revolt since May 1788 were granted an amnesty. The deputies were plainly anxious to cast a veil over deeds perpetrated during the interregnum between Lamoignon's 'despotic' action against the *parlements* and the construction of a properly constitutional regime. After a final speech by the king, the president uttered the words that all were waiting to hear: 'the National Constituent Assembly declares that its mission is fulfilled and its sessions are over'.[1] The break could not have been more sharply signalled and it applied to the deputies as well. For earlier that year they had passed a law rendering themselves ineligible for election to the next legislature. Most set off for home, in consequence; albeit with some apprehension as to what the future held in store. Since their departure for Versailles some two and a half years earlier the face of provincial France had been transformed, and deputies drawn from the old privileged orders, in particular, had good reason to feel vulnerable. A minority, meanwhile, remained in Paris to seek preferment under the new regime, or else to dabble in journalism. Since the abolition of the *octrois*, the capital had, after all, become a cheap as well as an agreeable place in which to reside. It was there rather than in his native Nîmes that the deputy Rabaut Saint Etienne picked up his pen to compose the first narrative account of the work of the National Assembly. While acknowledging that the scars formed by the removal of privilege had yet to heal fully, he still felt able to assert that 'the bulk of France is settled, the constitution is complete and the moment has come to write the history of the Revolution'.[2]

The Revolution did not stop in 1791, of course, precisely because

237

the excision of every vestige of privilege necessitated socio-economic as well as political surgery. Nevertheless, it is time to take stock for the end of our argument has been reached, if not the end of the Revolution. This book set out to provide a rounded account of the climactic years of the old regime and the preliminary years of the new. Nothing unusual in this perhaps, except for the fact that historiography decrees otherwise. The men and women of 1789, and many historians subsequently, denied the paternity of the *ancien régime*. The Revolution was an immaculate conception, an event without a past, without antecedents. As a result, studies of the *ancien régime* (as a system of government) and studies of the Revolution have tended to proceed along separate and unconnected paths. Indeed, the latter have come close to stifling the former in view of the general consensus that eighteenth-century, unlike seventeenth-century, Bourbon absolutism constitutes an historical cul-de-sac. True, matters are improving on this front, for a rehabilitation of Bourbon political practice in the latter part of the reign of Louis XV and that of Louis XVI is now under way.[3] Nonetheless, scholars rarely venture to cross the frontier of 1789 in the belief that Revolutionary experience must have been generically different from what came before.

Our study set out to move the chronological goal posts so as to make possible the exploration of two regimes which are traditionally viewed in isolation. It is for the reader to judge whether the resulting vision makes possible a satisfactory synthesis. In quizzing the 'rupture thesis' to which historians of very different persuasions cling, the intention is not to deny the specificity of the Revolution as an event. Clearly, the Revolution happened, and the men and women caught up in it quickly grasped that a force without parallel had barged into their lives. But at the same time it is surely instructive to embed the phenomenon of Revolution in the context from which it issued. For, rhetoric of rebirth notwithstanding, the early Revolutionaries were also tied to a process which was driven, in large measure, by the pre-1789 agenda of reforming absolutism. It is to his enduring credit that Alexis de Tocqueville, as historian and sociologist, recognised this fact. His unfinished masterpiece *The Ancien Régime and the Revolution* (1856) remains the best book ever written on eighteenth-century France and for two fundamental reasons. Unlike the actors in the drama of 1789 and many latter day scholars, he resisted the temptation to detach the Revolution from what came before (and after). On the contrary, he argued, the phenomenon unleashed in 1789 should be understood less as a repudiation of the *ancien régime* than as a confirmation of some of its most deep-seated tendencies. And the agent of continuity to which he drew attention was the state. For Tocqueville, the restless, centralising, energy of what we would nowadays term the 'fiscal-military state'[4] provides the key to an understanding of the process of reform and revolution.

It scarcely needs repeating that the conceptual scaffolding of Tocqueville's great work has influenced the arguments put forward in this book. For I, too, believe that the role of state power – in this instance the actions of the Bourbon monarchy – deserves fuller recognition than it has received hitherto in the process of launching political and societal change. In a study of what were plainly years of transition, it also seems to me to be fruitful to explore the unacknowledged as well as the acknowledged paternity of Revolutionary legislation. Nonetheless, it is true that Tocqueville's brilliance as a social prophet sometimes intrudes upon his qualities as a historian. For his elaboration upon the theme of state centralisation reads rather schematically in the light of recent research. Although the Bourbon monarchs may well have pursued consistently a policy of administrative centralisation and social homogenisation, their failure to make rapid progress owed much to other, contradictory, policies which they also pursued. On the subject of institutionalised privilege, for instance. The crown used privilege to buy out rivals in the political arena, according to Tocqueville. No doubt; but by the middle decades of the eighteenth century priorities had shifted. Thereafter, ministers sought increasingly to curtail privilege on the ground that it sapped the fiscal (and hence the military) capacities of the state. Yet almost until the end, they insisted that the integrity of the 'society of orders' was not at issue.

Tocqueville's insights are enormously valuable, then, but at the functional level of Bourbon rule the picture was more complicated than he supposed. State power ebbed and flowed in complex patterns: while the administrative personnel of the Caen intendancy nearly tripled in the course of the eighteenth century, the authority of the intendant in the adjacent capital of Rennes tended to decline. For Brittany was a land of Estates whose defining raison d'être was to place obstacles in the path of administrative monarchy. We must be wary of the suggestion that reforming absolutism constituted a force capable of sucking the life blood from local communities and vested interests, therefore. If it had done, revolution might actually have been averted. Rather, we need to pay attention to the tensions which the project to streamline Bourbon monarchy generated. Tensions which have been described as a conflict between 'ministerial' and 'jurisdictional' power. In other words the picture created by Tocqueville lacks depth, for the state was not the only player on the stage. And it was the vigour and sophistication with which those other players countered the allegedly despotic pretensions of government ministers that made the likelihood of civil commotions very much greater.

One question that Tocqueville did not explore is the political complexion of the centralising urge. Usually the policies pursued by successive reform ministers are portrayed in conservative colours, as fundamentally absolutist and anti-libertarian. By and large the *ancien-régime* monarchy remained 'a conservative force, assisting in the preservation of an extremely hierarchical society' writes the author of a standard textbook on the period.[5] In this formulation, the reforms mooted and implemented from the 1760s onwards were designed to shore up or to refurbish the structures of an absolute monarchy grown old and impotent since the demise of the Sun King. A task they signally failed to perform, it is further suggested. But our perspective, as will be clear by now, is rather different. It can be summarised in a phrase: state consolidation employing the power of consent. To be sure, the absolutism practised by Louis XVI, or even Louis XV, cannot be compared with the robust and coercive regime put in place by Louis XIV. By the 1760s most agents of government had ceased to view their mission solely in terms of tax extraction and the repression of discontent. Instead a milder, consensus-seeking style of absolutism was evolving which we have dubbed 'administrative monarchy'. The fiscal-military imperative was not lost, of course, rather it was pursued via welfarist policies which were designed to enhance the overall taxable wealth of the kingdom. The vestigial tendency to use coercive measures in order to extract revenue was now directed towards privileged elites rather than the common people. Therein lay much of the problem.

However, it is our contention that administrative monarchy displayed the potential to develop into something else. For, unlike Tocqueville, we believe that the crown made no systematic attempt to extinguish freedom. On the contrary, a number of ministers came to view the reinstatement of institutions embodying a spirit of liberty as beneficial to the purposes of government. In this sense, the advent of constitutional monarchy in 1789 should not surprise. It followed a decade of experimentation with quasi-representative bodies during which notions of consent and participation made rapid headway. The greater challenge is to explain why the final emergence of a limited form of monarchy was accompanied by the destruction of an entire social order. Of course, one of the difficulties facing this line of reasoning is that we know little about the attitudes of the monarch. What did Louis XVI want on acceding to the throne? How much flexibility would he show in the pursuit of his objectives? Dynastic obligations apart, Louis was certainly committed to upholding the power and pretensions of the monarchy in an age of ferocious international rivalries. However, it is much less certain that he was wedded to the ancestral practice of absolutism. Throughout his reign Louis showed that he was prepared to run the risks of reform, provided always that the gamble offered a reasonable prospect of return in terms of the enhancement of the powers of the crown. Thus, he posed no insuperable obstacle to the direction in which the machine of government was moving in any case. Ministers were able to persuade him that a measured amount of power sharing, covering matters such as tax collection, would serve only to strengthen his authority. What Louis was most reluctant to take was any formal step towards the effacement of the 'society of orders'. Yet critics among the privileged orders were quick to point out that the reform agenda of administrative monarchy tended precisely in this direction.

Thus the reform impulse set in place a dangerous illusion. By the end of 1787 streamlined absolute monarchy was no longer an option. Instead a revision of absolutism in the direction of aristocratic constitutionalism beckoned enticingly. Yet the farreaching changes which Louis had been persuaded to endorse, were predicated on a significant extension of the government's right to tax. This pushed privilege to the forefront of the debate and rendered those expecting to benefit from power sharing highly vulnerable. Meanwhile, the tried and hitherto trusted lieutenants of Bourbon state-building became the first casualties of the operation to reseat the authority of the monarchy. Having largely contributed to the growth of a reform constituency, the intendants were overtaken by the speed of events. Briefly, Provincial Assemblies contrived to mediate the tensions engendered by the transition from administrative to constitutional monarchy, but the ambiguities attendant upon their creation and composition raised doubts. They seemed insufficiently independent to serve as the progenitors of a neo-liberal regime, while at the same time appearing incapable of satisfying those who looked forward to the restoration of an older, particularist and pre-absolutist form of constitutional monarchy. In any case, they were swiftly shunted to one side when a complete refashioning of the kingdom became the order of the day in the autumn of 1789.

For the Revolution did not come to a halt with the regrouping of the deputies in a 'National Assembly' and the agreement of Louis XVI to rule henceforward as a constitutional monarch. This serves to remind us that a focus upon the high politics of reform will only explain so much. And, indeed, the other principal objective of this study has been to integrate the considerable and increasingly divergent researches of scholars of both the political and the social history of late eighteenth-century France. That is, to offer an appreciation of the 'political' which does not derive simply from base/superstructure modes of analysis, while at the same time allowing the 'social' dimension of the late *ancien-régime* crisis to emerge. The task is fraught with peril as a recent textbook author points out: 'scholars who have attempted a synthesis only manage to muddle and get muddled'.[6]

When searching for explanations of the extraordinary stamina displayed by the Revolution, two themes attract notice. One is the long- and short-term movement of the rural economy as revealed by Ernest Labrousse, the other is the social history of elites, both privileged and unprivileged. Each of these topics has been explored thoroughly in the preceding chapters, but it is worth restating the major points in order to make plain the connection with the events of 1789. Labrousse's concentration on the performance of the agricultural economy is vulnerable to criticism, but it does have the merit of directing attention to the structural frailties of the kingdom which Louis XVI inherited in 1774. After decades of growth and relative prosperity, the economy was entering a recession which would eventually spread to nearly all sectors: agriculture, industry and domestic, even international, trade. Moreover, this 'intercycle' was exacerbated by the increased frequency of climatic abnormalities which produced the poor harvests of 1782–3, the droughts of 1785–6 and the desperate combination of summer dearth and winter paralysis of 1788–9. The social repercussions of this economic downturn can be detected at every level, but it is the impact on the country dweller which is relevant here. Tenant farmers defaulted on their leases, plot holders were forced to sell up, whilst the lowest tier of the peasantry consisting of those dependent on agricultural or industrial wages were often driven into vagabondage.

Here we have the lineaments of a social crisis of the *ancien régime*, then. That is to say, a crisis which manifestly anticipated the 'political' collapse of absolute monarchy, and which would dramatically enlarge the consequences of that collapse. The researches of Georges Lefebvre and a host of scholars working within the parameters which he laid down leave little room for doubt on this score.[7] For the French peasantry were already on a mobile footing prior to 1789, and they had already identified their targets. It is therefore inexact to assert that the Revolution issued from a political duel between the monarchy and would-be power sharers, which just happened to coincide with an unfortunate socio-economic conjuncture. In reality, France fell victim to a multi-layered crisis: of the economy, of institutions and of state finance and credit-worthiness. If this can be accepted, it quickly becomes apparent why the Revolution did not end when, in late June 1789, Louis

XVI ordered the deputies of the clergy and the nobility to join in common session with the representatives of the Third Estate. For as soon as the constitutional agenda neared completion, a social agenda stood ready to take its place.

The problem of elites is simply stated. By the close of the *ancien régime* France possessed an array of elites, but they were imperfectly accommodated within the 'society of orders'. Indeed, juridical distinctions which no longer corresponded to the actual social structure of the country had become a source of frustration to all concerned. For good reasons of its own, the monarchy found the obligation to keep faith with a society constructed on the principle of institutional diversity increasingly onerous. As for the nobility they were divided over the real benefits conferred by prescriptive rights and suspicious, in any case, of the designs of the crown in this area. The clergy, likewise, contained too many fissures to think, and speak, as one. Meanwhile, an expanding layer of commoners (the 'bourgeoisie') found the rigid hierarchies of the *ancien régime* to be incapable of providing a niche appropriate to their talents and sense of self-worth. Why, then, did elites not rearrange themselves into 'natural' groupings based on wealth or occupation? The difficulty here was that the 'society of orders' retained considerable vitality. It was not a figment of legal treatises, but an ordering of society rooted in tangible concessions, exemptions and privileges.

The case for an intermingling of elites has been examined closely in chapter 2. That it fails ultimately to withstand scrutiny can be attributed to the tenacity of the 'society of orders'. At the pinnacle of each estate, prelates, aristocrats and wealthy commoners may well have mingled unselfconsciously. Much about their sources of wealth, lifestyles and cultural outlook drew them together. But privilege – the lubricant of particularism and diversity – continued to divide until the very end of the *ancien régime*, and even beyond. It also distorted the institutional economy, forcing entrepreneurs such as iron-master Pierre Babaud de la Chaussade to buy into the system in order to beat it.[8] That they were able to do so did not diminish the sense of frustration felt by the upwardly mobile at the way society was ordered. Ultimately, then, the health of *ancien-régime* society depended not on what accommodation may have been reached at the apex but on attitudes rooted at less exalted levels, that is to say, among the petty provincial nobility, the parish clergy and the small-town bourgeoisie. At these levels the possession or non-possession of privilege continued to count for a great deal. Even in 1789, amid near total acceptance of the need to terminate personal tax exemptions, it remained an open question whether the deputies attending the Estates General would use the occasion to force the issue of the 'society of orders'. In the end the decision was taken out of their hands by insurrectionary peasants and craftsmen. Nonetheless, it should be remembered that anachronistic distinctions of order continued to exert a powerful influence on political allegiances within the National Assembly, notwithstanding the hymns sung in praise of the 'new man'.

The work of the National Assembly provides a final opportunity to take stock of the arguments and the methods pursued in the writing of this book. If 1789 marked the 'birth of political modernity',[9] as has been claimed, there can be no room for ambiguity over the historic role performed by the deputies of France's first Revolutionary legislature. Indeed, three subsidiary arguments appear to flow from this conviction. First, the significance of the confrontation between administrative monarchy and its critics *before* 1789 can be downgraded as being literally without consequence. Since the Revolution generated its own ideological dynamic, the constitutional debates during what is commonly described as the Pre-Revolution are simply irrelevant. Second, the pioneer reputation of the National Assembly is not merely secured but greatly enhanced. Thus the editors of the influential *Critical Dictionary of the French Revolution* (1989) picture the Assembly as a body fired with a totalising vision of the new order from the very beginning.[10] Third, and by logical extension, it is suggested that the impetus for political and societal change therefore came from above. In other words, parliamentary history can alone provide a sufficient account of how the early Revolution developed.

However, it is my contention that none of these perspectives provides an entirely satisfactory framework within which to analyse the character of the new regime. The challenge posed by the phenomenon of 1789 is to understand what happened as *both* event and process. It is no answer to the conundrum simply to assert that the French Revolution was begotten not made. Plainly the deputies borrowed from the practices, policies, even the personnel, of the old regime to a considerable degree. Although they would not have formulated the relationship in quite these terms, they inherited and very largely implemented the reform agenda of the old monarchy. To suggest that they always built from scratch and with scant regard for past experience is frankly perverse and shows more respect for the flamboyant rhetoric of regeneration than for the detailed legislative record. But the point to grasp is that the National Assembly was so empowered as to overcome the limitations of reforming absolutism: cautious and piecemeal measures made way for root-and-branch solutions brooking no restraint or interference. Modest concessions in the direction of representation and accountability were overtaken by unstoppable forces demanding a full-blown separation of powers and a written constitution. Spotty reform of a ramshackle tax regime yielded in the face of an overwhelming urge to build a system of public contributions which treated all citizens alike and applied to the entire national territory. Hesitant steps to curb the wealth and prerogatives of the catholic church gave way to bold measures subordinating the spiritual power to the urgent financial needs of state and proclaiming the absolute value of religious toleration.

Yet, it is important to acknowledge that the National Assembly did not act simply as executor to the *ancien régime*. The deputies also turned their attention to areas of society and the economy which had barely registered among the reform objectives of administrative monarchy. Not since Maupeou had anyone considered seriously the feasibility of a wholesale reimbursement of venal offices, nor had anyone in government ever contemplated the extinction of seigneurial dues and the ecclesiastical tithe, save over a very long time span. As for the brusque and busybodying interference in the pastoral life of the church enshrined in the Civil Constitution of the Clergy, it is difficult to find any precedent in the buzzing hive of old-regime reformism. However, the sudden and ruthless assault on the 'society of orders' is what really marks out the extraordinary distance travelled in 1789. The reduction of sectional privilege had become part of the (largely surreptitious) project of administrative monarchy, it is true, but never in their wildest imaginings had ministers anticipated a cutting away of territorial, institutional and individual immunities on the scale of the operation which got under way during the evening session of 4 August.

How were the deputies able to perform this feat in contrast to the servants of so-called absolute monarchy whose fragile and piecemeal reforms often took years to enforce? It should be seen as a measure of the power of their ideology, more specifically of the energising myth of the nation, responds the historiographical establishment. I would not dissent from this general verdict. But it needs to be nuanced in several particulars, for otherwise there is a real danger of comprehending the ideology of the early Revolution as an autonomous and unidirectional force devoid of social flesh and bone, and detached from the tensions of day-to-day politics. It is well, for instance, to treat the 'miraculous' conception of the nation with a degree of scepticism. For the inspiring vision of the nation was not a unique product of collective political hallucination on the night of 4 August. It can be found in embryo in the torrent of speculation unleashed by Brienne's Provincial Assemblies edicts; in the pamphlet debates of 1788–9; and, of course, in the tense and impatient search for an escape route from stalemate in the Estates General. Moreover, the nation remained a fluid and controversial construct for many months after its promulgation. Indeed some provinces roundly condemned the ceaseless reiteration of 'all these big phrases empty of meaning' as one brochure put it.[11] In other words the ideological armature of the National Assembly did not fall into place in a flash, nor did it simply bulldoze all that lay in its path. The idea of the nation derived its potency from the power of consent, and consent, in turn, implied a process of negotiation with the country at large.

A vision confined to the parliamentary history of the years 1789–91 is apt to miss this point. For the vigour (and originality) of Revolutionary politics stemmed precisely from the scope for interaction in a greatly enlarged public sphere. While the legislators in Versailles, or Paris, endeavoured to control the agenda for change, they were repeatedly assailed and deflected by countervailing political forces. Thus it is both correct and incorrect to depict the National Assembly as the great propelling force of the early Revolution. By 1791 the deputies had willed into being a fully constitutional regime, and, by the same token, willed into oblivion the not inconsiderable achievements of reforming absolutism. But they had also been propelled into making changes which had not figured in the original project, and which amounted to the dissolution of an entire social order. It now behoves historians to recognise these twin political and social imperatives. For jointly they contrived the downfall of the old regime and the building of a new one to take its place.

Notes

The following abbreviations are used:

AAP   Archives de l'Assistance Publique
AD   Archives Départementales
AN   Archives Nationales
Annales ESC   *Annales, Economies, Sociétés, Civilisations*

INTRODUCTION

1. C. Lucas (ed.), *Rewriting the French Revolution: The Andrew Brown Lectures* (Oxford, 1991), p. vi.
2. See F. Furet and R. Halévi, 'L'Année 1789', *Annales ESC*, 44(1989), 4.
3. C. Lucas (ed.), *The French Revolution and the Creation of Modern Political Culture*, vol. II: *The Political Culture of the French Revolution* (Oxford, 1988), p. 241.
4. R. R. Palmer (ed.), *The Two Tocquevilles Father and Son: Hervé and Alexis de Tocqueville on the Coming of the French Revolution* (Princeton, N.J., 1987), p. 30.
5. A. Sorel, *Europe and the French Revolution: The Political Traditions of the Old Regime*, trans. and ed. A. Cobban and J. W. Hunt (London and Glasgow, 1970), p. 265.
6. E. Lavisse, *Histoire de France illustrée depuis les origines jusqu'à la Révolution* (9 vols., Paris, 1911), IX, pp. 313–400; P. Sagnac, *La Formation de la société française moderne* (2 vols., Paris, 1945–6), II, pp. 193–299.
7. See J. G. Gagliardo, *Enlightened Despotism* (London, 1968), p. 32.
8. O. Browning (ed.), *Despatches from Paris, 1784–1790* (2 vols. London, 1909–10), I, p. 147, Hailes to Carmarthen, 25 October 1786; also II, p. 30, *idem* to *idem*, 17 April 1788.
9. B. Stone, *The French Parlements and the Crisis of the Old Regime* (Chapel Hill and London, 1986), p. 169.
10. 'Le régime qu'une révolution détruit vaut presque toujours mieux que celui qui l'avait immédiatement précédé, et l'expérience apprend que le moment le plus dangereux pour un mauvais gouvernement est d'ordinaire celui où il commence à se réformer' (A. de Tocqueville, *L'Ancien Régime* (Oxford, 1969), p. 182.
11. See H. Grange, *Les Idées de Necker* (Paris, 1974); R. D. Harris, *Necker:*

Reform Statesman of the Ancien Régime (Berkeley, Calif., 1979); *idem, Necker and the Revolution of 1789* (Lanham, Md., 1986).

12. P. Renouvin, *Les Assemblées provinciales de 1787. Origines, développement, résultats* (Paris, 1921).

13. J. P. Boyd (ed.), *The Papers of Thomas Jefferson* (24 vols., Princeton, N.J., 1950–90), XII, p. 413, John Adams to Thomas Jefferson, 10 December 1787.

14. H. Carré, 'Le Mémoire de M. Necker sur les Assemblées provinciales, 1778–1781', *Bulletin de la Faculté des Lettres de Poitiers* (1893), p. 184.

15. Boyd (ed.), *The Papers of Thomas Jefferson*, XIII, p. 489, Thomas Jefferson to James Monroe, 9 August 1788.

16. F. Furet, *La Révolution de Turgot à Jules Ferry, 1770–1880* (Paris, 1988), pp. 26, 57.

17. See P. Gueniffey, 'Les Assemblées et la représentation', in Lucas (ed.), *The French Revolution*, vol. II: *The Political Culture of the French Revolution*, pp. 234.

I: GOVERNMENT

1. A. Young, *Travels in France during the Years 1787, 1788, 1789* (London, 1900), pp. lvi, 43.

2. R. Mousnier, *Les Institutions de la France sous la Monarchie Absolue, 1598–1789* (2 vols., Paris, 1974–80), II, p. 249.

3. See H. Le Bras and E. Todd, *L'Invention de la France: atlas anthropologique et politique* (Paris, 1981).

4. P. Doisy, *Le Royaume de France et les Etats de Lorraine* (Paris, 1753).

5. E.-G. Guyot, *Dictionnaire des postes* (Paris, 1754).

6. AD de la Lozère 2E 874 undated note.

7. P. Dawson, *Provincial Magistrates and Revolutionary Politics in France, 1789–1795* (Cambridge, Mass., 1972), pp. 71–2.

8. Young, *Travels in France*, p. 45.

9. M. Bordes, *L'Administration provinciale et municipale en France au XVIII siècle* (Paris, 1972), p. 105.

10. H. Fréville, *L'Intendance de Bretagne, 1689–1790: essai sur l'histoire d'une intendance en Pays d'Etats au XVIIIe siècle* (3 vols., Rennes, 1953), III, p. 193 n. 132.

11. See Harris, *Necker*, p. 181.

12. *Règlement sur la formation et la composition des assemblées qui auront lieu dans la province de Champagne en vertu de l'édit portant création des assemblées provinciales*, Versailles, 23 June 1787, *Assemblées municipales*: article 6.

13. E. Tambour, *Les Registres municipaux de Rennemoulin, juillet 1787 à floréal an IV* (Paris, 1903), p. 13.

14. C. Souchon, 'L'Assemblée d'élection de Laon et les "affaires du pays"', in *Actes du 111e Congrès national des sociétés savantes. Poitiers 1986. Section d'Histoire Moderne et Contemporaine* (3 vols., Paris, 1987), i, fascicle 1, p. 122 n. 13.

15. P. M. Jones, *Politics and Rural Society: The Southern Massif Central, c. 1750–1880* (Cambridge, 1985), p. 182.

16. Boyd (ed.), *The Papers of Thomas Jefferson*, XII, p. 59.
17. K. M. Baker, 'French Political Thought at the Accession of Louis XVI', *Journal of Modern History*, 50(1978), 289. See also, J. F. Bosher, *French Finances, 1770–1795: From Business to Bureaucracy* (Cambridge, 1970), pp. 130–3.
18. P. Ardascheff, *Les Intendants de province sous Louis XVI* (Paris, 1909), pp. 117–33.
19. F. Furet, *Penser la Révolution française* (Paris, 1978), p. 67.

2: SOCIETY

1. R. Mousnier, *The Institutions of France under the Absolute Monarchy, 1598–1789* (2 vols., Chicago and London, 1979–84), I, pp. 4–16.
2. G. Chaussinand-Nogaret, *The French Nobility in the Eighteenth Century: From Feudalism to Enlightenment* (Cambridge, 1985), p. 167.
3. G. J. Cavanaugh, 'Turgot: The Rejection of Enlightened Despotism', *French Historical Studies*, 6(1969), 32.
4. *Ibid.*
5. *Abbé* J.-J. Expilly, *Tableau de la population de la France* (Paris, 1780 (reprinted 1973)).
6. W. Doyle, *The Oxford History of the French Revolution* (Oxford, 1989), p. 34.
7. J. Dupâquier (ed.), *Histoire de la population française* (2 vols., Paris, 1988), II, pp. 70–1.
8. Chaussinand-Nogaret, *The French Nobility*, pp. 29–30.
9. G. Lefebvre, *The French Revolution* (2 vols., London and New York, 1964–5), I, pp. 43–9.
10. See Dupâquier (ed.), *Histoire de la population française*, II, pp. 71–2.
11. *Ibid.*, p. 72.
12. See W. Doyle, 'The Price of Offices in Pre-Revolutionary France', *Historical Journal*, 27(1984), 831–60.
13. Jones, *Politics and Rural Society*, p. 79 n. 13.
14. W. Doyle, *Origins of the French Revolution* (Oxford, 1980), p. 130.
15. See C. B. A. Behrens, *The Ancien Régime* (London, 1967), p. 46.
16. AN H¹ 1597.
17. M. P. Fitzsimmons, 'Privilege and the Polity in France, 1786–1791', *American Historical Review*, 92(1987), 270.
18. See AD Loire-Atlantique 2Mi25.
19. *Procès-verbal des séances de l'Assemblée générale des trois provinces de la généralité de Tours tenue à Tours, par Ordre du Roi, le 12 novembre 1787* (Tours, 1787), p. 111.
20. AN H¹ 1463, M. de Gourges, intendant of Montauban to controller-general, 2 June 1772.
21. See H. Guilhamon (ed.), *Journal des voyages en Haute-Guienne de J.F. Henry de Richeprey* (2 vols., Rodez, 1952–1967), II, pp. 311; AN DXIV 2, petition of inhabitants of Sainte-Croix, 29 May 1790.
22. D. Dakin, *Turgot and the Ancien Régime in France* (London, 1939), p. 63.
23. AAP Fonds Montyon *Carton 5: droit constitutionnel.*
24. Behrens, *The Ancien Régime*, p. 54.

25. For both of these examples, see A. Rioche, *De l'administration des vingtièmes sous l'Ancien Régime* (Paris, 1904), pp. 51, 138 n. 1, 172.
26. AD Puy-de-Dôme C7373 *Procès-verbal de l'assemblée de l'élection de Saint-Flour, Session du mois d'octobre 1788*, pp. 168–9.
27. Doyle, 'The Price of Offices in Pre-Revolutionary France', p. 833.
28. J. Necker, *De l'administration des finances de la France* (3 vols., n.p., 1785), III, p. 129.
29. G. Chaussinand-Nogaret, *Une Histoire des élites, 1700–1848* (Paris and The Hague, 1975), p. 22.
30. H. Guilhamon, *Origine et fortune de la bourgeoisie du Rouergue à la veille de la Révolution* (Rodez, 1921), p. 3.
31. W. Doyle, '4 August 1789: The End of Venality' (paper delivered to the George Rudé Seminar, University of Adelaide, Adelaide, July 1992).
32. A.-G. Maury, 'Les Ventes de seigneuries dans la région d'Issoire au XVIIIe siècle', in *Actes du 88e congrès national des sociétés savantes* (Clermont-Ferrand, 1963), pp. 819–28.
33. H. Guilhamon, 'Notes sur la noblesse du Rouergue à la fin du XVIIIe siècle', *Journal de l'Aveyron*, 15, 22 September 1918.
34. D. M. G. Sutherland, *France 1789–1815: Revolution and Counter-Revolution* (London, 1985), p. 18.
35. See Chaussinand-Nogaret, *The French Nobility*.
36. R. Forster, *The House of Saulx-Tavanes: Versailles and Burgundy, 1700–1830* (Baltimore and London, 1971), pp. 104–5.
37. See J. Dewald, *Pont-St-Pierre, 1398–1789: Lordship, Community and Capitalism in Early Modern France* (Berkeley, Calif., 1987), pp. 3–5. 285–8.
38. Chaussinand-Nogaret, *The French Nobility*, p. 87.
39. See G. Lewis, *The Advent of Modern Capitalism in France, 1770–1840. The Contribution of Pierre-François Tubeuf* (Oxford, 1993).
40. G. Gayot and J.-P. Hirsch (eds.), *La Révolution française et le développement du capitalisme* (Lille, 1989), p. 17.
41. W. Scott, 'Merchants and 1789: The Case of Marseille' (unpublished paper delivered to the George Rudé Seminar, University of New South Wales, Sydney, Australia, May 1982).
42. Boyd (ed.), *The Papers of Thomas Jefferson*, XII, p. 59.
43. See in particular the recent writings of K. M. Baker collected in *Inventing the French Revolution: Essays on French Political Culture in the Eighteenth Century* (Cambridge, 1990).
44. R. Chartier, *The Cultural Origins of the French Revolution* (Durham N.C., and London, 1991).
45. S. Bonin and C. Langlois (eds.), *Atlas de la Révolution française*, vol. II: *L'Enseignement, 1760–1815* (Paris, 1987), pp. 14, 17.
46. Dewald, *Pont-St-Pierre, 1398–1789*, pp. 42–4.
47. Chartier, *The Cultural Origins of the French Revolution*, p. 69.
48. *Ibid.*, p. 70.
49. *Œuvres complètes de Voltaire* (52 vols., Paris, 1883–5), XVIII, p. 11.
50. AAP Fonds Montyon *Carton 8: administration*.
51. See D. D. Bien, *The Calas Affair: Persecution, Toleration, and Heresy in Eighteenth-Century Toulouse* (Princeton, N.J., 1960 (reprinted 1979)).

52. Chartier, *The Cultural Origins of the French Revolution*, p. 27.
53. For a discussion of this concept, see *ibid.*, pp. 20–37, and R. Darnton, 'An Enlightened Revolution', *New York Review of Books*, 24 October 1991, 33–6.
54. J. Lough, *France on the Eve of Revolution: British Travellers' Observations, 1763–1788* (London, 1987), pp. 24–5.
55. D. Roche, *Le Siècle des lumières en province: académies et académiciens provinciaux, 1680–1789* (2 vols., Paris and The Hague, 1978), I, p. 57.
56. *Ibid.*, I, p. 189.
57. Dakin, *Turgot and the Ancien Régime in France*, pp. 80–1.
58. Chartier, *The Cultural Origins of the French Revolution*, pp. 162–3; J. M. Roberts, *The Mythology of the Secret Societies* (St Albans, 1974), p. 57.
59. Roche, *Le Siècle des lumières en province*, I, p. 197.
60. *Ibid.*, I, p. 189.
61. D. Echeverria, *The Maupeou Revolution: A Study in the History of Libertarianism, France, 1770–1774* (Baton Rouge, La., 1985), p. 72.
62. L. Villat, *La Corse de 1768 à 1789* (3 vols., Besançon, 1924), II, pp. 9–10.

3: ECONOMY

1. The view of Michel Morineau, summarised in F. Crouzet, *Britain Ascendant: Comparative Studies in Franco-British Economic History* (Cambridge and Paris, 1990), p. 100.
2. For example, the recent comments of J.-P. Poussou, 'Le Dynamisme de l'économie française sous Louis XVI', *Revue économique*, 40 (1989), 982–3.
3. C.-E. Labrousse, *Esquisse du mouvement des prix et des revenus en France au XVIIIe siècle* (2 vols., Paris, 1933 (reprinted 1984)), and *La Crise de l'économie française à la fin de l'Ancien Régime et au début de la Révolution* (Paris, 1944 (2nd edn, 1990)).
4. C.-E. Labrousse and F. Braudel (eds.), *Histoire économique et sociale de la France* (4 vols., Paris, 1970–6), vol. II: *Des derniers temps de l'âge seigneurial aux préludes de l'âge industriel, 1660–1789* (Paris, 1970).
5. See Labrousse and Braudel (eds.), *Histoire économique et sociale de la France*, II, p. 399; for an earlier calculation, see Labrousse, *Esquisse du mouvement des prix et des revenus en France au XVIIIe siècle*, II, pp. 598–9.
6. *Etudes et Documents* (Editions du Comité pour l'histoire économique et financière, Ministère des Finances), 2 (1990), 37.
7. J. K. J. Thomson, *Clermont-de-Lodève, 1633–1789: Fluctuations in the Prosperity of a Languedocian Cloth-Making Town* (Cambridge, 1982).
8. See P. N. Bamford, *Privilege and Profit: A Business Family in Eighteenth-Century France* (Philadelphia, 1988).
9. Labrousse and Braudel (eds.), *Histoire économique et sociale de la France*, II, p. 89.
10. J.-C. Toutain, 'Le Produit de l'agriculture française de 1700 à 1958: II, La Croissance', in *Cahiers de l'Institut de science économique appliquée*, supplement to 115 (1961), p. 276.
11. J. Goy and E. Le Roy Ladurie, *Les Fluctuations du produit de la dîme: conjoncture décimale et domaniale de la fin du Moyen Age au XVIIIe siècle* (Paris and The Hague, 1972), pp. 23–4.

12. See J.-M. Moriceau and G. Postel-Vinay, *Ferme, entreprise famille: grande exploitation et changements agricoles: les Chartier, XVIIe–XIXe siècles* (Paris, 1992).

13. G. Lemarchand, *La Fin du Féodalisme dans le pays de Caux: conjoncture économique et démographique et structure sociale dans une région de grande culture de la crise du XVIIe siècle à la stabilisation de la Révolution, 1640–1795* (Paris, 1989), p. 290. But note the reservations expressed by M. Morineau in his review of the same (*Revue d'histoire moderne et contemporaine*, 39 (1992), 335–9).

14. See G. Fourquin, *Les Campagnes de la région parisienne à la fin du Moyen Age du milieu du XIIIe siècle au début du XVIe siècle* (Paris, 1964), pp. 529–30, E. Le Roy Ladurie, 'History that Stands Still', in E. Le Roy Ladurie, *The Mind and Method of the Historian* (Brighton, 1981), pp. 1–27.

15. Figures taken from F. Bayard and P. Guignet, *L'Economie française au XVIe XVIIe et XVIIIe, siècles* (Paris and Gap, 1991), p. 168.

16. *Ibid.*, p. 169.

17. *Ibid.*, p. 170.

18. *Ibid.*, p. 172.

19. *Ibid.*, p. 171.

20. *Ibid.*, p. 174.

21. *Ibid.*, p. 172.

22. *Ibid.*, p. 45.

23. Dewald, *Pont-St-Pierre, 1398–1789*, p. 282.

24. J. F. Bosher, *The Single Duty Project: A Study of the Movement for a French Customs Union in the Eighteenth Century* (London, 1964), p. 14.

25. *Ibid.*, p. 23.

26. J. Bouteil, *Le Rachat des péages au XVIIIe siècle d'après les papiers du bureau des péages* (Paris, 1925), pp. 77, 119.

27. See above p. 67.

28. Thomson, *Clermont-de-Lodève*.

29. Labrousse and Braudel (eds.), *Histoire économique et sociale de la France*, II, p. 165; J.-C. Asselain, *Histoire économique de la France du XVIIIe siècle à nos jours*, vol. I: *De l'Ancien Régime à la Première Guerre mondiale* (Paris, 1984), p. 53.

30. Young, *Travels in France*, p. 50.

31. See J. Musset, 'Une source méconnue: les "mémoires municipaux" de l'élection ou département d'Argentan (1788)', *Bulletin de la société historique et archéologique de l'Orne*, 108 (1989), 65.

32. Asselain, *Histoire économique de la France*, p. 55.

33. *Ibid.*, p. 62.

34. *Ibid.*, p. 64; Bayard and Guignet, *L'Economie française au XVIe, XVIIe et XVIIIe siècles*, p. 136.

35. Browning (ed.), *Despatches from Paris, 1784–1790*, I, p. 16.

36. J. Tarrade, *Le Commerce colonial de la France à la fin de l'Ancien Régime: l'évolution du régime de 'l'Exclusif' de 1763 à 1789* (2 vols., Paris, 1972), II, p. 778.

37. Labrousse, *La Crise de l'économie française*.

38. The most recent are: Lewis, *The Advent of Modern Capitalism in France,*

1770–1840; J.-P. Hirsch, *Les Deux Rêves du commerce: entreprise et institutions dans la région Lilleoise, 1780–1860* (Paris, 1991); Lemarchand, *La Fin du Féodalisme dans le pays de Caux*; J.-P. Jessenne, *Pouvoir au village et Révolution: Artois, 1760–1848* (Lille, 1987).

39. See Asselain, *Histoire économique de la France*, I, pp. 25–6.
40. See G. Weulersse, *La Physiocratie à l'aube de la Révolution, 1781–1792* (Paris, 1985), p. 173.
41. *Procès-verbal des séances de l'Assemblée de Basse-Normandie tenues à Caen en novembre et décembre 1787* (Caen, 1788), p. 148.
42. Jessenne, *Pouvoir au village et Révolution*, pp. 25 n. 17, 26.
43. See J. A. Kington, 'Daily Weather Mapping from 1781: A Detailed Synoptic Examination of Weather and Climate during the Decade Leading up to the French Revolution', *Climatic Change*, 3 (1980), 24.
44. Boyd (ed.), *The Papers of Thomas Jefferson*, XVIII, pp. 159, 161.
45. Labrousse and Braudel (eds.), *Histoire économique et sociale de la France*, II, pp. 540–1.
46. Fréville, *L'Intendance de Bretagne, 1689–1790*, III, pp. 183–5.
47. AN H^1 1625, Lavoisier to unnamed correspondent, Frêchines, 31 July 1785.
48. Fréville, *L'Intendance de Bretagne, 1689–1790*, III, p. 184.
49. *Procès-verbal des séances de l'Assemblée de Basse-Normandie tenues à Caen en novembre et décembre 1787*, p. 148.
50. Poussou, 'Le Dynamisme de l'économie française sous Louis XVI', 966.
51. Browning (ed.), *Despatches from Paris, 1784–1790*, II, p. 76.
52. Boyd (ed.), *The Papers of Thomas Jefferson*, XVIII, p. 487.
53. *Mémoires d'agriculture, d'économie rurale et domestique publiés par la Société Royale d'Agriculture: année 1789* (Paris, n.d.), p. xxiv.
54. See J.-P. Hirsch, *La Nuit du 4 août* (Paris, 1978), p. 41.

4: REFORMERS AND THE REFORM CONSISTENCY

1. L. Gershoy, *From Despotism to Revolution, 1763–1789* (New York, 1963 (first edn, 1944)).
2. A. Cobban, *A History of Modern France* (3 vols., Harmondsworth, 1965).
3. *Ibid.*, I, p. 112.
4. See above, p. 10.
5. See above, p. 6.
6. J. Hardman, *Louis XVI* (New Haven and London, 1993).
7. Dakin, *Turgot*, p. 232.
8. Hardman, *Louis XVI*, p. 50.
9. See accounts given in Dakin, *Turgot*, p. 278, and Hardman, *Louis XVI*, p. 54.
10. K. M. Baker, *Inventing the French Revolution*, p. 192.
11. *Ibid.*, p. 191.
12. Harris, *Necker*, pp. 181–2.
13. Bosher, *French Finances*, p. 92.
14. M. de Lescure (ed.), *Correspondance secrète inédite sur Louis XVI, Marie-Antoinette, la Cour et la ville de 1777 à 1792. Publiée d'après les manuscrits de la*

Bibliothèque impériale de Saint Pétersbourg, avec une préface, des notes et un index alphabétique par M. de Lescure (2 vols., Paris, 1866), II, p. 92.

15. Hardman, *Louis XVI*, p. 138.
16. *Ibid.*
17. *Ibid.*, p. 136.
18. See AN H¹ 1596; H¹ 1601.
19. F. Mosser, *Les Intendants des finances au XVIIIe siècle: les Lefèvre d'Ormesson et le 'Département des Impositions'* (Geneva, 1978), pp. 149, 171 and n., 212–20.
20. *Ibid.*
21. AAP Fonds Montyon *Carton 8: administration.*
22. AN H¹ 94.
23. M. Bordes, 'Les Intendants éclairés de la fin de l'Ancien Régime', *Revue d'histoire économique et sociale*, 39(1961), 57–83.
24. See AAP Fonds Montyon *Carton 7: droit constitutionnel. Procès-verbal de l'assemblée provinciale de l'Isle de France. Année 1787*, pp. 101–34.
25. For the activities of the Chaumont de la Galaizière, see M. Antoine, *Le Gouvernement et l'administration sous Louis XV. Dictionnaire biographique* (Paris, 1978); G. Hottenger, *Les Remembrements en Lorraine au dix-huitième siècle* (Nancy, 1915), p. 42; AN 27AP *Dossier 2: papiers de François de Neufchâteau.*
26. Villat, *La Corse de 1768 à 1789*, II; M. Bordes, 'Un Intendant éclairé de la fin de l'Ancien Régime: Claude-François de Boucheporn', *Annales du Midi*, 74(1962), 177–94; T. E. Hall, 'Thought and Practice of Enlightened Government in French Corsica', *American Historical Review*, 74(1969), 880–905.
27. Bordes, 'Un Intendant éclairé de la fin de l'Ancien Régime', p. 193.
28. Quoted in C. B. A. Behrens, *Society, Government and the Enlightenment: The Experiences of Eighteenth-Century France and Prussia* (London, 1985), p. 134.
29. S. L. Kaplan, *Bread, Politics and Political Economy in the Reign of Louis XV* (2 vols., The Hague, 1976), I, p. xxvi.
30. *Ibid.*, I, p. 158.
31. P. Chevallier, *Loménie de Brienne et l'ordre monastique, 1766–1789* (Paris, 1959), p. 40.
32. J. W. Merrick, *The Desacralisation of the French Monarchy in the Eighteenth Century* (Baton Rouge, La., 1990).
33. *Ibid.*, p. 164.
34. T. Tackett, *Priest and Parish in Eighteenth-Century France* (Princeton, N.J., 1977), pp. 240–2.
35. T. Tackett, *Religion, Revolution and Regional Culture in Eighteenth-Century France: The Ecclesiastical Oath of 1791* (Princeton, N.J.), p. 131.
36. In this connection, note particularly the work of Dale K. Van Kley, *The Damiens Affair and the Unraveling of the Ancien Régime, 1750–1770* (Princeton, N.J., 1984), and *idem*, 'The Jansenist Constitutional Legacy in the French Revolution', in K. M. Baker (ed.), *The French Revolution and the Creation of Modern Political Culture*, vol. I: *The Political Culture of the Old Regime* (Oxford, 1987), pp. 169–201.
37. J. Millot, *Le Régime féodal en Franche-Comté au XVIIIe siècle* (Besançon, 1937), p. 134.

38. M. Marion, *Le Garde des Sceaux Lamoignon et la réforme judiciaire de 1788* (Paris, 1905), p. 64.

39. *Ibid.*, p. 215.

40. Quoted by J. F. Ramsey, 'The Judicial Reform of 1788 and the French Revolution', in F. J. Cox *et al.* (eds.), *Studies in Modern European History in Honor of Franklin Charles Palm* (New York, 1956), pp. 227–8.

41. Stone, *The French Parlements and the Crisis of the Old Regime*, p. 174.

5: TOWARDS 'A TRULY NATIONAL REPRESENTATION', 1787–1789

1. Stone, *The French Parlements and the Crisis of the Old Regime*, p. 15.

2. Quoted in J. Egret, *The French Prerevolution, 1787–1788*, trans. W. D. Camp (Chicago and London, 1977), p. 71.

3. *Encyclopédie ou dictionnaire raisonné des sciences, des arts et des métiers* (17 vols., Neufchâtel, 1765), XIV, p. 143.

4. J. Russell Major, *The Estates General of 1560* (Princeton, N.J., 1951), p. 73.

5. G. Bossenga, 'City and State: An Urban Perspective of the Origins of the French Revolution', in Baker (ed.), *The French Revolution and the Creation of Modern Political Culture*, vol. I, p. 117.

6. Gueniffey, 'Les Assemblées et la représentation'.

7. See M. de la Tremoïlle, 'L'Assemblée provinciale d'Anjou, d'après les archives de Serrant, 1787–1789', *L'Anjou historique*, 1(1900–1), 543.

8. *Ibid.*, 556.

9. F. Lebrun, *Parole de dieu et révolution: les sermons d'un curé angevin avant et pendant la guerre de Vendée* (Toulouse, 1979), p. 94.

10. See P. M. Jones, 'Reforming Absolutism and the Ending of the Old Regime in France', *Australian Journal of French Studies*, 29(1992), 227.

11. AD Maine-et-Loire C317.

12. AN H^1 1609.

13. A. Fillon, 'Louis Simon, étaminier, 1741–1820 dans son village du Haut-Maine au siècle des lumières' (2 vols., thèse de 3e cycle, University of Maine, 1982), II, p. 68.

14. Renouvin, *Les Assemblées provinciales de 1787*, p. 397.

15. AN H^1 1596.

16. Quoted in Egret, *The French Revolution, 1787–1788*, p. 162.

17. See J. Nicolas, *La Révolution française dans les Alpes: Dauphiné et Savoie* (Toulouse, 1989), p. 55.

18. See J. M. Roberts and J. Hardman, *French Revolution Documents* (2 vols., Oxford, 1966–73), I, p. 32.

19. Browning (ed.), *Despatches from Paris*, II, p. 99.

20. See Hardman, *Louis XVI*, p. 138.

21. Egret, *The French Revolution, 1787–1788*, p. 189. But see also, J. Egret, *Necker, ministre de Louis XVI, 1776–1790* (Paris, 1975), pp. 217–18.

22. Harris, *Necker and the Revolution of 1789*, p. 275.

23. AN H^1 1601.

24. Lescure (ed.), *Correspondance secrète*, II, p. 302.

25. Browning (ed.), *Despatches from Paris, 1784–1790*, II, p. 124.

26. Quoted in Doyle, *Origins of the French Revolution*, p. 147.

27. Estimates taken from M. Thénard, *Bailliages de Versailles et de Meudon. Les Cahiers des paroisses avec commentaires accompagnés de quelques cahiers de curés* (Versailles, 1889), p. xii; R. Halévi, 'La Monarchie et les élections: position des problèmes', in Baker (ed.), *The French Revolution and the Creation of Modern Political Culture*, vol. I, pp. 393–4.

28. Boyd (ed.), *The Papers of Thomas Jefferson*, XIV, p. 638.

29. Hirsch, *La Nuit du 4 août*, p. 42.

30. Furet, *Penser la Révolution française*, p. 62.

31. See B. F. Hyslop, *A Guide to the General Cahiers of 1789* (New York, 1936), p. 144.

32. Hirsch, *La nuit du 4 août*, p. 42.

33. See J. Markoff, 'Peasants Protest: The Claims of Lord, Church and State in the *Cahiers de Doléances* of 1789', *Comparative Studies in Society and History*, 32(1990), 427.

34. Chaussinand-Nogaret, *The French Nobility*, pp. 134–5.

35. *Ibid.*, p. 162.

36. See Tackett, *Religion, Revolution, and Regional Culture in Eighteenth-Century France*, p. 148.

37. *Cahiers des plaintes et doléances de Loire-Atlantique 1789. Texte intégral et commentaires. Cet ouvrage édité par le conseil-général de Loire-Atlantique ... sous la direction de Michel Le Mené et Marie-Hélène Santrot* (4 vols., Nantes, 1989), I, p. 76.

38. Boyd (ed.), *The Papers of Thomas Jefferson*, XV, p. 105.

39. E. Le Roy Ladurie, 'Révoltes et contestations rurales en France de 1675 à 1788', *Annales ESC*, 29(1974), 6–22.

40. See the report by G. Lemarchand, 'Troubles populaires au XVIIIe siècle et conscience de classe: une préface à la Révolution française', *Bulletin d'histoire de la Révolution française, années 1986–1989* (Editions du Comité des Travaux historiques et scientifiques, Paris, 1990), pp. 95–108.

41. See J. Markoff, *The Abolition of Feudalism: Peasants, Lords and Legislators in the French Revolution* (University Park, Pa., forthcoming).

42. Defined as 'an instance of twenty or more people of the countryside acting publicly and as a group, directly engaged in seizing or damaging the resources of another party or defending themselves against another party's claims upon them.' Markoff, *The Abolition of Feudalism*, p. 179.

43. C. A. Bouton, *The Flour War: Gender, Class and Community in Late Ancien Régime French Society* (Pennsylvania State University Press, 1993); *ibid.*, 'L' "économie morale" et la guerre des farines de 1775', in F. Gauthier and G.-R. Ikni (eds.), *La Guerre du blé au XVIIIe siècle: la critique populaire contre le libéralisme économique au XVIIIe siècle* (Paris, 1988), pp. 93–110.

44. Bouton, *The Flour War*, pp. 146, 156–8.

45. Nicolas, *La Révolution française dans les Alpes*, p. 53.

46. The preemptive acquisition of a holding by the seigneur on the death of a vassal whose children were no longer resident.

47. J. Egret, 'La Révolution aristocratique en Franche-Comté et son échec, 1788–1789', *Revue d'histoire moderne et contemporaine*, 1(1954), 268.

48. M. Cubells, *Les Horizons de la liberté: naissance de la Révolution en Provence, 1787–1789* (Aix-en-Provence, 1987), p. 64.

49. *Ibid.*, pp. 99–100.
50. *Ibid.*, pp. 94–6.
51. *Ibid.*, p. 151.
52. *Ibid.*, p. 136.

6: THE NATIONAL ASSEMBLY, 1789–1791

1. Fitzsimmons, 'Privilege and the Polity in France, 1786–1791', 281.
2. Young, *Travels in France*, p. 182.
3. *Ibid.*, p. 197.
4. For a reexamination of this episode, see M. Price, 'The "Ministry of the Hundred Hours": A Reappraisal', *French History*, 4(1990), 317–39, and Hardman, *Louis XVI*, pp. 149–58.
5. The most recent analysis is by C. Ramsay, *The Ideology of the Great Fear: The Soissonnais in 1789* (Baltimore and London, 1992).
6. Markoff, *The Abolition of Feudalism*, figure 6.7.
7. *Ibid.*, p. 293.
8. M. P. Fitzsimmons, 'The Committee of the Constitution and the Remaking of France, 1789–1791', *French History*, 4(1990), 27–8.
9. A. Mousset, *Un témoin ignoré de la Révolution: le Comte de Fernan Nuñez, ambassadeur d'Espagne à Paris, 1787–1791* (Paris, 1924), p. 66.
10. Boyd (ed.), *The Papers of Thomas Jefferson*, XV, p. 334.
11. Mousset, *Un témoin ignoré de la Révolution*, p. 66.
12. E. H. Lemay, *Dictionnaire des Constituants, 1789–1791* (2 vols., Oxford and Paris, 1991), II, p. 907.
13. R. Marx, *Recherches sur la vie politique d'Alsace pré-révolutionnaire et révolutionnaire* (Strasbourg, 1966), p. 114.
14. For this paragraph, see AD Loire-Atlantique C566–78; C add. 19–21.
15. AD Loire-Atlantique 2Mi25 (R2).
16. J. Godechot, *La Révolution française dans le Midi-Toulousain* (Toulouse, 1986), p. 96.
17. See Furet and Halévi, 'L'Année 1789', 3–24; S. Schama, *Citizens. A Chronicle of the French Revolution* (London, 1989), pp. 447–8, 859–61.
18. F. Mirouse (ed.), *François Ménard de la Groye, député du Maine aux Etats généraux. Correspondance, 1789–1791* (Le Mans, 1989), p. 234.
19. L. R. Berlanstein, *The Barristers of Toulouse in the Eighteenth Century, 1740–1793* (Baltimore and London, 1975), p. 171.
20. H. Carré (ed.), *Marquis de Ferrières: correspondance inédite, 1789, 1790, 1791* (Paris, 1932), p. 212.
21. AN 291AP *Dossier 2: papiers M. d'Aine, intendant.*
22. Decree of 4, 6, 7 and 11 August 1789, article one.
23. G. Guigne (ed.), *Procès-verbaux des séances de l'Assemblée Provinciale de la généralité de Lyon et de sa Commission Intermédiaire, 1787–1790* (Trévoux, 1898), p. 173.
24. AN 291AP *Dossier 2.*
25. E. Burke, *Reflections on the Revolution in France* (Harmondsworth, 1973), p. 286.
26. See P. M. Jones, *The Peasantry in the French Revolution* (Cambridge, 1988), p. 169.

27. See P. Renouvin, 'L'Edit du 22 juin 1787 et la loi du 22 décembre 1789', *La Révolution française*, 2(1911), 321.
28. Furet, *La Révolution de Turgot à Jules Ferry*, p. 98.
29. L'Esquieu and L. Delourmel, *Brest pendant la Révolution: correspondance de la municipalité avec les députés de la sénéchaussée de Brest aux Etats Généraux et à l'Assemblée Constituante, 1789–1791* (Brest, 1909), p. 64.
30. See T. W. Margadant, *Urban Rivalries in the French Revolution* (Princeton, N.J., 1992), p. 328.
31. J. Egret, *Le Parlement de Dauphiné et les affaires publiques dans la deuxième moitié du XVIIIe siècle* (2 vols., Grenoble and Paris, 1942), II, p. 356.
32. Quoted in N. Hampson, *Prelude to Terror: The Constituent Assembly and the Failure of Consensus, 1789–1791* (Oxford, 1988), p. 146.
33. Tackett, *Religion, Revolution and Regional Culture in Eighteenth-Century France*, p. 12.
34. Mirouse (ed.), *François Ménard de la Groye*, p. 379.
35. *Ibid.*, p. 388.
36. See F. Crouzet, *La Grande Inflation: la monnaie en France de Louis XVI à Napoléon* (Paris, 1993), pp. 62–5, 87–9.
37. *Ibid.*, p. 122.
38. AD Loire-Atlantique C563.
39. See Crouzet, *La Grande Inflation*, p. 85. A higher figure of 55m *livres* is proposed by M. Bruguière and J.-C. Asselain (*Revue économique*, special issue 6, 40(1989), 985–1000, 1156).
40. Guigne (ed.), *Procès-verbaux des séances de l'Assemblée Provinciale*, p. 150.
41. Lemay, *Dictionnaire des Constituants*, I, p. 23. Entry for P.-H. Anson.
42. J.-P. Gross, 'Progressive Taxation and Social Justice in Eighteenth-Century France', *Past and Present*, 140(1993), 107.
43. AN 291AP *Dossier 2*.
44. O. Browning (ed.), *The Despatches of Earl Gower, English Ambassador at Paris from June 1790 to August 1792* (Cambridge, 1885), pp. 79–80.
45. Lescure (ed.), *Correspondance secrète*, II, p. 458.
46. Hardman, *Louis XVI*, pp. 182–4.
47. See A. de Bacourt (ed.), *Correspondance entre le Comte de Mirabeau et le Comte de La Marck pendant les années 1789, 1790 et 1791* (3 vols., Paris, 1851), III, p. 30.
48. See Hardman, *Louis XVI*, p. 200.

7: THE POLITICAL CULTURE OF REVOLUTION

1. I. Woloch, *The New Regime: Transformations of the French Civic Order, 1789–1820s* (New York and London, 1994), p. 14.
2. Keith Baker defines the concept of political culture as follows: 'If politics, broadly construed, is the activity through which individuals and groups in any society articulate, negotiate, implement, and enforce the competing claims they make one upon another, then political culture may be understood as the set of discourses and practices characterising that activity in any given community' (see Baker (ed.), *The French Revolution and the Creation of Modern Political Culture*, I, p. xii).

3. AD Loire-Atlantique C563; *Procès-verbal de l'assemblée de la Bretagne et de l'Anjou tenue à Pontivy le 15 et autres jours de février 1790* (Paris, 1790), p. 25.

4. Quoted in J.-C. Bonnet (ed.), *La Carmagnole des Muses. L'Homme de lettres et l'artiste dans la Révolution* (Paris, 1988), p. 163.

5. AN DIV 17.

6. See P. Goujard, 'Les Pétitions au Comité Féodal: loi contre loi', in *La Révolution et le monde rural. Actes du colloque tenu en Sorbonne les 23, 24, et 25 octobre 1987 à l'initiative de l'Institut National de la Recherche Agronomique et de l'Institut d'Histoire de la Révolution Française* (Paris, 1989), p. 76.

7. Quoted in Y. Le Gall, 'Les Consultations générales en Loire-Inférieure, 1789–an VIII' (2 vols., thèse pour le doctorat en droit, University of Angers, 1976), I, p. 299.

8. Quoted in E. Hartmann, *La Révolution française en Alsace et en Lorraine* (Paris, 1990), pp. 168–9.

9. AN DIII 27, *mémoire* of Dufour, *médecin* of Nant.

10. The most recent estimate is M. Edelstein, 'Electoral Behavior during the Constitutional Monarchy, 1790–91: a "Community" Interpretation', in R. Waldinger, P. Dawson and I. Woloch (eds.), *The French Revolution and the Meaning of Citizenship* (Westport, 1993), p. 105.

11. *Ibid.*, p. 107. See also M. Edelstein, 'Integrating the French Peasants into the Nation-State: The Transformation of Electoral Participation, 1789–1870', *History of European Ideas*, 15(1992), 321.

12. J. R. Censer and J. D. Popkin (eds.), *Press and Politics in Pre-Revolutionary France* (Berkeley, Calif., 1987), p. viii.

13. Quoted in J. D. Popkin, 'The Provincial Newspaper Press and Revolutionary Politics', *French Historical Studies*, 18(1993), 434.

14. *Ibid.*

15. Young, *Travels in France*, p. 153.

16. J. R. Censer, *Prelude to Power: The Parisian Radical Press, 1789–1791* (Baltimore and London, 1976), p. 8; C. Hesse, *Publishing and Cultural Politics in Revolutionary Paris, 1789–1810* (Berkeley, Calif., 1991), p. 173.

17. H. Gough, 'L'Image de la Révolution dans la presse provinciale', in M. Vovelle (ed.), *Bicentenaire de la Révolution française, 1789–1989. L'image de la Révolution française. Communications présentées lors du Congrès Mondial pour le Bicentenaire de la Révolution, Sorbonne, Paris, 6–12 juillet 1989* (4 vols., Oxford, 1990), I, p. 140.

18. See J. Boutier, P. Boutry and S. Bonin, *Atlas de la Révolution française*, vol. VI: *Les Sociétés politiques* (Paris, 1992), p. 12.

19. *Ibid.*, p. 14.

20. *Ibid.*, p. 9.

21. See F. Patard, 'Bernay et le Fédéralisme dans l'Eure. Quel Enjeu?', in *A Travers la Haute-Normandie en Révolution, 1789–1800* (Rouen, 1992), p. 169.

22. Boutier, Boutry and Bonin, *Les Sociétés politiques*, p. 11.

23. B. Combes de Patris, *Procès-verbaux des séances de la société populaire de Rodez* (Rodez, 1912), p. 17.

24. *Ibid.*, pp. 79–80.

25. Boutier, Boutry and Bonin, *Les Sociétés politiques*, p. 63.

26. See L. Hunt, *Politics, Culture and Class in the French Revolution* (London, 1986), part II; M. Edelstein, 'Electoral Participation and Sociology of the Landes in 1790' (forthcoming); *idem*, 'The French Revolution and the Creation of Modern Political Culture' (paper delivered to the Annual Meeting, American Historical Association, Washington DC, 1992).

CONCLUSION

1. See J.-P. Rabaut Saint Etienne, *Précis historique de la révolution française: Assemblée Constituante* (5th edn, Paris, 1809), p. lxxxvi.
2. *Ibid.*, p. 4.
3. See, in particular, Van Kley, *The Damiens Affair*; Echeverria, *The Maupeou Revolution*; Merrick, *The Desacralisation of the French Monarchy*; Baker (ed.), *Inventing the French Revolution*; Hardman, *Louis XVI*; and most recently B. Stone, *The Genesis of the French Revolution: A Global-Historical Interpretation* (Cambridge, 1994).
4. The phrase comes from J. Brewer, *The Sinews of Power: War, Money and the English State, 1688–1783* (London, 1989).
5. M. Beloff, *The Age of Absolutism, 1660–1815* (London, 1963), p. 50.
6. T. C. W. Blanning, *The French Revolution: Aristocrats versus Bourgeois?* (Atlantic Highlands, N.J., 1987), p. 7.
7. For a summary, see P. M. Jones, 'Georges Lefebvre and the Peasant Revolution: Fifty Years On', *French Historical Studies*, 16(1990), 645–63.
8. See above p. 83.
9. See above, p. 2.
10. F. Furet and M. Ozouf (eds.), *A Critical Dictionary of the French Revolution*, trans. A. Goldhammer (Cambridge, Mass., 1989). In this connection, see the perceptive review essay by I. Woloch, 'On the Latent Illiberalism of the French Revolution', *American Historical Review*, 95(1990), 1452–70.
11. *Réclamations des provinces contre les opérations de leurs députés* (n.p., 1790), p. 32.

Bibliography

MANUSCRIPT SOURCES

ARCHIVES NATIONALES, PARIS

H^1 94	*Généralité de Bourges, 1782–8*
H^1 1462	*Correspondance sur l'agriculture, 1785–7*
H^1 1463	*Finances, 1709–88*
H^1 1593	*Assemblées provinciales et assemblées d'arrondissement, 1787–8*
H^1 1596	*ibid.*
H^1 1597	*ibid.*
H^1 1600	*Correspondance et mémoires sur les assemblées provinciales, 1779–88*
H^1 1601	*ibid.*
H^1 1609	*Affaires diverses*
H^1 1625	*Correspondance et mémoires sur l'agriculture, 1770–85*
H^1 1626	*ibid.*
DIII 27	*Comité de Législation: Aveyron*
DIV 17	*Comité de Constitution: Ardèche*
DXIV 2	*Comité des Droits Féodaux: Charente, Charente-Inférieure, Cantal*
27 AP	*Dossier 2: papiers de François de Neufchâteau*
291 AP	*Dossier 2: papiers M. d'Aine, intendant*

ARCHIVES DE L'ASSISTANCE PUBLIQUE, PARIS

Fonds Montyon	*Carton 2: sociologie politique*
	Carton 5: droit constitutionnel
	Carton 7: droit constitutionnel (suite)
	Carton 8: administration

ARCHIVES DEPARTEMENTALES DE LOIRE-ATLANTIQUE, NANTES

C563	*Etats Généraux: convocations, vœux, délibérations, 1788–90*
C566	*Cahiers de doléances et procès-verbaux d'assemblées paroissiales, mars–septembre 1789*
C567	*ibid.*

C568   *ibid.*
C569   *ibid.*
C570   *ibid.*
C571   *ibid.*
C572   *ibid.*
C573   *ibid.*
C574   *ibid.*
C575   *ibid.*
C576   *ibid.*
C577   *ibid.*
C578   *ibid.*
(nota: C566–78 = 2Mi25 (microfilm reels 1–3)
C add. 19–21

ARCHIVES DEPARTEMENTALES DE LA LOZERE, MENDE

2E 874   *Titres des communautés d'habitants: Le Malzieu*

ARCHIVES DEPARTEMENTALES DE MAINE-ET-LOIRE, ANGERS

C315   *Intendance: organisation des municipalités, 1788–90*
C316   *ibid.*
C317   *ibid.*

ARCHIVES DEPARTEMENTALES DU PUY-DE-DOME, CLERMONT-FERRAND

C7373   *Procès-verbal de l'assemblée d'élection de Saint-Flour, Session du mois d'octobre 1788*

PRINTED PRIMARY SOURCES

Bacourt, A. de (ed.) *Correspondance entre le Comte de Mirabeau et le Comte de La Marck pendant les années 1789, 1790 et 1791*. 3 vols., Paris, 1851
Boyd, J. P. (ed.) *The Papers of Thomas Jefferson*. 24 vols., Princeton, N.J., 1950–90
Browning, O. (ed.) *The Despatches of Earl Gower, English Ambassador at Paris from June 1790 to August 1792*. Cambridge, 1885
   Despatches from Paris, 1784–1790. 2 vols., London, 1909–10
Burke, E. *Reflections on the Revolution in France*. Harmondsworth, 1973
Cahiers des plaintes et doléances de Loire-Atlantique 1789. Texte intégral et commentaires. Cet ouvrage édité par le conseil-général de Loire-Atlantique . . . sous la direction de Michel Le Mené et Marie-Helène Santrot. 4 vols., Nantes, 1989
Carré, H. (ed.) *Marquis de Ferrières: correspondance inédite, 1789, 1790, 1791*. Paris, 1932
Champion, E. (ed.) *Qu'est-ce que le Tiers Etat? Par Emmanuel Sieyès, précédé de l'Essai sur les privilèges*. Paris, 1888
Combes de Patris, B. *Procès-verbaux des séances de la société populaire de Rodez*. Rodez, 1912

Doisy, P. *Le Royaume de France et les Etats de Lorraine*. Paris, 1753

Duvergier, J.-B. *Collection complète des lois, décrets, ordonnances, règlements et avis du conseil d'état*. 78 vols., Paris, 1824–78

Encyclopédie ou dictionnaire raisonné des sciences, des arts et des métiers. 17 vols., Neufchâtel, 1765

Esquieu, L., and Delourmel, L. *Brest pendant la Révolution: correspondance de la municipalité avec les députés de la sénéchaussée de Brest aux Etats Généraux et à l'Assemblée Constituante, 1789–1791*. Brest, 1909

Expilly, *abbé* J.-J. *Tableau de la population de la France*. Paris, 1780 (reprinted 1973)

Guigne, G. (ed.) *Procès-verbaux des séances de l'Assemblée Provinciale de la généralité de Lyon et de sa Commission Intermédiaire, 1787–1790*. Trévoux, 1898

Guilhamon, H. (ed.) *Journal des voyages en Haute-Guienne de J. F. Henry de Richeprey*. 2 vols., Rodez, 1952–67

Guyot, E.-G. *Dictionnaire des postes*. Paris, 1754

Lescure, M. de (ed.) *Correspondance secrète inédite sur Louis XVI, Marie-Antoinette, la Cour et la ville de 1777 à 1792. Publiée d'après les manuscrits de la Bibliothèque impériale de Saint-Pétersbourg, avec une préface, des notes et un index alphabétique par M. de Lescure*. 2 vols., Paris, 1866, II

Mémoires d'agriculture, d'économie rurale et domestique publiés par la Société Royale d'Agriculture: année 1789. Paris, n.d.

Mirouse, F. (ed.) *François Ménard de la Groye, député de Maine aux Etats généraux. Correspondance, 1789–1791*. Le Mans, 1989

Necker, J. *De l'administration des finances de la France*. 3 vols., n.p., 1785

Œuvres complètes de Voltaire. 52 vols., Paris, 1883–5, XVIII

Procès-verbal de l'assemblée de la Bretagne et de l'Anjou tenue à Pontivy le 15 et autres jours de février 1790. Paris, 1790

Procès-verbal de l'assemblée provinciale de l'Isle de France. Année 1787. N.p., n.d.

Procès-verbal des séances de l'Assemblée de Basse-Normandie tenues à Caen en novembre et décembre 1787. Caen, 1788

Procès-verbal des séances de l'Assemblée générale des trois provinces de la généralité de Tours tenue à Tours, par Ordre du Roi, le 12 novembre 1787. Tours, 1787

Rabaut Saint Etienne, J.-P. *Précis historique de la révolution française: Assemblée Constituante*. 5th edn, Paris, 1809

Réclamations des provinces contre les opérations de leurs députés. n.p., 1790

Règlement sur la formation et la composition des assemblées qui auront lieu dans la province de Champagne en vertu de l'édit portant création des assemblées provinciales. Versailles, 23 June 1787

Roberts, J. M., and Hardman, J. (eds.) *French Revolution Documents*. 2 vols., Oxford, 1966–73

Tambour, E. *Les Registres municipaux de Rennemoulin, juillet 1787 à floréal an IV*. Paris, 1903

Thénard, M. *Bailliages de Versailles et de Meudon. Les Cahiers des paroisses avec commentaires accompagnés de quelques cahiers de curés*. Versailles, 1889

Young, A. *Travels in France during the Years 1787, 1788, 1789*. London, 1900

SECONDARY SOURCES

Antoine, M. *Le Gouvernement et l'administration sous Louis XV. Dictionnaire biographique.* Paris, 1978

Ardascheff, P. *Les Intendants de province sous Louis XVI.* Paris, 1909

Asselain, J.-C. *Histoire économique de la France du XVIIIe siècle à nos jours,* vol. I: *De l'Ancien Régime à la Première Guerre mondiale.* Paris, 1984
  'Continuités, traumatismes, mutations', *Revue économique,* special issue 6, 40 (1989), 1137–85

Baker, K. M. 'French Political Thought at the Accession of Louis XVI', *Journal of Modern History,* 50 (1978), 279–303

Baker, K. M. (ed.) *The French Revolution and the Creation of Modern Political Culture,* vol. I: *The Political Culture of the Old Regime.* Oxford, 1987
  Inventing the French Revolution: Essays on French Political Culture in the Eighteenth Century. Cambridge, 1990

Bamford, P. N. *Privilege and Profit: A Business Family in Eighteenth-Century France.* Philadelphia, 1988

Bayard, F., and Guignet, P. *L'Economie française au XVIe, XVIIe et XVIIIe siècles.* Paris and Gap, 1991

Behrens, C. B. A. *The Ancien Régime.* London, 1967
  Society, Government and the Enlightenment: The Experiences of Eighteenth-Century France and Prussia. London, 1985

Beloff, M. *The Age of Absolutism, 1660–1815.* London, 1963

Berlanstein, L. R. *The Barristers of Toulouse in the Eighteenth Century, 1740–1793.* Baltimore and London, 1975

Bien, D. D. *The Calas Affair: Persecution, Toleration, and Heresy in Eighteenth-Century Toulouse.* Princeton, N.J., 1960 (reprinted 1979)

Blanning, T. C. W. *The French Revolution: Aristocrats versus Bourgeois?* Atlantic Highlands, N.J., 1987

Bonin, S., and Langlois, C. (eds.) *Atlas de la Révolution française,* vol. II: *L'Enseignement, 1760–1815.* Paris, 1987

Bonnet, J.-C. (ed.) *La Carmagnole des Muses. L'Homme de lettres et l'artiste dans la Révolution.* Paris, 1988

Bordes, M. 'Les Intendants éclairés de la fin de l'Ancien Régime', *Revue d'histoire économique et sociale,* 39 (1961), 57–83
  'Un Intendant éclairé de la fin de l'Ancien Régime: Claude-François de Boucheporn', *Annales du Midi,* 74 (1962), 177–94
  La Réforme municipale du contrôleur-général Laverdy et son application, 1764–1771. Toulouse, 1968
  L'Administration provinciale et municipale en France au XVIIIe siècle. Paris, 1972

Bosher, J. F. *The Single Duty Project: A Study of the Movement for a French Customs Union in the Eighteenth Century.* London, 1964
  French Finances, 1770–1795: From Business to Bureaucracy. Cambridge, 1970

Bossenga, G. 'City and State: An Urban Perspective on the Origins of the French Revolution', in K. M. Baker (ed.), *The French Revolution and the Creation of Modern Political Culture,* vol. I: *The Political Culture of the Old Regime.* Oxford, 1987, pp. 115–40

The Politics of Privilege: Old Regime and Revolution in Lille. Cambridge, 1991

Bouteil, J. *Le Rachat des péages au XVIIIe siècle d'après les papiers du bureau des péages*. Paris, 1925

Boutier, J., Boutry, P., and Bonin, S. *Atlas de la Révolution française*, vol. VI: *Les Sociétés politiques*. Paris, 1992

Bouton, C. A. 'L'"économie morale" et la guerre des farines de 1775', in F. Gauthier and G.-R. Ikni (eds.), *La Guerre du blé au XVIIIe siècle: la critique populaire contre le libéralisme économique au XVIIIe siècle*. Paris, 1988, pp. 93–110

The Flour War: Gender, Class and Community in Late Ancien Regime French Society. Pennsylvania State University Press, 1993

Brewer, J. *The Sinews of Power: War, Money and the English State, 1688–1783*. London, 1989

Bruguière, M. 'Révolution et finances: réflexions sur un impossible bilan', *Revue économique*, special issue 6, 40 (1989), 985–1000.

Cabourdin, G., and Viard, G. *Lexique historique de la France d'Ancien Régime*. Paris, 1978

Carré, H. 'Le Mémoire de M. Necker sur les Assemblées provinciales, 1778–1781', *Bulletin de la Faculté des Lettres de Poitiers* (1893), 174–85

Cavanaugh, G. J. 'Turgot: The Rejection of Enlightened Despotism', *French Historical Studies*, 6 (1969), 31–58

Censer, J. R. *Prelude to Power: The Parisian Radical Press, 1789–1791*. Baltimore and London, 1976

Censer, J. R., and Popkin, J. D. (eds.) *Press and Politics in Pre-Revolutionary France*. Berkeley, Calif., 1987

Chartier, R. *The Cultural Origins of the French Revolution*. Durham, N.C., and London, 1991

Chaussinand-Nogaret, G. *Une Histoire des élites, 1700–1848*. Paris and The Hague, 1975

The French Nobility in the Eighteenth Century: From Feudalism to Enlightenment. Cambridge, 1985

Chevallier, P. *Loménie de Brienne et l'ordre monastique, 1766–1789*. Paris, 1959

Cobban, A. *The Social Interpretation of the French Revolution*. Cambridge, 1964

A History of Modern France. 3 vols., Harmondsworth, 1965

Crouzet, F. *Britain Ascendant: Comparative Studies in Franco-British Economic History*. Cambridge and Paris, 1990

La Grande Inflation: la monnaie en France de Louis XVI à Napoléon. Paris, 1993

Cubells, M. *Les Horizons de la liberté: naissance de la Révolution en Provence, 1787–1789*. Aix-en-Provence, 1987

Dakin, D. *Turgot and the Ancien Régime in France*. London, 1939

Darnton, R. 'An Enlightened Revolution', *New York Review of Books*, 24 October 1991, 33–6

Dawson, P. *Provincial Magistrates and Revolutionary Politics in France, 1789–1795*. Cambridge, Mass., 1972

Dewald, J. *Pont-St-Pierre, 1398–1789: Lordship, Community and Capitalism in Early Modern France*. Berkeley, Calif., 1987

Doyle, W. *Origins of the French Revolution*. Oxford, 1980

'The Price of Offices in Pre-Revolutionary France', *Historical Journal*, 27 (1984), 831–60

The Oxford History of the French Revolution. Oxford, 1989

'4 August 1789: The End of French Venality' (paper delivered to the George Rudé Seminar, University of Adelaide, Adelaide, July 1992)

Dupâquier, J. (ed.) *Histoire de la population française*. 2 vols., Paris, 1988

Echeverria, D. *The Maupeou Revolution: A Study in the History of Libertarianism, France, 1770–1774*. Baton Rouge, La., 1985

Edelstein, M. 'Integrating the French Peasants into the Nation-State: The Transformation of Electoral Participation, 1789–1870', *History of European Ideas*, 15 (1992), 319–26

'The French Revolution and the Creation of Modern Political Culture'. Paper delivered to the Annual Meeting, American Historical Association, Washington DC, 1992

'Electoral Behavior during the Constitutional Monarchy, 1790–91: A "Community" Interpretation', in R. Waldinger, P. Dawson and I. Woloch (eds.), *The French Revolution and the Meaning of Citizenship*. Westport, 1993

'Electoral Participation and Sociology of the Landes in 1790', forthcoming

Egret, J. *Le Parlement de Dauphiné et les affaires publiques dans la deuxième moitié du XVIIIe siècle*. 2 vols., Grenoble and Paris, 1942

'La Révolution aristocratique en Franche-Comté et son échec, 1788–1789', *Revue d'histoire moderne et contemporaine*, 1 (1954), 245–71

Necker, ministre de Louis XVI, 1776–1790. Paris, 1975

The French Prerevolution, 1787–1788. Trans. W. D. Camp, Chicago and London, 1977

Etudes et Documents (Editions du Comité pour l'histoire économique et financière, Ministère des Finances), 2 (1990)

Fillon, A. 'Louis Simon, étaminier, 1741–1820 dans son village du Haut-Maine au siècle des lumières (2 vols., thèse de 3e cycle, University of Maine, 1982)

Fitzmaurice, E. (ed.) *Lettres de l'abbé Morellet à Lord Shelburne, depuis Marquis de Landsdowne, 1772–1803*. Paris, 1898

Fitzsimmons, M. P. 'Privilege and the Polity in France, 1786–1791', *American Historical Review*, 92 (1987), 269–95

'The Committee of the Constitution and the Remaking of France, 1789–1791', *French History*, 4 (1990), 23–47

Forster, R. *The House of Saulx-Tavanes: Versailles and Burgundy, 1700–1830*. Baltimore and London, 1971

Fourquin, G. *Les Campagnes de la région parisienne à la fin du Moyen Age du milieu du XIIIe siècle au début du XVIe siècle*. Paris, 1964

Fréville, H. *L'Intendance de Bretagne, 1689–1790: essai sur l'histoire d'une intendance en Pays d'Etats au XVIIIe siècle*. 3 vols., Rennes, 1953

Furet, F. *Penser la Révolution française*. Paris, 1978

La Révolution de Turgot à Jules Ferry, 1770–1880. Paris, 1988

Furet, F., and Halévi, R. 'L'Année 1789', *Annales ESC*, 44 (1989), 3–24

Furet, F., and Ozouf, M. (eds.) *A Critical Dictionary of the French Revolution*. Trans. A. Goldhammer, Cambridge, Mass., 1989

Gagliardo, J. G. *Enlightened Despotism*. London, 1968

Gayot, G., and Hirsch, J.-P. (eds.) *La Révolution française et le développement du capitalisme*. Lille, 1989

Gershoy, L. *From Despotism to Revolution, 1763–1789*. New York, 1963

Godechot, J. *La Révolution française dans le Midi-Toulousain*. Toulouse, 1986

Gough, H. 'L'Image de la Révolution dans la presse provinciale', in M. Vovelle (ed.), *Bicentenaire de la Révolution française, 1789–1989. L'image de la Révolution française. Communications présentées lors du Congrès Mondial pour le Bicentenaire de la Révolution, Sorbonne, Paris, 6–12 juillet 1989*. 4 vols., Oxford, 1990, I, pp. 140–5

Goujard, P. 'Les Pétitions au Comité Féodal: loi contre loi', in *La Révolution et le monde rural. Actes du colloque tenu en Sorbonne les 23, 24, et 25 octobre 1987 à l'initiative de l'Institut National de la Recherche Agronomique et de l'Institut d'Histoire de la Révolution Française*. Paris, 1989, pp. 67–81

Goy, J., and Le Roy Ladurie, E. *Les Fluctuations du produit de la dîme: conjoncture décimale et domaniale de la fin du Moyen Age au XVIIIe siècle*. Paris and The Hague, 1972

Grange, H. *Les Idées de Necker*. Paris, 1974

Gross, J.-P. 'Progressive Taxation and Social Justice in Eighteenth-Century France', *Past and Present*, 140 (1993), 79–126

Gueniffey, P. 'Les Assemblées et la représentation', in C. Lucas (ed.), *The French Revolution and the Creation of Modern Political Culture*, vol. II: *The Political Culture of the French Revolution*. Oxford, 1988, pp. 234–57

Guilhamon, H. 'Notes sur la noblesse du Rouergue à la fin du XVIIIe siècle', *Journal de l'Aveyron*, 15–22 September 1918
Origine et fortune de la bourgeoisie du Rouergue à la veille de la Révolution. Rodez, 1921

Halévi, R. 'La Monarchie et les élections: position des problèmes', in K. M. Barker (ed.), *The French Revolution and the Creation of Modern Political Culture*, vol. I: *The Political Culture of the Old Regime*. Oxford, 1987, pp. 387–402

Hall, T. E. 'Thought and Practice of Enlightened Government in French Corsica', *American Historical Review*, 74 (1969), 880–905

Hampson, N. *Prelude to Terror: The Constituent Assembly and the Failure of Consensus, 1789–1791*. Oxford, 1988

Hardman, J. *Louis XVI*. New Haven and London, 1993

Harris, R. D. *Necker: Reform Statesman of the Ancien Régime*. Berkeley, Calif., 1979
Necker and the Revolution of 1789. Lanham, Md., 1986

Hartmann, E. *La Révolution française en Alsace et en Lorraine*. Paris, 1990

Hesse, C. *Publishing and Cultural Politics in Revolutionary Paris, 1789–1810*. Berkeley, Calif., 1991

Hirsch, J.-P. *La Nuit du 4 août*. Paris, 1978
Les Deux Rêves du commerce: entreprise et institutions dans la région Lilleoise, 1780–1860. Paris, 1991

Hottenger, G. *Les Remembrements en Lorraine au dix-huitième siècle*. Nancy, 1915

Hunt, L. *Politics, Culture and Class in the French Revolution*. London, 1986

Hyslop, B. F. *A Guide to the General Cahiers of 1789*. New York, 1936

Jessenne, J.-P. *Pouvoir au village et Révolution: Artois, 1760–1848*. Lille, 1987

Jones, P. M. *Politics and Rural Society: The Southern Massif Central, c. 1750–1880.* Cambridge, 1985

The Peasantry in the French Revolution. Cambridge, 1988

'Georges Lefebvre and the Peasant Revolution: Fifty Years On', *French Historical Studies*, 16 (1990), 645–63

'Reforming Absolutism and the Ending of the Old Regime in France', *Australian Journal of French Studies*, 29 (1992), 220–8

Kaplan, S. L. *Bread, Politics and Political Economy in the Reign of Louis XV.* 2 vols., The Hague, 1976

Kington, J. A. 'Daily Weather Mapping from 1781: A Detailed Synoptic Examination of Weather and Climate during the Decade Leading up to the French Revolution', *Climatic Change*, 3 (1980), 7–36

Labrousse, C. E. *Esquisse du mouvement des prix et des revenus en France au XVIIIe siècle.* 2 vols., Paris, 1933 (reprinted 1984)

La Crise de l'économie française à la fin de l'Ancien Régime et au début de la Révolution. Paris, 1944 (2nd edn, 1990)

Labrousse, C. E., and Braudel, F. (eds.) *Histoire économique et sociale de la France.* 4 vols., Paris, 1970–6

Lavisse, E. *Histoire de France illustrée depuis les origines jusqu'à la Révolution.* 9 vols., Paris, 1911

Le Bras, H., and Todd, E. *L'Invention de la France: atlas anthropologique et politique.* Livre de poche, 1981

Lebrun, F. *Parole de dieu et révolution: les sermons d'un curé angevin avant et pendant la guerre de Vendée.* Toulouse, 1979

Lefebvre, G. *The French Revolution.* 2 vols., London and New York, 1964–5

Le Gall, Y. 'Les Consultations générales en Loire-Inférieure, 1789–an VIII' (2 vols., thèse pour le doctorat en droit, University of Angers, 1976)

Lemarchand, G. *La Fin du Féodalisme dans le pays de Caux: conjoncture économique et démographique et structure sociale dans une région de grande culture de la crise du XVIIe siècle à la stabilisation de la Révolution, 1640–1795.* Paris, 1989

'Troubles populaires au XVIIIe siècle et conscience de classe: une préface à la Révolution française', *Bulletin d'histoire de la Révolution française, années 1986–1989*, éditions du Comité des Travaux historiques et scientifiques, Paris, 1990, 95–108

Lemay, E. H. *Dictionnaire des Constituants, 1789–1791.* 2 vols., Oxford and Paris, 1991

Le Roy Ladurie, E. 'Révoltes et contestations rurales en France de 1675 à 1788', *Annales ESC*, 29 (1974), 6–22

'History that Stands Still', in E. Le Roy Ladurie, *The Mind and Method of the Historian.* Brighton, 1981, pp. 1–27

Lewis, G. *The Advent of Modern Capitalism in France, 1770–1840. The Contribution of Pierre-François Tubeuf.* Oxford, 1993

Ligou, D. *La Première année de la Révolution vue par un témoin, 1789–1790.* Paris, 1961

Lough, J. *France on the Eve of Revolution: British Travellers' Observations, 1763–1788.* London, 1987

Lucas, C. (ed.) *The French Revolution and the Creation of Modern Political*

Culture, vol. II: *The Political Culture of the French Revolution*. Oxford, 1988

Rewriting the French Revolution: The Andrew Browning Lectures. Oxford, 1991

Margadant, T. W. *Urban Rivalries in the French Revolution*. Princeton, N.J., 1992

Marion, M. *Le Garde des Sceaux Lamoignon et la réforme judiciaire de 1788*. Paris, 1905

Dictionnaire des institutions de la France aux XVIIe et XVIII siècles. Paris, 1923 (reprint 1972)

Markoff, J. 'Peasants Protest: The Claims of Lord, Church and State in the *Cahiers de Doléances* of 1789', *Comparative Studies in Society and History*, 32 (1990), 413–54

The Abolition of Feudalism: Peasants, Lords and Legislators in the French Revolution. University Park, Pa., forthcoming

Marx, R. *Recherches sur la vie politique d'Alsace pré-révolutionnaire et révolutionnaire*. Strasbourg, 1966

Matthews, G. T. *The Royal General Farms in Eighteenth-Century France*. New York, 1958

Maury, A.-G. 'Les Ventes de seigneuries dans la région d'Issoire au XVIIIe siècle', in *Actes du 88e congrès national des sociétés savantes*. Clermont-Ferrand, 1963, pp. 819–28

Merrick, J. W. *The Desacralisation of the French Monarchy in the Eighteenth Century*. Baton Rouge, La., 1990

Millot, J. *Le Régime féodal en Franche-Comté au XVIIIe siècle*. Besançon, 1937

Moriceau, J.-M. and Postel-Vinay, G. *Ferme, entreprise, famille: grande exploitation et changements agricoles: les Chartier, XVIIe–XIXe siècles*. Paris, 1992

Morineau, M. Review of Lemarchand, *La Fin du Féodalisme*, in *Revue d'histoire moderne et contemporaine*, 39 (1992), 335–9

Mosser, F. *Les Intendants des finances au XVIIIe siècle: les Lefèvre d'Ormesson et le 'Département des Impositions'*. Geneva, 1978

Mousnier, R. *The Institutions of France under the Absolute Monarchy, 1598–1789*. 2 vols., Chicago and London, 1979–84

Mousset, A. *Un témoin ignoré de la Révolution: le Comte de Fernan Nuñez, ambassadeur d'Espagne à Paris, 1787–1791*. Paris, 1924

Musset, J. 'Une source méconnue: les "mémoires municipaux" de l'élection ou département d'Argentan (1788)', *Bulletin de la société historique et archéologique de l'Orne*, 108 (1989), 55–72

Nicolas, J. *La Révolution française dans les Alpes: Dauphiné et Savoie*. Toulouse, 1989

Palmer, R. R. (ed.) *The Two Tocquevilles Father and Son: Hervé and Alexis de Tocqueville on the Coming of the French Revolution*. Princeton, N.J., 1987

Patard, F. 'Bernay et le Fédéralisme dans l'Eure. Quel Enjeu?', in *A Travers la Haute-Normandie en Révolution, 1789–1800*. Rouen, 1992, pp. 163–74

Popkin, J. D. 'The Provincial Newspaper Press and Revolutionary Politics', *French Historical Studies*, 18 (1993), 434–56

Poussou, J.-P. 'Le Dynamisme de l'économie française sous Louis XVI', *Revue économique*, 40 (1989), 965–84

Price, M. 'The "Ministry of the Hundred Hours": A Reappraisal', *French History*, 4 (1990), 317–39

Ramsay, C. *The Ideology of the Great Fear: The Soissonnais in 1789*. Baltimore and London, 1992

Ramsey, J. F. 'The Judicial Reform of 1788 and the French Revolution', in F. J. Cox *et al.* (eds.), *Studies in Modern European History in Honor of Franklin Charles Palm*. New York, 1956, pp. 217–38

Renouvin, P. 'L'Edit du 22 juin 1787 et la loi de 22 décembre 1789', *La Révolution française*, 2 (1911), 289–321

Les Assemblées provinciales de 1787. Origines, développement, résultats. Paris, 1921

Richet, D. *La France moderne: l'esprit des institutions*. Paris, 1973

Rioche, A. *De l'administration des vingtièmes sous l'Ancien Régime*. Paris, 1904

Roberts, J. M. *The Mythology of the Secret Societies*. St Albans, 1974

Roche, D. *Le Siècle des lumières en province: académies et académiciens provinciaux, 1680–1789*. 2 vols., Paris and The Hague, 1978

Russell Major, J. *The Estates General of 1560*. Princeton, N.J., 1951

Sagnac, P. *La Formation de la société française moderne*. 2 vols., Paris, 1945–6

Schama, S. *Citizens. A Chronicle of the French Revolution*. London, 1989

Scott, W. 'Merchants and 1789: The Case of Marseille' (unpublished paper delivered to the George Rudé Seminar, University of New South Wales, Sydney, Australia, May 1982)

Sorel, A. *Europe and the French Revolution: The Political Traditions of the Old Regime*. Trans. and ed. A. Cobban and J. W. Hunt, London and Glasgow, 1970

Souchon, C. 'L'Assemblée d'élection de Laon et les "affaires du pays"', in *Actes du 111e Congrès national des sociétés savantes. Poitiers, 1986. Section d'Histoire Moderne et Contemporaine*. 3 vols., Paris, 1987, i, fasicle 1, pp. 105–24

Stone, B. *The French Parlements and the Crisis of the Old Regime*. Chapel Hill and London, 1986

The Genesis of the French Revolution: A Global-Historical Interpretation. Cambridge, 1994

Sutherland, D. M. G. *France 1789–1815: Revolution and Counter-Revolution*. London, 1985

Tackett, T. *Priest and Parish in Eighteenth-Century France*. Princeton, N.J., 1977

Religion, Revolution and Regional Culture in Eighteenth-Century France: The Ecclesiastical Oath of 1791. Princeton, N.J., 1986

'Nobles and the Third Estate in the Revolutionary Dynamic of the National Assembly', *American Historical Review*, 94 (1989), 271–301

Tarrade, J. *Le Commerce colonial de la France à la fin de l'Ancien Régime: l'évolution du régime de 'l'Exclusif' de 1763 à 1789*. 2 vols., Paris, 1972

Thomson, J. K. J. *Clermont-de-Lodève, 1633–1789: Fluctuations in the Prosperity of a Languedocian Cloth-Making Town*. Cambridge, 1982

Tocqueville, A. de *L'Ancien Regime*. Oxford, 1969

Toutain, J.-C. 'Le Produit de l'agriculture française de 1700 à 1958: II, La Croissance', in *Cahiers de l'Institut de science économique appliquée*, supplement to 115 (1961), pp. 1–287

Trémoïlle, M. de la 'L'Assemblée provinciale d'Anjou, d'après les archives de Serrant, 1787–1789', *L'Anjou historique*, 1 (1900–1), 439–69, 542–71, 662–706; 2 (1901–2), 40–70

Van Kley, D. K. *The Damiens Affair and the Unraveling of the Ancien Régime, 1750–1770*. Princeton, N.J., 1984

'The Jansenist Constitutional Legacy in the French Prerevolution', in K. M. Baker (ed.), *The French Revolution and the Creation of Modern Political Culture*, vol. I: *The Political Culture of the Old Regime*. Oxford, 1987, pp. 169–201

Villat, L. *La Corse de 1768 à 1789*. 3 vols., Besançon, 1924

Vovelle, M. *The Fall of the French Monarchy*. Cambridge, 1984

Weulersse, G. *La Physiocratie à l'aube de la Révolution, 1781–1792*. Paris, 1985

Woloch, I. 'On the Latent Illiberalism of the French Revolution', *American Historical Review*, 95 (1990), 1452–70

The New Regime: Transformations of the French Civic Order, 1789–1820s. New York and London, 1994

Index